Selected Letters of W. D. Howells

Volume 2

1873 – 1881

The William Dean Howells Family
ca. 1875

W. D. HOWELLS

Selected Letters

Volume 2: 1873-1881

Edited and Annotated by
George Arms and Christoph K. Lohmann

Textual Editors
Christoph K. Lohmann and Jerry Herron

TWAYNE PUBLISHERS

Boston

1 9 7 9

*This volume of Selected Letters is also published as
Volume 9 of A Selected Edition of W. D. Howells*

*Editorial expenses for this volume have been supported by grants from
the National Endowment for the Humanities administered through
the Center for Editions of American Authors of the Modern Language Association*

*Published in 1979 by Twayne Publishers, A Division of G. K. Hall & Co.,
70 Lincoln Street, Boston, Massachusetts 02111*

*.Printed on permanent/durable acid-free paper and bound in
the United States of America*

First Printing

Library of Congress Cataloging in Publication Information

*Howells, William Dean, 1837–1920.
Selected letters.*

*(His A Selected edition of W. D. Howells; v. 4–)
Includes index.
CONTENTS: v. 2. 1873–1881.
1. Howells, William Dean, 1837–1920—Correspondence.
2. Novelists, American—19th century—Correspondence.
I. Arms, George Warren, 1912–
II. Title.
PS2020.F68 vol. 4, etc. [PS2033.A4] 818'.4'09 78–27247
ISBN 0–8057–8528–0*

Acknowledgments

We are grateful for permission to print the letters in this volume, as given by William White Howells and the heirs of W. D. Howells. The following individuals and institutions have also permitted the use of letters in their collections: George Arms, Albuquerque, New Mexico; The Trustees of the Boston Public Library; Mark Twain Papers, Bancroft Library, University of California (Berkeley); Cincinnati Historical Society; Columbia University Libraries; Connecticut Historical Society, Hartford; Cornell University Library; Duke University Library; Folger Shakespeare Library, Washington, D. C.; Harvard College Library; Rutherford B. Hayes Library, Fremont, Ohio; Huntington Library, San Marino, California; Milton S. Eisenhower Library, Johns Hopkins University; The Mark Twain Memorial, Hartford, Connecticut; Massachusetts Historical Society, Boston; New-York Historical Society; Northwestern University Library; Ohio Historical Society, Columbus; Princeton University Library; Rutgers University Library; Henry W. and Albert A. Berg Collection, New York Public Library, Astor, Lenox and Tilden Foundations; Willard S. Morse Collection, University of Southern California Library; Humanities Research Center, University of Texas at Austin; Trinity College Library, Hartford, Connecticut; George W. Cable Collection, Tulane University Library; William Dean Howells Collection, Clifton Waller Barrett Library, University of Virginia Library; State Historical Society of Wisconsin, Madison; Collection of American Literature, Beinecke Rare Book and Manuscript Library, Yale University; E. N. Zeigler, Florence, South Carolina.

Special thanks also go to our research assistants, William J. Henning and Jerry Herron, as well as to Bainbridge Bunting, University of New Mexico, Albuquerque; Gerard Flynn, University of Wisconsin, Milwaukee; Ginette de B. Merrill, Belmont, Massachusetts; Roger W. Robbins, Geneva, Illinois; and Richard G. Wilson, University of Virginia, Charlottesville.

Contents

A NOTE ON EDITORIAL PRACTICE   xi

I.   Toward a New Fiction (1873–1876)   1

     Introduction
     Letters and Notes

II.   Emerging Novelist and Busy Editor (1877–1881)   147

     Introduction
     Letters and Notes

TEXTUAL APPARATUS

     Introduction   305
     Textual Record   311
     Word-Division   341

LIST OF HOWELLS' CORRESPONDENTS   345

INDEX   349

A Note on Editorial Practice

Two basic principles inform the treatment of the texts of the Howells correspondence which have been selected for publication in these volumes: one, the contents of the original documents are reproduced as fully and correctly as possible; and, two, all physical details of the manuscripts necessary for accurate reconstruction of the text are reported, though without encumbering the reading text itself. Consistent with these principles, the printed versions of the letters which form the body of these volumes retain the eccentricities of Howells' spelling, punctuation, and occasionally elliptical epistolary style, and are presented without such editorial appurtenances as brackets, arrows, virgules, and *sic*'s. The printed text is, insofar as possible, that of the finished letter, after Howells revised it either locally or generally by writing over, crossing out, and interlining. Howells' errors, except for inadvertent repetitions of words or syllables, are printed as they appear in the holographs, so long as the sense of the text can be discerned.

In accordance with the principle of reporting significant manuscript information, each letter is represented by a full itemization of cancellations, interlineations, the unusual placement of postscripts and marginal comments, and the presence of nonauthorial notes and comments believed to be contemporary with the composition or receipt of the letter, as well as of those editorial revisions necessary to insure comprehension. The reader should be aware, therefore, that some few words, letters, and marks of punctuation printed in this text are not in the original letters (or in transcriptions which have been employed when the originals are no longer extant or accessible). The full record of emendations, editorial comments, textual details, and Howells' revisions is provided in the Textual Apparatus, the introduction to which explains the symbols and abbreviations used to allow for the printing of the maximum of evidence in a minimum of space. Several exceptions, however, should be noted. Howells frequently failed to lift his pen when moving from one word to the next; thus, he often joined words that were not meant to be joined. Occasionally, though not always, he would repair such errors by separating these inadvertently joined words with a vertical line. Conversely, he sometimes lifted his pen while writing a single word, or he disconnected compounds that appear elsewhere as one word. In such cases, no notation of these irregularities has been included in the apparatus, while an attempt has been made, through comparisons among the letters, to render Howells' texts as nearly as possible in the form that he seems likely to have intended.

Given the wealth of references to personal and public events in the letters and the relevance of the letters to the shape and movement of Howells' career, annotation is potentially endless. The policy of these volumes is to present only the basic information which will make the context of the letters understandable and the letters themselves useful to both scholar and general reader. Annotation is thus restricted to explanation and clarification of references to people, places, events, literary works, and other such primary data. Interpretive comment is excluded.

Since the letters in this series represent only a portion of the extant Howells correspondence, it is also important that their relationship to each other and to letters not printed in these volumes be indicated. Cross references to other letters printed in the series simply identify correspondent and date: e.g., "Howells to Comly, 7 July 1868"; references to annotation accompanying letters add to this citation the specific footnote number: e.g., "Howells to Comly, 7 July 1868, n. 4." Manuscript letters not printed in this edition but cited or quoted are identified by correspondent and date, followed by the library location or collector's name in parentheses: e.g., "(MH)" for Harvard University or "(Ray)" for the collection of Gordon N. Ray.[1] Special collections within libraries are not indicated. When manuscripts of texts cited are also available in major printed collections (e.g., *Mark Twain–Howells Letters*), publication information follows the library symbol. Publication information appearing without notation of manuscript location should be assumed to designate texts extant only in published form. Quotations from letters in annotations follow the final, revised forms, and do not include a record of internal revisions. In addition, to avoid the proliferation of annotation, information necessary to the understanding of such quoted letters is provided within brackets at appropriate points within the quotations.

To further reduce the bulk and duplication of annotation, several other conventions have been adopted. People, events, and literary works are identified in footnotes at the points where their first significant mention appears in the whole series of letters. Further annotation of these same details is provided only where the context of a specific letter demands elaboration. The basic information can be located by using the indexes to the individual volumes or the cumulative index in

---

1. Libraries are indicated by the abbreviations detailed in *Symbols of American Libraries*, 10th ed. (Washington: Library of Congress, 1969).

the final volume of letters, where major references are distinguished by the printing of the appropriate page numbers in italic type. References to books give the year of first publication; however, books reviewed in dated articles should be assumed to have been published in the same year as the review, unless information to the contrary is provided. Whenever possible, references to books by Howells identify volumes published in "A Selected Edition of W. D. Howells," signaled by the abbreviation "HE" immediately following the title; references to works not available in this form generally cite the American first edition, which is identified by date of publication.

The editors have followed a consistent policy in the use of ellipses in quotations. If the first period is close up to the word preceding it, it stands for an end-of-sentence period in the original, with the omission following it. Thus, "invention. . . . develop" indicates that there is a period in the original after "invention," with the omitted portion of the text following it. However, "hereafter . . . . Good lord!" indicates that there is more text in the same sentence after "hereafter."

Titles of most secondary sources are given in full, but a number of them are cited so often in this series that the following list of short titles has been adopted.

Cady, *Howells*, I	Edwin H. Cady, *The Road to Realism: The Early Years, 1837–1885, of William Dean Howells* (Syracuse, N. Y.: Syracuse University Press, 1956)
Cady, *Howells*, II	Edwin H. Cady, *The Realist at War: The Mature Years, 1885–1920, of William Dean Howells* (Syracuse, N. Y.: Syracuse University Press, 1958)
Gibson-Arms, *Bibliography*	William M. Gibson and George Arms, *A Bibliography of William Dean Howells* (New York: New York Public Library, 1948; reprinted, New York Public Library and Arno Press, 1971)
James Letters	*Henry James Letters*, ed. Leon Edel, 2 vols. (Cambridge, Mass.: Harvard University Press, Belknap Press, 1974–1975)
Life in Letters	*Life in Letters of William Dean Howells*, ed. Mildred Howells, 2 vols. (Garden City, N. Y.: Doubleday, Doran & Co., 1928)

Lynn, *Howells*

Kenneth S. Lynn, *William Dean Howells: An American Life* (New York: Harcourt Brace Jovanovich, 1971)

Norton, *Lowell Letters*

Letters of James Russell Lowell, ed. C. E. Norton, 2 vols. (New York: Harper & Brothers, 1894)

Transatlantic Dialogue

Transatlantic Dialogue: Selected American Correspondence of Edmund Gosse, ed. Paul F. Mattheisen and Michael Millgate (Austin: University of Texas Press, 1965)

Twain-Howells

Mark Twain-Howells Letters, ed. Henry Nash Smith and William M. Gibson, 2 vols. (Cambridge, Mass.: Harvard University Press, Belknap Press, 1960)

Woodress, *Howells & Italy*

James L. Woodress, Jr., *Howells & Italy* (Durham, N. C.: Duke University Press, 1952)

C. K. L.
D. J. N.

I

Toward a New Fiction

1 8 7 3 – 1 8 7 6

Introduction

THE years 1873–1876 were a fulfilling and happy period in Howells' life. The members of his immediate family (including the recent addition of Mildred) were healthy; there were no deaths or crises at home or in his father's household; Howells led an active (perhaps too active) social life; his own reputation as a critic and editor was firmly established; and he arrived at an important new insight about his development as a novelist. He, Elinor, and the three children moved into their comfortable new house at 37 Concord Avenue, Cambridge, in the summer of 1873. Elinor had designed it herself, and the family probably thought that they had found a home for many years to come, perhaps for life. The library served as Howells' study, and his description of it in a letter to his father of 20 July 1873 presents a detailed picture of the solid respectability the novelist had achieved since assuming the editorship of the *Atlantic* two years earlier:

> The ceiling is richly frescoed; below the cornice, and down to the chair-board running the room is a soft buff paper and then dark red to the floor. The book-casing, drawers and closets are heavy chestnut; the hearth is of tiles, and the chimney-piece rises in three broad shelves almost to the cornice. This is the glory of the room, and is splendidly carved, and set with picture-tiles and mirrors; on either jamb of the mantel is my monogram, carved, and painted by Elinor, who modified and improved the carpenter's design of the whole affair.

But despite such comforts the family escaped during the summers from the notorious heat and humidity of the Boston area to the cooler climate of Jaffrey, New Hampshire, and Shirley Village, Massachusetts (where Howells observed the ways of a Shaker community), or to the tranquillity of Townsend Harbor, Massachusetts. All of these retreats were carefully selected so that the ever busy editor could easily take "the cars" to his editorial offices in Cambridge.

Howells' father, his sisters Victoria, Aurelia, and Annie, as well as his mentally retarded brother Henry moved from Jefferson to Quebec, the elder Howells having received an appointment as American consul in 1874. This came as a great relief to Howells partly because it provided his father with badly needed income, partly because Howells had become more and more aware of his sisters' discontent with life in the provincial "West." He visited Quebec several times, and faithfully maintained his weekly correspondence with his father or one of his sisters. Some of the most interesting family letters of this period are addressed to Annie, who was trying to establish herself as a reviewer and author of fiction in her own right. Her brother Will supported her in that endeavor, presumably remembering his own salad days in Ohio. But there were also times when his Victorian sense of female propriety qualified his enthusiasm for her activities. Thus he expressed, in a letter to his father, his dislike of her conduct as a review writer for the Chicago *Inter-Ocean*: "I return Annie's letter which I confess presented a picture I didn't like of her life at the newspaper office among all those editors. I heartily wish she would give up her room there . . . . It's the only decorous way for her to do" (16 February 1873). Nevertheless he encouraged her—especially in her writing of fiction—and used his influence with the editors of several "Western" newspapers (his old friend J. M. Comly of the *Ohio State Journal* among them) to take her book notices on a regular basis.

The social life of the Howellses was extremely demanding; their schedule often left them exhausted and longing for the peace and quiet of a country home. By the mid-1870s the *Atlantic* editor had "arrived" in the good society of Boston and Cambridge, an achievement that was signaled by his election to the Saturday Club in November 1874. One letter to Victoria speaks—with perhaps some slight exaggeration—of a dinner party in "the most exclusive Boston circles" (18 January 1874); other letters mention a dinner with Thomas Appleton (9 January 1875), one at Longfellow's (18 June 1876), and one arranged by Henry Adams in honor of Lord Houghton (27 November 1875). Many of these affairs were important to Howells' career as an editor, and thus attendance was more often obligatory than a matter of personal preference. What aggravated this situation was the frequency with which people called at the new house: "Besides visitors we have constant callers," he complained to his father, "and I dread to hear the bell ring: I average two or three interruptions each morning, and it almost worries my life out . . ." (27 June 1875).

It is remarkable that under these conditions Howells managed to establish himself as an important critical voice, an authoritative editor, and a novelist who saw with increasing clarity the particular kind of fiction. he should write. Ever since he had taken over the editorship of the *Atlantic* from James T. Fields, Howells had worked tirelessly and imaginatively to make the magazine into the best critical authority in the country. At least by his own estimate he had largely succeeded in achieving his goal only two years later. Writing to his sister Annie on 3 February 1873, Howells proudly asserted that "The Nation often has good notices, but on the whole I think The Atlantic's the best in the country—" adding rather tongue-in-cheek, "even though I don't always write them." And several months later, explaining to Thomas Wentworth Higginson his philosophy of reviewing, Howells again let it be known how well he thought of his enterprise: "We have limitations which no one dislikes more than I, but we are in some sort a critical authority, in a country where criticism is rare..." (18 October 1873). The price of this ambition was total dedication to editorial duties, leaving little time for casual reading, family affairs, or other pleasures.

Writing letters to established and prospective contributors and in other ways pursuing contacts to develop and maintain literary relationships were essential to the successful accomplishment of Howells' mission. He made sure that the older generation of New England writers—Lowell, Longfellow, Emerson, Whittier, and Holmes—would retain their connection with the *Atlantic*. But he also reached out for younger writers from other parts of the country, including Bret Harte (in whose official welcome to Boston Howells had played a major part in 1871), Paul Hamilton Hayne, H. H. Boyesen, and—closer to home—Charles Dudley Warner and Sarah Orne Jewett. Boyesen he considered his protégé, and the letters to the Norwegian-American writer are full of good advice from an already experienced editor who saw with increasing clarity the kind of fiction he was later to advocate so outspokenly. Again and again he admonished Boyesen to be less diffuse and to use his own experiences and observations as the basis of fiction. "It rests with yourself to be a writer of tame, pleasant-enough spun-out fiction," Howells wrote to Boyesen on 19 September 1876, laying out the alternatives of romantic mediocrity and realistic mastery, "or to take your place with such concise dramatic poets as Tourgueneff and Björnson." With Miss Jewett, whose Deephaven stories Howells liked immensely, he was gentler in suggesting improvements: "It's very 'brightly' written—that is to say, you wrote it—but there is no climax...; and then it appears to me impossible that you should do successfully what you've undertaken in it: assume a young man's character in the supposed narrator" (10 June 1876). But it is in the brief advice given Charles Dudley Warner for sharpening some of his travel sketches from the Near East that we see most clearly Howells' insistence on specific and accurately observed detail: "I would rather have one good Turk or dirty Jew got by heart than a whole generalized population" (5 January 1876).

There were two literary relationships, however, that stand out from the rest, not only because they have a special significance for the development of American fiction in the late nineteenth century, but because they grew into lifelong friendships—Howells' somewhat distant and never entirely easy association with Henry James, and his deep and close friendship with Mark Twain.

James and Howells had gotten to know each other in 1865 or 1866, at a time when both young men were trying to establish themselves as professional writers—Americans who had both experienced Europe and were searching for new ways of using that encounter in literature. They took walks together in and around Cambridge, rowed on Fresh Pond, and were in each other's company in the large James household on Quincy Street, presided over by Henry James, Sr., whose Swedenborgianism made Howells feel at home, quite as if he were still with his father in Ohio. During the years 1873–1876 James was mostly in Europe, except for a one-year sojourn in Cambridge and New York during 1874–1875, but the distance between the two friends did not stop their exchange of comments on each other's works. As James received and read the serial installments of *A Chance Acquaintance* he wrote at length about his reactions to it, and Howells in return commented on his intentions. Howells encouraged James in his literary efforts not only by praising his works (although suggesting at times less prolixity), but also by reporting on the favorable popular and critical response to them in America. Above all, he offered ample space in the *Atlantic* for James's stories, sketches, and novels and tried hard to keep James from succumbing to the siren song of *Scribner's Monthly*, the *Atlantic*'s chief competitor: "I hope you wont send any of your stories to Scribner's. We have of course no claim upon you, but we have hitherto been able to print all the stories you have sent, and so it shall be hereafter. Scribner is trying to lure away all our contributors..." (5 December 1873). How successful Howells' effort turned out to be is evident from the serialization of James's first two major novels in the *Atlantic*—*Roderick Hudson* and *The American*.

Howells' friendship with Mark Twain, which began with a chance encounter in the editorial offices of the *Atlantic* in 1869, is reflected in the frequent exchange of letters beginning in 1874—some 135 for the period 1874–1876 alone. They are the first part of a long and brilliant, rich and revealing record that has been fully printed and explored in the *Mark Twain–Howells Letters*.[1] But even the few letters by Howells that have been selected for inclusion here give a taste of the intensity and significance of this association between two men whose personalities could hardly have been more different, but who complemented

1. *Mark Twain–Howells Letters*, ed. Henry Nash Smith and William M. Gibson, 2 vols. (Cambridge: Harvard University Press, Belknap Press, 1960).

and depended on each other as no two other authors in the history of American literature. The frequent exchange of visits between Cambridge and Hartford, the long walks together, the hours of laughing, storytelling, and planning of joint literary ventures (often until deep into the night) testify to the enjoyment Howells and Clemens derived from being in each other's company. Their epistolary comments on each other's works reveal both the respect they had for the integrity of their art and the honesty with which they offered advice. Howells, for example, gently suggested some changes in the first of the "Old Times on the Mississippi" sketches, which he had been fortunate to get for the *Atlantic*: "The sketch of the low-lived little town was so good, that I could have wished ever so much more of it; and perhaps the tearful watchman's story might have been abridged—tho this may seem different in print" (23 November 1874). More important, however, was Howells' contribution to the final version of *Tom Sawyer*, which Clemens wished him to read and edit in manuscript. "It's altogether the best boy's story I ever read," he wrote on 21 November 1875, after having sat up late marking the manuscript with his comments. "It will be an immense success. But I think you ought to treat it explicitly *as* a boy's story. . . . I have made some corrections and suggestions in faltering pencil, which you'll have to look for. They're almost all in the first third. When you fairly swing off, you had better be let alone." It is perhaps this willingness to comment fully and frankly on each other's writings, yet to "let alone" when the personal, innermost qualities of each writer's style and vision were at stake, that best characterizes the literary relationship between Howells and Mark Twain.

The fictional output was not very great during this period of Howells' life, but the step he took from *A Chance Acquaintance* to *A Foregone Conclusion* was an important one in his development as a realist—so important, in fact, that Howells once referred to the latter as "My first novel."[2] After having published the first four installments of *A Chance Acquaintance*, he recognized that he had accomplished one major goal, if nothing else: "it sets me forever outside of the rank of mere *culturists*, followers of an elegant literature, and proves that I have sympathy with the true spirit of Democracy" (20 April 1873). With *A Foregone Conclusion* Howells continued his interest in the truthful portrayal of common people, but he abandoned both the American setting and the travel format that had served him so well up to this time. His new interest focused more sharply on the analysis of character and on the ways in which characters interact and affect each

---

2. Edwin H. Cady, *The Road to Realism: The Early Years 1837–1885 of William Dean Howells* (Syracuse: Syracuse University Press, 1956), p. 187.

other. This brought him a long and complimentary letter from John William De Forest, who compared Howells favorably with George Eliot and Ivan Turgenev. Because Howells considered De Forest to be the first great American realist, and because he thought as highly of Turgenev at this time in his life as he was to admire Tolstoy a dozen years later, the letter praising *A Foregone Conclusion* must have given him particular pleasure.

The only other novelistic enterprise Howells undertook during these years was *Private Theatricals*, which ran in the *Atlantic* from November 1875 to May 1876, but did not appear in book form until 1921—then with the title *Mrs. Farrell*. Instead of revising the serial, Howells turned to writing a campaign biography of Rutherford B. Hayes, an Ohio Republican squarely in the tradition of the Western Reserve Republicanism in which Howells had grown up. As a cousin of Elinor Howells, furthermore, Hayes deserved the novelist's support for personal as well as political reasons. The month of August at Townsend Harbor was spent writing the *Sketch of the Life and Character of Rutherford B. Hayes*, and it was finished early in September. But it was not until the beginning of 1877 that Howells was certain of having helped elect the new president—a political success that was a distinct asset to Howells' social and professional status. If one adds to these rather slim literary accomplishments the translation of Tommaso Salvini's *Sansone*, two short plays—*The Parlor Car* and *Out of the Question*—and such abortive projects as a history of Venice and what Howells in one letter refers to as the "New Medea" (24 September 1876), one gets the clear impression of an author groping for a new and challenging subject for fictional treatment.

For the time being, though the search remained unsuccessful, Howells had no doubt about the *kind* of fiction he wanted to write. "I understand," he wrote to Charles Dudley Warner on 4 September 1875, "that you want me [to] try a large canvass [sic] with many peop's in it. Perhaps, some time. But isn't the real dramatic encounter always between two persons only? Of three or four at most? If the effects are in *me*, I can get them into six numbers of The Atlantic, and if they aren't, I couldn't get 'em into twenty. Besides, I can only forgive myself for writing novels at all on the ground that the poor girl urged in extenuation of her unlegalized addition to the census: it was such a very *little* baby!" The realization that the small canvas was the most congenial fictional form for him, that he should deal with the psychological drama resulting from the encounter of a small set of characters, was Howells' major achievement in his development as a novelist up to 1877. If that was not a particularly visible accomplishment, he could always comfort himself by thinking about his large circle of friends and acquaintances, by reminding himself of the excellent quality and reputation of the *Atlantic,* and by sitting in his handsomely appointed library at 37 Concord Avenue contemplating with satisfaction the sight of his monogrammed mantel.

C. K. L.

2 JANUARY 1873, BOSTON, TO PAUL H. HAYNE

>   ... *The Atlantic Monthly*, ...
>   *Boston*, Jan. 2, *1873*.

My dear Mr. Hayne:[1]

I accept your delicate poem, The Wood Lake,[2] with pleasure, and will ask them to send you a check to-morrow. With your leave, I think I shall omit the stanza I have marked, because it does not heighten the whole effect, and is of an exaggerated expression in its imagery. Pray return me the poem.

I am a thousand times obliged for your fotograf. At forty-one how do you keep so fresh and young a face? My wife and I are both charmed with it, and she fancies that she sees in it a likeness to myself as she first saw me. But at thirty-five I look much your senior.—You have a good, kind, sensitive face, on which I like to look and feel that you are my friend; and I should know you for a poet anywhere. Are you tall or short? I see you are not stout, as I am getting to be. Are your eyes and hair northern or southern?

For your Christmas greeting I send you a Happy New Year with all my heart.

>   Yours ever
>   W. D. Howells.

1. Paul Hamilton Hayne (1830–1886), a South Carolina poet, was a leading member of the Russell's Bookstore Group in Charleston, along with William Gilmore Simms, Henry Timrod, and others. Howells praised Hayne's poems and opened the *Atlantic* to him and other young Southern writers, and Hayne in turn wrote Howells, on 21 May 1873 (OFH), of his own "*high, & exceptional esteem* wherewith I regard *you*; an esteem strengthened & sanctified by *affection* ...." See Cady, *Howells*, I, 173; J. D. Ferguson, "A New Letter of Paul Hamilton Hayne," *American Literature* 5 (1934), 368–70.
2. "The Wood Lake," *Atlantic*, April 1873.

5 JANUARY 1873, CAMBRIDGE, TO CHARLES D. WARNER

>   Cambridge, Jan. 5, 1873.

Dear Mr. Warner:

If it were not for your Backlog Studies[1] I should doubt your literature after the promptness and fidelity with which you kept your promise to send me those *raids* on Snap and Murray.[2] But I enjoyed them both—especially that on his Reverence, whom I do not love. My heart went with you also against Snap, though my sectional sensibilities were wounded at the expression: "even in the West." "Even in the West," quotha! I will yet have this out of Connecticut—yea, Hartford's self shall repay it.

Perhaps a fine revenge, worthy of all the Charles Lambs of America[3] (what a fold there *is* of us!) would be to take you at your word, and come down there to visit you. *Happy thought.* Do it!

We *did* have a good time, didn't we?[4] The gods themselves cannot take that away from us. But I remunerated for it, by taking a frightful cold (in Twain's room, I suppose,) and it settled in the form of a stiff neck, and now I go round with my head tilted sarcastically upon one side, looking as if I were about to flash out something very satirical—a thing I can't do, for the life of me, under a week's notice. With love to Clemens,

Yours truly
W D Howells
(Established 1837.)[5]

1. *Backlog Studies* had just been published by J. R. Osgood & Co., and Howells wrote Warner on 28 January 1873 (CtHT): "I read your book with the greatest pleasure, and have tried to say so in the March Atlantic. But these things are hard to manage: it's much easier to say what you think of the book you don't like than of the book you do like. I had no fault whatever to find with yours—it was light and pleasant, every page. Some community of framework I thought well to mention in order to illustrate its utter unimportance." Actually Howells wrote a new review and published it in the *Atlantic*, April 1873. See Howells to C. D. Warner, 3 February 1873 (CtHT).

2. Howells had probably requested Warner to write two book reviews, which turned out to be sharply critical. One was most likely a review of William Henry Harrison Murray's *Music-Hall Sermons,* a collection of very popular sermons delivered over a three-year period (1869–1873) in the Boston Music Hall. Perhaps Howells' comment about not loving "his Reverence" indicates that he attended some of these meetings, which were organized by the Independent Congregational Church. Snap has not been identified, and neither review was published in the *Atlantic*, probably because of Howells' wish not to offend the religious feelings of his audience.

3. Howells' review of *Backlog Studies* begins with the following sentence: "Among the Charles Lambs of America, whom the book-noticers have given us in such number that we can no longer count the humorous fold upon the fingers of both hands, we believe that we like none so well as Mr. Warner...."

4. Howells had visited Hartford several days earlier to see both Warner and Clemens. On 3 January 1873 (CSmH) he wrote Charles W. Stoddard: "I lunched the other night with Mark Twain, and we had some 'very pretty conversation,' as Pepys says. Yourself was among the topics."

5. Howells is here referring to the year of his birth.

3 FEBRUARY 1873, BOSTON, TO ANNE T. HOWELLS

> ... *The Atlantic Monthly,* ...
> *Boston,* Feb. 3, *1873.*

Dear Annie:

Your notice of "Sibylle"[1] is very good indeed, well expressed and interesting, and with little lively turns which I needn't point out to you. The notices crossed out I suppose are not yours; the rest are so slight that there isn't much to say of them; but they're all graceful and pleasant. Only, I *never* would say, as you do of Hale, "the name of the author is a guaranty," etc. That's begging the question.

In regard to all my notices, I should seek, if I were you, to make them *entertaining,* and thoroughly worth the reader's while. This you can do by sketching the plot, or else by giving some passage or point that he can enjoy without having read the book. The passage should be characteristic of the author; and there ought always to be some extract, if possible. You will be most pleasing and brilliant when you do your best to set the author honestly before the reader. If you don't like an author, say *why,* and let him *show* why. Never try to be funny at his expense; that's poor, cheap, cruel business. Read a book, or else don't write of it.

The Nation often has good notices, but on the whole I think The Atlantic's the best in the country—even though I don't always write them. For the rest, trust yourself and don't be afraid. Most newspaper notices are rubbish, and you can easily make your department conspicuous.

Do you still board at the Smiths'? Miss Bross somehow understood that you were going to *her* place.[2]—We had Milly[3] Christened on Saturday, before all the ladies of the neighborhood.—We are all well except colds for Winny and Bua.—We are of course absorbed with the new house,[4] which has been somewhat delayed by the terribly cold weather.—I have met the Brosses a good deal, and I think they are both charming.—Do you hear anything said of "A Chance Acquaintance"?[5] I dont expect much effect from it till the fourth number; then I hope people will begin to understand the characters, and to mis-guess the end. I've worked steadily on it for more than a year; but I don't expect it to be so well liked as Their Wed. Journey.[6]—That's quite funny about the preaching clown.[7] Elinor joins me in love.

> Your affectionate brother,
> Will.

How terribly sad is Aunt Hannah's death![8]

1. Annie's review of Octave Feuillet, *The Story of Sibylle* has not been located; it did not appear in *Inter-Ocean*, a Chicago daily for which Annie began to work in August 1872. Feuillet's novel was translated from the French and published by Osgood & Co. in 1872. Howells' subsequent reference to Annie's notice of a book by Hale suggests that she also reviewed Edward Everett Hale, *His Level Best and Other Stories*, also published by Osgood (1873).

2. Annie probably boarded with the family of W. H. Smith in Chicago; Miss Bross was a friend of Annie's, whom Howells mentioned in his letter to his father, 1 December 1872 (MH): "I've called on Miss Bross a very pleasant Chicago friend of hers [Annie's] who is staying in Boston for the winter...." In a somewhat later letter to W. C. Howells, 22 December 1872 (MH), he wrote that "Miss Bross said she hoped Annie was going to board at the same place with her when she [Annie] left Mrs. Smith's." Miss Bross was traveling with her aunt.

3. Mildred Howells was born 26 September 1872. She was the last of Howells' three children, Winifred ("Winny") being the oldest and John ("Bua") the second.

4. See Howells to W. C. Howells, 22 September 1872, n. 2.

5. *A Chance Acquaintance* was serialized in the *Atlantic*, January–June 1873, and published in book form by J. R. Osgood & Co. late in May 1873. Howells had written his father on 19 January 1873 (MH): "In preparing the successive installments of my story, I've done almost as much work on it as in first writing it, and so with my editorial business, I've found no chance to write on anything else, though I've got two things planned. The story seems to have a fair chance in the newspapers, but I don't expect any marked impression till the third number is published."

6. *Their Wedding Journey* was published in December 1871 with an 1872 imprint.

7. Howells' reference has remained obscure.

8. Hannah K. Howells was the third wife of Henry C. Howells, a brother of William Cooper Howells.

5 FEBRUARY 1873, BOSTON, TO WILLIAM C. HOWELLS

> ... *The Atlantic Monthly,* ...
> *Boston*, Feb. 5, *1873*.

Dear father:

We did find the cheese, at once, and it adds to my shame about the whole transaction that I didn't send you Elinor's thanks for it, as she bade me. It's capital, and we're both greatly obliged to you. I send $2 to pay for the nuts.

I wish you would write me at once in regard to the Englishman of whom I spoke in my last.[1] I really think you could make him useful to you. He could turn his hand to a good many things.

—Now in regard to my story,[2] and the resemblances you fancy. It seems to me that if you look at the structure of the plot again you'll see that these do not exist. However, perhaps I had better say that I have no idea of portraying any of your characters in it. There are some faint outlines of Annie in "Kitty," and I have used her little adventure of coming on without preparation to Quebec.[3] There all resemblance, except of the most casual kind, ceases. The "girls" at Erie are Kitty's *aunts*, represented as 15 or 20 years older; she as born in Illinois; the two Ellison boys were officers in the army, as, I'm sorry to say, none of your boys were. All that you have to do is simply to say that there is nothing of any supposed likeness between the Ellison family and our own, as in fact there is not. It isn't a question of our girls at all, or of my opinion of them. Consequently, I can't model the Ellison girls upon them, though I don't see at all how I have treated the Ellison girls with any sort of slight. On the contrary I conceived of them with the greatest respect. I beseech you to dismiss forever from your mind the notion that I regard either Vic or Aurelia as inferior to Annie, or had any intention to exhibit them in the Ellisons

affectionately
Will.

1. Howells had written to his father, 2 February 1873 (MH): "By the way, have you any use in Jefferson for a starving Englishman of good education who has seen better days? I have at present such a character on my hands. He was at Oxford (Eng.) when his mother lost her fortune, and for the last six years he's been in Nebraska. He writes well enough, and has had a little newspaper experience. He's not a printer; but he knows a little about book-keeping, and it's just possible that he might turn out generally useful to you. You could get him for little or nothing. He's about 30." The Englishman has not been further identified.
2. *A Chance Acquaintance.*
3. See Howells to Anne T. Howells, 6 March 1873.

16 FEBRUARY 1873, BOSTON, TO WILLIAM C. HOWELLS

...The Atlantic Monthly,...
Boston, Feb'y 16, *1873.*

Dear father:

We have had rather an anxious week here, on account of Bua, who has had a very bad cold, with swollen tonsils. He is now almost quite well again, but for forty-eight hours he suffered a great deal, especially at night. He could not breathe at all through his nose; he talked continually in his sleep, and he would wake dizzy and terrified. Dr. Wyman[1] said this was because the swollen tonsils caused a great pressure of blood on the brain. Doesn't this throw a good deal of light on poor Henry's case?[2] His trouble began in much the same way, and I believe his tonsils remained swollen for years, maintaining that constant pressure. Doesn't it almost seem as if he might have been relieved and restored to sanity, by an operation on the tonsils, which is very common? You know he always seemed to suffer pain in his head.—We have very little news beyond this. I haven't seen the novel by Riddle of which you speak, but I dare say it will be sent to the magazine.[3]

I'm sorry that Harvey[4] bought my books—for I should been so glad to send him a set, if I hadn't rather stupidly supposed that he had them. I wrote him last week in reply to a letter which I got a long time ago. I'm glad to hear that he feels friendly towards me, for he had some reason to feel otherwise.—I return Annie's letter which I confess presented a picture I didn't like of her life at the newspaper office among all those editors. I heartily wish she would give up her room there, and do her reviewing, as she far better might—at her boarding-house. It's the only decorous way for her to do. I'm sorry she ever thought of taking a room at the office. It makes her life altogether too public.[5]—The story[6] seems to be gaining in popularity, each month, though it never will be so much liked as Their Wedding Journey. The three last parts are the best. I'd like now to take up the Eureka business;[7] but I'm afraid of treading on the family corns!—All join me in love. Elinor has been kept from writing, by Johnny's sickness.

Your affectionate son
Will.

1. Dr. Morrill Wyman (1812–1903), a Cambridge physician, distinguished himself by developing an effective operation to cure pleurisy, and by founding Cambridge Hospital.

2. Howells' youngest brother was mentally retarded, apparently as a result of a childhood accident.

3. Albert Gallatin Riddle, *Bart Ridgeley: A Story of Northern Ohio* (1873).

4. Probably Harvey Green, editor of the Medina *Gazette* and a former boarder in the Howells household at Jefferson. The basis of Howells' statement about Green's feelings toward him is not known.

5. See Howells to Anne T. Howells, 3 February 1873, n. 1. In a subsequent letter to his sister, 28 February 1873 (MH), Howells apologized for this criticism of Annie's conduct: "I am very sorry indeed if what I said offended you, for I never meant it to do so. I never dreamt that you would cheapen yourself; but our circumstances are what they are in effect, in spite of us.... It was your position that I thought disadvantageous, only, for you know well enough how much I admire your good sense and personal dignity. I never knew you to do a silly thing, and I merely hated the publicity of your having a room at the office."

6. *A Chance Acquaintance.*

7. In October 1850, W. C. Howells moved with his family and several of his brothers to Eureka Mills, near Xenia, in order to establish a Utopian community whose economic basis was to be a paper mill. In the fall of 1851, the Howells family abandoned the venture and moved to Columbus. This experience loomed large in Howells' memory and imagination, and for many years he contemplated some fictional treatment of it until the publication of *New Leaf Mills* (1913). It is also reflected in several of his autobiographical writings: *My Year in a Log Cabin* (1887), *My Literary Passions* (1895), and *Years of My Youth*, HE, pp. 39–56. See Cady, *Howells*, I, 34–37, and Lynn, *Howells*, pp. 59–62.

6 MARCH 1873, CAMBRIDGE, TO ANNE T. HOWELLS

Cambridge, March 6, 1873.

Dear Annie:

This morning I wrote you a letter which has strangely vanished; perhaps the postman took, it, but I'm afraid it was stolen by an Italian pensioner of mine from the place where I put it for the postman. However, it was chiefly to advise decidedly against your use of A Tour in a Basket, because it certainly *would* identify you with Kitty, and might be a great annoyance to both of us.[1] I acknowledge that it was rather selfish of me to employ that little adventure of yours, but you know your sketch had lain unfinished for nearly two years. But besides identifying you, in the eyes of the large public who only see the surface and striking points, with Kitty, I really think it would not be so well for you, seeing that Quebec has already been fully treated by me, to publish anything about that place.

I'm merely repeating what I've already written, and it's quite likely you'll have got my other letter.

I'm so glad you like my story,[2] for it's cost me far more work than anything I've ever written. Some day I'd like to explain why, as a matter of curious literary experience. One of the great difficulties was in having so few characters, and another in taking a plot that I could hardly bring to the surface in a dramatic way at all.

I trust you wont use your sketch. If I can make you any reparation for my selfishness in gobbling the subject I should like to do so. Can't you send me your story in Ms.—the one you speak of?[3]

Your aff'te brother
Will.

Tell me if you got both my letters.

1. Annie had written a story based on her trip to Quebec in 1870; it told of her making do with no more baggage than a single basket taken along for what had originally been planned as a much shorter excursion. In writing *Their Wedding Journey*, Howells already wanted to use the basket episode, but finally decided to leave it out. See Howells to W. C. Howells, 3 December 1871, n. 3.

2. *A Chance Acquaintance.*

3. Annie's story has not been identified.

10 MARCH 1873, CAMBRIDGE, TO HENRY JAMES

Cambridge, March 10, 1873.

My dear James:

I hope you'll be properly affected by the size of this sheet: it's extent is an emblem of my friendship for you, for I'm reducing the size of my notepaper generally.

First let me thank you with all my heart for your criticism on my story—rather, on my heroine. It came too late for the magazine; but I have been able to check the young person a little before handing her down to the latest posterity in book form.[1] Her pertness was but another proof of the contrariness of her sex: I meant her to be everything that was lovely, and went on protesting that she was so, but she preferred being saucy to the young man, especially in that second number. Afterwards I think she is at least all I profess for her. I like her because she seems to me a character; the man, I own is a simulacrum. Well or ill advisedly I conceived the notion of confronting two extreme American types: the conventional and the unconventional. These always disgust each other, but I amused myself with the notion of their falling in love, which would not be impossible, if they were both young and good looking. Now conventionality is, in our condition of things, in itself a caricature; I did my best for the young man, but his nature was against him, and he is the stick you see. Of course the girl must be attracted by what is elegant and fine in him, and provoked to any sort of reprisal by his necessary cool assumption of superiority. She cannot very well help "sassing" him, though she feels that this puts her at a disadvantage, and makes her seem the aggressor. I have tried to let this explain itself to the reader as much as I can; but it is a kind of thing that scarcely admits of dramatic demonstration, and I feel that the whole thing is weighed down with comment. However, I've learnt a great deal in writing the story, and if it does not destroy my public, I shall be weaponed better than ever for the field of romance. And I am already thirty pages advanced on a new story,[2] in which, blessed be heaven, there is no problem but the sweet old one of how they shall get married. In this case I'm sorry to say they don't solve it, for the hero is a Venetian priest in love with an American girl. There's richness! And now peace to me and my work. I've been burning to tell you how much I like your "Madonna,"[3] and to report the undissenting voice of acclaim with which it has been hailed. Ever so many people have spoken of it, the Delphic Dennett alone remaining mum.[4] Truly it has been a success, and justly, for it is a bravely solid and excellent piece of work. All like the well-managed pathos of it, the dissertations on pictures, the tragic, most poetical central fact, and I hope that many feel with me its unity and completeness. Every figure in it is a real character, and has some business there. The sole blemish on it to my mind is the insistance on the cats and monkeys philosophy.[5] I don't think you ought to have let that *artista* appear a second time, and, I confess, to have the cs and ms for a refrain at the close, marred the fine harmony of what went before, till I managed to forget them. I have your Roman romance, and I shall print it very soon.[6] I like it, but I shall tell you more about it when I get it in print. I'm glad that we're to hear from you every month, and I rejoice that you think of doing a serial for next year.[7] Whether you'll find Venice a good working climate, I'm not sure. I'd rather do my loafing there. But it's delicious in early summer, and with sea-baths, I don't see why you shouldn't get on.—All the family at Casa Howells are well; but they have had their colds and other woes this winter. My wife in particular has been very delicate, though with a little promise of spring she's at least gaining courage if not health again. She agrees with you about Kitty's pertness, and is otherwise my terriblest critic, as always. The children are all that a fond papa could desire. The two oldest you know, but little maid Mildred is the jolliest and prettiest of all. She is really a little beauty, and as amiable as the day is long.—The house gets on as well as could be expected in a winter which has forbidden plastering. It's all finished outside, and we're to be in it—if we put our faith in carpenters—by the first of June.—You divine truly that I have seen no one this winter. The other night I went to one of the Rev. Peabody receptions, and to-morrow we're invited to the Golden Wedding of Dr. and Mrs. Palfrey.[8] About once in three weeks Mr. Longfellow has regularly taken pity on me, and had me to dinner. This is the whole story. I don't know whether anything's been going on or not, but I love all my fellow men here as heartily as if I had met the whole human family once a week. I thank you for not telling me too much about Rome. Such things are hard to bear. I hate the American in Europe,—because I am not he. At times the longing is almost intolerable with me, and if I could see any way of keeping the bird in the hand while I clutched at those in the bush, I should go. I have a scheme for work some day in Italy which I hope to carry out.[9] It would take me there just about the time the children should be studying French and music, and keep me there five years. M'aspetti! Intanto Le reverisco![10] Mrs Howells and the children join me in love.

Yours ever
W D Howells.

P. S. I'm glad Osgood is to get out a volume for you.[11]

Imagine getting up this morning and finding a heavy snow storm in full blast. It was almost heart-breaking. We've now had three months of snow, and sleighing.

1. James's letter commenting on the serial version of *A Chance Acquaintance* has not been located; see, however, Howells to James, 12 May 1873, n. 3, and Howells to James, 5 December 1873, n. 4. The extent of Howells' effort to "check" Kitty Ellison in the book can be seen in the Emendations section of *A Chance Acquaintance*, HE, pp. 175–84.

2. *A Foregone Conclusion*, which was published the following year.

3. "The Madonna of the Future," *Atlantic*, March 1873.

4. John R. Dennett was the literary critic of the *Nation*.

5. Toward the end of his story, James introduces a vulgar and commercial artist—the opposite of the supreme artistic idealist who is the central character—who offers for sale grotesque little statues of cats and monkeys in various human poses. He says to the narrator: "Speaking, signore, to a man of imagination, I may say that my little designs are not without a philosophy of their own. Truly, I don't know whether the cats and monkeys imitate us, or whether it's we who imitate them." At the very end, the narrator encounters the same character again, hearing him murmur: "Cats and monkeys, monkeys and cats; all human life is there!"

6. "The Last of the Valerii," *Atlantic*, January 1874.

7. James's first serialized novel was *Roderick Hudson*, *Atlantic*, January–December 1875.

8. Andrew P. Peabody (1811–1893), like John Gorham Palfrey (1796–1881), was a Unitarian minister and former editor of the *North American Review* (1852–1861).

9. Howells' reference here is probably to his plans for writing a history of Venice, which he pursued for many years but finally left unfinished.

10. The correct Italian sentence would read: "M'aspetti! Intanto La reverisco!" It means "Wait for me! Meanwhile I send you my regards!"

11. Both *A Passionate Pilgrim* and *Transatlantic Sketches* were published early in 1875 by J. R. Osgood & Co.

16 MARCH 1873, BOSTON, TO WILLIAM C. HOWELLS

. . . The Atlantic Monthly, . . .
Boston, March 16, 1873.

Dear father:

The weeks persist in imitating each other so closely that it might as well be last Sunday as this, for all the news that I have to tell you. The best is that our snow is going—there! I heard a crow cawing as he flew over,—and that the spring does faintly promise to come. But it is a very slow thaw, as you may judge from the fact that the ice is still a foot thick the whole length of our street. The severity of this winter and the prodigious expense that it has entailed simply on the fact of existence, has made us talk and think a great deal of the possibility of some easier and better kind of life in a friendlier climate.[1] It costs me now every cent that I can earn: how will it be when I shall have to pay for the foolish and costly education of the children? It may be that I shall have sufficiently advanced myself in literature to meet the increased expense, but woe to me if I haven't. The worst of my present life is that it leaves me no time for reading or study. You have no idea how busy I am, and how the work constantly piles up on my hands. Of course I write a great deal, and of a kind that causes me immense labor, and the editorial duties are alone sufficient to occupy one person. If I only were sure of enough without editing! But I couldn't risk that yet awhile.—Elinor's health improves, and yesterday she went into Boston in the horse-cars for the first time *in eight months.* She had been in before two or three times in a carriage. She went with me also the other day to Dr Palfrey's Golden Wedding—a very charming and beautiful affair. The Doctor wore the gloves in which he was married, and he and his wife were radiantly happy. The Parsonses[2] are to have their golden wedding in May.—The plastering of our house is to begin this week, for we hope that we are now beyond the reach of frost. Tell Joe[3] I shall answer his kind letter soon. Elinor joins me in love to all.

Your affectionate son
Will.

1. In his letter to Henry James, 10 March 1873, Howells had written of his longing for Italy and his plans to return there for several years.
2. The Harvard law school professor, Theophilus Parsons (1797–1882), and his wife, from whom Howells had purchased a lot at 37 Concord Avenue, Cambridge; they became neighbors when the Howellses moved to their new house in July.
3. Joseph A. Howells.

20 MARCH 1873, BOSTON, TO CHARLES W. STODDARD

... *The Atlantic Monthly,* ...
Boston, March 20, *1873.*

Dear Mr. Stoddard:

As Osgood has probably written you already of his acceptance of your book and its forthcomingness,[1] I judge you are in a state to bear a little adversity, and so I send you back your poem.[2] I wish that I found more "to it," but it begins and stops in such an unauthorized, inconsequent way, and it is so altogether alien to the general reader's intelligence, that I can't venture upon it. But do send me the other ones that you speak of.[3] As to the volume of poems, let me suggest to you to let that rest till the 5th thousand of the prose is sold—you must be used to advice, and will like this. Seriously.

I've just finished reading your first theatrical paper.[4] Were you sensible of straining more in its composition than in that of your Tahiti things, or is it my fancy? If I'm right, don't do it! I imagined a certain pressure and anxiety in it, which seemed quite foreign to you. Perhaps I have n't caught your mood yet. I think so, and I wait for the second paper, before saying more.

I think your book will succeed.

Yours very cordially
W. D. Howells.

Should you mind writing on thicker paper?

1. *South-Sea Idyls*, a volume of sketches based on Stoddard's voyages to Hawaii and Tahiti, was published by Osgood in 1873. On 3 January 1873 (CSmH), Howells had written to Stoddard: "Send on the copy of your book. I have spoken to Osgood about it, and I know that it will have a fair and favorable chance."

2. The poem has not been identified.

3. None of the poems Stoddard submitted were published in the *Atlantic*. That Stoddard seems to have accepted Howells' advice to publish prose rather than poetry is suggested by the fact that the only book publication of his poetry besides *Poems* (1867) was a 1917 collection edited posthumously by Ina Coolbrith.

4. Howells had requested Stoddard on 13 November 1872 to write about his experiences on the stage, and three articles on this subject were published in the *Atlantic* during 1874, even though Howells wrote Stoddard on 2 June 1873 (CSmH): "I like your theatrical articles well enough . . . , but I had pitched my hopes of them by the Prodigal in Tahiti, and they fall below that. This is what I ought to have said long ago; but I am already too old an editor to be sure of any thing, and I'm not at all certain that your papers may not be a great hit in the magazine."

27 MARCH 1873, BOSTON, TO HJALMAR H. BOYESEN

. . . *The Atlantic Monthly,* . . .
Boston, March 27, *1873*.

My dear Boyesen:

I send back the two poems I have not printed. The legend you can easily prepare for publication, and I dare say sell to the Galaxy. The idyll I should like for myself if you could once put it in shape.[1] But it is very *wordy*, and will require a good deal of work, yet. Perhaps you can let it rest till you come on here, in June, and then we can fight it out together. I shall print the Bergsoe review as soon as I can find a place for it.[2] About the short story I can't now speak certainly;[3] I'm crowded almost to death.—I thought St. Olaf's Fountain one of your best poems;[4] Mr. Longfellow praised it to me, and he knows good poetry.—Perhaps, if you are going to Norway this summer, it is as well to have laid by your Legend of the M. S.[5] Without doubt your fancies will all be freshened by the sight of old scenes, and you will go forward the more vigorously with it, for the delay. You ought never to be really down-cast about your future. That is assured, if you live—and live in America. There is no doubt of your power—your genius, as you know I may call it without intending to flatter you; and you have already won your public. One thing, however, I would say to you quite earnestly: study a condensed expression both in prose and verse. It strikes me more and more that your chief fault is diffuseness.[6] It's a bad fault, but it's one of the most curable, and the remedy lies with yourself. Study your "idyll" in the light of my disgusting frankness. They've begun to put A Chance Acquaintance into type for book publication. I'm glad that it has pleased you and that the Sewalls are reading it.[7] I'm now well launched upon another story, every scene of which is clearly before me.[8] I've never foreseen anything else so fully.—I long to *umarm*[9] you.—Mrs. Howells and the children join me in regard.

> Ever yours
> W. D. Howells.

1. Neither the two poems nor the "idyll" has been identified. The "legend" is probably Boyesen's poem, "Necken," Galaxy, May 1874, the story of a young girl who drowns herself after having read a book of legends that impress upon her a sense of loss of heroism in the modern world.

2. Boyesen's review of Wilhelm Bergsöe, I Sabinerbjergene (Copenhagen, 1871), an epistolary account of life in the Sabine Mountains, appeared in the Atlantic, July 1873.

3. The "short story" has not been identified.

4. "St. Olaf's Fountain," Atlantic, April 1873.

5. Apparently Boyesen never published what Howells here refers to as the "Legend of the M. S."

6. Howells was not only critical of Boyesen's writing; he also commented on the Norwegian's character in a letter to W. C. Howells of 15 June 1873 (MH): "We have had a great deal of Boyesen here, this week, but not half so much as Boyesen has had. He's full of himself, to bursting, and doesn't by any mistake, touch any subject that isn't more or less related to himself. But it's a very amiable and harmless egotism, and much like my own. I think it would amuse a third person to hear Boyesen and me trying to be generous to each other's supreme self-contemplation."

7. Mr. and Mrs. Francis Sewall of Urbana, Ohio.

8. A Foregone Conclusion, of which Howells had already written thirty pages by 10 March. See Howells to James, 10 March 1873.

9. German for "embrace."

6 APRIL 1873, BOSTON, TO WILLIAM C. HOWELLS

> ... *The Atlantic Monthly,* ...
> Boston, April 6, *1873.*

Dear father:

Bua has been in doubt lately whether he should be a soldier, a sailor, or an artist; but this morning he came swaggering into the library and said he was not going to be either of those: "I'm to be *just a common man*,—like you, papa!" This rather stung my vanity, and I made him understand, as well as I could that to be an author was not to be a common man, at all. So he is going to be an author, he says. But I really think his destiny is art in some form. He has the quickest and most correct eye, and he is always observing lines and shapes. He goes about with two pencils in his pocket, and is always drawing something.—Have any of you at home been reading Middlemarch?[1] We are now reading it aloud, with ever growing amazement at its greatness. I think it's very badly executed, as a piece of literary art, but as an intellectual achievement, it is wonderful. It's richly worth reading.—I see by the last Sentinel that you've been having trouble over Garfield's vote on the salaries.[2] It looks like quackery on the part of those who assail him; but it's a pity that he had not at once refused to take his back pay. But I don't agree with you that the salaries were sufficient before. As things go, they were not living salaries, and must have continually tempted members to large and small stealings. But the trouble is far back of all that. I'm afraid that the people themselves have corrupt and loose ideas and principles.—Luxury has undermined everything. That sort of race redemption for which old James hopes is not at hand yet;[3] perhaps we're just now being "let into our evils" as a preliminary to it.

—Our house has the first coat of plastering on it at last, and it begins to look like a house in earnest. It's very pretty, and I wish you could see it.—Is Annie still boarding with the Smiths? I can't learn this from anybody. Her friend Miss Bross was here the other day, and said she thought she was still with the Smiths.[4]—The children all keep well. Elinor has grown much better since the open weather began. With united love to all,

Your aff'te son
Will.

1. George Eliot's *Middlemarch* was first serialized in *Blackwood's Magazine*, December 1871–November 1872; the first American edition has an 1872–1873 imprint. The review that appeared in the *Atlantic*, April 1873, is by A. G. Sedgwick; Howells did not comment on it in print until *Heroines of Fiction* (1901).

2. On 3 March 1873 James A. Garfield had voted for H. Rept. 2991, an appropriations bill that increased salaries and compensations of Representatives from an average of approximately $6,000 to roughly $7,500 per year. See *Congressional Globe*, 42d Cong., 3d sess., 1873, pt. 3, pp. 2103–5. W. C. Howells commented on the issue of Congressional salaries, though not specifically on Garfield's vote, in the *Sentinel*, 3 April 1873.

3. Henry James, Sr., strongly under the influence of Swedenborgianism, believed in the idea that God is immanent in the unity of mankind, and he made it the foundation of his doctrine of redemption, as it is expressed in *Society the Redeemed Form of Man, and the Earnest of God's Omnipotence in Human Nature* (1879).

4. See Howells to Anne T. Howells, 3 February 1873, n. 2.

20 APRIL 1873, BOSTON, TO WILLIAM C. HOWELLS

> *...The Atlantic Monthly,...*
> *Boston, April 20, 1873.*

Dear father:

Annie writes me that she goes home at the end of the month,[1] and that she intends to keep on at her book-noticing there if possible. This is a good idea; and I hope she will be able also to take up some branch of story-writing, for which I think she is even better fitted than for criticism. If I were you and Joe, I would exempt her as much as possible from demands on her time, so that she can have a good opportunity for her own work. I was particularly struck with the good sense and ability of her notice of old Cushing's book on the Geneva conference.[2]—We have been greatly retarded by the weather in getting the house finished. The second coat of plastering is not all on yet, and it dries very slowly, these east-windy days. I doubt if we shall get in, now, before the 1st of July. We've got our parlor mantel-piece up: it's of a lavender-colored marble, with arabesque designs in gold. The other mantels, except one, are all to be of wood.—I got a letter from Boyesen, the other day. I imagine he would like to stop at Jefferson on his way east. You know he's going to Norway, this summer. I doubt if he'll return to Urbana; he'll probably go to Cornell, where he's had a professorship offered him.[3]—My story is decidedly gaining favor, and I should not be surprised if the sale were quite good.[4] People speak to me of it more than of Their Wedding Journey. I am glad I have done it for one reason if for no other: it sets me forever outside of the rank of mere *culturists,* followers of an elegant literature, and proves that I have sympathy with the true spirit of Democracy. Sometimes I've doubted whether I had, but when I came to look the matter over in writing this story, I doubted no longer.—By the way, do you think that farmers' rebellion against the railroads will spread into Ohio?[5] I'm glad of any union amongst them, for I hope it may lead to some sort of communism and society which is the only thing that can save them from becoming mere peasants.

All join me in love to all.

> **Your aff'te son**
> **Will.**

1. Annie Howells had been living in Chicago for several months, and Howells had become increasingly uneasy about her way of life there. See Howells to Anne T. Howells, 3 February 1873, n. 1, and Howells to W. C. Howells, 16 February 1873.
2. Annie's notice of Caleb Cushing, *The Treaty of Washington: Its Negotiation, Execution, and the Discussions Relating thereto* (1873) has not been located; it may have appeared in *Inter-Ocean.* See Howells to James, 12 May 1873, n. 5.
3. After his departure from Urbana University, Urbana, Ohio, and his voyage

to Europe, Boyesen was appointed to a professorship of Germanic literature and language at Cornell University (1874–1880).

4. *A Chance Acquaintance*, which Howells at first thought would not be as popular as his first novel.

5. The arbitrary manner in which railroads imposed exorbitant and inequitable freight rates especially on farm products was the cause of widespread discontent. On 20 March 1873 the *Nation* reported that "In Illinois and Iowa, local organizations, known as Farmers' Clubs or Granges, are said to have been formed, and to have succeeded in making the railroad question more prominent than any which has occupied public attention since the close of the war."

12 MAY 1873, BOSTON, TO HENRY JAMES

> *...The Atlantic Monthly,...*
> *Boston*, May 12, *1873*.

My dear James:

"A Roman Holiday" (which I have butchered your Carnival to make) is cast for the July number,[1] and it was put in type for June, but it came out eleven pages instead of five or six. I can only keep my word to you to print a contribution every month if you keep within bounds. I want to have your name appear regularly, but it is a brute matter of space, and not an affair of the heart, with the printers, though *I* would willingly give you half the magazine. I liked the A R. H. very much indeed, and the Roman Rides are still better—more in the vein, and richer-toned. That is delicious, about that infernal scoundrel's experience as héros de roman![2] If the black drop of envy could kill, he lives no longer. But alas! it is not Rome alone that works such wonders; youth helps, which is going; money which I never had, nor social courage. It is a plebeian as well as a senile spite that I vent.—Your paper was good all through, and this I said to myself before your letter came to confirm me in my liking by its generous praises of my story.[3] It will go into the August Atlantic.—I'm glad you liked that IV part, and I needn't be ashamed to own that I thought it well managed.—If you have been vexed by Dennett's curt and most unfair treatment of your Gautier,[4] let me tell you that it has united all other voices in your favor and honor. It has been universally liked by everybody here.

Events are much rarer than great genius in Cambridge, as you know. However, we have the divine Keeler back again, and that is something.[5] He comes back from the arbitration of the Alabama claims with a formulated philosophy of Epicurean type, and is really delightful joking. Aldrich, Perry, Fiske and the rest are very well; I will pass round your messages. Fiske will probably go abroad in August. Mrs. Edwards, one of his sectaries, gives him $1000 towards his expenses.[6] Isn't that handsome?—I hope Perry will be able to keep the North American; they have at least made no other arrangement about it.[7]—We dined with the Aldriches at your father's, the other day, and had a merry time.—There has been a slight rash of dinners and parties in Cambridge, this spring, but the eruption has yielded to treatment, and all is now quiet again. We look soon to have the Nortons back.[8] I rowed on Fresh Pond with Keeler, last week, and to-day, I rode round it with my wife. It's very well, let me tell you, though it's not Roman. The landscape was in the tender beauty of its most virginal green; the low western sun struck across the grass in the orchards (where scarcely a stubborn bough has budded yet,) and it was fairly *ridente*[9]—but with tears somewhere, too. O it breaks my heart to have the spring again—what a rapture, what a pang it is!—The Howellses are well, and united in their love to you.—The new house, which is pretty enough, is hurrying forward.—I have written nearly a hundred and fifty pages of my new story,[10] and am getting the people together. It goes just now no smoother than true love's course, but I hope and strive.—Don't make your sketches more than 30 pages of your Ms., if you can help.

> Yours ever
> W. D. Howells.

Thank you again with all my heart for what you say of my story. You see with kind eyes; but I really hoped that I had put something to be seen. That chapter cost me infinite pains.

1. "A Roman Holiday," *Atlantic*, July 1873; apparently James's original title had been "A Roman Carnival."

2. Early in "Roman Rides," *Atlantic*, August 1873, James introduces a character who says that a day's experience of Rome and the Campagna is like "reading an odd chapter in the history of a person very much more of a *héros de roman* than myself."

3. Presumably *A Chance Acquaintance*, which was then appearing in the *Atlantic*; but James's letter to Howells has not been located. However, on 22 June 1873 (MH; *James Letters*, I, 395–97), James resumed his praise of Howells' serialized novel: "your work is a Success & Kitty a creation. I have envied you greatly, as I read, the delight of feeling her grow so real and complete, so true & charming. I think in bringing her through with such unerring felicity, your imagination has *fait ses preuves*." *A Chance Acquaintance* was published in book form two days after Howells wrote his father on 18 May 1873 (MH): "It was to have been published yesterday, but the first edition of 3000 was exhausted by advance orders before it was put into the market, and it was postponed till Tuesday, and 1500 more printed immediately.... Of course, we are greatly elated, and I have gone round silently celebrating for the last three days. It's by far the greatest success that I've yet made...." On 25 May 1873 (MH), Howells informed his father of continuing good sales: "They issued the third edition of my book yesterday, and the sale still prospers."

4. James's review of *Théâtre de Théophile Gautier: Mystères, Comédies et Ballets* (1872), *North American Review*, April 1873, is a general essay on the French author. John R. Dennett's criticism of the review has not been located.

5. Ralph Keeler had returned from Europe, where, in 1871–1872, he had reported the proceedings of the international Tribunal of Arbitration in Geneva, which was to settle the so-called *Alabama* claims of restitution for damages suffered by the

United States as a result of England's support of the Confederacy during the Civil War. The Tribunal was established by the Treaty of Washington.

6. For additional details about Mrs. M. A. Edwards' patronage of John Fiske, see John Spencer Clark, *The Life and Letters of John Fiske* (Boston: Houghton Mifflin, 1917), I, 406–7; and Milton Berman, *John Fiske: The Evolution of a Popularizer* (Cambridge, Mass.: Harvard University Press, 1961), p. 133.

7. Thomas Sergeant Perry was briefly editor of the *North American Review* before Henry Adams assumed the editorship early in 1874.

8. C. E. Norton and his family had spent several years in Europe.

9. Italian for "laughing."

10. *A Foregone Conclusion.* On 27 April 1873 (MH), Howells had written his father: "I have resumed my Venetian story, which was interrupted for a month by other work. It seems to be something that I can write, when I've a chance, about as fast as I can make copy."

6 JUNE 1873, BOSTON, TO FRANCIS PARKMAN

... *The Atlantic Monthly,* ...
Boston, June 6, *1873.*

My dear Mr. Parkman:

I am more delighted than I should like to "let on," by your very kind letter. I thank you with all my heart for liking my book, and I beg you to express my gratification to the lady who sent me that charming message.[1] I don't know whether I could bear many such messages, so human is man, and yet, for once I think I may enjoy without being spoiled.

—How graceful it was of Le Moyne to dedicate his Album du Touriste to you. The words in which he did it had a prettier turn than anything else that caught my eye in the book—so I quoted them in my notice of it for the July number.[2] In the same number, I print one of the two chapters you gave me, with the title, "Some early Canadian Miracles and Martyrs," and I shall use the second chapter very soon.[3] I should have sent you a proof, but I thought you were in Quebec. However, I think we've got it clean. As for the matter, I needn't tell you that I like it all the better for reading it again.

Many thanks for the invitation—which we shall accept—to look in on you at Jamaica Plain. At what moment do your rose-trees most abundantly break forth in blossoms and nightingale's music?

Yours truly
W. D. Howells.

1. In his letter of 3 June 1873 (MH), Parkman had written Howells of his pleasure in reading *A Chance Acquaintance*: "The truth, freshness, subtle penetration of character, kindly satire, and wholesome genuine feeling that fill it throughout, make it charming. ... One ... [lady], an extremely intelligent person ... said,

'Tell Mr. Howells that I am an old blazée novel reader, and that his book has made me think myself a young and fresh one again.'"

2. Howells reviewed J. M. Le Moine, *L'Album du Tourisme* in the *Atlantic*, July 1873.

3. "Early Canadian Miracles and Martyrs," *Atlantic*, July 1873; "A Great Deed of Arms," *Atlantic*, December 1873.

8 JUNE 1873, BOSTON, TO ANNE T. HOWELLS

...The Atlantic Monthly,...
Boston, June 8, 1873.

Dear Annie—

According to my frugal wont, as regards handwriting, I must make this letter serve for an answer both to you and father. Your fotograf is wonderfully good: a very fortunate likeness, and a lovely picture. Does it flatter you, or are you really so handsome as that? Elinor and I are extremely proud of it, and I thank you for it.—If you have anything ready in the way of a sketch or short story, you can send it to me without waiting to hear from the editor of Hearth and Home: I suppose the editor has merely forgotten to write. He's a very good friend of mine,[1] and I'm sure doesn't mean any neglect. You know the kind of short story they print in H. and H., and can guess what will suit them.— I confess that I should be sorry to have you take another place on a newspaper, for it seems to me that would be simply delaying your real work, which is something higher; and yet I don't venture to advise. I suppose that you get very little chance to work at home. If you're still in Jefferson, the latter part of August, we can talk this matter thoroughly over.—If Boyesen's calculations were right, he is with you to-day, and before you get this letter he will be in Cambridge, and bring me the latest news of you all. His story reads very well in print,[2] and for so young a man he has a very enviable reputation.—I wish very much that you could see our house, as it advances from day to day towards its final perfection. The grounds about it have been put in order, and it looks exquisitely neat. It will be an extremely pretty house, inside and out. Yesterday afternoon Elinor and I spent in a vain search for parlor carpets, and our failure quite took the glory off our wall-paper triumph of last week. We have almost decided to put down our old p. cs. but then we should have buy new carpets for the chambers.—I continue to receive letters from people imploring me to go on with A Chance Acquaintance. The last appeal is from Illinois: very few States—loyal States—have not joined in the petition—but I am quite inexorable.[3] By the way, Kitty's getting those letters at the last moment was merely an occasion for her to waiver a instant, and then stick the closer to her decision: it was not meant as a hint towards any sequel.—Some of the notices are very amusing: the *most* amusing is from the Rochester Democrat, which says the book "is redolent of snobbery," and evidently attributes all of Mr. Arbuton's principles to me.[4] It isn't best to be as ironical as you can.—My new story is about one third done.[5] I read it to my most terrible critic, Elinor, the other day, and she likes it very much.— I'm extremely gratified that you approve of Kitty's behavior in that last scene. You can imagine what a most difficult thing it was to manage. I wrote it four or five times, and then let it go to press with a shudder of apprehension.—All unite in love to all.

Your aff'te brother
Will.

Elinor sticks to her old *stylish* weight of 82 pounds. Anything beyond that is not lady-like.—I hope father is feeling all right now, and poor old Henry is better. Tell him that Bua has a soldier's cap.

1. George Cary Eggleston (1839–1911), younger brother of the better known Indiana author, Edward Eggleston, whom he succeeded in the editorship of *Hearth and Home*. Howells was at this time trying to help Annie in her search for a suitable position with a newspaper. He wrote his father on 11 May 1873 (MH): "Here is a letter in answer to one that I wrote the editor of Hearth and Home a few days ago about a vacancy on his paper. I thought Annie would like to see it, and I hope she will be able to do some work if he applies for it. I have sent him to-day her address. There is now so great a demand for writing, that she need not be long without a salaried position if she cares enough about it to make herself known. I often think how very different these things are since I began to write, and how many years I had to struggle before I could get any sort of recognition. At present, it is so easy to get into print, and to be paid for being there."

2. *Gunnar*, which began serialization in the *Atlantic*, July 1873.

3. Some of these letters, imploring Howells to let Kitty Ellison marry Miles Arbuton, are still extant. One is by Margaret Sangster, the associate editor of *Hearth and Home*, who wrote: "after creating for us such a sweet womanly girl as Kitty, and getting us all to loving her, how could you think of ending it *so*? . . . [¶] Do be persuaded to write a bye and bye chapter some day with a gentler afterthought for poor Mr Arbuton—" See her letter to Howells, 20 May 1873 (MH). The editor of the same magazine, however, was of a different opinion: "we have had nothing American, as yet, quite equal to Their Wedding Journey and A Chance Acquaintance. Perhaps I ought not to say this, in a letter to you, but I have been thinking it ever since I read Kitty's final decision last night . . . ." See G. C. Eggleston to Howells, 4 June 1873 (MH); also Howells to James, 26 August 1873.

4. The review has not been located.

5. *A Foregone Conclusion*, which Howells had begun early in March.

11 June 1873, Boston, to Charles D. Warner

> ... *The Atlantic Monthly,* ...
> Boston, June 11, *1873.*

My dear Warner:

I do not merit the kindness of your notice:[1] I'm anything that you like, in connection with that visit which my soul longs to make, but is kept back from by a vile, unworthy body. We are now putting the finishing touches on a house and our happiness, and I can't leave either till both are done for. But I'll tell you what: I'm going West in the latter part of August, and coming back in the same part of September, and either going or coming, I really do think I shall try to stop at Hartford—if you still want me to do so. Till then, write me as one that loves his fellow-men too well to keep his promises. A visit *is* an awful thing, now, isn't it? Come, you wouldn't do it yourself, would you? It is all very well for the women, whose cooks go and off and leave them at the slightest symptom of hospitality; but it's hard for men. Just think of being tagged round by me a couple of days! How would you entertain a guest who doesn't play whist, or billiards, nor smoke, nor swear? There is eating and drinking; but I should die if I ate and drank all I wanted. I'm sure you haven't looked at the thing in all its bearings.

I do hope you'll give me something for next year.[2] Don't you go and let anybody else announce you, any way.

Tell the young lady who plays Italian so beautifully that I'm dusting up my foreign languages, and shall be ready by Christmas *any* way.[3]

> Yours evanescently
> **W. D. H.**

1. In his letter of 26 May 1873 (MH), Warner expressed disappointment at Howells' inability to come for a visit to Hartford. About Howells' most recent novel he wrote: "We are all in a state about your Chance Acquaintance. Of course I did not say in my notice [which has not been located] what I thought about it, lest I should be considered gushing. The Nation sets us an example of criticism. I should have said, following this style, that the C. A. is a very clever thing in its way, and will probably please those who like this sort of thing. [¶] Well, I am delighted at the success of your story. If it does sell up among the large thousands it will give me an increased respect for the good taste of my native land." The review in the *Nation,* 12 June 1873, was quite favorable, stating that "we regard 'A Chance Acquaintance' as a step towards the production of 'the great American novel.'"

2. *Baddeck and That Sort of Thing* was published in the *Atlantic,* January–May 1874.

3. Warner had written Howells on 26 May: "There is a young lady with us now who plays the piano like the Venus of Milo, and can converse with you in your own Italian."

20 July 1873, Cambridge, to William C. Howells

> ... *The Atlantic Monthly.*
> *Boston,* July 20, *1873.*

Dear father:

This is the first letter I write in my beautiful new library, which is more charming than I could make you understand by the longest description.[1] The ceiling is richly frescoed; below the cornice, and down to the chair-board running the room is a soft buff paper and then dark red to the floor. The book-casing, drawers and closets are heavy chestnut; the hearth is of tiles, and the chimney-piece rises in three broad shelves almost to the cornice. This is the glory of the room, and is splendidly carved, and set with picture-tiles and mirrors; on either jamb of the mantel is my monogram, carved, and painted by Elinor, who modified and improved the carpenter's design of the whole affair. This splendor was all a present to me from the builder, and was kept a secret until Friday afternoon when I was allowed to behold it for the first time.—The work on the other rooms is nearly finished, now, and nothing remains but the papering of one parlor.

Joe, Bua and I started for Deer Isle on Monday evening, and arrived there next day at 3. p. m.[2] The whole trip is as charming as it can be, and Deer Isle is perfectly lovely—I could not imagine a more delightful spot. But the cooking at the captains is enough to kill: pie, preserves and three kinds of cake three times a day, and no fresh meat. We carried them a ham, and I left Joe a pot of condensed beef for beaf-tea, and so with what fish he catches and plenty of soft-boiled eggs, I think he can manage. They're very good kind people, and seem very fond of him; and he is pretty well lodged. Fortunately, too, the air is health itself. But the food is dreadful—there's no hiding the fact.—I expected to stay a day longer, but found that if I waited till Friday, I couldn't get home till this morning, and I didn't think I ought to be so long away from Elinor, who, in fact, used herself up so that this morning she had quite a sharp attack of dearrhoea. She's all right now.—I suppose Joe has told Eliza of his consulting our Doctor. The Dr. said again to-day that Joe had no trouble of the kidneys or bladder except what came from his dyspepsia, the best cure for which would be a long vacation, and complete change of habits of work.

I've read with great pleasure your letters from the Ohio river country—especially that from St. Clairsville.[3] It was very well put indeed, and quite carried me back. I notice that you twice misspell *Arcadia.* Acadia (without the *r*) was the French settlement in Nova Scotia, a totally different thing.—Bua enjoyed the voyage to Deer Isle and back beyond description. Returning, we had very heavy weather on the steamer, but he was not sea-sick, and slept for the whole boat, for nearly every one else was up, sick and scared—myself included. I was Bua's Providence; but where was mine? That is one of the advantages of happy childhood—to have your infallible refuge handy. Joe will enjoy himself, I think, though all the captain's men folks are away fishing. He talks of going to St. John's.[4]

All join in love to you all

> Your affectionate son
> Will.

1. On 7 July the Howells family had moved into their new house at 37 Concord Avenue, Cambridge.

2. Deer Isle is located in Penobscot Bay, off the shore of Maine. Joseph A. Howells had arrived in Cambridge on 11 July, and the purpose of his visit appears to have been medical, as is indicated by Howells' later comment about Joe's visit to the Howells family physician, Dr. Wyman.

3. W. C. Howells had recently visited Belmont County, where he had lived some forty years ago. In an earlier letter to his father, 29 June 1873 (MH), Howells had written: "I'm glad that you enjoyed your visit to the old places so much." He indicated that in the fall he too might look up some old friends in St. Clairsville, across the Ohio River from Wheeling, West Virginia, where his parents had briefly lived after their marriage in 1831. W. C. Howells published five reports on his trip in the *Sentinel*, 19 and 26 June, 3, 10, and 17 July 1873; the last one is from St. Clairsville.

4. St. John, New Brunswick, a harbor town on the Bay of Fundy.

20 JULY 1873, CAMBRIDGE, TO JAMES M. COMLY

Cambridge, July 20, 1873.

My dear Comly:

Nothing has gratified me more for a long time than your letter and the paragraph in the accompanying State Journal.[1] I had seen the statement on which it was based, and had written you a letter making light of it, but suppressed the letter because it seemed too serious to write of it at all—that is, for me to do so—and might have looked like asking some denial from you. Of course it vexed me, for I knew it wasn't true; but indeed my love for my old Columbus friends did not depend upon their reading my scribbles. I thank you all the same for the cordiality with which you speak of me.—Your lecture I haven't read yet; I got back only two days since from a little excursion to the coast of Maine, and plunged at once into the cares of finishing the new house which I've been building, and which we've just moved into. But I'm promising myself the pleasure soon, and I'm glad you have spoken in favor of what seems to me a just cause.—Horton *is* a good fellow, and I was awfully sorry to have him go away from Cambridge.[2] Is he destined to politics? Or is he something of a dilettante in his treatment of public matters? He's an able fellow, and might have succeeded in sculpture or literature.

I'm sorry to hear of Mrs. Libby's suffering, which the Mitchells had already told me about. Please remember me very cordially to her.[3]

When I visit Columbus—sometime in September—I shall bring my oldest girl, Winifred, with me. She is nearly ten, now, and I'm going to introduce her to all my old acquaintances. She's a great reader, and has quite romantic ideas about visiting her papa's youthful haunts. How I long to hear those old brick pavements ring again under my heels! Will you take some Rhine wine and Swiss cheese with mustard with me at 11 p.m. some night? Or are you past all that? I get a student now and then to debauch that way—but they treat me too respectfully, confound them!—as if I were a middle-aged man.

Good-bye. Love to the Doctor and all the family.[4]

Yours affectionately
W. D. Howells.

1. The *Ohio State Journal*, 14 July 1873, printed a brief item which begins with the observation that "A writer in the Graphic recently stated that 'it was a singular fact that no copy of Howells's "Venetian Life" had ever been sold in Columbus, Ohio—his native place.'" After correcting the error about Howells' place of birth, the writer (presumably Comly) notes that Howells' works have been selling well in Columbus, and he concludes: "The Graphic person would do well to visit Columbus and see how well Howells is honored in his own country, hereabouts. He could not be more thought of if he was a dead poet, instead of a live one."

2. Edwin J. Horton, a fellow Ohioan, sometimes talked with Howells about their home state. See Howells to Comly, 7 July 1868.

3. Libby was the nickname of Comly's wife, Elizabeth Smith Comly; Mr. and Mrs. John G. Mitchell were mutual friends in Columbus.

4. Dr. Samuel M. Smith, Howells' friend, physician, and benefactor during his Columbus days, and Comly's father-in-law.

18 August 1873, Boston, to William C. Bryant

...*"The Atlantic Monthly,"...*
Boston, Aug. 18, 1873.

Dear Sir:

I have for some time wished to ask you to write for The Atlantic a series of articles—the more autobiographical the better—on such phases of our literary, social and political past as have most interested you; and in making this application now I venture to thank you personally for the very great pleasure that the reading of your newly published volume of Orations and Addresses has given me.[1] Of course I could not reasonably ask work so carefully studied and treated as your criticisms of Cole, Cooper and Irving; I should be contented with papers far more sketchy and desultory, and more in the character of reminiscences, though I should not expect anything like a gossipping chronicle from you. I necessarily write in ignorance of your engagements and inclinations, but I trust that my suggestion may not strike you unfavorably.[2]

Very respectfully yours,
W. D. Howells.

W. C. Bryant, Esq.

1. Bryant's *Orations and Addresses* had just been published by G. P. Putnam's Sons, New York.
2. Bryant replied on 22 August 1873 (OFH): "I cannot say that I will undertake the task, nor yet that I will not. At my time of life the love of ease is not easily overcome, and it may be that my recollection of past occurrences will not be sufficiently distinct to enable me to write any thing with which I shall be satisfied.... So I must for the present leave the matter where it is and trust to time to decide it." On 9 October 1873 (MH), Bryant informed Howells that "I have been thinking over the literary intimacies of my past life, and have feared that the recollection which I have of them is too dim and vague to allow them to be set down in an interesting manner...."

26 AUGUST 1873, BOSTON, TO HENRY JAMES

... *"The Atlantic Monthly," ...*
Boston, Aug. 26, 1873.

My dear James:
I have just finished your Chain of Cities, which with the Villeggiatura, I shall publish before the year's out.[1] The last is much the best, for the Chain is a little too much drawn out in the direction of things that cannot be felt by the many readers who have never seen them; it's meagre, too, whereas the Villeggiatura is richly full, and has certain luxuries of sentiment that gave me a poignant pleasure. They are both good enough; but I wish you would write for the Atlantic as unlaboriously as you seem to write your Nation letters, putting all the minor observation and comment that you can into them.[2]—Your brother tells me that you are not so well as you have been, which I'm truly sorry to hear, but I hope it's merely *cose passagiere*.[3] Here, we are in very reasonable repair, but for a sprinkling of whooping-cough among the children. We are in our new house, with which we are vastly content. We have done some aesthetic wall-papering, thanks to Wm. Morris whose wall papers are so much better than his poems;[4] and my library is all in chestnut, with a three-story mantel-piece, after Eastlake[5]—set with tiles, and standing very solidly on a tiled hearth, while overhead is a frescoed ceiling. I try not to be proud.—Directly after I got your last

letter I sent you my book, which I hope you received.[6] You would be amused at the letters I get—some forty, now—from people unknown to me—begging for a sequel. The trouble is that they are of such various minds as to what the end ought to be.[7] Miss Lane writes us from Quebec that half a dozen gentleman have called, to see the rooms in which Kitty lived.[8] This, I take it, is being a novelist in dead earnest, and I am pushing forward my Venetian priest's story all I can; but I shall hardly begin printing it before next summer.[9] In the meantime Osgood is going to bring out a volume of poetry for me in October.[10]—I have seldom known Cambridge so empty as this summer—possibly because I've been in it all the time. Just now when the crickets are prophesying autumn with heart-breaking solemnity, I'm getting ready to go west for three weeks, with Winny.—Next year we are to have new type for the magazine, and it is otherwise to be brightened up. What is to be done with the North American—whether it is to be left with Perry, or to be given to Norton or Adams—isn't decided.[11] I believe they're all three willing to take it. Of Perry one has only very brief glimpses at rare intervals; he spends all his time at Miss Cabot's country retreat.[12]

Mrs. Howells and all the children join me in love to you.—I wish this were not such a stupid letter.

Affectionately yours,
W. D. Howells.

1. "A Chain of Italian Cities," *Atlantic*, February 1874. By "Villeggiatura" Howells probably meant three pieces on summer travel in Italy, the last of which James sent on 22 June; it was published as "Roman Neighborhoods," *Atlantic*, December 1873.

2. In his reply to this letter, dated 9 September 1873 (MH; *James Letters*, I, 400–403), James wrote: "So my Chain of Cities did arrive. I'm sorry it seems 'meagre'— an idea that makes me weep salt tears. This, however, I fondly hope, was less owing to my own poverty than to a constant fear to amplify and make it too long. . . . I shall send you more things in these coming months, and I shall heed your advice about unlaboriousness. I know I'm too ponderous. But the art of making *substance* light, is hard."

3. Italian for "a passing thing."

4. William Morris (1834–1896) revolutionized standards and concepts of interior decoration in England after founding the firm of Morris, Marshall, Faulkner & Co. in 1861. In the *Atlantic*, March 1873, Howells had reviewed Morris's *Love is Enough*, calling it a "skilfully attenuated triviality . . . too dull for any words of ours to tell . . . ." He objected to "its inexorable dreariness, its unrelenting lengthiness, and serious vacuity."

5. Sir Charles Eastlake (1793–1865), the British painter, who became president of the Royal Academy in 1850.

6. For James's comments on *A Chance Acquaintance*, see Howells to James, 5 December 1873, n. 4.

7. See Howells to Anne T. Howells, 8 June 1873, n. 3.

8. Miss Lane kept a boardinghouse in Quebec, at 44½ Anne Street, where Howells' father stayed when he became American consul at Quebec. See Howells to W. C. Howells, 17 June 1874 (MH), and 9 July 1874, n. 1.

9. *A Foregone Conclusion*, about which Howells had written his father on 17 August 1873 (MH): "I have been very much interrupted on my story by moving, and so on, so that I have advanced it very little, this summer, and I suppose that I cannot do any real work on it before I get home from Ohio. Still, it has gone forward, somewhat."

10. *Poems*, Howells' first volume of collected poems since 1860, was published in October.

11. Thomas Sergeant Perry edited several issues of the *North American Review* during 1873; but early in 1874 Henry Adams assumed the editorship. Howells wrote to C. E. Norton on 20 July 1873 (MH) that he had seen J. R. Osgood, who "said that the arrangement with Perry was not a permanent one, and had never been so regarded on either side.... There was no one to take charge of the Review when Lowell and Adams went away, and I have reason to believe that it was through my very strong urgency that Perry was asked to take charge of it. He and I often talked of the impermanent nature of his charge, and so I felt that I was not compromising his interests, by going directly to Osgood with your letter. I suppose Mr. Osgood's letter will refer in great part to the necessity of getting the Review inexpensively edited, for it is still a gentleman in adversity, and pays chiefly in honor. I myself never thought it so good as when you had it, and I heartily wish it was in your hands again, with Mr. Perry as your assistant, until Lowell's return."

12. Lilla Cabot, daughter of Dr. Samuel and Hannah Jackson Cabot of Boston, married Perry in April 1874.

18 OCTOBER 1873, BOSTON, TO THOMAS W. HIGGINSON

> ... *The Atlantic Monthly,* ...
> Boston, Oct. 18, *1873.*

My dear Higginson:

I thank you for writing me so frankly about Mr. Channing's Thoreau.[1] I did not know—or rather did not remember—your relation to the author or I should not have asked you to notice the book.[2] I will turn to Sanborn,[3] as you suggest.—As to not having your own book reviewed in The Atlantic I think you are in error,[4] though I respect the feeling that governs you. We have limitations which no one dislikes more than I, but we are in some sort a critical authority, in a country where criticism is rare, and I do not see why a notable book such as yours is should seem to be ignored by us. I try to make The Atlantic a place where a man's merit, if I feel it, shall be recognized, and I am willing that any competent critic who feels the merit of an author when I don't, should recognize it there. For the appearance of puffery, I don't care a straw so I keep my conscious clear of the sin. But I will be ruled by you if what you say is finally your wish. I think some of those Oldport papers among the most charming essays we have; but the stories I did not like so well.

I suppose I shall seem dull when I confess that I see nothing wrong with the last line of Forlorn,[5] and that I don't at all understand your feeling about it. *Gatto ci cova*,[6] I dare say, but I don't find it. Yet I have sometimes thought that my smell for an anti-climax was good. To be sure, this anti-climax is my own—if it *is* one.

Yours truly
W. D. Howells.

1. Howells had written Higginson on 12 October 1873 (NN): "Have you a mind to review Channing's new book on Thoreau for The Atlantic? I am not in sympathy with either of them, but I'm quite willing to believe that there are good and fine things which I don't like, even in literature." Higginson's reply to this letter has not been located. See G. S. Hellman, "The Letters of Howells to Higginson," *Twenty-Seventh Annual Report of the Bibliophile Society 1901–1929* (Cedar Rapids, Iowa: Torch Press, [1929]), pp. 32–33.

2. Higginson was William Ellery Channing's second cousin, and he married Channing's sister Mary in 1847.

3. Franklin B. Sanborn's review of Channing's *Thoreau: The Poet-Naturalist* (1873) appeared in the *Atlantic*, February 1874.

4. *Oldport Days* (1873) was reviewed in the *Atlantic*, January 1874. The review contains the following interesting passage: "There is an art we modern Americans need, and that is to go deeper than imitation,—to take nature as a base and scaffolding, but build thereon somewhat as the poets love to build. For the poet sees the literal and the ideal as in one stereoscopic view. . . . But sometimes we feel the bare actual to be the best; and though this author's genius loves the poetic aspects of things, it delights at times no less in strict realism."

5. Howells' poem "Forlorn" was first published in the *Nation*, 16 August 1866, and included in the 1873 volume of poetry. The last two lines read: "Over the threshold, not the less, forever / He felt her going on his broken heart."

6. A colloquial Italian expression equivalent to "I smell a rat."

21 OCTOBER 1873, BOSTON, TO ANNE T. HOWELLS

Boston, Oct. 21, 1873.

Dear Annie:

I send back the letters you enclosed, and with them a letter from the editor of the Buffalo Courier, who promises to take two letters a month from you.[1] This gives you $80 a month, without counting the Inter-Ocean, which I wish you would give up because I know that Crocker who writes for it needs the money it brings him, and because he is a malignant fellow who would probably make himself very offensive to you if you got the correspondence away from him.[2] I'm quite in earnest on this point, and I hope you will yield it to me even if you do not see it in the same light.—I count the Commercial at $20, the Courier at $20, the Herald at $20, and the Hearth and Home and State Journal at $10 each.[3] This seems a good deal of money; but you must not expect it to go far in Boston. I inquired for rooms to-day at Ainsworth's and they had none; at Mrs. Brown's (Miss Nourse's sister's, a very nice place) you can get board and a very modest back room for

$13 a week.[4] Two rooms, or a parlor bedroom, at any respectable house would cost you $20 or $25 a week.—I think $13 more than you ought to pay, so I shall look for something else for you. I had set $10 as the outside, for I think you wont find yourself able to write 2 letters a week, and may want to drop some of your engagements, or may lose some of them. Please look at the subject seriously in every light. Suppose you keep up your income of $80, and pay $55 or $60 for a month's board and washing (for I doubt if I can get it for much less than $12 a week) you wouldn't have much left for clothes and incidentals. Consider, also, whether with 2 letters a week, you would be able to write on your story at all, and whether you would really be advancing yourself by coming here as correspondent. Of course, there is a chance that you might make yourself so acceptable to the Hearth and Home or the Commercial that one of them would offer you a place; and of course if you find your experiment a failure, we shall only be too glad to have you finish up with a good long visit to us. But I want you to think the whole matter over again. Then if you believe yourself equal to the work, and the economy, come by all means.

Your aff'te brother
Will.

1. Howells was helping Annie to establish herself as the Boston correspondent of several newspapers and a New York magazine. He wrote to J. M. Comly, the editor of the *Ohio State Journal*, on 28 September 1873 (OHi): "My sister Annie, who formerly wrote for the Inter-Ocean, is probably coming to Boston for the winter, and would be able, if you want anything of the kind, to write a letter twice a month—or oftener—for the Journal. Her facilities for knowing what is going on here in literature, art, and other Boston interests, would be good, and I think she could make acceptable letters." Also, on 26 October 1873 (MH), he wrote his father: "I sent Annie the letter of the editor of the Buffalo Courier, which I hope she has answered in the affirmative. Has she heard again from the Commercial? The editor of Hearth and Home writes that he trusts she will be here in time to do the December magazines for him. I wish she would fix the time for her coming, definitely . . . ." Annie arrived in Boston sometime between 26 October and 19 November, the date on which Howells requested two press tickets to the Symphony concert series for his sister. (See Howells to J. S. Dwight, 19 November 1873 [MH]; also Howells to W. C. Howells, 18 October 1874.) She returned to Jefferson on about 1 May 1874, as is indicated in Howells' letter to H. H. Boyesen, 7 May 1874 (ViU): "My sister went home a week ago. She had a very agreeable winter in Boston, but I don't know whether she will return next winter. She can do something so much better than newspaper work, that I hate to have her spend her time on it."

2. Most likely Samuel R. Crocker (d. 1878), editor and publisher of the Boston *Literary World*, which he founded in 1870.

3. The *Commercial* and the *Herald* were newspapers in Cincinnati and Cleveland respectively; the "State Journal" was of course the *Ohio State Journal*.

4. According to Howells' letter to his sister Aurelia, 12 January 1873 (MH), the Howells family had at one time boarded at Ainsworth's boardinghouse, but he added: "We never see them any more."

5 DECEMBER 1873, BOSTON, TO HENRY JAMES

> . . . *The Atlantic Monthly,* . . .
> Boston, **Dec. 5,** *1873.*

My dear James:

Today, I met your mother on the Corso, in the vicinity of the Mercato Tom-Brewero,[1] and she gave me your news, as you Italians say. Part of these was that you had been writing a notice of my poetry for the North American, but that you had been anticipated by another "party"—and the review was at home, in MS. and I might read it there before it was sent off to seek its fortune.[2] This I did with great consolation and thankfulness, for the leaf that has been commonly bestowed upon my poetical works by the critics of this continent has not been the laurel leaf—rather rue, or cypress.[3] You have indeed treated my poor little book with a gracious kindness which I shall not forget; and I hope it isn't immodest to add with the first real discernment that has been shown by its critics. Thanks; and whilst I am in the way of it let me thank you also for what you say in your last letter both in praise and in blame of A Ch. Acq.[4] Your strictures are fairly made, and I know that I ran along the edge of a knife-blade to reach that dénouement. Sometimes it seems to me all clumsily wrong; and again I have the motive as clearly before me, as I had at first, and feel that nothing could drive me from that conclusion. But much is to be said against it, and you have said it very justly. As to the new story,[5] it draws near the end, with I hope, a gathering intensity. I long to get it all once fairly on paper, so that I can view it as a whole, and begin to clean it up a bit. The effects are still so much in the rough, so much at loose ends, that I have a certain *brivido*[6] in touching it, and I should like to jump the rest down at once. I have to work at it so interruptedly, too, that the pleasure of working at it is greatly marred.—Excuse, as Artemus Ward says,[7] the apparent egotism.—I have your Last of the Valerii in the January no.,[8] and I like it very much. It did not strike me so favorably in MS. as it does in print; but now I think it excellent. By the way, I hope you wont send any of your stories to Scribner's. We have of course no claim upon you, but we have hitherto been able to print all the stories you have sent, and so it shall be hereafter. Scribner is trying to lure away all our contributors, with the syren song of Doctor Holland, and my professional pride is touched.[9] Your Chain of Cities goes into the February, and your Siena, which is charming, into the March no.[10]— And what do you think of our dear old Atlantic's being sold! But it changes nothing but the publisher's imprint; even the editor remains the same. Aldrich and I had a Black Thursday when we heard our periodicals were in a state of barter,[11] and scarcely knew whether we were to be sold with them or not. But we were both made over. I am sorry to part with Osgood, who was a good master; but Hurd and Houghton promise me fair, and you know they were my first publishers.[12] The printing will hereafter be done at the Riverside Press; and if you were again in Cambridge, I hope we should have many a stretch across the flats together. In one's own company it is not a merry walk, especially in winter. But I console myself with thinking that it is business and not pleasure, anyway.—The social season in Cambridge opens with some sprightliness. I was at your brother Wilkie's Infare, which was full of enjoyment for me, and apparently for everybody else.[13] I seem to be dining out a good deal, too; even to-night I am going to Col. Dodge's on Quincy street.[14] Dinner at 7—what do you think of that for our simple Cambridge?—I haven't fairly got used yet to the Nortons' being at home,[15] and I haven't seen Charles more than twice. He is better in health, but he comes home with a dreadfully high standard for us all. We may attain it as blessed spirits a thousand years hence.—The fall-and-winter English-man is beginning to appear. I have met him twice—at your house and at the Gurney's:[16] a very peaceful Briton, indeed, and disposed to inform himself. To this end he has bought my "works", as I'm given to know. There is also a Russian amongst us, studying bugs with Agassiz—one Baron Osten—something, whom I want to be calling Gregory Ivanovich, out of Turgénieff.[17]—Our babes are all well, and Mrs. Howells sends you her warmest regards.—My sister Annie, whom perhaps you remember is spending the winter in Boston as a correspon-dent for some western papers.[18]—No more at present.

Affectionately yours
W. D. Howells.

Love to your brother.

1. According to Mildred Howells, the " 'Mercato Tom-Brewero' was an Italian version of the shop where most of literary Cambridge did its marketing." See *Life in Letters*, I, 179–80.

2. The *North American Review*, January 1874, published a brief, generally favor-able notice of Howells' *Poems*. James's longer review appeared in the *Independent*, 8 January 1874 (reprinted in *Literary Reviews and Essays*, ed. A. Mordell [New York: Twayne Publishers, 1957], pp. 215–21). While James praised the style of Howells' poetry, he considered it light in substance, referring to the poems he liked best as "poems about nothing" and "slender effusions of verse."

3. Although in several letters Howells mentioned the negative reviews *Poems* received (e.g., to Annie A. Fields, 6 October 1873 [CSmH] and to J. M. Comly, 8 October 1873 [OHi]), there is little evidence of harsh treatment by the reviewers. Perhaps the least favorable comment appeared in the Boston *Literary World*, Novem-

ber 1873, a fact that may explain Howells' unfriendly remarks about its editor, S. R. Crocker, in his letter to Anne Howells, 21 October 1873. See Howells to Stedman, 27 December 1873, n. 3.

4. In his letter of 9 September 1873 (MH; *James Letters*, I, 400–403) James wrote to Howells: "It gains largely on being read all at once and certain places which at first I thought amenable to restriction (or rather certain features—as zum beispiel a want of interfusion between the 'scenery' element in the book & the dramatic) cease, quite, to seem so in the volume. But your people are better than their background; you have done your best for the latter but your story is intrinsically more interesting.... Vivid figures will always kill the finest background in the world.—Kitty is certainly extremely happy—more so even than I feel perfectly easy in telling you; for she belongs to that class of eminent felicities which an artist doesn't indefinitely repeat.... The successful thing in Kitty is her *completeness*; she is singularly palpable and rounded and you couldn't, to this end, have imagined anything better than the particular antecedents you have given her.... Arbuton I think, now that I know the end, decidedly a shade too scurvy. The charm of Kitty, as one thinks of her, is that she suggests a type—a blessed one, and the interest of the tale as one gets into it is the foreshadowing of a conflict between her type and another. But at the last, the man's peculiar shabbiness undermines this interest by making you think that she had simply happened to get hold of a particularly mean individual— one, indeed, that she wouldn't have even temporarily felt any serious emotion about. I know that a great part of the idea of the story is that she shall be impressed by his unessential qualities; but as it stands, you rather resent her drama— her own part in it being so very perfectly analysed—having a hero who was coming to *that*! I was hoping that it was she who was to affront him. She does, indeed, by her shabby clothes; but this is an accident; that she should have done something, I mean, which even had she been dressed to perfection, would have left him puzzled, at loss, feeling that she wasn't for him. This wouldn't, indeed, have, necessarily implied his being snubbed, but was that inherent in your plan? Your drama, as you saw it, I suppose was the irreconcilability of the two results of such opposed antecedents & not a verdict on one or the other."

5. *A Foregone Conclusion.*

6. Italian for "shudder."

7. The particular lecture or sketch in which Ward (Charles Farrar Browne) used this phrase has not been identified.

8. James was apparently eager to get something of his printed in the January 1874 issue of the *Atlantic*, but he feared that "The Last of the Valerii" (the "Story" referred to below) would be too long. He had written Howells from Florence on 18 October 1873 (MH): "If it suits you to have me figure in your january [sic] number, if my two last sketches are printed & my story is too long for the purpose— if all this is blessed fact—there's your chance. Siena, you'll see is my theme & I have tried to remain brief. My only fear is you'll find me too brief. Bald, however, I have tried not to be, nor yet too artfully curled and anointed." See n. 10 below.

9. Dr. Josiah Gilbert Holland (1819–1881) was founder, part-owner, and editor of *Scribner's* (1870–1881). As a popular lecturer and sentimental novelist, he was perhaps Howells' most formidable adversary in the fight for literary realism. See Cady, *Howells*, I, 122–25, 169–70; Lynn, *Howells*, p. 152; and Howells to Stedman, 8 December 1874. In his reply to this letter, James wrote from Florence on 9 January 1874 (MH): "Let me explain without further delay, the nature of the package which will go with this, in another cover. It is the 1st half of a tale in two parts ["Eugene Pickering," *Atlantic*, October–November 1874], for use at your convenience.... I was on the point of sending it to Scribner, but your words in deprecation of this course have made me face about. I am much obliged for the esteem implied in them; but it remains true, in a general way, that I can't really get on without extracting tribute from that source. It's a mere money question. The *Atlantic* can't publish as many stories for me as I ought & expect to be writing.

At home, it could, for then I needed scantier revenues. But now, with all the francs it takes to live in these lovely climes, I need more strings to my bow and more irons always on the fire. But I heartily promise you that the *Atlantic* shall have the best things I do ...."

10. "A Chain of Italian Cities" was published in February, but "Siena" did not appear until June 1874.

11. Thomas Bailey Aldrich was editor of *Every Saturday* (1866–1874), which, like the *Atlantic*, was owned by James R. Osgood & Co. and sold to H. O. Houghton & Co.

12. *Venetian Life* was published by Hurd & Houghton, 1866.

13. Garth Wilkinson James (1845–1883) was in the railway business in Wisconsin, where he married Caroline Eames Cary in November 1873; the young couple then visited the James family in Cambridge. The infare was probably given at the family residence on Quincy Street.

14. Theodore A. Dodge (1842–1895), brevetted colonel in the U. S. Army (1865), was the author of several books on the Civil War.

15. C. E. Norton had spent several years in England and Europe.

16. Ephraim W. Gurney.

17. Carl Robert Romanovich von der Osten-Sacken (1828–1906), a member of the Russian legation to the United States (1856–1862) and Russian consul general at New York (1862–1871), was then doing research with Louis Agassiz. Howells' reference to "Gregory Ivanovich" is probably a mistake; he may have had in mind Gregory Mikhailovitch Litvinof in Turgenev's novel *Smoke*, which appeared in English translation in 1872.

18. See Howells to Anne T. Howells, 21 October 1873.

11 DECEMBER 1873, BOSTON, TO THOMAS B. ALDRICH

...The Atlantic Monthly,
Boston, Dec. 11, 1873.

Dear Aldrich:

I don't know whether you've changed this since I read it in Ms., but it seems vastly better—more Aldrichy.[1] It's charming now. Some of the points pierced quite into the laughter, with me, who smile not easily at a brother's wit. If—

> "Your murder cry for usage, and
>   your heart their plainings hear,"[2]

come round with the proof, and giggle—in the afternoon.

Yours
W. D. H.

1. Perhaps the second installment of *Prudence Palfrey*, *Atlantic*, January–June 1874, which was probably in proofs by the date of this letter.

2. The source from which Howells quoted these lines has not been identified.

12 DECEMBER 1873, CAMBRIDGE, TO JAMES M. COMLY

...The Atlantic Monthly,...
Cambridge, Mass., Dec. 12, *1873.*

Dear Comly:

I'm greatly obliged for your interest in me, and I'm glad to say that the change of ownership makes no difference whatever in my relation to the magazine. I am still sole "master of the situation." If it comes convenient to you, I wish you would say in the Journal that the Atlantic becomes in nowise a New York magazine, except that it will have greater facilities of distribution from Hurd and Houghton's place there. It still continues of Boston, Bostony—with a shade of Buckeye. The magazine was "sold for no fault," but because Osgood was offered a handsome price, and had gone off on heliotypes so far that he found it hard to look after his magazines.[1]

I'm working towards the end of my story,[2] and it "grows upon me." I wish you were here to listen to certain chapters of it. I believe I've got a very mannish man in it, and I hope a couple of probable women.

Please tell Mrs. Smith that I dreamt of her last night, and she was *so* natural—took a small joke of mine about her being a German gräfinn, in a way that made me 14 years younger, and invoked the shade of Ferguson to help laugh.[3]

Annie has brought out her Journal letter for me to see, and I hope you'll like it, for I think it's quite above the average.[4] If there are any suggestions that you have to make after reading it, for her guidance hereafter she will be very glad of them. I think her letters will constantly grow better; but there are points that each editor knows will please his readers, and that she might miss. Of course it will be desirable to her to be paid on receipt of each letter. You know her address, 9 Boylston Place, Boston.

With love to all of you—

Affectionately yours
W D Howells.

Don't forget your promised article.[5]
Please send 2 copies to Annie, and one to father at Jefferson.

1. For a discussion of J. R. Osgood's interest in the new heliotype process of printing a wide variety of pictorial art, see Ellen B. Ballou, *The Building of the House* (Boston: Houghton Mifflin, 1970), pp. 167–70.
2. *A Foregone Conclusion.*
3. Mrs. Smith was the wife of Dr. Samuel M. Smith; [Thomas?] Ferguson was one of Howells' Columbus friends.
4. See Howells to Anne T. Howells, 21 October 1873, n. 1.

5. According to the index to the *Atlantic*, Comly never published an article in that journal.

17 DECEMBER 1873, CAMBRIDGE, TO WHITELAW REID

> ... *The Atlantic Monthly,* ...
> *Cambridge, Mass.,* Dec. 17, *1873.*

My dear Reid:

I am quite willing that you should print Mr. Webb's Life and Sufferings in the Tribune if you like to do so;[1] and I hope you wont let my saying that I should be far from publishing the same amount of mere abuse of you in the Atlantic, interfere with your wish in the matter.

Mr. Webb has no grievance from me, and if, as you think, his Autobiography is partly deserved, it must be because I erred in charitably naming him with men he had so long struggled to be remembered with. It was an error of the heart and not of the head; for I knew better than to have done it.

There will be no reply from me, and Aldrich asks me to thank you and to say that he is quite indifferent.

> Yours ever
> W. D. Howells.

Dear Hay:[2]

Who after this shall say the sweetest nature hasn't plenty of vinegar in it?

> WR

Did you think he would like it?

> H.

1. Reid had sent Howells a six-column item printed for the New York *Tribune* but apparently never published, in which Charles Henry Webb (using the pseudonym "John Paul") indignantly argued that he was not a "Californian Humorist" as he had been referred to in Howells' review of C. W. Stoddard's *South-Sea Idyls*, *Atlantic*, December 1873. Along with it Reid sent a letter (15 December 1873 [OFH]), in which he asked: "Can you and Aldrich stand this sort of thing without too much groaning? It's amusing, and I think half deserved [i.e., Webb's criticism of Aldrich and Howells as self-appointed literary arbiters], and in the eloquent language of the country press 'our columns are always open to a courteous reply.'" Charles H. Webb (1834–1905), after three years in New York, edited *The Californian* (1864–1866) and then returned to New York.

2. Reid's note and the reply to it indicate that he forwarded Howells' letter to John Hay.

27 DECEMBER 1873, CAMBRIDGE, TO EDMUND C. STEDMAN

>...*The Atlantic Monthly,*...
>*Cambridge, Mass.,* Dec. 27, *1873.*

Dear Stedman:

Thanks for your manly, straightforward, friendly letter, which makes me sorry that I didn't like everything in your book.[1] To be as honest, I think my review of you *is* more considered and more well-intentioned than any you are likely to get in other magazines. Every bit of the praise, I heartily meant, and I tried to keep the blame from being nasty.

That *Little Muriel* is a lovely poem—worthy of the very sweetest mood of Wordsworth. If the author will send me something, she shall have early justice.[2]

—I am not sure that my poems are pearls, except that they seem mostly to have been thrown before swine. Some of them on a sober revision are *not* pearls, I find; but about the pigs there can be no doubt.[3]

>Yours ever
>W. D. Howells.

Love of mine to all of yours. Have you altogether abandoned The Atlantic.

1. Howells published a review of *The Poetical Works of Edmund Clarence Stedman* (1873) in the *Atlantic,* January 1874, and Stedman wrote Howells on 25 December 1873 (OFH; see also C. Duffy, "An Unpublished Letter: Stedman to Howells," *American Literature* 30 [1958], 369–70, an exceedingly inaccurate transcription), thanking him "for what seems to me...a scholarly, careful, judicial, examination of my collected poems."

2. Stedman had enclosed "a little poem by a friend of mine, a sweetly *natural* poet, which please glance at & keep her name in your mind." The author may have been Annie Rankin Annon, whose poems were occasionally published in the *Atlantic*; the first, "An After-Thought," appeared in April 1874. "Little Muriel" has not been identified as being by her.

3. On 5 November 1873 (NIC), Howells had written to Bayard Taylor: "My poems have done fairly, though it is but honest to say that their best friends seem not to love 'em so well as their prose relations. The bitterest pill that I have had to swallow is an accusation of imitating Bret Harte in The Pilot's Story, written in 1860. There is nothing like criticism." See Howells to James, 5 December 1873, n. 3.

28 DECEMBER 1873, CAMBRIDGE, TO CHARLES D. WARNER

> ...*The Atlantic Monthly*,...
> *Cambridge, Mass.*, Dec. 28, *1873*.

Dear Warner:

Up to the time old Hawkins dies your novel[1] is of the greatest promise—I read it with joy—but after that it fails to assimilate the crude material with which it is fed, and becomes a confirmed dyspeptic at last. Still it is always entertaining; and it kept me up till twelve last night, though I needed sleep. I was particularly sorry to have Sellers degenerate as he did, and none of the characters quite fulfill their early promise. I will withold my public opinion altogether if you like, and if on revision of the book, it does not strike me more favorably, I should prefer to do so; though I should be able to praise parts of it with heartiness and sincerity.[2]

> Yours ever
> W. D. Howells.

1. S. L. Clemens and C. D. Warner, *The Gilded Age* (1873).

2. Howells' private criticism of *The Gilded Age* came in response to Warner's request of 26 December 1873 (MH): "I am a little troubled about The Gilded Age. Most of the few papers whose notices of it I have seen, say it is not much as a novel. but that it is entertaining. Only one cub says it is a dreary failure *ab suo ad malum*. Is it? I know it is raw in spots, and the satire (dealing with facts so recent) is laid on with a trowel. But it does seem to me decent in spots. Now, if you have looked into it, won't you tell me right off in a line, if it is worthless? You need not fear to hurt my feelings. Only if you find nothing good in it, I hope you can defer your *public* condemnation of it a little." Apparently Howells did not think better of *The Gilded Age* after revision, for he did not publish a review of it.

28 DECEMBER 1873, CAMBRIDGE, TO BAYARD TAYLOR

> ...*The Atlantic Monthly*,...
> *Cambridge, Mass.*, Dec. 28, *1873*.

My dear Taylor:

I will take four articles of you on such Weimarish and other like topics as interest you,[1] at $150 apiece—which is the price you indicate in your letter—and I will take as many poems as I can get of the kind I like from you. This business of pronouncing on the Atlanticability of a man's verse has, if you like, no true relation to its merit; but I have never declined any poem of yours save for the reason that it did not strike me as suitable. Your name is so valuable that I sh'd be glad to have it in every number; but I could not take the rejected poems you mention even if I had the chance again. The extract from *Lars*—a poem I very greatly like—did not sufficiently detach itself from the context to be useful in the magazine.[2] Let me assure you while I speak thus frankly that no one feels the honor you do the name of American literature more than I. You are one of the few Americans who do serious and noble work in a dignified way; and the record of your latest years is the proudest of your whole life. When the true criticism takes the place of mere nastiness in our journals, these facts will be more generally recognized. The idea of my presuming to hold you in any sort of tutelage is laughable.[3]

—We have a report that poor Keeler is drowned at Santiago de Cuba, but I cannot help doubting it—it's too shocking. For my part I could better have spared many better men—though indeed, I don't know any such great harm of Keeler.[4]

—You'll see by this letter-head that the Atlantic has been sold. It was inconceivable to me that Osgood should give it up; but I suppose he needed money. H. and H.,[5] you know, were my first publishers, and so I don't feel strange with them; and they leave me utterly untrammeled, in the management of the magazine.

—Taylor, I want you to do me a favor, namely, ask old Tauchnitz to put my *Venetian Life* and *Italian Journeys* in his editions. You can tell him something of their American and English standing (they were favorably reviewed by all the London idiots) and how there is a steady sale for them to travellers. Do this only if quite convenient and agreeable to yourself, and if he will pay me something for each book. For mere bays and laurels and other brush I don't care—at his hands.[6]

Give my love to the Grahams.[7] Remember us affectionately to your wife and daughter, and believe me ever

Sincerely yours
W. D. Howells.

1. In his letter to Howells of 30 November 1873 (MH) Taylor had offered to supply the *Atlantic* every month with "a prose article of a dozen pages on Life in Weimar, with a good deal of local coloring and gossip...." On 14 September 1874 (NIC) Howells was still negotiating with Taylor about these contributions: "When you get to work on the Weimar paper, stretch it to *three* of ten or twelve Atlantic pages each." Finally, on 28 September 1874 (NIC) Howells acknowledged receipt of the first of three articles that were eventually published in the *Atlantic*, January and August 1875, and January 1877.

2. On 30 November Taylor had responded rather heatedly to Howells' earlier request (5 November 1873 [NIC]) for more contributions to the *Atlantic*: "Since I left home, 18 months ago, I have sent you 4 poems, (including the passage from Lars), two of which you have accepted. Does this indicate that one poem in 9 months is about your need of the B. T. ingredient in the salad? Or, does what you publish indicate your own personal taste in the matter of poetry? I can't quite imagine the latter, but must assume that (for instance) Mrs. Thaxter's heavy-footed

lyrics are welcome to a much larger number of readers than I have yet found.... I am getting a little tired of the rôle of a beginner in literature ... can't you make an estimate and say: so many poems and so many prose sketches a year will be acceptable?... I *should* have some recognized literary value at my age. Editors should have confidence that, if I undertake certain tasks, I will do them at least fairly, and that my articles will be presentable in any case. I stand on this footing with the New-York magazines...."

3. In his reply of 6 February 1874 (MH), Taylor responded in kind to Howells' conciliatory tone: "I am glad you did not misinterpret the spirit of my letter. I have told you (more than once, I fancy,) that I am engaged in the somewhat desperate task of burying such reputation as I had ten years ago several thousand fathoms deep, and creating a new one. I have always felt that you cordially recognized this endeavor...." He then agreed to Howells' offer to accept four articles a year, giving a rather detailed description of his financial problems.

4. Keeler was on assignment as special correspondent for the New York *Tribune* when he died on 17 December 1873. On 9 January 1874 (OHi) Howells wrote to J. M. Comly: "Isn't it too bad about poor Keeler? He was in this room the Sunday before he sailed, and we were joking about the chances of his ever getting back.... His death is a real sorrow to Aldrich and me, for though he had some deplorable limitations, still he was a man to be greatly liked, and ... honored for much." Howells' obituary notice, "Ralph Keeler," appeared in the *Atlantic*, March 1874.

5. Hurd and Houghton had published *Venetian Life* in 1866; H. O. Houghton & Co. published the *Atlantic* as of January 1874.

6. Taylor wrote in his 6 February 1874 letter: "I'll willingly talk to Tauchnitz about your books. I shall have to go to Leipzig for a fortnight, in May.... I met T. ten years ago, at the Duke's dinner-table, where he was rather snobbish. He's not popular, but they say he has good qualities. However, don't expect much, as to pay for the books...." Five months later, on 14 July 1874 (NIC), Howells reminded Taylor of his request: "Did you ever see Baron Tauchnitz on my behalf?" Apparently Taylor did see or write to the German publisher and informed Howells in a letter, now lost, sent from Hamburg sometime in August; Howells replied on 6 September 1874 (NIC), closing with the following remark: "All right about old Tauch.!" Both *Venetian Life* and *Italian Journeys* were eventually published by Tauchnitz (Leipzig, 1883).

7. Mr. and Mrs. James Lorimer Graham.

9 JANUARY 1874, CAMBRIDGE, TO MELANCHTHON M. HURD

The Atlantic Monthly,
Jan. 9, 1874.

Dear Hurd:

I'm glad that Stedman's going to send me something, and I hope that Stoddard will do so by and by.[1] He never has sent more than one poem during the eight years I've been here: that I declined not for literary reasons, but because it was calculated to trouble our religious readers. Harper could have printed it with impunity; but the *Atlantic*, with its repute for scepticism, could not.[2] As for putting him on the same footing with Emerson and Longfellow, I should do that willingly if he were as great.

I'm glad you like the February number. I hope to make that for

March still better; and in fact I've got good material for the whole year.—I'm afraid that the *Polaris* is now rather past as a sensation;[3] though without doubt if some survivor of it could tell his story it would be intensely interesting. I don't think a series would do: the Arctic business has been exploited a great deal, already.

I've not yet seen Aldrich's paper on Keeler,[4] though I know what it is. Poor fellow! It does seem too sad to lose him in that way. He was a man who had ever so much kindness in him, and his death is a real tragedy. You know he left with me his narrative of Owen Brown's escape from Harper's Ferry, dictated to him by O. B. himself—one of the most intensely interesting things I've ever read. I hope to print it in March or April.[5] It's entirely nonpartizan.

In March we shall have a poem from Emerson—the first contribution for four or five years.[6]

I wish you'd write me each month what you think of the magazine, and any very pertinent comment, for or against, that you hear.—I have always been a faithful reader of all notices of the mag., and I'm anxious to know as much of public opinion as I can; though I don't rely greatly upon it—it's fickle.

Mrs. Howells joins me in regards to you and yours.

Very sincerely,
W. D. Howells.

1. Stedman's poem was "The Lord's-Day Gale," *Atlantic*, April 1874, and Howells notified Stedman of its acceptance on 20 January 1874 (NNC). Stoddard apparently did not send a contribution.

2. Howells frequently expressed his concern about offending the religious sensibilities of the *Atlantic*'s readers. On 25 February 1874 (CtHT), for example, he wrote to Warner, referring to an installment of *Baddeck and That Sort of Thing*: "your remarks on church-going will lose us nearly all our paying subscribers. Dead-heads will hang on to see our going down. Keep those blasphemies for Scribner's, which we wish to have a bad name." See also Howells to Garrison, 25 August 1874, and to Clemens, 8 September 1874.

3. The *Polaris* was the vessel used by Charles Francis Hall (1821–1871) on his recent Arctic exploration. The expedition left New London, Connecticut, on 3 July 1871 and returned in the summer of 1873 without Hall, who had died only a few months into the venture.

4. On 20 January 1874 (MH) Howells wrote Aldrich that he was returning his notice of Ralph Keeler with the comment that he wished he could have it in expanded form for the *Atlantic*.

5. "Owen Brown's Escape from Harper's Ferry," *Atlantic*, March 1874.

6. See Howells to Emerson, 22 January 1874.

18 January 1874, Cambridge, to Victoria M. Howells

> *. . . The Atlantic Monthly, . . .*
> *Cambridge, Mass.,* Jan. 18, *1874.*

Dear Vic:

It seems as if I were not quite able to manage two letters home a week, and so I must make this serve for father and you both. And in the first place please tell father that Welch and Bigelow have five or six hundred pounds of the old Atlantic bourgeois which he can get very cheap.[1] Ask him to tell me at once how much he wants, and I'll attend to having it sent. Also, let him say how much he expected to pay.

I went last night to that dinner at Mr. Coolidge's,[2] which I mentioned before. It was a men's dinner, and it appears that it was given for me. The people there were Dr. Holmes, Messrs. Curtis, Amory and Gray, all distinguished laywers, and Mr. Coolidge's son-in-law, and son.[3] The party represented one of the most exclusive Boston circles, but I found them very charming people, and what amused me most of all was that they had every one read A Chance Acquaintance, and were delighted with the way Boston was hit off in it. They evidently wanted me to talk about it; but I concluded I would let the record stand, and so fought shy of the subject. Mrs Coolidge,—Jefferson's granddaughter—elaborately expressed her satisfaction with Kitty, and said that such a character was a compliment and honor to the whole sex. Wasn't it funny? But you should see the people to appreciate the thing fully.—Annie was out here on Thursday with two letters (Herald and State Journal) for me to run over.[4] Her letters are good, but not so good as she might make them. They're too newspapery—I dare say she writes home much better letters than she prints. Still its a difficult thing to manage such a various correspondence. Annie's perfect calm in all circumstances amuses me—she's quite the little Cobbin of old.[5]— Don't think I've forgotten your letter about Henry. I think I shall wait till he has another seizure before seeing Dr. Clarke.[6] I'm glad he seems so much better.—Two children have died of scarlet fever in our neighborhood, and of course we're anxious though there are no symptoms of it our family, and the children are all quite well.

We unite in love to all. I hope father is over his colic.

> Your affectionate brother
> Will.

---

1. Welch and **Bigelow**, of Cambridge, had been the printers of the *Atlantic* until January 1874, when the new owners of the magazine, H. O. Houghton & Co., took over the printing process.
2. Howells' host at the dinner was Joseph Randolph Coolidge, who was married to

Eleanora Wayles Randolph, a granddaughter of Thomas Jefferson. Howells and Coolidge apparently got to know each other as a result of a series of articles in the *Atlantic* on Jefferson by James Parton. One of these, "Thomas Jefferson's Last Years," *Atlantic*, October 1873, contained some unflattering statements about Jefferson's descendants, and it prompted Coolidge to enlist the help of O. W. Holmes in trying to get into the *Atlantic* an "article which contradicts one of Mr. Parton's witnesses in many respects . . . ." Holmes also advised Howells to treat Coolidge with utmost respect: "He is, of course, an old man, (75 years) and old men like a courteous phrase or two now and then—none better than Joseph Coolidge Esq." See Holmes to Howells, 10 December 1873 (MH); also Howells to Parton, 17 December 1873 (Arms).

3. The company at the Coolidge dinner was of high social distinction. Benjamin R. Curtis (1809–1874), associate justice of the U. S. Supreme Court (1851–1857), had become famous for his dissenting opinion in the Dred Scott case (1857) and for being chief defense counsel in the impeachment trial of Andrew Johnson (1868). Thomas C. Amory (1812–1889) had been active in the municipal government of Boston, wrote on historical subjects, and published a volume of poetry. Horace Gray (1828–1902) was associate justice (1864–1873) and chief justice (1873–1881) of the Massachusetts Supreme Court and associate justice of the U. S. Supreme Court (1882–1902).

4. See Howells to Anne T. Howells, 21 October 1873, n. 1.

5. "Cobbin" was probably a family nickname for Annie; it may have been derived from "cob," a person who excels as a result of hard work.

6. Edward H. Clarke (1820–1877) was professor of materia medica at Harvard (1855–1872), a distinguished Boston physician, and author of the controversial *Sex in Education* (1873), in which he argued that women are constitutionally unfit for the intellectual demands of higher education.

22 January 1874, Cambridge, to Ralph Waldo Emerson

> *. . . The Atlantic Monthly, . . .*
> *Cambridge, Mass.*, Jan'y 22, *1874.*

My dear Sir:

I hope that on looking at the enclosed proof you may still find it possible to let me have yr poem for the March Atlantic.[1] It seems to me that its interest depends only in the very slightest degree upon the occasion to which it refers. Of course this is a matter for you decide: but I venture to say that none of your readers would attach more or less value to *any* poem of yours because it was printed a month sooner or later.[2]—I shall be very sorry indeed if I lose your poem, but I should regret still more the appearance of having been at all wanting in consideration. Let me explain, therefore, that three or four days passed before you consented even conditionally to let me have the piece; a week or more passed then, and when I wrote for your final decision you did not answer me. Finally, on the 5th of January, when the last forms of the February no. were ready for stereotyping, and the proof-reading of your poem would have delayed the magazine several days, you sent the poem. I see now that I should have returned it and asked your consent to its use in the March no., but I never thought you would object. However, the mortification of losing it now will be sufficient penance with me for my over-anxiety to keep it.

I will return the ms. as soon as I go to the printers.

Very respectfully
W. D. Howells.

Mr. Emerson.

1. Howells had requested the poem in a letter dated 17 December 1873 (MH): "Can you not give me for publication in The Atlantic the poem which you read at the Boston Tea-Party?" Emerson had read his poem, "Boston," at the celebration of the historic event on 16 December 1873 in Faneuil Hall. On 5 January 1874 (MH) Emerson sent "the verses read at Faneuil Hall" and indicated that he might make some changes in the poem after getting proof. Then, on 19 January 1874 (MH), Emerson asked Howells to "send me back my verses and break up the form," since he did not wish to have publication delayed until the March *Atlantic*. See R. L. Rusk, ed., *The Letters of Ralph Waldo Emerson* (New York: Columbia University Press, 1939), VI, 254–55.

2. The soundness of Howells' argument is indicated by the fact that "Boston" was published in a much later issue of the *Atlantic*, that of February 1876. This suggests that Mildred Howells' later comment, written in the margin of a draft of this letter, is substantially correct: "Holmes & Emerson wrote poems on the same subject, and Emerson would not appear in the same number with Holmes or after him, so he withdrew his poem, M. H." Howells' draft, dated 22 January 1874 (MH), differs in some minor details from the final letter, but one difference is of interest. In line 19, after "were ready for" the draft reads: "casting, and when, if I had thought it well to put it in near Dr. Holmes's poem, the proof-reading...." Apparently Howells realized that the propinquity of a Holmes poem might cause problems with Emerson.

24 JANUARY 1874, CAMBRIDGE, TO HJALMAR H. BOYESEN

Cmbrdge, Jan'y 24, 1874.

My dear Boyesen:

We have been eating your health, as it were, in that delicious Norwegian cheese which I imagine tastes of the sorter, and of the hand of the lovely Hulder[1] who made it. Many thanks for it.—And by the way why could you not get the better of the Hulder in a fantastically realistic sketch of some sort? Say a young Norwegian returns from America, and finds Christiania all agog about a beautiful singer or danseuse, whose origin is quite obscure—and he marries her, and she turns out to be the Hulder, according to some, and according to others, not. Leave it in a sort of undecided, Hawthornish way.—I send back *Necken* and *Aslang*.[2] The former I do not care for, and the latter needs a great deal of working over, before it is put in type. I'll send you a proof of The Ravens of Odin,[3] which doesn't require much correction.—I'm delighted that you like Ithaca so much and that it likes you. You ought to be very happy and very industrious there, and I shall expect high things from you.—Don Ippolito is dead.[4]—Mrs. Howells sends regards and the children their love.

Mrs. Moulton "gushes" about you.[5]

> Very affectionately
> W. D. Howells.

1. See Howells to Boyesen, 19 March 1872, n. 6.
2. "Necken" was published in the *Galaxy*, May 1874; "Aslang" has not been identified.
3. "The Ravens of Odin," *Atlantic*, June 1874.
4. This comment indicates that Howells just completed chapter 17 of *A Foregone Conclusion*.
5. Ellen Louise Chandler Moulton (1835–1908), the popular Boston journalist, poet, and author of children's stories.

6 FEBRUARY 1874, CAMBRIDGE, TO BEN W. LACY

> *... The Atlantic Monthly, ...*
> *Cambridge, Mass., Feb'y 6, 1874.*

Dear Sir:

The pleasure with which I hear that your club has done me the honor to discuss my writings is mixed with very grave alarm at the nature of the question which you refer to me.[1] I am not so good authority on such a point as you seem to imagine; for my experience is that one's characters take themselves into their own hands to a great extent, and refuse allegiance to their author in quite a surprising way.

Colonel Ellison, if I may make bold to speak of him, seemed to me a person who while very lazily good-natured had a perfect conception of his wife's character, and was constantly amused by it. I do not think he ever had any idea of comparing her with any one else, and he was as much in love with her unreason as anything else in her. Perhaps I am mistaken, but he appeared to be a person who would not care in the least what others thought of her, and would not be afflicted by any absurdities of hers.

But I really speak of these matters with diffidence, and a sincere regret that I cannot say something more conclusive. I feel that I have scarcely done anything to earn the pleasure your letter gave me.

> Yours very truly
> W. D. Howells.

Mr. Lacy.

1. Ben W. Lacy of Dubuque, Iowa, had written Howells on 30 January 1874 (Lacy's own copy at MH): "A half dozen men, at their club meeting this week, honored themselves by taking as the subject of their evening's conversation, 'Mr. Howells [sic] Characteristics as a Writer'.... when 'A Chance Acquaintance' was taken up, it became apparent that there were two theories held regarding the character of Colonel Ellison." Lacy then sets forth the two theories and finally sums up: "In short, is the Colonel good natured and blind [to his wife's "drawbacks"], or can he see well enough, but philosophically shuts one eye?"

17 FEBRUARY 1874, CAMBRIDGE, TO CHARLES D. WARNER

...The Atlantic Monthly,...
Cambridge, Mass., Feb. 17, *1874.*

My dear Warner:

Mrs. Howells wishes me to thank you very cordially on her part, and to say that she is out of the question. She has let me ask Osgood, however, to fill up the list, and Osgood has consented. So if Providence does not happen before the 5th of March, pray expect me and my former owner in the afternoon. You can parcel us out any way you like.¹—I see that the G. A.² will not be allowed to flash its meretricious splendors in The Galaxy. And now Lady Wentworth Higginson is out in the Woman's Journal with the opinion that if I am going to leave The Atlantic, all the better for The A.!³ We have fallen upon a hard-hearted and scurrilous age. But let us try to worry along. We know very well what will become of some people in the next world. With kindest regards to Clemens,

Yours sincerely
W. D. Howells.

1. The negotiations concerning Howells' visit to Hartford also involved Mark Twain, and the ensuing complications are explained in *Twain-Howells*, pp. 14–15. As this letter indicates, however, Warner invited Howells in an earlier letter (now lost) than that of 19 February, and Howells already proposed to come with Osgood instead of Elinor in this letter, not in that of 25 February 1874.

2. *The Gilded Age* was published by the American Publishing Co., Hartford, and was not serialized before book publication.

3. In 1872–1873 T. W. Higginson was an associate editor for *Woman's Journal*, which advocated the principles of the American Woman Suffrage Association. In the issue for 14 February 1875 an unsigned article criticizes the quality of Howells' editorship: "The *Literary World* says that after July next, Mr. Howells will surrender the editorship of the *Atlantic Monthly* to Mr. H. G. [sic] Scudder, formerly of the *Riverside Magazine*. It will be interesting to see whether that lowering of the literary standard of the magazine (to meet a supposed popular demand) which has been so conspicuous under Mr. Howells, will be continued under the new editorship; or whether an upward step will be taken."

17 MARCH 1874, CAMBRIDGE, TO CHARLES D. WARNER

> *... The Atlantic Monthly, ...*
> *Cambridge, Mass.,* March 17, *1874.*

My dear Warner:

I hope to send you a proof of Baddeck V in a few days.[1]

You have so completely removed my prejudice against the subscription-book publication that I should now be very glad to hear from Mr. Bliss.[2] My notion is a very romantic and vivid history of Venice, which could be plentifully illustrated and which I could tell in epochs, and mostly in sketches of heroic lives. I shall have very little to do with politics, and very much with men and usages, getting in every thing I can of heroic and sentimental, at the same time making an honest and trusty book. It would be more a history of the *city* than of the Republic, and I should *place* everything intelligibly through my familiarity with the place. It would probably, as history divide itself into

I   *The Heroic Age.*

Foundation of the city by the exiles of Padua—formation of Democratic governmt—Wars with Pirates—The Crusades—The Conquest of Constantinople, etc. up to 1297.

II   *The Glorious and Prosperous Prince.*

Aristocratic Governmt—Wars with Genoa and the Turks—Conquests and repelled Invasions—Growth of the Arts and Commerce. Up 1700.

III   *The Decay of Venice.*

Social Corruption and Political Decline. Up to 1796.

IV   *Subject Venice.*

Venice under the Austrians. Up 1866. With full accounts from my own life there.

I give political outlines, but the substance of the history would be social; and I should make the pudding all plums,—as nearly as I could.

If Mr. Bliss writes to me I'll unfold the scheme at length to him.[3]

—I am merely living here in exile. My true home is Hartford. Mrs. Howells joins me in love to both of you.

> Very sincerely yours
> W. D. Howells.

1. Five days earlier Warner had sent Howells the last installment of *Baddeck and That Sort of Thing.*

2. During his recent visit with Warner, Howells apparently discussed the possibility of writing a history of Venice, a project he had been contemplating for at least ten years. The plan was to have the book published on a subscription basis by Elisha P. Bliss's American Publishing Co., Hartford. Warner wrote Howells on

12 March 1874 (MH): "And I have talked with Bliss...and made him anxious to get you on his string....Indeed he was anxious to get you the moment I mentioned your having been here. He wanted me to write to you and remove your prejudices against publishing by subscription." On 24 January 1875 (MH) Howells wrote his father: "I'm stalled, a little, on my Venetian history. I find it will take a vast deal more reading than I had allowed for, and so I must read as I can, and write at something else." See also Howells to W. C. Howells, 19 March 1865 and 18 October 1874; Howells to Norton, 28 December 1874; and Howells to Warner, 4 June 1875.

3. Although Warner kept prodding Bliss and advised Howells on the terms he should propose (Warner to Howells, 25 and 26 March 1874 [MH]), Howells had not heard from Bliss when he wrote to Warner on 31 March 1874 (CtHT): "I'm glad you think well of my plan for The Story of Venice—the notion has grown so attractive to me that I think I shall write the book whether Bliss wants it or not." On 11 April 1874 (CtHT) he wrote again to Warner that "Mr. Bliss has written, and I have replied that Barkis is willin'." Bliss, however, did not respond to Howells' inquiry into terms, as is indicated in a further letter to Warner, 19 April 1874 (CtHT). Finally, Bliss and Howells had a meeting in Boston on 14 August 1874, but they did not come to an agreement. See Howells to Warner, 13 August and 18 August 1874 (CtHT).

21 MARCH 1874, CAMBRIDGE, TO JAMES M. COMLY

Cambridge, March 21, 1874.

My dear Comly:

Many thanks for your news of the doctor[1] and your family. It's all so sad that it's hard to realize now how much better it is than it has been. You say very little of yourself, my dear old fellow: I hope that your health endures the tremendous strain on it.—I send back the dispatch, thinking you'd perhaps like to keep it.[2]

Did I speak in my last of the charming visit I'd had with Warner and Mark Twain at Hartford.[3] It seemed to me quite an ideal life. They live very near each other, in a sort of suburban grove, and their neighbors are the Stowes and Hookers,[4] and a great many delightful people. They go in and out of each other's houses without ringing, and nobody gets more than the first syllable of his first name—they call their minister *Joe* Twitchell.[5] I staid with Warner, but of course I saw a great deal of Twain, and he's a thoroughly good fellow. His wife is a delicate little beauty, the very flower and perfume of *ladylikeness*, who simply adores him—but this leaves no word to describe his love for her. As for Warner and his wife they are all that you could desire them. O I *hope* you'll be able to come on here some day, and see all the nice people I'm saving up for you! With our united love to your wife,

Yours ever
W. D. H.

1. Dr. Samuel M. Smith, Comly's father-in-law, had recently fallen quite ill, and Howells expressed his deep concern over his former benefactor's condition in a letter to Comly of 12 March 1874 (OHi).

2. The enclosure has not been located.

3. Howells, Elinor Howells, and J. R. Osgood had visited the Warners during the first week of March. See Howells to Warner, 17 February 1874, n. 1.

4. Calvin E. Stowe (1802–1886) and his wife, Harriet Beecher Stowe (1811–1896); John (1816–1901), a lawyer, and Isabella Beecher Hooker (1822–1907), a reformer.

5. Joseph H. Twichell (1838–1918), Congregational minister in Hartford (1865–1912), was Mark Twain's lifelong friend.

24 MARCH 1874, CAMBRIDGE, TO HJALMAR H. BOYESEN

. . . The Atlantic Monthly, . . .
Cambridge, Mass., March 24, *1874.*

My dear Boyesen:

I've just sent your story to Scribner's with a most praiseful note, and I know they'll take it.[1] By the way, how long will your long story be, and when shall you have it done? I should like to consider it as a serial for 1875—*bien entendu* that the testing of the pudding is in the tasting thereof, and that I now promise nothing.[2]

—I don't think you quite understand my position about Tourguénieff. I'm in no haste to have him praise my books,—but he's had Venetian Life about six months, and if he'd liked it he'd have said so in his letter to you. It has occurred to me more than once that my books are just the sort he would not and could not like. I have never lifted a finger for any man's favor—especially any foreigner's—and it seems to me that if I sent him Their W. J. it would be something like asking him to speak of it to me—and that's simply impossible for me. Let the matter rest for the present, I beg you.[3]

Ever cordially yours,
W. D. Howells.

I'll put those black birds of yours into the June, I think.[4] They croak at me every day.—I should think the N. A. Review *would* like your Ibsen business.[5]

1. The next story by Boyesen to appear in *Scribner's* was "The Story of an Outcast," November 1874. As Howells explained in a letter to Boyesen of 20 April 1874 (ViU), he had accepted a story (probably this one) for publication in the *Atlantic,* but could offer only $50, whereas *Scribner's* might pay $75.

2. The "long story" was probably *A Norseman's Pilgrimage, Galaxy,* December 1874–May 1875, the only serialized piece by Boyesen at this time.

3. See Howells to Boyesen, 10 June 1874.

4. "The Ravens of Odin," *Atlantic,* June 1874.

5. The first of several published articles by Boyesen on the Norwegian playwright was "Henrik Ibsen," *Century,* March 1890.

27 March 1874, Cambridge, to James Maurice Thompson

> ... *The Atlantic Monthly,* ...
> *Cambridge, Mass.,* March 27, *1874.*

My dear friend:

I keep the *Atalanta,* from which I hope you will let me blot the second and last stanzas, which add nothing to its beauty. The last makes the *thought* of the poem unsimple, and "a splendid hand of song" is not good.—I should like ever so much to keep *A Wild Flower* too. It has greater beauties than *Atalanta.*[1] But several of its images and the final meaning seem strained.—You will forgive me, I hope, for not answering your letter sooner,[2] when I tell you that I have written about four hundred letters to contributors during the past four months, and that this was but a small part of my work, for I have been finishing a new story of my own,[3] reading proofs, MSS. by the cord, and writing criticisms. Your letter interested me greatly, and I put myself in your place without trouble—in fact it was a very familiar place to me. What shall I say? You're not going to be discouraged, I see that; and I saw in the first thing you sent me the divine spark—which you so often manage to cover up with smoke. I should like to know how you work, and what your methods of self-criticism are.—As to that letter to Longfellow, he is the best and purest and kindest heart in this world, and he wouldn't misunderstand you. If he didn't answer your letter, it was because he could not, probably; or he may have mislaid it.—Nobody says anything about what shall go into The Atlantic but myself, least of all, Col. Higginson, who lives sixty miles away, and is no friend of mine—though *that* may be nothing against him.[4] Aldrich lives in Cambridge, and we see each other pretty often. He's a good fellow, and is making a good story, I think. He will be interested to know that you had hit upon the same fancy as himself in M'lle Zabriskie.[5]—Do you know Eggleston?[6] He was here to-day. Sometime I hope to see you in Cambridge—how I wish I could see you in Crawfordsville![7]

Remember me to Gen. Wallace,[8]

> Cordially yours
> W. D. Howells.

Mr. Thompson.

---

1. "Atalanta," *Atlantic,* May 1874; "A Wild Flower" has not been identified.
2. Thompson's letter, presumably a reply to Howells' of 5 February 1874 (OFH), is no longer extant.
3. *A Foregone Conclusion.*

4. T. W. Higginson lived in Newburyport, Massachusetts, about 25 miles from Cambridge. See also Howells to Warner, 17 February 1874, n. 3.

5. The "good story" refers to *Prudence Palfrey*, which was then appearing in the *Atlantic*. "Mademoiselle Olympe Zabriski" is one of the humorous stories in *Marjorie Daw* (1873); its central character is a wealthy New York bachelor of Dutch ancestry whose fascination with a beautiful trapeze artist ends in disappointment when the acrobat in the end turns out to be a young man in female disguise.

6. Howells is probably referring to George Cary Eggleston, rather than to his brother Edward Eggleston. In an earlier letter Howells calls G. C. Eggleston his "very good friend." See Howells to Anne Howells, 8 June 1873.

7. Howells' wish became reality on 30 April 1881, the day he arrived in Crawfordsville, Indiana, to observe the divorce case that he used in *A Modern Instance*. See Howells to Winifred Howells, 1 May 1881.

8. Lew Wallace (1827–1905), the Indiana author, practiced law in Crawfordsville.

22 APRIL 1874, CAMBRIDGE, TO EDWIN D. MEAD

... The Atlantic Monthly....
Cambridge, Mass. April 22, 1874.

Dear Eddy:[1]

You glad my soul by the reported copyright.[2] But O, you're sure you're not mistaken? My wildest dream was but $200. And $600! Confirm my faltering faith with an early check! A score of bills,—as it were a nest of callow grocers, butchers, coalmen, fishmongers,—gape for the dainty greenbacks.

> "If you be what I think you, some sweet dream,
> I would but ask to fulfil yourself;
> But if you be that Copyright I knew,
> I ask you nothing; only, if a dream,
> Sweet dream, be perfect. I shall dine to-night.
> Swoop down and seem to pay me ere I dine."[3]

Yours ever,
W. D. H.

1. Edwin Doak Mead (1849–1937), a relative (perhaps a cousin) of Elinor Howells, then worked in the counting room of Fields, Osgood & Co.; Howells had been instrumental in obtaining this position for him. He later edited the *New England Magazine* (1890–1901) and became director of the World Peace Foundation (1910–1917).

2. It is unclear what copyright arrangement Mead had reported.

3. Howells' parody of Tennyson's *The Princess*, VII, 130–35:

> If you be, what I think you, some sweet dream,
> I would but ask you to fulfill yourself:
> But if you be that Ida whom I knew,
> I ask you nothing: only, if a dream,
> Sweet dream, be perfect. I shall die tonight.
> Stoop down and seem to kiss me ere I die.

25 May 1874, Cambridge, to James R. Lowell

> ...*The Atlantic Monthly....*
> *Cambridge, Mass.* May 25, 1874.

Dear Mr. Lowell:

It made me very happy to get a letter from you to-night.[1] It came just in time to be read aloud at tea to Mrs. Howells; and we said, with that disposition to kiss your hand which we have whenever we think of it, that this letter looked exactly like that letter you wrote me at Venice accepting my Recent Italian Comedy:[2] I got it from the *postiere* in Campiello dei Squellini, and we both went up to heaven at once. But that letter had a blue envelope and this a white one.—My wife and all the children join me in love to you and Mrs. Lowell.

—I've sent your message to Aldrich whom I haven't the least idea you've offended in any way.[3] We've often talked of you, and he simply seemed loth to trouble you with letters. But I've no doubt he'll write now.—It was by pure accident that your name was left out of the list of contributors, and we all gnashed our teeth over the omission. As for the new proprietors, they were only too proud and happy to get your poem, and will be glad of anything more you can give us.[4] I wish we might have a contribution from you every month. Mr. Houghton is wise enough to think there is no one like you. The Agassiz got us repeated orders from the news-companies.[5]

—I have written to Osgood, and as soon as I learn that the poem is in the printer's hands, I'll make the corrections you give me.

—We go to Jaffrey, N. H. for the summer, but I shall run down to see you, when you come. I'm immensely glad you've set the time for returning, though I don't wonder you hate on some accounts to turn your back on the Mother-World. But America is worth a thousand of her, after all, in spite of the cynical utterances of a certain poet who shall be nameless,[6] and I would not on any account go back—for less than a ten years' stay. You see what it is to be a true patriot. In fact it comes very natural at this time of year in Cambridge to love one's country. The apple-blossoms are worth all that past of which Mr. Norton sighs to find us disinherited. There is one apple-tree in Miss Wyman's backyard worth the whole of the middle-ages.[7] And only imagine the orioles tilting the cups of blooms, and draining the honeyed heel-taps every where. A rivederci presto!

W. D. Howells.

1. Lowell had written Howells from Paris on 13 May 1874 (MH; printed in Norton, *Lowell Letters*, II, 121–23).

2. See Howells to Lowell, 21 August 1864, n. 1, and Howells to W. C. Howells, 25 August 1864.

3. Lowell's letter reads in part: "I wrote Aldrich in answer to a note from him & have never had a line from him since. I have puzzled my wits with conjecturing how I might have offended him—but in vain. You young fellows are 'kittle cattle to shoe behind,' & I trust you will find nothing to quarrel with me for in this." Then he added this postscript: "If I *have* offended Aldrich in some way to me inscrutable, do, pray, convince [him] that I did it in all unwittingness. Life is too short for misunderstandings, if too long in some other respects." These two passages are omitted in Norton's edition of Lowell's letters.

4. Having noticed that his name had been omitted from the list of the regular *Atlantic* contributors, Lowell thought that H. O. Houghton & Co. deliberately dropped him when they became the owners of the magazine.

5. Lowell's long poem, "Agassiz," appeared in the *Atlantic*, May 1874.

6. For Howells' comment about Lowell's criticism of America, see *Literary Friends and Acquaintance*, HE, p. 185.

7. Miss Elizabeth Wyman lived at 3 Craigie Street, very near Howells' house at 37 Concord Avenue.

10 JUNE 1874, JAFFREY, NEW HAMPSHIRE, TO HJALMAR H. BOYESEN

Jaffrey, N. H. June 10, 1874.

My dear Boyesen:

It gave me the greatest delight to get your letter with that extract from Turgénieff's.[1] It made me so proud that I forgot I was getting to be an old fellow, and ought to be insensible to praise: I ran with it in the silliest way to my wife, who raves about T.'s books, and we triumphed together over it. Many thanks for your right conception of what might have seemed my whimsicality:[2] I could not bear that a man whom I valued so much as Turgénieff should seem to be urged by me to speak of my books. When I go down to Boston, I'll send him Their W. J., and in the meantime pray write him my regards and gratitude in your next letter. Tell him that scarcely a month passes but we burn incense to him in The Atlantic. The subtitle of the magazine should be changed so as to read: "Devoted to Turgénieff, Science and Art."[3]—I expect to be at home in Cambridge before the 1st of the month, to remain till after the Fourth.

Father has been made Consul at Quebec, and I may run up there week after next to help him choose a house.[4] Isn't it pleasant for him? My sisters are of course enraptured.

This is a pleasant place, with mosquitoes so large that you can see them tuning their harps and sharpening their daggers on the top of Mt. Monadnock, four miles away. What is left of the family sends love.

I shall expect to see you in Cmbdge.[5]

Yours ever
W. D. Howells.

1. In his letter to Howells of 1 June 1874 (MH), Boyesen quoted the following passage from a letter, dated 11 May 1874, he had received from Turgenev: "I have read 'Venetian Life' & 'A Chance Acquaintance', and like both books very much indeed. I think I even prefer the former. There is in both a delightful freshness & *naturel*—and a gay, subtle, artless, elegant humor, which I enjoyed thoroughly. Please to present my best compliments to Mr. Howells, & tell him that I would be very glad to receive a copy of 'Their Wedding Journey' from his hands." See Howells to Boyesen, 30 November 1874; also P. E. Seyersted, "Turgenev's Interest in America . . . ," *Scando-Slavica* 11 (1965), 25–39.

2. That is, his decision not to send Turgenev *Their Wedding Journey*, and to ask Boyesen to "let the matter rest." See Howells to Boyesen, 24 March 1874. In his 1 June letter, Boyesen assured Howells that he had "acted strictly according to your injunctions, and have said nothing about you or 'Their W. Journey' . . . ."

3. The actual subtitle was "A Magazine of Literature, Science, Art, and Politics."

4. Howells went to Quebec on 30 June 1874, having promised his father in a letter of 17 June 1874 (MH) to stay with him "over three or four days, so as to take the brunt of the house-hunt with you." See also *Twain-Howells*, p. 18.

5. While Elinor and the children stayed in Jaffrey for the summer, Howells frequently commuted to Cambridge, a distance of nearly 100 miles.

9 JULY 1874, JAFFREY, NEW HAMPSHIRE, TO WILLIAM C. HOWELLS

Jaffrey, July 9, 1874.

Dear father:

My thoughts keep running back to you, and of course they're anxious thoughts. I do hope that you're quite yourself again by this time, and that you've got your office moved, at least. You will be living at 4 Lorne Terrace by Saturday, I suppose.[1] I think you can't do better than take those things of Casey's[2]—they're cheap and good. How I wish I could have staid to see you settled! Some things, father, I wish to urge upon you. When you are once in your own office, don't move from it to do business of any kind. When any one wants a consular service, of whatever nature, *make him come to you. It is below your office to run about after people*, and it will tire you out, very soon. Remember that the whole U. S. reside with you at Quebec.[3]

If you cannot cash my check, send it back, and I'll send the money up *by express*. I wonder we didn't think of this before.

Don't get excited. Take things calmly. You've really got an easy, pleasant and honorable period of residence before you.

I got here last night, and this afternoon I go down to Boston to see a tragedian who wants me to translate one of Salvini's Italian plays for him. I think I shall.[4]

All well, here, and the children delighted with their presents. They join me and their mother in love to you and Aurelia.

Regards to the Lanes.

Your aff'te son
Will.

Buy the old high-post bedstead, and I'll take it of you.

1. The day before, Howells had returned from his trip to Quebec. He expressed his anxiety about his father's health and financial condition in a letter to Joseph Howells, 6 and 8 July 1874 (MH). The elder and the younger Howells stayed at the Lanes' boardinghouse, 44½ Anne Street, while looking for a house suitable as a consular office and residence. They rented one located at 4 Lorne Terrace for $370 per year, as Howells wrote Longfellow on 11 July 1874 (KyU).

2. Casey has remained unidentified.

3. Howells advised his father about many things at this time. Writing to his brother Joe on 6 August 1874 (MH), he asked him to omit the faulty French headings his father used in "Familiar Letters from the Editor" in the *Sentinel*: "I'd write to him and point out the mistake, but I'm afraid it would hurt his feelings, and he's too old to be persuaded out of his eccentricities. I've had to lecture him a good deal already."

4. The agreement of 9 July 1874 (MH), in Howells' handwriting and signed by Charles R. Pope, stipulates that Pope will take Howells' English translation of Ippolito d'Aste's *Sansone* (*Samson*) for a payment of "$400 outright, on acceptance of his translation, $100 additional when the play has run fifty nights, and $1.00 a night for every night the play shall run thereafter." Pope (1832–1899) was a highly successful actor, theatrical producer, and manager, to whom Howells had been referred by Mark Twain. See Howells to Clemens, 11 July 1874. After many years of professional life throughout the United States, Pope built and managed Pope's Theatre in St. Louis (1879–1888) and after retiring from the stage became U. S. consul at Toronto. Howells refers to the play as Salvini's because the well-known Italian actor Tommaso Salvini (1829–1915) had recently toured the United States with *Sansone*.

11 JULY 1874, CAMBRIDGE, TO SAMUEL L. CLEMENS

... The Atlantic Monthly....
Cambridge, Mass. July 11, 1874.

My dear Clemens:

Your letter and telegraph[1] came to our mosquitory bower whilst I was away in Canada, and I failed to see Mr. Pope, here. But Thursday I ran down to Boston to call on him, and I've arranged to translate the play for him.[2] As it is owing to your kindness that I'm thus placed in relations with the stage,—a long-coveted opportunity—I may tell you the terms on which I make the version. He pays me $400 outright on acceptance of my version, and $100 additional when the play has run fifty nights; and $1. a night thereafter as long as it runs. When my translation is done, I'm to tell him, and he will send his check for $400 to you, and I'll submit my Ms to him. If he likes it, you send me the check, if he doesn't you return it to him.[3]

You perceive this isn't hard on Mr. Pope. The terms were my own— he would have given me $500 down, but I didn't think he ought to buy a pig in a poke, and I felt that I ought to take some risk of a failure.[4] I liked Mr. Pope very much, and I should be glad of his acquaintance, even if there were no money in it. As it is, imagine my gratitude to you!

My regards to all your family.

Yours ever
W. D. Howells.

1. Clemens' letter and telegram are no longer extant.

2. See Howells to W. C. Howells, 9 July 1874, n. 4.

3. Howells finished the translation on 12 August, and he wrote to Pope the same day (MH): "I will send the Mss. to you as soon as I hear that your check for $400 has reached Mr. Clemens, whom please ask to notify me of its coming.... [¶] In making this version I have of course gone deeply into the spirit of the play, and I shall annotate some of the passages in pencil giving my notion of the author's conception." As Clemens informed Howells on 22 August 1874 (NN; *Twain-Howells*, pp. 21–22), Pope liked the first act of the play, which Howells had sent earlier. On 4 September (MH), Pope accepted the play, writing to Howells: "...I cant express to you how greatly in [sic] am pleased with your work. I could wish for nothing better, and I believe no one could have done it better."

4. In his reply dated 15 (actually 25) July 1874 (ViU; *Twain-Howells*, pp. 20–21) Clemens wrote Howells that he should have held out for the larger payment; but he felt proud about Howells' "gaudy manliness" in driving a sound bargain.

14 AUGUST 1874, CAMBRIDGE, TO HENRY W. LONGFELLOW

... The Atlantic Monthly....
Cambridge, Mass. August 14, 1874.

Dear Mr. Longfellow:

I'm very sorry indeed to return this poem—no! I don't reject it, but I think that in the last stanza it loses the wild, delicate grace of the preceding strains and becomes commonplace—*albumish*. If Mr. Ward will leave that off—it has as unpleasant a tang as a moral—I'll be glad to print the poem.[1]

—I could find no fault with your pen and ink except that they were not writing poetry for The Atlantic Monthly.[2]—I'm going back to Jaffrey, to-morrow, after two weeks' of the hardest kind of work. In the first place you must know that I've been translating one of the Salvini plays (the *Sansone*) for an American actor (who was sure that he would "get a good article" from me).[3] Then I found literally a wheelbarrow load of MSS., and I've been steadily scattering heartbreaks all over the Union in letters of rejection. Then, I've finished copying A Foregone Conclusion, happily marrying the lovers at the end—but *which* lover, I leave you to do me the honor of guessing.[4]

—I expect to return with my family about the 1st of September,—alas!

for all reasons that it should be so near!—and then I hope it wont be long till I see you again. (These heartfelt sentiments are very contentious.)

Very sincerely yours
W. D. Howells.

1. The poem is Samuel Ward's "Nocturne," *Atlantic*, November 1874. It was published after Longfellow himself "lopped off" the last stanza, feeling "quite sure that the author will not object to it." See Longfellow to Howells, 16 August 1874 (MH).

2. The *Atlantic* had not published a poem by Longfellow since "The Rhyme of Sir Christopher," in the September 1873 issue; but Howells' campaign to get more contributions was eminently successful. "Cadenabbia" appeared in December 1874, and another four poems in the first five numbers in 1875, among them "The Old Bridge at Florence," for which Howells had specifically asked Longfellow in a letter of 11 November 1874 (ViU).

3. See Howells to W. C. Howells, 9 July 1874, n. 4.

4. Howells had written his father on 26 July 1874 (MH) that he had finished *A Foregone Conclusion* and only needed to copy the last part.

16 AUGUST 1874, JAFFREY, NEW HAMPSHIRE, TO AURELIA H. HOWELLS

Jaffrey, Aug. 16, 1874.

Dear Aurelia:

I got back to Jaffrey last night, after a fortnight of exceedingly hard work in Cambridge. The last week I was so busy that after letting Sunday slip by without writing to father, I could not afterwards find the mood and the moment together.[1] Elinor sent me your letter giving an account of the visit to the French frigate, and you may be sure that we shared your pleasure fully. It is a great privilege for you to see this elegant and splendid phase of life after your long seclusion in Jefferson, and I know how keenly you appreciate it all.[2] Elinor was greatly entertained with your letter, and felt that it quite cast all our consular experiences into the shade.—I hope that you're going quite earnestly into the study of French. Have you a grammar? Have you a French housemaid? You ought to have both. And a dictionary. Annie has already some little knowledge—about $5's worth of French—and you might help each other. You ought to begin reading some easy French book, looking out the words in the dictionary, and writing down your translation; then turn this back into French without looking at the original, and see how near you come to it. Don't let father get off any of his patent sixteen-bladed, corkscrew-attachment theories upon you; but take your grammar, your dictionary and your reading-book, and hammer it out for yourself. I hope you wont forget what I suggested to you about keeping full notes of all the strange things you see and hear.—I don't know of anybody who gives so much good advice to his sisters, unasked, as I do; or has so little of it taken.

There isn't much news, to write. I found Elinor and the children well. We leave here on the 29th, and may possibly go for a week to Newport after that—Elinor and I alone; but this isn't certain. Boyesen said he was very sorry that he couldn't go to Q., but he had to send money to his brother and uncle, and found that he could not afford it. He went back to Ithaca on Tuesday. Willy Howells[3] reached Cambridge on Monday, and left Thursday afternoon, after visiting Salem and South Reading.— I want Vic and Annie to write me about their adventures and your final housekeeping arrangements in Quebec; especially I want to know how Vic likes it.

Elinor joins me in love to all, and will write as she has a chance.

> Your affectionate brother
> Will.

1. At about this time Howells wrote of his extremely busy schedule also to C. E. Norton in a letter dated "Tuesday morning" (MH): "I find no time to read anything but proofs, manuscripts and books for review. Of reading as a high delight, I have lost almost all consciousness...."

2. Aurelia had moved to Quebec with her father when he became American consul there.

3. William Dean Howells II, the son of Joseph and Eliza Howells, was then seventeen years old.

25 AUGUST 1874, JAFFREY, NEW HAMPSHIRE, TO FRANCIS J. GARRISON

Jaffrey, Aug. 25, 1874.

Dear Garrison:[1]

I should be very glad if Mrs. Child would *offer* us something, but if I asked her to write I should feel bound to take what she wrote, and she has sometimes contributed things that alarmed the religious fears of the readers, and I don't want to embarrass the magazine with that kind of writing.[2]

I'll go myself to see Mr. Peirce when I get back.[3]

Will you please send me a check for $96?

I return some of the notices—the rest will follow. By the way, don't we exchange with the Hartford Courant? I've never seen a notice from that paper since the magazine was transferred to H. & H.[4]

—I must say for your private ear (though I don't know why I should trouble you with the matter) that A Foregone Conclusion does not seem to make much impression with the magazine-noticers. They're not people whom I greatly revere, but I did hope the story would help the

Atlantic, and it is to help it through them if at all. None of them seem to get the "hang" of it. *Is* it too fine-drawn, or obscure, or simply dull? What do you hear said of it? Nothing? In these wilds no echo of opinion reaches me.[5]

Pray don't let my anxieties pass your own knowledge.[6]

Yours ever
W. D. Howells.

1. Francis Jackson Garrison (1848–1916), son of William Lloyd Garrison, the abolitionist, assisted his father in editing *The Liberator* and later joined H. O. Houghton & Co. to work at the Riverside Press. He was coauthor with his brother Wendell Phillips Garrison of *The Life of William Lloyd Garrison* (1885–1889).

2. Lydia Maria Child (1802–1880), the abolitionist and author of historical romances, had published articles on religious subjects in earlier issues of the *Atlantic*. For Howells' concern about the treatment of religion in the magazine, see also Howells to Hurd, 9 January 1874, and to Clemens, 8 September 1874.

3. Since Garrison's earlier letter is not extant, and no man by that name had any contributions in the *Atlantic* at this time, the identity of Peirce and the nature of Howells' errand remain unclear.

4. M. M. Hurd and H. O. Houghton, the new proprietors of the *Atlantic*.

5. Even if Howells did not see any published comments on the serialization of *A Foregone Conclusion* while he was vacationing at Jaffrey, several of his friends wrote him their private opinions of the new novel. James Parton in his letter of 18 June 1874 (MH): "Also I must tell you that I listened last night to a reading of your opening number of A Foregone Conclusion. The comparison is with the first instalment [sic] of A Chance Acquaintance—opening with opening—and the verdict was, that the new story surpasses the other in every respect. There is more directness, more of that which the surfeited story-reader wants, without any less of finish or truth." Mark Twain wrote on 21 June 1874 (MH; *Twain-Howells*, pp. 17–18): "I have only been re-reading the Foregone Conclusion, & it does seem such absolute perfection of character-drawing & withal so moving in the matter of pathos now, humor then, & both at once occasionally, that Mrs Clemens wanted me to defer my smoke & drop you our thanks...." Clemens again on 22 August 1874 (NN; *Twain-Howells*, pp. 21–22): "you have even outdone yourself. I should think that this must be the daintiest, truest, most admirable workmanship that was ever put on a story." Harriet W. Preston on 6 July 1874 (MH): "I like *Foregone Conclusion*, *very* much—all but what may be called the *optical* portions to wit—the red rim round the heroine's eyes... and the fun you make of the poor dear silly mother's eye-glasses, wh[ich] a near-sighted person somehow feels bound to resent[.]" Finally, J. W. De Forest, in a long letter of 21 July 1874 (OFH), compared Howells favorably with George Eliot and Ivan Turgenev. Of the characters in the novel he says, summing up: "On the whole, they are four real people, as real as anybody's people."

6. Apparently Garrison was candidly critical in his response, now lost; that much can be inferred from Howells' letter to him of 29 August 1874 (NjP): "Many and sincere thanks for your kind frankness. I hope for your increased liking of Miss Vervain in the fourth installment, and my hopes of due effect with the public are built on the fifth. I intended that her proud love for her mother should touch people, and I have desired that they should see a great nobleness of nature in her amidst the confusions of her ignorance and innocence. I could not make this come out early in the story without forcing the character.—I'm glad you liked Mrs. V. What I wished to show in her was a winning good heartedness united to babbling weak-headedness...."

1 SEPTEMBER 1874, CAMBRIDGE, TO BRET HARTE

> *... The Atlantic Monthly....*
> *Cambridge, Mass.* Sept. 1, 1874.

My dear Harte:

Please send back immediately the proof of your poem *Ramon*.[1]

I've just got home from the country, to find your letter of the 28th, and have telegraphed you to send me the ms. of your new story for examination. *Any* story by you or any other writer would not be worth $500, "unsight unseen," but a particular story might be worth that sum. It is indispensible that I should see this story before asking the publishers to buy it at an extraordinary price.[2]

Of course, if you were writing exclusively for us, it would be another matter, but as matters stand, why it *isn't*!

I beg you to be as prompt as you can about answering my other letters. It is a main object with us to know *before the 7th of September* whether you engage yourself to us or not. After that it will not be so important.[3]

> Yours ever,
> W. D. Howells

1. "Ramon," *Atlantic*, October 1874. The problems Howells had in dealing with Harte are evident in Harte's letter of 14 May 1874 (MH; printed in B. A. Booth, "Bret Harte Goes East: Some Unpublished Letters," *American Literature* 19 [1948], 331), in which he complains about several corrections Howells made in the poem "For the King," *Atlantic*, July 1874: "So little do I value that kind of criticism, wh. you have, I know in perfect goodness, indicated I might receive for these irregularities, that I would have been perfectly satisfied had you printed the poem as I sent it.... I would always prefer that such infelicities should be left for me to defend. I know, my dear Howells, that your suggestions are kindly, but it vexes me sorely that even in kindness, you should voice the 'blameless priggism' of a certain kind of criticism."

2. The letter from Harte of 28 August is not extant, but his exasperation with the low payments made by the *Atlantic* for his contributions is expressed in his letter to Howells of 8 September 1874 (MH; also printed in *American Literature* 19 [1948], 332).

3. None of the correspondence mentioned is extant, and "Ramon" was the last of Harte's contributions printed in the *Atlantic*.

8 SEPTEMBER 1874, CAMBRIDGE, TO SAMUEL L. CLEMENS

> *... The Atlantic Monthly....*
> *Cambridge, Mass.* September 8, 1874.

My dear Clemens:

I'm going to settle *your* opinion of the next installment of A Foregone Conclusion by sending back one of your contributions.[1] Not, let me hasten to say, that I don't think they're both very good. But The Atlantic, as regards matters of religion, is just in that Good Lord, Good Devil condition when a little fable like yours wouldn't leave it a single Presbyterian, Baptist, Unitarian, Episcopalian, Methodist or Millerite *paying* subscriber—all the dead-heads would stick to it, and abuse it in the denominational newspapers. Send your fable to some truly pious concern like Scribner or Harper, and they'll extract it into all the hymn-books. But it would ruin *us*.

I've kept the True Story which I think extremely good and touching with the best and reallest kind of black talk in it. Perhaps it couldn't be better than it is; but if you feel like giving it a little more circumstantiation (you didn't know there was such a word as that, did you?) on getting the proof, why, don't mind making the printers some over-running.

The fotografs were most welcome, and I'm sorry that I can't send back anything but thanks. I admire the attitude and the asthma,[2] and the whole landscape, and I've put them all three up on the mantelpiece where I can look at them whenever so dispoged.[3]

There are parts of the Fable that I think wonderfully good even for you—that touch about Sisyphus and Atlas being ancestors of the tumble-bug, did tickle me.[4]

Pope writes back and pretends to be overjoyed with the version of Samson.[5]

My best regards to Mrs Clemens, for whose speedy recovery I devoutly wish.

Yours ever
W. D. Howells.

1. Mark Twain had sent Howells "Some Learned Fables, for Good Old Boys and Girls" and "A True Story, Repeated Word for Word as I Heard It"; only the latter appeared in the *Atlantic*, November 1874. Howells' objections to the former are explained in *Twain-Howells*, p. 863; his recollection of accepting "A True Story" was later included in "Recollections of an Atlantic Editorship," *Atlantic*, November 1907.

2. Only one of the three photographs Clemens sent has been located at Harvard; it shows him seated at his desk, and on the back he wrote: "Do you mind that attitude? It took me hours to perfect that." Probably one of the other photographs bore an inscription that would explain the "asthma" reference.

3. If this reading is correct, Howells appears to be adopting Sairy Gamp's speech in Dickens' *Martin Chuzzlewit*.

4. The story as printed in *Mark Twain's Sketches, New and Old* (1875) does not contain the passage Howells liked.

5. See Howells to Clemens, 11 July 1874, n. 3.

24 SEPTEMBER 1874, CAMBRIDGE, TO JOHN B. O'REILLY

> ... *The Atlantic Monthly*. ...
> *Cambridge, Mass.* Sept. 24, 1874.

My dear Mr. O'Reilly:[1]

I am very glad indeed that you have written me your criticism privately, because this enables me to reply to it: public criticism, when it does not affect my personal character, I hope never to answer.[2]

Let me say at once that I have no such sense of Don Ippolito's character as you have imagined. I do not think he has a superior mind, but a delicate, uncertain, vacillating mind, quite other than strong. I hoped this had already appeared; I'm sure it will appear explicitly before the end. I pondered over the passage you cut out, and let it stand because it seemed to me that what followed in Don Ippolito's own confession as to the perfect justice and kindness of his treatment by his clerical teachers would keep any one from thinking it of general application. Don Ippolito speaks solely for himself, and so does each of the characters: for example, Ferris in his talk about the priesthood. My own standpoint is quite outside of the operation of the story. Do you remember the nun called *the Signora* in Manzoni's *Betrothed*? (*I Promessi Sposi*.)[3] Well, I do not mean to have Don Ippolito accepted as a type, any more than that good man and good Catholic, Manzoni, meant to have the Signora accepted as a type.—I beg you to have patience with my story to the end; then if you pronounce me unfair, I shall be disappointed. I thank you for writing to me, for nothing could disgust me more than to be supposed to be making an onslaught on your church.

> **Yours sincerely**
> **W. D. Howells.**

1. John Boyle O'Reilly (1844–1890), a poet, editor, and militant Irish patriot, had escaped to the United States from penal servitude in Australia in 1869. He joined the editorial staff of the Boston *Pilot* and was its owner and editor (1876–1890).

2. O'Reilly wrote Howells on 23 September 1874 (MH), criticizing the character of Don Ippolito in *A Foregone Conclusion*. He attached a clipped passage from the October installment (p. 137 of the 1875 edition), in which the priest says that to be a priest is to live a lie; then O'Reilly continued: "I know you are sketching the working of an abnormal mind; that you make the poor wretch say that his life is a lie, that he is not a Catholic and all that. But I cannot help thinking that you mean to show that *because* this priest has a very superior mind, naturally devoted to scientific considerations, therefore he is a poor Catholic, or rather no Catholic at all."

3. Alessandro Manzoni's novel was published 1825–1827.

3 OCTOBER 1874, CAMBRIDGE, TO MELANCHTHON M. HURD

...The Atlantic Monthly....
Cambridge, Mass. Oct. 3, 1874.

Dear Mr. Hurd:

With the greatest wish to like Mr. Lanier's poem, I am sorry to say that I don't find it successful.[1] The reader would be mystified as to its purpose and meaning, and would hardly know how or why to connect the final bit of narrative with the preceding apostrophe. Neither is striking enough to stand alone.

Perhaps you'll be kind enough to show this note to Mr. Lanier, whom I should be glad to count among our contributors. His worst danger is a vein of mysticism running through all he writes.

Yours ever
W. D. Howells.

1. Sidney Lanier had asked Hurd to act as his intermediary in submitting "Corn" to the *Atlantic* perhaps because Howells had already rejected two earlier poetic contributions by Lanier. In retrospect Lanier saw Howells' repeated rejections as a "chagrin" which convinced him of his own deep commitment to poetry, and he resented Howells' coolness towards him, as he explained in a letter to Bayard Taylor of 25 February 1877: "I sent 'Corn' to Mr Howells: and, upon his refusing it, I tried, some time afterwards, a couple of sonnets, accompanied by a note asking (poor green goose that I was! as if an editor had time for such things,—but I really knew no better) if he would not do me the favor to point out in these a certain 'mysticism' of which he had complained in 'Corn'. This he did not answer: only returning the two poor little sonnets with the usual printed refusal. [¶] This looked so much like a pointed invitation to me to let him alone that I have never had the courage to trouble him since." See C. R. Anderson and A. H. Starke, ed., *Centennial Edition: Sidney Lanier* (Baltimore: Johns Hopkins Press, 1945), IX, 186–87, 434, and X, 341–42; also A. H. Starke, "William Dean Howells and Sidney Lanier," *American Literature* 3 (1931), 79–82.

18 OCTOBER 1874, CAMBRIDGE, TO WILLIAM C. HOWELLS

...The Atlantic Monthly....
Cambridge, Mass. Oct. 18, 1874.

Dear father:

It's chiefly from the force of habit that I write to you this morning, for there is nothing new to tell you. My cold is slowly passing off, but is not quite gone, yet; and I'm thinking of running down to Newport to finish it up, though I shall not do this if I can help it. The weather was very lovely all last week, but is rainy this morning, and I suppose an entire change of air would be good for me. The cough doesn't trouble me much, but I feel languid and weak.—I've begun reading in earnest for my Venetian history, and find myself very much interested in the subject, which I think I shall be able to treat in the way I wanted.[1] The story—A Foregone Conclusion—is nearly all stereotyped in book form, and the labor of it is done, so that I have a fair field for the other work.— By the way, I have two copies of Parkman's Canada under the Old Régime, and I'm going to send you one, for I know that you and the girls will greatly enjoy it.[2]—The last Sentinel had two of your letters, and I thought them the best you had yet written.[3] You ought to give a full account of your winter experience in the paper: it would be very entertaining. It's a pity that some of you shouldn't keep a diary in which you sketched down all the odd things and odd people that you see.

Elinor wants me to excuse her to you all, and to say that she is going to write very soon.—I was looking out of the attic windows yesterday, and thinking that it was a little later than this last year that Annie came to seek her fortune in Boston. How many strange changes since then! I'm glad that she's at home with you in Quebec, much as I'd like to have her here; for I know that last winter was a hard one for her.

Elinor joins me in love to all.

Your affectionate son
Will.

1. See Howells to Warner, 17 March 1874.

2. Howells had just completed a study of Francis Parkman's works, which was published as "Mr. Parkman's Histories," Atlantic, November 1874. In a letter to Parkman of 8 September 1874 (MHi), he requested further information about the "general design" of the histories, beyond what could be ascertained from the prefaces; he also expressed his enjoyment of The Old Regime in Canada (1874): "I have just read—perhaps I ought to say gulped—your last volume with the greatest enjoyment, which nothing marred but the fact that it was not twenty volumes; and now I'm writing that long-projected article on all your histories."

3. Some of the earlier "Familiar Letters from the Editor" had caused Howells to remonstrate about his father's misuse of French. He wrote to Victoria and Annie Howells on 6 September 1874 (MH): "I hope you'll soon learn enough French to correct the extraordinary Gallicisms of father's Sentinel letters; or it would be better still if you could get him not to use them. Nobody understands them, they're almost invariably misspelled and misprinted, and I don't see what possible comfort they give him. The letters are full of agreeable information, but father's French quite kills my joy in them." See also Howells to W. C. Howells, 9 July 1874, n. 3.

24 OCTOBER 1874, NEWPORT, RHODE ISLAND, TO ANNE T. HOWELLS

Newport, Oct. 24, 1874.

Dear Annie:

I at last made up my mind yesterday to run down here, and try to finish up the cold and cough which have been hanging on with me for the last six weeks, and which the doctor thought a change of air would rid me of. But before I left home I finished your story,[1] which was even better than I expected as to the writing and the development of characters. The analysis of motive and of feeling was very subtly as well as very dramatically made, and many of the situations were powerful. In fact, I shouldn't object to any of them, artistically, except the last, which is quite unworthy of the rest.

I should say that with that ending the story was a failure. It is violent and feeble at the same time, and I strongly advise you to invent some other denouement. To have Dale struck by lightning and Agnes go mad is a mere *coup de théâtre*, to which you ought not to resort. Besides you owe it to Agnes and to your own ideal of womanly character, not to let her succumb to an unworthy passion, which she does as effectively in losing her wits for Dale's death as if she had run away with him. To my mind she does not behave with great self-respect in her relations with Dale, until she finally repulses him, and sends him off. A right and natural climax of the story would be her humble recognition of her rescue by Providence in his death, and her devotion to duty that would thereafter wean her from an ignoble sorrow. Dale was simply a selfish, reckless man, not worthy of Jeanette, and certainly not worthy of any good woman. In hastening to Agnes with the news of her husband's death, he shows himself coarse and obtuse in unpardonable degree; and your opportunity would be to let the true nobleness of her husband's delicate and gentle conduct contrast itself in Agnes's mind with Dale's behavior until with lapse of time, a real love for her husband fills her heart. I do n't think that even this love could make her worthy of him, but it would content the reader and make him more forgiving towards her than any right-minded reader can now feel. You know that in dealing with such a problem as this you are handling very delicate matters, and false morality here, is false art. I could wish that you had chosen some simpler and wholesomer phase of human-nature, which would also be fresher; but since you have taken this, you must make your triumph the greater, by treating it from the loftiest ground. Women will read your story as innocently as it is written, but men will think evil if you give them the slightest occasion. Now Dale's death is an escape for Jeanette as well as Agnes, and you ought so to intimate by the catastrophe. I think your story would be stronger by a thousandfold, if you ended the present last chapter simply with Stone's announcement of Dale's death. Then begin a new chapter, in which you take Agnes up after a lapse of years, and briefly indicate the processes of mind and heart by which she reaches a penitent tranquillity. She need never tell Jeanette, who may have meantime married; she may or may not have told her husband—let this point work itself naturally out in your mind. But in the end every trace of love for Dale should have left her.

I sketch this plan roughly, but you can see its sense. Now, I'll do what you wish with your Ms. I will send it to the Galaxy as it is, or I will send it back for revision.[2] I have never exercised patience in my life, but I have afterwards been most humbly glad of it, and I urge you to reconsider your work. It is already too late to get it into any magazine for the beginning of the year, but the G. might accept it to begin say in July. If you take it back, you'll see how I've modified some passages.

With much love to all

> Your affectionate brother
> Will.

1. "Reuben Dale," *Galaxy*, December 1875–April 1876. On 10 October 1874 (MH) Howells wrote Victoria about Annie's forthcoming story: "I'm curious to see her story, which I suppose she's finishing as fast as possible. She needn't care for my criticism, which of course can be only most affectionately meant—at least she needn't be in dread of it. What I read of her story seemed to me very well done. But if she sends the ms. to me, am I to forward it to the editor of the Galaxy whether I like it or not?"

2. Apparently Howells sent it to the *Galaxy*. In his letter of 17 November 1874 (NN) to its editor, probably Francis P. Church (but possibly his brother, William C. Church), he responded to suggestions Church made for revisions: "I shall strongly urge upon Miss Howells the revision of her novelette according to your suggestion. I thank you for her and I can assure you that your letter will occasion greater excitement and joy in one house at Quebec than probably ever was known in that city." Church's suggestions apparently did not agree with Howells' proposed revisions. Annie left the ending of the story as she had originally conceived it, ignoring her brother's objections. It is evident that the moral argument here advanced by Howells expresses only part of his dislike for the last episode; the melodramatic ending certainly must have offended his literary taste as well. In later years he would attack such writing by calling it "romanticistic."

14 NOVEMBER 1874, CAMBRIDGE, TO JOHN AUGUSTIN DALY

> *... The Atlantic Monthly....*
> *Cambridge, Mass.* Nov. 14, 1874.

My dear Sir:[1]

Do not suppose from the great deliberation with which I answer your obliging letter that I was not very glad indeed to get it.[2]

I have long had the notion of a play, which I have now briefly exposed to Mr. Clemens, and which he thinks will do.[3] It's against it, I suppose that it's rather tragical, but perhaps—certainly, if you've ever troubled yourself with my undramatic writings,—you know that I can't deal exclusively in tragedy, and I think I could make my play in some part such a light affair that many people would never know how deeply they ought to have been moved by it.

I have also the idea of a farce or vaudeville of strictly American circumstance.[4]

Of course I'm a very busy man, and I must do these plays in moments of leisure from my editorial work. I'm well aware that I can't write a good play by inspiration, and when I've sketched my plots and done some scenes, I shall, with your leave send them for your criticism.

Yours very truly
W D Howells.

1. John Augustin Daly (1838–1899) began as a drama critic in New York, wrote and produced plays, and became owner and manager of the Fifth Avenue Theatre and Daly's Theatre. He was one of the most successful theater entrepreneurs of his time.

2. Daly had written Howells on 3 November 1874 (MH), urging him, at Mark Twain's suggestion, to write a play. The letter concludes with this sentence: "I am ready at all times to do my share towards fostering a Native drama, & I shall be very glad indeed to have an opportunity of producing a play from your pen." Clemens had earlier asked Howells: "Shan't I drop Daly a line & hint to him that it isn't likely you would want to bother with a play but that possibly you *might* if persuasively tackled?" See *Twain-Howells*, p. 33.

3. Howells had in mind a dramatization of *A Foregone Conclusion*, which was just about to appear in book form. There is no extensive correspondence between Howells and Clemens concerning this matter, but Mark Twain had been to a party at the Howellses on the evening of 13 November, and on the day Howells wrote this letter to Daly, Clemens gave a supper at Young's Hotel in Boston for Howells and a few other friends. See *Twain-Howells*, p. 77, and Howells to Clemens, 23 November 1874. Also, on 13 December 1874 (MH) Howells wrote his father: "Just now, Elinor and I are talking over the project of dramatizing the story. If I could make a good play of it, I should 'fill my purse right quick.' "

4. This is the first reference to *The Parlor Car*, which was not written until 1876.

23 NOVEMBER 1874, CAMBRIDGE, TO SAMUEL L. CLEMENS

... The Atlantic Monthly. ...
Cambridge, Mass. November 23, 1874.

Dear Clemens:

The deliberation with which I respond to your letters of Friday is but a faint token of the delight that their coming gave me.[1] I hope you're going to let me keep the letter from Limerick: at any rate I'm going to keep it till I've showed it round—especially to Aldrich and Osgood. I quite agree with Twitchell about its deliciousness. (You not like Lamb! When the L. in your name stands for Lamb, and you know very well that you were christened Charles, and afterwards changed it to Solomon, for a joke.) Mrs. Howells is simply absurd about it, and thinks it better than the most tragical mirth in A Foreg. Conc.

The piece about the Mississippi is capital—it almost made the water in our ice-pitcher muddy as I read it, and I hope to send you a proof directly. I don't think I shall meddle much with it even in the way of suggestion. The sketch of the low-lived little town was so good, that I could have wished ever so much more of it; and perhaps the tearful watchman's story might have been abridged—tho this may seem different in print. I want the sketches, if you can make them, *every month*.[2]

Don't say another word about being late at lunch. I hope we know how to forgive a deadly injury,—especially when we know what is going to happen to the person when he dies.

Mrs. Howells thanks you ever so much for the fotografs. We both admire the babies, who seem to have behaved uncommonly well under fire of the fotografer, and to have come out seriously charming. We think they and the house the prettiest in the world. Give our best regards to Mrs. Clemens and the Twitchell.

Your visit was an inexpressible pleasure.[3] We hope for that great day when you shall bring your wife.

> Yours ever
> W. D. Howells.

1. On Friday, 20 November, Howells apparently received three letters from Clemens: one was probably a copy of a letter to Olivia Clemens, which purported to have been written at Limerick in 1935; the second was an apology for coming late to lunch on Monday, 16 November; the third was a brief note accompanying the MS. of the first installment of "Old Times on the Mississippi." See *Twain-Howells*, pp. 37–42.

2. "Old Times on the Mississippi," *Atlantic*, January–June and August 1875.

3. In a letter to his father of 15 November 1874 (MH), Howells gave an account of a party that took place the evening of Mark Twain's and Joseph Twichell's arrival in Boston after their celebrated abortive "pedestrian tour" from Hartford: "On Friday evening we had a few people to meet them [Larkin G. Mead, Jr., and his wife], and Mark Twain and his minister, Rev. Mr. Twitchell [sic] came out from Boston. They had started from Hartford to walk to Boston, the day before, and made 28 miles; Friday they made six, and then took to the railroad. I never saw a more used-up, hungrier man, than Clemens. It was something fearful to see him eat escalloped oysters." Howells remembered this incident thirty-five years later when he wrote *My Mark Twain*. See *Literary Friends and Acquaintance*, HE, p. 284.

29 NOVEMBER 1874, CAMBRIDGE, TO WILLIAM C. HOWELLS

> ... *The Atlantic Monthly*. ...
> Cambridge, Mass. Nov. 29, 1874.

Dear father:

I had an old-fashioned sick-headache last Sunday and could not write; and when Sunday was once past my chance of writing at all seemed gone.

What I have been thinking a cold turns out to be something with a much harder name—pharyngitis, a disease of the tube that takes the food into the stomach rather than the air into the lungs. It's in fact more a symptom of a low physical condition generally than a disorder of itself, and it must pass off slowly as I build up my health. I'm taking baths, and a little homeopathic medicine, and I've left off every sort of stimulant. Without knowing it, I've probably overworked during the past years.

My book came out yesterday, and I think will do well, tho of course there's no *furore* as there was about A Ch. Acq. There were about 1000 advance orders, and Osgood expects to sell 5000 before Xmas.[1] I should be sorry to have him disappointed.—We've quite lost the date of my beginning this story, and I wish if you have any of my letters of the beginning of 1873, & to the middle of that year, you'd see if I make any reference to it.[2] It's provoking to have forgotten it all so soon.—Dora Howells was here yesterday with a young Worcester whom she bro't to call.[3] He remembered you from your first visit to Waltham, but had the idea that you were my uncle.—Yesterday I was elected a member of the Saturday Club, Henry James, senior, proposing me, and Ralph Waldo Emerson seconding me. I had been twice proposed and blackballed before that. The vote for admission must be unanimous.[4]

Vic's account of your impecuniosity was very amusing, but what I wanted was a list of Quebec prices: butter, eggs, flour, sugar, beef, cabbage, mutton, pork, etc.—I suppose in great straits you console yourselves by remembering that you're not obliged to live in Quebec, and if absolute starvation threatens that you can retreat. When this quarter is over you'll probably have no difficulty.

We have had no cold weather yet. Yesterday was very mild and sunny, and to-day a soft Southwest wind is blowing.—I don't know that we have any news. The family continue well, and all unite in love to all of you.

Your affectionate son,
Will.

1. The controversial ending of *A Chance Acquaintance* had caused enough stir to boost advance sales to 3,000 copies (see Howells to James, 12 May 1873, n. 3); but Osgood's projected sales figure for *A Foregone Conclusion* suggests Howells' popularity even without such a *"furore."* As Howells informed his father on 6 December 1874 (MH), 2,000 copies were sold the first week; two weeks later sales went up to 3,000. See Howells to W. C. Howells, 20 December 1874.

2. See Howells to James, 12 May 1873, n. 10, and 26 August 1873, n. 9.

3. Theodora Howells, a first cousin, was probably living in Chicago; the "young Worcester" was most likely a son of Thomas Worcester. See Howells to W. C. Howells, 9 January 1875, n. 2.

4. "This Club ... came into existence in a very quiet sort of way at about the same time as the 'Atlantic Monthly,' and although entirely unconnected with that magazine, included as members some of its chief contributors. ... It offered a wide

gamut of intelligences, and the meetings were noteworthy occasions.... The vitality of this Club has depended in a great measure on its utter poverty in statutes and by-laws, its entire absence of formality, and its blessed freedom from speech-making." Oliver Wendell Holmes as quoted in B. Wendell, *A Literary History of America* (New York: C. Scribner's Sons, 1931), p. 438. The elder James formally notified Howells of his election on 30 November 1874 (MH), concluding his brief letter with this sentence: "I ought to add perhaps that when your name was proposed last month for membership, a more than usual alacrity (as it seemed to me) was manifested to second the motion."

30 NOVEMBER 1874, CAMBRIDGE, TO HJALMAR H. BOYESEN

... The Atlantic Monthly....
Cambridge, Mass. Nov. 30, 1874.

My dear Boyesen:

I acknowledged by postal card your first Romantic School article as soon as it came, and now I have just read it, with great pleasure. It is well written and very interesting; and I've no doubt the succeeding papers will be as good. I shall probably begin the series in the April number.[1]

Thanks for your good words about my story, which is now before the public. Some people think the end a falling-off: all that I can say is that it was thoroughly considered and fully intended, and that nothing could make me change it.[2] Already the letters from unknown correspondents have begun to come in.[3]

I had a very sweet and flattering note, the other day, from Tourguéneff, who, poor man! will think you've loosed the whole eternal Yankee nation upon him.[4]

I'm afraid that Perry has got hold of the same books in German as you send me reviews of. Pray look at his notice in January.[5]

Are you better in health? I have had a wretched autumn, but at last see daylight again.

Yours affectionately
W. D. Howells.

The Galaxy has accepted a long story of my sister Annie's.[6]

1. The series consisted of three *Atlantic* articles: "Social Aspects of the German Romantic School" (July 1875); "Novalis and the Blue Flower" (December 1875); and "Literary Aspects of the Romantic School" (May 1876).

2. This statement about *A Foregone Conclusion* is somewhat inconsistent with that in Howells' letter to C. E. Norton, 12 December 1874 (MH): "If I had been perfectly my own master—it's a little droll, but true, that even in such a matter one isn't—the story would have ended with Don Ippolito's rejection. But I suppose that it is well to work for others in some measure, and I feel pretty sure that I deepened the shadows by going on, and achieved a completer verity, also."

3. Neither Boyesen's letter nor any of those written by "unknown correspondents" is extant. A few days later Harriet W. Preston, a frequent contributor to the *Atlantic*, wrote of her "delight in the subdued and delicately tinted close" of the novel (6 December 1874 [MH]). For E. C. Stedman's comments, see Howells to Stedman, 8 December 1874, n. 1.

4. After Howells had sent Turgenev *Their Wedding Journey* at Boyesen's suggestion (see Howells to Boyesen, 10 June 1874), the Russian novelist wrote to Howells on 28 October 1874 (MH; printed in *Scando-Slavica* 11 [1965], 32–33): "Your litterary physionomy [sic] is a most sympathetic one: it is natural, simple, and clear—and in [sic] the same time—it is full of unobtrusive poetry and fine humour.—Then—I feel the peculiar american [sic] stamp on it—and that is not one of the least causes of my relishing so much your works."

5. T. S. Perry reviewed only one German book in the *Atlantic*, January 1875; it was G. Brandes, *Die Hauptströmungen der Literatur des neunzehnten Jahrhunderts* (1872). Later, on 4 December 1874 (ViU), Howells asked Boyesen to see whether he and Perry were covering the same ground in their notices of this book.

6. See Howells to Anne T. Howells, 24 October 1874, n. 1.

5 DECEMBER 1874, CAMBRIDGE, TO JAMES M. COMLY

> *... The Atlantic Monthly....*
> *Cambridge, Mass.* December 5, 1874.

My dear Comly:

I have just chanced upon a newspaper notice of Dr Smith's death, of which I now learn for the first time.[1] Amidst the sorrow in which you are, I ought not perhaps to say what a grief his loss is to me; but I cannot help making some sign to let you know that I have never ceased to think of him with affection and gratitude.

I have heard of your trials from time to time, and you have had my full sympathy, which I did not feel authorized to express without some indication that it would be less a pain than a comfort to you. God knows how sorry I am for you. I wish, if you ever have the heart to do so you would send me a line to say how you are.

Is it true that Charley also is dead? Where is Fanny?[2] How is Mrs. Smith?

—There is one thing that I hope it isn't indelicate for me to mention at this time. Doctor Smith must have been kind to every body; he was *very* kind to me, and when I left Columbus, he would n't take any money for treating me in diphtheria.[3] I hope you wont scruple to receive the enclosed check in payment of this debt, which will still remain undischarged in my loving remembrance of him. You can use it for some purpose or other, whatever are the circumstances in which he's left his family.[4]

Give my love to them all, and believe me as ever

> Your affectionate
> W. D. Howells.

1. Dr. Samuel Smith of Columbus, Comly's father-in-law, died on 30 November "aged fifty-eight years, of paralysis, after a long illness." See Ashtabula *Sentinel*, 3 December 1874.

2. Charley and Fanny were Dr. Smith's son and daughter.

3. Smith had also lent Howells some money when the young man set out on his voyage to Venice in 1861. See Howells to Anne T. Howells, 19 December 1861, n. 4.

4. Howells sent a check for $50, and Mrs. Susan E. Smith wrote him on 3 March 1875 (MH): "I will use it with pleasure—all the more pleasure from the *positive fact* that off [sic] all those for whom the Dr has done acts of kindness & that too with his heart in it—you my friend are the *first one* who has reciprocated it as the hearts [sic] outgoing toward his family!—Not only the first but also the last!"

8 DECEMBER 1874, CAMBRIDGE, TO EDMUND C. STEDMAN

. . . The Atlantic Monthly. . . .
Cambridge, Mass. Dec. 8, 1874.

Dear Stedman:

You wont think it in immediate return for your kind words that I send you my book, for I had it in my mind to do so ever since it came out. But I *am* glad of your praise, and I thank you for offering to review me in Scribner's. I'm rather amused than otherwise at the attitude of the Doctor.[1] If he would only do me the favor to write a good poem, I should exult to commend it in The Atlantic, though he had just been making an attempt on my life. In fact, I've tried several people of taste with The M. of the M.,[2] and nobody would promise to praise it or even to spare it, so I tho't it best to let it go unvexed. I knew very well that they wouldn't print anything friendly about me or anything *by* me from my experience with the Aldrich biography, which I offered to do out of pure good will to him, and which the Doctor denied me the high privilege of doing under threats to his publishers of resignation. I suppose he can say now with a good conscience that I'm angry because Scribner's rejected one of my articles.—As a matter of advantage or disadvantage, I really care very little about reviews anywhere, unless they can come from men who like yourself have thought and felt artistically; I'm in a perfect maze of doubt as to what the effect of criticism on a book may be. Arthur Bonnicastle, ignored by all the critical *authorities*, sells 25,000; Turguéneff's Liza, 1000, with the acclaim of all people of taste.[3] Come si fa?[4]

—Thanks for your insight into my processes. No man ever felt his way more anxiously, doubtfully, self-distrustfully than I to the work I'm now doing.

—Yu shal hav the Wūster spelling of cors, if yu līk.[5] For my ōn part, I so detest al idl and unecesary leters in riting, that I wūd willingly banish them from print, and I think that by going over the various English spellings of the past, one cŭd realy arive at somthing līk a sens of uniformity strugling with the pedantry of the lexicografer, and cŭd construct a tru orthografy from the authors of the midle period. But it is the Atlantic publishers ho hav introduced the Webster spelling, not I. I wil kēp the stanza you spōk of; no dout, yu'r rīt.

Yurs ever

W. D. Howels

1. In his letter of 7 December 1874 (location of MS. unknown), Stedman wrote that he liked *A Foregone Conclusion* the best of all the books Howells had written. "Indeed it has been of curious interest to me to see your *gradual* but steady progress in *construction*—invention of plot and management of separate characters.... Each of your books has had a little more *story* to it, and this is a story throughout and therefore the best of all." He then continued by explaining that he had offered to write a review for *Scribner's*, but that J. G. Holland declined the offer, just as Howells would not review Holland's poetry in the *Atlantic*. The conflict between Dr. Holland and Howells prompted Stedman to add the following witty verse:

> H. number I will not review
> The poems of H. number II,
> Because he can't defend 'em;
> H. number II has nothing done
> With novels of H. number I,
> For fear he must commend 'em!

See L. Stedman and G. M. Gould, eds., *Life and Letters of Edmund Clarence Stedman* (New York: Moffat, Yard, 1910), I, 526–27.

2. Holland's long poem, *The Mistress of the Manse* (1874).

3. Holland's novel *Arthur Bonnicastle* was first published in 1873, the same year in which the English translation of Turgenev's *Liza; or, A Nest of Nobles* appeared.

4. Italian for "What's to be done?"

5. Howells is here referring to the controversy over the authoritativeness of two rival dictionaries: Joseph E. Worcester's *Comprehensive Pronouncing and Explanatory Dictionary of the English Language* (first ed., 1830) and Noah Webster's *American Dictionary of the English Language* (first ed., 1828). Apparently Stedman, in reading the proof of "The Skull in the Gold Drift," *Atlantic*, February 1875, used Worcester. In an earlier letter to Stedman, 4 December 1874 (NNC), Howells had suggested to delete the sixth stanza of that poem; but Stedman replied that he considered it essential to the meaning.

15 DECEMBER 1874, CAMBRIDGE, TO WENDELL P. GARRISON

...*The Atlantic Monthly*....

Cambridge, Mass. Dec. 15, 1874.

Dear Mr. Garrison:[1]

I suppose we shall not want to keep on firing away at each other all winter; but I must say that you take altogether more for granted than any editorial experience would justify. As a matter of fact I never saw Mr. Barry; his hand-writing was that of an educated person and a practiced writer; and as for the thinness of his comment on his fact, I have frequently found that men of small philosophy are capable of compiling interesting material of the sort he had got together. There was absolutely no clew to the fraud, and you might as well blame me for having my pocket picked in a crowd or being knocked on the back of the head in the dark.[2]

It will not do to attribute my victimization to personal journalism; for the worst trick ever played on us was in Mr. Lowell's time when he published an article on Meteorology so absurdly false and ignorant and quackish that he was obliged to admit an answer from Prof. Rogers in the next number.[3] He took the ground that I do in regard to Old Trees, and said that he felt a prey to his contributor because he knew nothing about the subject. Yet we both live as it were in the very bosom of botany and meteorology. (If that's the way it's spelt.)

Besides I don't find any publication that is more continually finding itself mistaken than the impersonally edited Nation.

If you mean to imply that I admitted Mr. Barry's article from some personal motive of my own, I hope you perceive your error, and I have to regret that you should have formed so mean an opinion of me and my motives generally. I don't know why you should.

Very truly yours
W. D. Howells.

1. Wendell Phillips Garrison (1840–1907) was literary editor of the *Nation* (1865–1906). See also Howells to J. F. Garrison, 25 August 1874, n. 1.

2. In "The Magazines for December," *Nation*, 10 December 1874, Garrison showed that John S. Barry's "Old Trees," *Atlantic*, December 1874, was "lifted" from an article by Ása Gray on the "Longevity of Trees," *North American Review*, July 1844. Garrison argued that "Mr. Barry's own padding is absolutely worthless, and ought to have furnished the *Atlantic*'s editor a clew to the real character of the article." In an earlier letter to Garrison, 12 December 1874 (NjP), Howells rejected this criticism, asking: "How? Why? Will you put your hand on your heart and say that you know anything about the old numbers of the North American, generally speaking?"

3. In July 1860, J. R. Lowell, then the editor of the *Atlantic*, had printed D. W. Bloodgood's article on "Meteorology." Two months later Lowell wrote an apologetic introduction to William Barton Rogers' devastating exposure of Bloodgood's many errors. See "July Reviewed by September," *Atlantic*, September 1860.

18 DECEMBER 1874, CAMBRIDGE, TO THE EDITOR OF THE "EVENING TRANSCRIPT"

To the Editor of The Transcript:

Dear Sir:

In the friendly account you gave last night of the Atlantic Dinner, it seemed to me that my jesting allusion to Mr. Fields took another color from that I meant it to have.[1] I had been praised, in the toast to which I spoke, for rejecting my own contributions, and I was merely sharing these honors with some of my predecessors, when I mentioned Mr. Fields. I ought to have added that in the vastly greater number of cases, he was quite right in sending back my contributions.

Very respectfully yours
W. D. Howells.

Cambridge, Dec. 18, 1874

1. The Boston *Evening Transcript* of 17 December 1874 carried a front-page story about the *Atlantic* dinner that took place two days earlier. The paragraph to which Howells' letter refers reads as follows: "During the evening Mr. Howells was toasted as 'The Editor of the Atlantic: Such is his impartiality that he has been known to reject his own contributions.' It gave him the opportunity for a most characteristic little speech, in the course of which he retorted on those critics who sometimes find the magazine dull. He said they little knew how dull he might have made it if he had chosen. 'They have no idea of the master-pieces of inanity and absurdity which are each month withheld from them. They cannot understand what strong restraint the editor places upon his own gifts for their sake, and how continually he rejects his own contributions.' At a later stage Mr. Howells referred to his first contributions to the Atlantic, in 1860, which were accepted by Mr. Lowell, and stated that Mr. Fields uniformly rejected everything he sent." The dinner was the first of four such occasions given by H. O. Houghton & Co. for a select group of contributors.

19 DECEMBER 1874, CAMBRIDGE, TO BELTON O. TOWNSEND

... *The Atlantic Monthly*....
Cambridge, Mass. Dec. 19, 1874.

Dear Sir:[1]

I could not forgive myself if I did not try to answer your letter in your own frank spirit, for I have not often been so much interested by an appeal to my very fallible judgment.[2]

I have just been reading your article, in which it seems to me that there is the promise of success, but of which I think neither the subject nor the method is such as to make it successful in itself. It strikes me as the work of a clear and earnest mind, done remote from criterions and incentives, and in material not now very interesting to readers of literary criticism. Macaulay is now so far from being a power in literature that imitation of him would not help you to anyone's liking. But a man capable of thinking critically—and you are so—ought not to imitate any other; there is but one precept in such matters: say out simply, distinctly, directly what you have to say. *Avoid* cramming into every point all you know about it; adduce nothing that does not throw the strongest light on it. Have you had any practice in book-noticing? That is good, for it teaches you to shorten the distance between yourself and your reader, and it makes known to you the most recent literature.

But as you are so far from literary centres, why do you not employ yourself with some other sort of writing? I have asked many southerners to write something about the present social state of their section—and quite vainly. Can't you do this for at least one neighborhood of one State? Pray think of it.[3]

I write with much work at my back, and not so fully as I would like. It is a real regret with me to send back your Ms.

Very truly yours
W D Howells.

Mr. Townsend.

1. Belton O'Neall Townsend, a lawyer with literary aspirations, lived in Florence, South Carolina. In 1884 he published a slender volume of poetry, *Plantation Lays and Other Poems*, with a dedication to W. D. Howells; it begins with the following paragraph: "Not only am I indebted to you more than to any other literary friend for assistance, kindness and attention, but also for frequent encouraging and flattering expressions such as these: 'I have no doubt that your destiny is literature.... You have already made an impression which few men of your age have done, and you have but to go on in the course you have taken.... Do you know that they [my prose productions, anonymous or under *noms de plume*] have been made the subject of wide editorial comment in the North?'" The dedication is dated "Feb'y 22, 1884." For Howells' opinion of the volume see Howells to Townsend, 14 May 1884, and *Twain-Howells*, pp. 488–89.

2. Neither Townsend's letter nor his article has been located.

3. Howells' suggestions, encouraging the young writer to take up an interesting subject matter and treat it in a direct, personal manner, resulted in a series of articles on South Carolina in the *Atlantic*: "The Political Condition of South Carolina" (February 1877); "South Carolina Morals" (April 1877); "South Carolina Society" (June 1877); and "The Result in South Carolina" (January 1878).

20 DECEMBER 1874, CAMBRIDGE, TO WILLIAM C. HOWELLS

...The Atlantic Monthly....
Cambridge, Mass. Dec. 20, 1874.

Dear father:

Our Atlantic dinner on Tuesday was very successful and happy.[1] There were about thirty contributors present, and we had speeches from nearly all. I was prepared with a written speech, which I read. Mark Twain spoke twice, and so did several others. I sat at one end of the table, with him and Aldrich near me, and we had a particularly jolly time. After the dinner, Aldrich and I staid all night with Clemens at the Parker

House, and sat up talking it over till two o'clock in the morning. The only drawback was the absence of some of the older contributors, who were all but Doctor Holmes, detained by one fatality or other.[2]—From your printed and written accounts of it, I should think the sort of weather you've been having in Quebec was perfection. I'm really astonished at the capabilities of your hall stove. We little thought in bargaining for it last summer, what an engine it was.—Perhaps you think now, with the older Quebeckers, that winter is their best season.—You perceive that I haven't a word of news. I'm glad you like the Parkman so well.[3] My book has sold 3000, already, and is still in lively demand. It hasn't had one adverse notice, yet.[4]—Did Vic's poplin arrive in safety? I hope so. All join me in love to all of you.

Your affectionate son
Will.

1. See Howells to Editor, Boston *Evening Transcript*, 18 December 1874, n. 1.
2. For the correspondence between Howells and Clemens regarding the *Atlantic* dinner, see *Twain-Howells*, pp. 51–57.
3. Francis Parkman, *The Old Regime in Canada*. See Howells to W. C. Howells, 18 October 1874, n. 2.
4. *A Foregone Conclusion*.

28 DECEMBER 1874, CAMBRIDGE, TO CHARLES E. NORTON

...The Atlantic Monthly....
Cambridge, Mass. Dec. 28, 1874.

Dear Mr. Norton:

Many thanks for the Desiderius, of which I've just read the very sweetly written preface. It seems from Allibone that Howel died in Newgate (where he was imprisoned for a non-juring pamphlet) in 1725, and from the dates it is very possible that he made this translation while in jail—No, I see that I'm mistaken: the version must have been made before 1716.[1] All the same, however, the association, or confusion, of ideas, gives an illogical pleasure to an inexact man like me. It is just this kind of thing which is to give a lifelike warmth and color to a projected sketch of Venetian Life in History.[2]

Did you say you had Sanudo?[3] The more I read history the more I'm astonished at the historians—for being so much deader than of the people they write about. Hazlitt, for example, is delightfully dead.[4] O for a lot of old chroniclers, with some flesh on their bones! A brief anecdote, the slightest instance, from one of them makes my blood dance. I shall have Filiasi, Marcello, Sabellico and Sansovino in a fortnight,[5] but that fool Hazlitt (as Cellini would have said) refers to Mss., the thought of the preciousness of which is enough to madden one. I am simply boiling to go back to Venice and do this book. And I can't, I can't! I have a salary and a wife and three children, and I can't desert either of them.

But thanks again for father Laurence. I wish I could promise not to pass a day without reading some part of the Desiderius, as was his fashion. But I shouldn't keep the promise—though I don't know why that need hinder me from making it.

Yours ever
W. D. Howells.

1. S. Austin Allibone, *Critical Dictionary of English Literature and British and American Authors* (1858) contains an entry that reads in part: "**Howel, Laurence,** d. 1720, a learned Non-juring divine, educated at Jesus Coll., Camb., ordained . . . in 1712, was imprisoned in 1717 for writing a pamphlet entitled (1.) The Case of Schism in the Church of England truly stated, Lon., 1715, 8vo. Anon. He died in Newgate,—to the great disgrace of his persecutors. Howel was also the author of . . . Desiderius, or The Original Pilgrim; a Divine Dialogue from the Spanish, 1717, 8vo. . . ." Miguel Comalada was the author of *Desiderius*; Howel translated it and probably wrote the preface.

2. See Howells to Warner, 17 March 1874.

3. Probably Marino Sanudo, *La Spedizione di Carlo VIII in Italia* (1873); the more important *Diarii*, an extensive journal covering the years 1496–1533, was published in fifty-eight volumes between 1879 and 1903.

4. William C. Hazlitt, *The History of the Origin and Rise of the Republic of Venice* (1858).

5. Giacomo Filiasi, *Memorie storiche de'Veneti primi e secondi* (1796–1798); Pietro Marcello, *De Vitis principum et gestis Venetorum compendium* (1502); Marco Antonio Coccio Sabellico, *Rerum Venetarum ab orbe condito decades IV* (1487); Francesco Sansovino, *Venetia, città noblissima et singolare descritta in XIIII libri* (1581).

8 JANUARY 1875, CAMBRIDGE, TO THOMAS B. ALDRICH

. . . *The Atlantic Monthly.* . . .
Cambridge, Mass. Jan'y 8, 1875.

My dear Aldrich:

I read your story about as soon as I got it,[1] and merely delayed writing until I could speak with Mr. Houghton and say with authority that you could of course have your price for it—$200. It's well understood that I like it—that bit you read me when I was down at Ponk,[2] affectioned me fully and finally, and I'm only sorry that your own candid appreciation of it leaves me so little to say: you've plagiarized my emotions in regard to it, and so fatally expressed me, that I feel like finding fault with it, now.[3] Why didn't you make it longer, for one thing? I wanted you to keep right on amusing me, and so will the public, I give you fair warning. It's a vein that would have borne working a great deal deeper; but perhaps you've done the best thing, after all.

I'll give you the first place in the April number: will that do?

—Were you honest about all those photographs of Clemens? It's characteristic of him, and most funny.[4]

—By the way don't you think Scudder showed a certain lack of originality in his twin business? He's an awfully tickled man; but when it comes to having a double-barreled wet-nurse in his attic, he wont go round smiling as far as he can make himself seen. You must be sure to write him. You know he's out of the concern?[5]

—Your Italian plurals are right.[6] With love to all the Poggers,

Yours ever
W. D. Howells.

1. "A Midnight Fantasy," *Atlantic*, April 1875.

2. Aldrich lived at Ponkapog, Massachusetts, and Howells had visited him there in late December 1874.

3. On 1 January 1875 (location of MS. unknown) Aldrich wrote Howells: "I send you herewith the new story.... In conception and workmanship this is an advance on anything I have done,—a love story with a dimple. The dimple being the sly burlesque which here and there breaks the surface of a serious poetical narrative. I have softly lifted the tragic element out of two tragedies, and dovetailed them into a genteel comedy. It is a burlesque that is not coarse. It is a *new* thing. (You will pardon my candid self-appreciation. We 'Californian Humorists,' you know, were never too modest.)" See F. Greenslet, *Life of Thomas Bailey Aldrich* (Boston: Houghton Mifflin, 1908), pp. 116–17; and Howells to Reid, 17 December 1873, n. 1, for an explanation of the reference to "Californian Humorists."

4. In the same letter Aldrich reported having received from Clemens a photograph a day for two weeks and finally "*twenty* separate photographs" in one mail.

5. Horace E. Scudder (1838–1902), a writer of juvenile literature and editorial assistant at the Riverside Press, became a member of the firm of Hurd & Houghton in 1872, but retired from the partnership in 1875 to concentrate on editorial work. In later years he edited the *Atlantic* (1890–1898). His wife had recently given birth to twin daughters.

6. Aldrich had asked Howells about the proper Italian plural forms for Capulet (*Capeletti*) and Montagu (*Montecchi*) in connection with writing "A Midnight Fantasy."

9 JANUARY 1875, CAMBRIDGE, TO WILLIAM C. HOWELLS

Cambridge, Jan'y 9, 1875.

Dear father:

I forgot Vic's play again last week, but now I have it wrapt up and addressed, and I don't think there will be any failure to get it off tomorrow.[1] We have had a very full week, as to society; I was out four times and Elinor twice, and we had invitations to parties or dinner every night in the week, I believe. I don't know any harder work than this sort of enjoyment, and I was fairly used up by last night. I don't know why it shd be so unsatisfactory. So far as I can see, society in Cambridge is as sanely and morally organized as it can be; people are amiable and benevolent, and yet it always leaves a bad taste in the mouth. I suppose there was reason at the bottom of the austerity of several of the sects, like the Puritans and Quakers: a great amount of quietness is necessary to the possession of one's soul, and to the protection of one's self against one's self.—One of the parties was at the James's, a very simple and pleasant affair, of not a large number of people. I was talking to the old gentleman, and asked him if he had seen Dr. (Waltham) Worcester's little book on "Animals in Heaven."[2] "No, poor man," said he; "I wish he was among them."—I dined Friday night with Longfellow, Holmes, Norton, and poor old Greene at Mr. Tom Appleton's in Boston[3]—the best dinner-giver there, and a man of many tastes and travels. He is recently home from Egypt, and his house was full of oriental bric-a-brac,—wonderful things for richness and beauty.—On Wednesday evening we went to Private Theatricals at Mr. Longfellows. The play was Queen of Hearts,[4] and very charmingly done. As you have had the same play in Quebec, I send the cast for the satisfaction of the girls.

The weather continues very mild, and we are all well. With our united love to all,

                                              Your affectionate son
                                              Will.

The fotos. of Henry and Annie are very good, and we are glad to have them. Annie's is quite picturesque. Has she got any money yet for her story? I wrote to Church some weeks ago in her behalf. If she hasn't, she'd better write herself.[5]

1. Victoria, like Annie, had literary ambitions; the play referred to here may have been "The Sheriff's Daughter," mentioned by R. J. Hinton in "The Howells Family," New York *Voice*, 15 July 1897. See also Howells to W. C. Howells, 26 December 1875, n. 1.

2. The Reverend Thomas Worcester (1795–1878) was the minister of the Swedenborgian Society in Waltham, Massachusetts (1818–1868). He devoted his life to the study of Swedenborg's writings and was well known in theological circles, but the "little book" mentioned by Howells has not been identified. He appears to have been a friend of Howells' father. See Howells to W. C. Howells, 19 January 1878.

3. George W. Greene and Thomas G. Appleton.

4. *The Queen of Hearts* (1875), by James B. Greenough, a resident of Cambridge and professor of Latin at Harvard, was subtitled "A Dramatic Fantasia. For Private Theatricals." Howells reviewed it in the *Atlantic*, May 1876.

5. See Howells to Anne T. Howells, 24 October 1874, n. 1 and n. 2.

31 JANUARY 1875, CAMBRIDGE, TO WILLIAM C. HOWELLS

... The Atlantic Monthly....
Cambridge, Mass. Jan'y 31, 1875.

Dear father:

Elinor wants me to say to Annie that she inquired the other night of a whole dressing-room full of ladies, and none of them had a place for Marie. I will ask at the James's to-day, and they may know of some place. You had better send us Marie's address, and if we hear of anything, we can let her know. She could easily get a place by advertising, and we should be most glad to take her ourselves if we were not already so well provided for. I thought she was an extremely nice girl.—It was at the house of Mr. Houghton of the Riverside that Elinor met all those ladies. We had gone to hear old Mr. James read his locally famous paper on Carlyle,[1] whom he loathes. It was a bitterly personal reminiscence. One of the stories he told was of Carlyle and Tennyson. Carlyle was wishing Duke William (as he called Wm the Conqueror) back again, and Tennyson said, "Yes, have back your Duke William, to cut off eleven hundred Cambridgeshire gentlemen's legs, to keep them from bearing arms against him!" "Ah! that was a vera sad thing for Duke William to do. But apparently he thought he had a right to do it, and upon the whole I think he had." "Well! If your Duke William comes back again, he'd better keep out of my way, I can tell you, or he'll find my knife in his guts." The only consoling thing, says James, that he heard said that evening.

You don't tell me whether Henry approves or not of the long "snug" winter you're having. Does he go out every day? Bua and Winny were talking of him at breakfast, this morning, and lamenting that it was so long since they had seen him.—Pillà[2] has a very curious passion for a little white ermine reticule (with the creature's head on) which we got for Winny in Quebec. She goes to sleep with it every night, and as soon as she wakes, she calls for her "mou"—mouse, and she talks to it by the hour.

Last week we were without water, except as we carried it from the neighbors', from Sunday morning till Thursday evening, the pipes being frozen in the street, at a depth of nearly five feet. How deep do they lay them in Quebec? Do they ever freeze there?—Dr. Nichols[3] made us a very pleasant call some days ago. Mrs. Wesselhoeft[4] had been sick of a fever.—I haven't heard from Boyesen since he left. Elinor paints his defects somewhat boldly, but he's undoubtedly a sponge—a finer sort of sponge, but a sponge. However, I don't think he'll find much more moisture in me.

We all unite in love,

> Your aff'te son
> Will.

1. Henry James, Sr., "Some Personal Recollections of Carlyle," *Atlantic*, May 1881, which contains the Carlyle-Tennyson anecdote mentioned in the next sentence.
    2. Pillà was Mildred Howells' nickname.
    3. Probably James Robinson Nichols (1819–1888), who had received an honorary M. D. degree from Dartmouth (1867) for his contributions to chemistry and pharmacy. He founded the Boston pharmaceutical firm of J. R. Nichols & Co. in 1857 and was editor of the *Boston Journal of Chemistry*.
    4. The wife of Howells' physician, Dr. Walter Wesselhoeft, a general practitioner of homeopathic medicine in Cambridge. Like his brother, Conrad, he was a professor at the Boston University School of Medicine. His residence in 1879 was 97 Mt. Auburn Street.

10 FEBRUARY 1875, CAMBRIDGE, TO THOMAS B. ALDRICH

> Cambridge, Feb'y 10, 1875.

My dear Aldrich—

I'm sorry of course to have your poems "go out of the family," but I'm honestly glad you got $100 from Harper, and that he has the taste to want more. I take the "Pine and the Walnut" at $50, and I let you have "Rococo" again because it doesn't seem so full of meaning as the others, and—well, all the other offensive reasons.[1] Can you forgive me? I think I could forgive you in the like case, but I pray heaven not to try me. One thing I object to is the continued pectoral imagery of the poem. First you had a jewel rise and fall on Mabel's bosom, then you asked to have your poems hid in a young maid's bosom (like King David in his old age,) in the proof herewith, you wish to be a mignonette in order to observe the bloom on a young lady's bosom, in the "Rococo" you place a small flower on her haughty heart, and warn it not to be so stuck-up. My dear friend, is it not time to expose some other portion of her person?—I wonder if you're getting mad, or laughing? You know I mean only a presentation of facts that is the·last to make itself to the author.

I've not read over James's book, yet.[2]—When are you coming up to Boston?

The proof of the long poem in a few days.[3]

> Yours ever
> W. D. Howells.

1. "The Pine and the Walnut," *Atlantic*, May 1875. "Rococo" appears to have remained unpublished.
    2. *A Passionate Pilgrim and Other Tales*, which Howells reviewed in the *Atlantic*,

April 1875. James's response to this review was conveyed to Howells in a letter dated "Friday evening"—either 19 or 26 March 1875 (OFH; *James Letters*, I, 475): "I read this morning your notice of A P. P. &—well, I survive to tell the tale! If kindness could kill I should be safely out of the way of ever challenging your ingenuity again. Never was friendship so ingenious—never was ingenuity of so ample a flow! I am so new to criticism (as a subject,) that this rare sensation has suggested many thoughts, & I discern a virtue even in being overpraised. I lift up my hanging head little by little & try to earn the laurel for the future, even if it be so much too umbrageous now. Meanwhile I thank you most heartily. May your fancy never slumber when you again read anything of mine!"

3. The "long poem" is probably "Spring in New England," *Atlantic*, June 1875, which Howells had advised Aldrich to add to a number of other poems so as to fill eight magazine pages, worth $300.

28 FEBRUARY 1875, CAMBRIDGE, TO SAMUEL L. CLEMENS

> ... *The Atlantic Monthly*....
> *Cambridge, Mass.* Feb. 28, 1875.

My dear Clemens:

Your giving up that river-trip has been such a blow to me that I have not been able to write until now.[1]

Mrs. Howells and I expect to appear at Hartford on Thursday, March 11, to afflict you very briefly. As Mrs. H. and Mrs. Clemens are both tearing invalids, don't you think it would be better not to give that ball *this* visit? Let us have just a nice sit-down, quiet time. Of course if the date named wont do, you can temporize: we're unsuspecting people. I want you to give me all the Pilot experiences you can in conscience.[2] It'll help your book to have had them talked about beforehand. I know that our pay is small, comparatively.[3]

We missed you dreadfully at the dinner, the other day, where we had a beautiful time.[4]

> Yours ever
> W. D. Howells.

Mrs. H. expects to go on to N. Y. the Saturday after her arrival in Hartford.[5]

1. Howells and Clemens had been corresponding about a joint voyage down the Mississippi to New Orleans for more than two months, when Howells wrote on 16 February 1875 (CU) that he was too far behind in his work, because of a stubborn cold all winter, to go away for four weeks. On 20 February (MH) Clemens replied: "I give up the river trip, *now*, because I find our mother cannot remain here with my wife...." In April, Clemens appears to have offered to pay Howells' expenses if he came along on the trip sometime in the course of the summer; but Howells declined. See *Twain-Howells*, pp. 66–67, 79.

2. Clemens sent the fifth installment of "Old Times on the Mississippi" (*Atlantic*, May 1875) on 10 February, and he informed Howells on 20 February that he will "trim up & finish 2 or 3 more river sketches for the magazine...."

3. The rate of pay for Clemens' sketches was $20 per page, which was probably less than what other magazines could have offered.

4. The dinner was given by J. R. Osgood at the Nautilus Club on 24 February in honor of T. B. Aldrich, who was to leave for Europe on 24 March 1875.

5. Elinor Howells' sister Joanna (Mrs. Augustus D. Shepard) lived in New York.

7 MARCH 1875, CAMBRIDGE, TO WILLIAM C. HOWELLS

> *... The Atlantic Monthly. ...*
> *Cambridge, Mass.* March 7, 1875.

Dear father—

The mou' came yesterday morning, and you ought to have seen with what rapture she was received.[1] I don't think that Pillà at first realized that she was not the old, lost mou'. She rubbed her all over her face, then hugged her under her chin, and hailed her with every loving name. I told her to introduce her new mou' to the mock-mou' (an audacious figment of canton flannel,) and she did this in due form, but hasn't touched the mock-mou' since. Altogether, it's the drollest little passion I've ever seen; and we're very thankful to you for attending to the purchase so soon. I hope that I sent money enough.

Elinor and I plan to start on Thursday. We intend to stop at Hartford with the Mark-Twains till Saturday;[2] then I'm to come back, and Elinor is to go on to New York. In an another week or ten days I shall follow her there with the children, and then we'll proceed to Bethlehem together.[3] I feel that I need the change, for though my cough is about gone, I have no *tone*, and can't keep up to my work. Elinor commonly has a break-down at this time of year, which we hope to avert by going into different air.—I have begun a new story, the scene of which is in some such place as that where we stayed last summer. I think I shall call it *The Hero of a Summer*, and I mean it to be something shorter than my last.[4]—Has a lull come in your social gayeties at Quebec, or aren't you going out so much as you were earlier in the winter? You mustn't deprive us of your gossip, though I confess we give you very little in return.

We unite in love to all.

> **Your affectionate son**
> **Will.**

1. On 28 February 1875 (MH) Howells had written his father: "I want to ask you or such one of the girls as can venture outdoors to go to some furriers and buy a little ermine purse or bag, like the enclosed work of art, with the creature's head on. It should be about 5 inches long by 3 broad; we paid $1 for such a one in Quebec in 1870—perhaps Annie'll remember it; and Pillà has played with it so much that she's nearly worn it out. She calls it her mou' (mouse) ...."

2. In a later letter to his father, 14 March 1875 (MH), Howells wrote: "We had a really charming visit, not marred by anything. The Clemenses are whole-souled hosts, with inextinguishable money, and a palace of a house, to which, by the way I really prefer ours,—and we met all the pleasant people whose acquaintance I made last year, except the Warners, who are now up the Nile." For another comment on the Clemens mansion, see Howells to W. C. Howells, 19 March 1876.

3. The family arrived in the Pennsylvania Moravian settlement on 27 March, after having spent two days in Scotch Plains, New Jersey, visiting Elinor's mother. They returned to Cambridge on 13 April.

4. "The Hero of a Summer" later became "Private Theatricals," *Atlantic*, November 1875–May 1876. This study in the moral and social decay of New England was posthumously published in book form as *Mrs. Farrell* (1921). See Cady, *Howells*, I, 192–94.

6 APRIL 1875, BETHLEHEM, PENNSYLVANIA, TO HENRY W. LONGFELLOW

Sun Inn
Bethlehem, April 6, 1875.[1]

Dear Mr. Longfellow:

If it is true, as I hear, that you are to write a poem for the Lexington or Concord centennial, will you not give it me for the June Atlantic? I shall try to have some account of those *feste* in that number.[2]

Bethlehem is everything that my fancy painted it—mine being a fancy that uses the soberer tints. It is quaint and strange, and yesterday I saw a constable stopping the boys from playing base-ball, who might have been ordered to his duty by a burghermaster of mid-Germany a hundred years ago. "Dutch" is the prevailing tongue, so that in a long walk one evening I heard not a word of English from all the people I met.

We hope to be at home again one week from to-day. I don't find the view from 37 Concord Avenue excelled by the Lehigh Valley scenery, though that too is very pretty in is way.

Very truly yours
W. D. Howells.

1. Howells described the community and the inn for his father in a letter of 29 March 1875 (MH): "We arrived here Saturday evening, and found a quaint old brick and stone town in one of the loveliest regions of country....[¶]... Yesterday morning I got up at 4 o'clock to go to the sunrise Easter service in the Moravian church. After the ceremony was over in the building, we all went to the graveyard, where the trombone players were stationed, and where the people sung a hymn. It was very touching, but it was plainly a decaying custom, and the Moravians are doubtless secularizing....[¶] We are here at the Sun Hotel, which as the Sun Inn was founded in 1754, and which has sheltered all the notables of Revolutionary and Colonial history. It used to be the best tavern in the country, and is still admirably kept."

2. Among Longfellow's contributions to the *Atlantic* in 1875, none has the Revolutionary Centennial as a subject. The June number, however, contains J. R. Lowell's "Ode Read at the Concord Centennial."

25 APRIL 1875, CAMBRIDGE, TO AURELIA H. HOWELLS

> *... The Atlantic Monthly. ...*
> *Cambridge, Mass.* April 25, 1875.

Dear Aurelia:

My letter even in prospect seems to have had such a happy effect in Annie's case that I will try writing on you, this Sunday, and I hope in all seriousness my dear girl that it will find you quite well again. Have you all over-enjoyed yourselves this past winter, or does your disrepair come from the natural hardships of the spring break-up? I suppose that even in the midst of your freezing and thawing you don't sigh for the delights of Jefferson?—How good it is to hear of poor Joe's recovery! I'm only afraid now that some dreadful consequence of the fever may remain with the children. Our children have had *no* sickness this winter; but the scarlet fever has been and still is in our neighborhood, and we tremble for them.—I wish you would look about you for rooms in your neighborhood, so that if Henry should find us intolerable visitors, we can still be near you. We are anxious not to make our stay a burden to you, or a disturbance in anyway. There's plenty of time, for we don't expect to leave Cambridge till August.—After all, I didn't get to Concord or Lexington. The trains were packed inside and out so that Clemens and I judged it best to try to go in a carriage, and of course we couldn't get a carriage. So we walked and horse-carred it to Arlington, where I tried to sponge a ride from the Committee as a volunteer guest of the town. The committee could not take my view of the matter, and just as we had resolved to walk to Lexington, Clemens began to have a colic. We came home, and spent the Centennial in my library.[1] I suppose you had no observance of the battle of Lexington in Quebec at all.—Give our love to all, and let us hear soon that you are well again.

> Your affectionate brother
> Will.

1. For Howells' lively reminiscence of his and Mark Twain's unsuccessful attempt to witness the Concord and Lexington Centennial on 19 April 1875, see *My Mark Twain*, in *Literary Friends and Acquaintance*, HE, pp. 280–82; see also *Twain-Howells*, pp. 72–75.

2 MAY 1875, CAMBRIDGE, TO WILLIAM C. HOWELLS

... The Atlantic Monthly. ...
Cambridge, Mass. May 2, 1875.

Dear father:

I have had no letter from you this week except the one I found in the Sentinel,[1] but I hope in the absence of bad news that you're all well. Here we are very well, though the scarlet fever is everywhere about us in the neighborhood, and we're anxious for the children. We had to take them from their school because the fever was in a house just opposite that where they were going to school. It is of a mild type, and as the season advances, I suppose there is less and less danger.—Last night we had rain after a trying drought of three weeks, during which the Cambridge dust became almost insufferable, and the grass could scarcely start. The storm isn't over yet, apparently.—I went yesterday afternoon to Mark Twain's play of Colonel Sellers,[2] and was immensely pleased. The character is the whole piece, nearly, but it is quite enough. There was one delicious scene in court, where Sellers is witness in behalf of the young lady who has killed her bigamous husband, which was ineffable. He delivers his testimony in a stump speech, and every now and then becomes so carried away by his own eloquence that he turns round and addresses the jury. "Why, gentleman of the Jury!" and it takes the whole force of the law to stop him. He would be a good witness for the Beecher trial.[3] I wish Vic had been with me, yesterday; she'd have enjoyed it better than she did Sir Simon Simple.[4]—We rather expect a call from Dora Howells this morning—we've not seen her for a long time. I suppose you know that Henry Howells of New York has lost his new house at Flushing by fire;[5] it was entirely burned up. I have no news of any kind, except that I'm getting on with my new story very well.[6]

All of us join in love to you.

Your affectionate son
Will.

I've accepted Rev. Erasmus Jones's paper on the Welsh.[7]

1. "Familiar Letters from the Editor," Ashtabula *Sentinel*, 29 April 1875; W. C. Howells' letter was dated Quebec, 20 April 1875.

2. Howells wrote about Mark Twain's "Colonel Sellers: A Drama in Five Acts" (1874) in "Drama," *Atlantic*, June 1875, after having seen the Boston performance by John T. Raymond, the popular actor whose real name was John O'Brien (1836–1887). See *Twain-Howells*, pp. 80–83.

3. The sensational New York trial of Henry Ward Beecher (1813–1887), in which he had been charged with adultery, ended later that year with a hung jury. In an undated note to F. J. Garrison (NjP), Howells wrote: "Somebody keeps the *supple-*

ment belonging to the N. Y. Tribune sent me, and so I know nothing about the Beecher. I cannot remain ignorant of this great moral spectacle, and edit the Atlantic properly."

4. *Not Such a Fool as He Looks* by Henry James Byron (1834?–1884) was frequently referred to by the name of one of the main characters, Sir Simon Simple. The play was first performed on 4 December 1868 at the Theatre Royal in Manchester, England.

5. Theodora and Henry were Howells' first cousins.

6. "Private Theatricals."

7. Erasmus W. Jones, "The Welsh in America," *Atlantic*, March 1876.

28 MAY 1875, CAMBRIDGE, TO GEORGE H. WARNER

. . . The Atlantic Monthly. . . .
Cambridge, Mass. May 28, 1875.

Dear Mr. Warner:[1]

I *was* in earnest when I made the remark you quote against me, but I now see that I was also emotionally insane.[2] No impossible thing could please me more than the one you propose. I also told Clemens,— with the recklessness of a maniac,—that I would run down to see him on any & every Saturday he would name in the spring, and he has done nothing but name Saturdays since, without the least effect that I can perceive. The truth is, I'm writing another story,[3] and the unavoidable interruptions are so many that I dare not add any others at present— or till I get the pot fairly boiling. I fear this will be with the help of a July sun.

Many and many cordial thanks; but I can't come. Mrs. Howells joins her regrets and regards with mine.

Where shall I address a letter telling your brother how perfectly charming I find his Passing the Cataract (July Atlantic)?[4]

I'm going to send your P. S. to Mrs. Piatt.[5] She's a woman of exquisite genius, I think.

Yours sincerely
W. D. Howells.

1. George H. Warner (1833–1919), brother of C. D. Warner, worked for many years for the American Land Emigrant Company, located in New York and Des Moines. See E. C. Salsbury, *Susy and Mark Twain* (New York: Harper & Row, 1965), p. 435.

2. Warner's letter to Howells, 22 May 1875 (Mark Twain Memorial, Hartford), begins with the question whether Howells was serious when he suggested he might come to take some wagon rides in the hills around Hartford.

3. "Private Theatricals."

4. See Howells to C. D. Warner, 4 June 1875, n. 1.

5. Warner praised Mrs. S. M. B. Piatt's poem "Folded Hands," *Atlantic*, June 1875.

4 JUNE 1875, CAMBRIDGE, TO CHARLES D. WARNER

...The Atlantic Monthly....
Cambridge, Mass. June 4, 1875.

My dear Warner:

I think your Passing the Cataracts—which I've got in the July number —is one of the most delightful pieces of writing that I've read for a long time. It is not only charming literature with just that right flavor and color of humor, but it was to me a thoroughly intelligible account of the thing described. I enjoyed every word of it, and I'm looking to its success with the public in confident expectation. I hope you'll soon be sending me another paper.[1]—You'll be interested to know that I've an assistant on the magazine at last: Lathrop, whom you suggested last fall. He comes back from New York very well contented to have returned, and I think it will be a good thing for both of us.[2] It will give me a chance to push forward my own story, which I've got about one third written.[3] I was obliged to give up the notion of writing a sketch of Venetian history for the present: the reading became alone so formidable, that I saw I could never find time for that and for the magazine, too.[4]—The Atlantic prospers this year, and I've just been able to add a delightful "card" to our attractions—no less than the Autobiography of Frances Anne Kemble.[5] I have the first installment, and it's charming.—Mark Twain's Mississippi papers have been a great success as they richly deserved to be.—Longfellow, you'll be sorry to hear, is still a sufferer from neuṛalgia in his head.—Lowell, whom I saw yesterday, is very well. I wonder if you'll see his Centennial Ode.[6] It's greatly thought on, here.— I met your friend Dr. Gray,[7] the other day and he made cordial inquiries about you both. He was very glad to know of your forthcoming paper.— There isn't a great deal of literary news, that I can think of. You'll have heard, perhaps, that Godkin has lost his wife, and has come to live in Cambridge.[8] Centennials are the rage with us, at present. They eclipse even the Beecher-trial[9]—if a bad smell can be said to be eclipsed. I suppose that our Bunker Hill Centennial is going to be the greatest celebration there ever was in the whole history of man,[10] or of woman either, and every little place where anybody was scared in the British is centenning away with all its might.—Mrs. Howells is not at all well, and hasn't been for months, but she sends her love with mine to both of you, and the children theirn. Just think of your getting this in Venice! Why don't I poison the page?

Yours ever
W. D. Howells.

1. C. D. Warner was on an extensive voyage to Egypt and other parts of the Middle East and Europe. "Passing the Cataract of the Nile," *Atlantic*, July 1875, was one in a series of articles on his experiences and observations.

2. George Parsons Lathrop (1851–1898) was assistant editor of the *Atlantic* until 1877; he later married Rose Hawthorne, edited Nathaniel Hawthorne's works (1883), and was the author of travel books and works of fiction. He had apparently been recommended to Howells by Richard Watson Gilder, editor of *Scribner's*, whom Howells thanked for his support of the young man in a letter dated 26 May 1875 (NN).

3. "Private Theatricals."

4. See Howells to Warner, 17 March 1874, n. 2.

5. Fanny Kemble (1809–1893), the famous actress and author of autobiographical books, had recently submitted to the *Atlantic* a number of poems. See Kemble to Howells, 21 and 30 April [n.y.] (MH). In his response, Howells apparently invited her to write something autobiographical instead. In a letter dated "Wednesday 5th" (5 May 1875; MH) she replied: "With regard to your proposal of publishing prose of the nature of memoirs reminiscences etc [sic] of mine in your magasine [sic] I should be happy to furnish you with such matter of which I have a considerable collection....I have written very little for any Periodicals & know nothing of the business arrangements of such publications but I have heard that their Editors consider themselves at liberty to omit and occasionally alter matter that is forwarded to them to neither of which operations should I be willing to submit my MSS...." Her memoirs were published as "Old Woman's Gossip," *Atlantic*, July–November 1875, January 1876–April 1877.

6. "Ode Read at the Concord Centennial," *Atlantic*, June 1875.

7. Probably Asa Gray (1810–1888), the eminent botanist, who had been Fisher Professor of Natural History at Harvard and president of the National Academy of Arts and Sciences until 1873. After his retirement he retained charge of his extensive herbarium, which he later donated to Harvard University together with his personal library.

8. E. L. Godkin, the editor of the *Nation*.

9. See Howells to W. C. Howells, 2 May 1875, n. 3.

10. The celebration was to take place on 17 June 1875, and Howells mentioned it in his weekly letter to his father on 20 June 1875 (MH): "We had a great day here on the 17th. Winny and I went to see the parade, which lasted five hours, and was really a most magnificent spectacle."

27 JUNE 1875, CAMBRIDGE, TO WILLIAM C. HOWELLS

...The Atlantic Monthly....
Cambridge, Mass. June 27, 1875.

Dear father:

It's so hot a morning that I have hardly the nerve to begin the usual letter-writing, but I dare say I shall get through a short note.

Eliza came Friday evening with Mary and Beatrice on her way to Deer Isle, and she goes on tomorrow afternoon.[1] None of them seem very well, but I think they will get through all right. We have Mrs. and Mary Mead, and are, for the present, fourteen in family. In fact, what with one person and another visiting us (I don't complain of the present incumbents,) our house isn't our home in the summer, (it's a boarding-house and the bills are frightful) and we shall not try to stay here, after this, later than the end of May. Besides visitors we have constant callers, and I dread to hear the bell ring: I average two or three interruptions each morning, and it almost worries my life out; so that we're thinking quite seriously of going into the country for the month of July.

As nearly as we can now fix the time, it will be the middle of August before we reach Quebec; and I think I must say that if Elinor is not quite strong I shall not try to bring her, but will come with one of the children. The expense of the journey is something I can't perfectly well afford, though I'd gladly assume that for the sake of any pleasure you might have in seeing us all together; but the possibility of having her worse for the trip instead of better is too much of a load. It isn't the difficulty of the up-stairs rooms, that dismays me,[2] but the journey: she stood the journey from Bethlehem very poorly. You understand, then, that if all things are favorable, we will all come at the time named; and that we do gratefully appreciate and feel your kindness in wanting us all to come.

Boyesen is here in the usual abundance. He complains that "Miss Annie" doesn't write to him. By the way, tell Annie that it's no more use for me to write to the Galaxy than for her to do so; but I've no doubt her story will soon appear.[3] Here's a letter I thought she'd like to see. Elinor will write to both the girls. She joins me in love to all.

> Your affectionate son,
> Will.

If we find Elinor cannot go, I may come sooner.

1. Eliza was the wife of Howells' older brother Joe; Mary (1864–1892) and Beatrice (1869–1942) were her two daughters. See also Howells to W. C. Howells, 20 July 1873, n. 2.
2. Howells had written his father on 20 June 1875 (MH) about Elinor's poor health: "She has been more than usually feeble this summer, and has had almost constantly a pain in her side, which we think came from the many stairs she had to climb at the hotel in Bethlehem. It's quite necessary that her bed-room should not be more than one flight up . . . ."
3. The *Galaxy* began the serialization of "Reuben Dale" in December 1875.

18 JULY 1875, CAMBRIDGE, TO ANNIE A. FIELDS

Cambridge, July 18, 1875.

Dear Mrs. Fields:

Mrs. Howells, is not well, and she asks me to answer your very, very kind letter.[1] The tops of our heads are altogether too callous for searing by *any*body's coals of fire; but we wonder all the same at your unerring instinct in choosing the unworthiest people in the world for the pleasure you offer us; and nothing but the cumbrous state of our family and the fact that we have arranged to go into the country this week,[2] prevents us from abusing your goodness with our usual shameless alacrity.

We are going for six weeks to a house on the Shaker Farm at Shirley (kept by a tenant of the Shakers)[3] and then we are to visit my father at Quebec. After that, if you are still at Manchester, and will let us run down to see your woods red in October, we shall be very glad; but we wont come in the force nor for the time you propose. You are quite good enough without that discipline. If you have returned to Boston, we shall hold your invitation in terror over you for next summer.

The whole family joins in love to both of you, and with our sincere gratitude, I am

Yours very truly
W. D. Howells.

1. The letter of invitation has been lost.

2. The Howells family was making plans for spending the summer at Shirley Village, Massachusetts, a Shaker community about thirty-five miles northwest of Cambridge. They probably left Cambridge on 26 or 27 July; moved on to Chesterfield, New Hampshire, sometime between 4 and 8 September; arrived in Quebec toward the end of that month; and returned to Cambridge on 8 October.

3. For Howells' description of the Robinson family, see his letter to Garrison, 2 August 1875.

29 JULY 1875, CAMBRIDGE, TO WHITELAW REID

. . . The Atlantic Monthly. . . .
Cambridge, Mass. July 29, 1875.

My dear Reid:

I cannot help expressing to you the regret I feel at the sort of misunderstanding which has grown up between The Atlantic and The Tribune; and I wish to assure you, from my own knowledge, that in the series of vexatious accidents by which other newspapers have been enabled to notice the magazine in advance of you, our publishers have been entirely blameless, and have been extremely annoyed. You must see how absurd it would be on their part deliberately to aggrieve you by giving less important journals an advantage which your regard for their own requests kept you from seizing. Hereafter every effort will be made to prevent the precedence by which you have been annoyed.

At the same time I wish to say that for my own part, I never desire the magazine noticed except as a matter of literary interest, and I should not presume to think you had neglected The Atlantic for the past three months except for its want of that interest, if you had not printed allusions to its contents under the distant and mysterious character of material appearing in "a magazine." I own that I was annoyed by your failure to give us credit for Lowell's Concord Ode, and still more vexed that you would not connect us with the publication of Mrs. Kemble's memoirs,[1] which I had prided myself on getting her to publish in an American magazine. It was a sort of slight which I am sure you would not think justifiable except in reprisal for a supposed indignity.

I am heartily sorry that The Atlantic notices must be treated as matters of *news*, and I wish it could be noticed with the other magazines, from which it differs only in quality. But this is your affair. Whether you chose ever to speak again or not of the magazine I conduct, I still wish to tell you that its publishers have tried their best to meet your wishes[2]— which, you will allow, sometimes take a mandatory form not pleasant to people.—I give you this assurance because I think it due you from me as an old friend; and I may add that if any other editor took your attitude towards us, I should be very far indeed from offering him such an assurance, or troubling him with a letter of any sort.

> Yours ever
> W. D. Howells.

1. Lowell's "Ode" appeared in the *Atlantic*, June 1875; Fanny Kemble's "Old Woman's Gossip" began in July.

2. Reid's letter, in which his wishes were apparently conveyed, has probably been lost.

2 AUGUST 1875, SHIRLEY VILLAGE, MASSACHUSETTS, TO FRANCIS J. GARRISON

> *...The Atlantic Monthly....*
> *Cambridge, Mass.* August 2, 1875.

Dear Mr. Garrison:

I am very reluctantly obliged to ask you to pay in advance for two articles by John Fiske, Cambridge ($200) and $100 to G. W. Greene, East Greenwich, R. I. Fiske's are on The Unseen Universe, and Greene's on De Kalb. They have both written me dunning letters, and I don't know how to put them off. I shall use their papers this year.[1]

I am getting material here for a very interesting paper on the life of a Shaker Village, which I hope to write this month if—as I expect—I get my story done.[2]

In the house, here, I have thrust under my nose the material of a domestic romance. On Friday night I was invoked to assist at a family quarrel between our landlord and his daughter on one side, and the land-lady and her son on the other, the children being half-brother and sister.

It had come to something very like fisticuffs, and you may imagine it made a pleasant prospect for a man seeking the quiet of the country for an opportunity of work. I have persuaded the old man to send his daughter (a regular old Sairy Gamp of a monthly nurse)[3] out of the house; and at present there is peace. He has gone to Boston with her—his wife thinks for a divorce, in which form of marital separation he has already had experience. In the meantime, we wait. I wonder if your father doesn't know of him?—Christopher Robinson, old abolitionist and temperancer of Lynn.[4] He seems quite childish now, in some ways.—We may be obliged to leave here, if this matter grows worse.[5]

Yours truly
W. D. H.

1. George Washington Greene, "General John De Kalb," *Atlantic*, October 1875; John Fiske, "The Unseen World," *Atlantic*, February–March 1876.

2. Howells was in the process of completing "Private Theatricals." "A Shaker Village" did not appear in the *Atlantic* until June 1876.

3. Sarah Gamp, a disreputable old nurse, is a character in Dickens' *Martin Chuzzlewit* (1844).

4. Formerly a shoe manufacturer in Lynn, Massachusetts, Christopher Robinson became involved in the abolitionist and temperance movements in the 1840s. He appears to have been the publisher of *The Pioneer*, a temperance paper edited by Henry Clapp, Jr. See Howard P. Walthall, "Abolitionism in Lynn ... (1820–1860)" (Honors thesis, Harvard University, 1964).

5. Although the Robinson family affair did not get worse, the situation was less than ideal. "Matters have settled into a sort of sullen quiet here," Howells wrote Garrison on 4 August 1875 (NjP), "and the old ass is not so recalcitrant on his return as I feared he might be. But it is a tragedy, dreary and squalid beyond conception. Still, the vegetables and cream are of the first quality." On 8 August 1875 (NjP) he referred to the matter again in writing to Garrison: "the old misery continues unrelieved. Your father's knowledge of R.'s history confirms my own suspicions of something deplorable in the past of both these people, though the woman is a foolish, amiable person, with incomplete ideas of right and wrong, rather than positively evil. In the meantime they do us no harm, and they keep the peace." Finally, on 15 August 1875 (MH), Howells wrote again about it to his father, calling the situation "one of those tragico-comic episodes to which fate seems bent on bringing me to witness for the express, if not direct, advantage of literature." See Howells to Warner, 4 September 1875, n. 3.

4 September 1875, Shirley Village, Massachusetts,
    to Charles D. Warner

Shirley Village, Mass. Sept. 4, 1875.

My dear Warner:

Thanks to your kindness the two volumes of Carducci came promptly to hand:[1] they were just what I wanted, and if the debt cannot be decently forgotten, why I suppose I must some day pay you for them.—I directed

the Riversiders to send you all the Atlantics for this year, and I hope
that you have got them by this time. I supposed of course you were
getting them, all along.—We are here, in the country, where we have been,
for the past six weeks, near the Shakers, with whom we are on intimate
terms of friendship, and about whose strange life I'm going to make a
little paper for the magazine.[2] They present great temptations to the
fictionist, and as Mrs. Howells has charged me not to think of writing
a story with them in it, I don't see how I can help it.[3]—The new pre-
maturity is called Private Theatricals, and is, as you conjectured, a six-
monthser.—I gulped all your flattering fault-finding with the innocence
which authorship is never rid of. I understand that you want me try
a large canvass with many peop's in it.[4] Perhaps, some time. But isn't
the real dramatic encounter always between two persons only? Or three
or four at most? If the effects are in *me*, I can get them into six numbers
of The Atlantic, and if they aren't, I couldn't get 'em into twenty. Besides,
I can only forgive myself for writing novels at all on the ground that the
poor girl urged in extenuation of her unlegalized addition to the census:
it was such a very *little* baby!—I've got your first chapter (*manners*—to
make you wait all this time, while I was gabbing about myself!) which
appears in the Nov. Atlantic under the gifted title of *Orienting*.[5] When I
return about the first of next month, I'll get all you've sent him, and try to
run you into every number.—By the way I heard you were going to write a
story for Scrib.[6] If it's true, it's a mean shame, and you will suffer for it.—
Lee & Shepherd have failed—*badly*. It hits Osgood, but it wont break
him.[7]—I was down at Cambridge yesterday, but saw nobody except
Lathrop,[8] who is doing well on the magazine.—Mrs. Howells sends love
to Mrs Warner. She is a little better. We go on Monday to Chesterfield
N. H., and then to Quebec. My devotion to Venice.

Yours ever
W. D. H.

Orienting is delightful!

1. On 4 July 1875 (CtHT) Howells had asked Warner "to buy me ... the poems
of Giosué Carducci...." Since, according to Warner, there were two editions on the
market, he sent both. See his letter to Howells, 1 August 1875 (MH). Carducci (1836–
1907) had established himself as one of the leading Italian poets with the publication of a volume of lyrics, *Levia Gravia* (1865); further volumes followed in 1871
and 1872.
2. "A Shaker Village," *Atlantic*, June 1876.
3. Howells eventually used the Shaker village setting in *The Undiscovered
Country* (1880) and in *The Vacation of the Kelwyns* (1920).
4. In his letter of 1 August, Warner praised Howells on the basis of just having
reread *Italian Journeys*, and then offered this advice: "it is time you quit paddling
along shore, and struck out into the open.... The time has come for you
to make an *opus*—not only a study on a large canvas but a picture. Write a long

novel, one that we can dive into with confidence, and not feel that we are to strike bottom in the first plunge."

5. The title used in the *Atlantic*, November 1875, is "At the Gates of the East." The series of articles was continued in July 1876. See also Howells to Warner, 24 October 1875, n. 1.

6. Howells is of course referring to *Scribner's*, the magazine edited by his arch rival, Dr. J. G. Holland.

7. Lee & Shepard, a Boston publishing firm, had been foundering for several years, and J. R. Osgood was one of their major creditors. See E. Ballou, *The Building of the House* (Boston: Houghton Mifflin, 1970), pp. 224–34.

8. G. P. Lathrop, the assistant editor of the *Atlantic*.

17 SEPTEMBER 1875, CHESTERFIELD, NEW HAMPSHIRE, TO DAVID A. WELLS

Prospect House,
Chesterfield, N. H. Sept. 17, 1875.[1]

Dear Mr. Wells:[2]

I think we ought not to recur to the Free Trade matter in the form of controversy; if we let you take Mr. Wharton's skin off, he would certainly want to induce a new growth with small patches of yours, and there would be no end to the waste and repair. I'm very sorry, but I don't see how I can accept your proposed reply.—I wish now to present both sides of the currency question—paper and specie.[3] Do you know any stronger hard money man than that Col. Grosvenor of St. Louis,[4] who is now making speeches in Ohio? Whom else would you suggest? How would Pendleton do for the paper side?[5] If we got him for paper, I thought it would be best to have some Western man answer him. What do you think?

Yours truly
W. D. Howells.

1. The Howells family had left Shirley Village sometime between 4 and 8 September, probably because of the unpleasant quarrel in the Robinson family. See Howells to Garrison, 2 August 1875.

2. David A. Wells (1828–1898) became well known as the author of a widely read political essay, "Our Burden and Our Strength" (1864). He served in a number of public offices related to revenue matters in Washington and New York, and gradually became a strong advocate of free-trade policies. In 1872 he became a lecturer in political science at Yale. His article, "The Creed of Free Trade," appeared in the *Atlantic*, August 1875. The opposite position was presented by Joseph Wharton in "National Self-Protection," *Atlantic*, September 1875. In an earlier letter to Wells, 19 January 1875 (DLC), Howells had written: "I don't see any reason why we shouldn't publish the free trade article you propose; and even if it did not exactly represent the opinions of The Atlantic management, you alone would be responsible for it. I rather think it would be interesting to have you express yourself with all possible distinctness, and then have the protection side given by some tariff cham-

pion, not in the way of answer or controversy, but for the purpose of getting both phases of the matter clearly before the reader." Howells' interest in publishing different positions on public issues is also indicated in other letters soliciting contributions on the subject of public schools and the use of public funds for the support of parochial schools. These articles, however, never did appear.

3. See Howells to Garfield, 6 October 1875, n. 2.

4. Perhaps this is Charles H. Grosvenor (1833–1917) of Ohio, who became a brevet colonel and brigadier general during the Civil War, served in the Ohio House of Representatives (1874–1878), and was a member of Congress (1885–1891, 1893–1907). However, there seems to be no connection with St. Louis in his career.

5. George H. Pendleton (1825–1889), a prominent Ohio politician since the 1850s, was the Democratic candidate for vice-president (1864), and a U. S. senator (1879–1885).

6 OCTOBER 1875, QUEBEC, TO JAMES A. GARFIELD

Quebec, Oct. 6, 1875.[1]

Dear General Garfield:

Your article will be in good time if it comes by the 1st of December; and I'm very glad that you can do it.[2] I should like it to be mainly affirmative, but of course, you can't affirm truth without denying falsehood, and I want you to write it after your own notion. I think it would be interesting to review briefly the ground and events of the present canvass in Ohio, where the rag-money men have made boldest front, and to consider their principal fallacies;[3] from that, you could go on to a general consideration of the subject. You could introduce the Ohio election because it is probably a type of future contests. But I want to leave you free to do it in any way you think best.

My father and sisters join Mrs. Howells and myself in kindest regards. The Howellses here are sorry you could not have paid them a visit this summer. They are very pleasantly situated in every way, and they cherish the remembrance of your kindness in promoting father's appointment.

Very truly yours
W. D. Howells.

I go home to Cambridge on Friday.[4]

1. The Howells family arrived in Quebec from Chesterfield, New Hampshire, sometime during the last days of September.

2. Howells had written Garfield on 25 September 1875 (DLC): "We wish to treat in The Atlantic the question of Hard and Soft Money, as we have already treated that of Free Trade, from opposite sides, and I apply to you first to write us the Hard Money Article. Your opponent will not see your article till his own is in our hands, for we want to present the two sides, without entering into controversy." Garfield's article, "The Currency Conflict," appeared in the *Atlantic*, February 1876; its counterpart was Henry C. Baird's "Money and Its Substitutes," *Atlantic*, March 1876. The order in which these two articles were published was the reverse of that preferred by

Howells. As he repeatedly indicated to Garfield—on 5 and 14 December 1875 (DLC)—he wanted the "right side" (the hard-money argument) to have the last word.

3. Garfield did not follow this suggestion although he quoted from a campaign speech by Governor William Allen (1806–1879), who lost in his bid for reelection to Rutherford B. Hayes. Allen was the foremost advocate of the soft-money theory, which came to be known as the "Ohio idea."

4. Friday was 8 October.

24 OCTOBER 1875, CAMBRIDGE, TO CHARLES D. WARNER

... The Atlantic Monthly....
Cambridge, Mass. Oct. 24, 1875.

My dear Warner:

I have arranged with Bliss and your brother to have chapters of your Syrian material, the Egyptian being just about to be used in a book. This will suit me just as well, if not better,—not but that I have greatly liked your Egyptian chapters; the last was even better than the first. Syria, however, is less bewritten than Egypt. Your brother says from Bliss that Scribners are not to have any of the material, and so I am doubly content.[1] I hope you are.—Aldrich is at home again, and we went down to Ponkapog on Friday to see him. He has enjoyed his European trip vastly; but to my mind he lost money by travelling with so rich a man.[2] That is, they always had dinner in a private room, and they always went first-class, which cut them off from about the only contact with one's fellow men that one has in travelling. Aldrich is full of literary plans, which seem promising.—Harry James breakfasted with me just before sailing again for Europe, and I was able to let him read what you said of him, the postman having just brought your letter.[3] He was delighted, and charged me with the expression of his pleasure. I'm sorry he's gone again, but that was the logical sequence of his coming home. He's to be in Paris, as the correspondent of the N. Y. Tribune.[4] He has been "poorly" all summer, but is ... happy in knowing what ails him, namely, not gout in the stomach, but trouble of the liver.—Longfellow is better, and has just now printed a little book of the loveliest verse he's ever written.[5]—Gilder's volume is peculiar; I can't tell yet whether I like it.[6]— The great talk is Bret Harte's novel which begins (to the disadvantage of mine) in the November Scribner.[7] I've not read the beginning.—I'm glad you like the Atlantic so well. I think we shall do even better next year. Lathrop is a great help, and such a thoroughly right fellow that I'm greatly content with him.—Our painted autumnal world is all about our feet to-day, thanks to the still dim air, that brings the leaves down faster than the wind.—We returned two weeks ago, after ten lovely days in dear old Quebec. Our joint love to both of you.

Write![8]

1. The complications about the use of Warner's travel accounts arose from his using some of them for a book, *Among the Mummies and the Moslems, My Winter on the Nile* (1876), that was to be published by Elisha P. Bliss's American Publishing Co. Also there was the possibility that some of the pieces would appear in *Scribner's.* At Warner's suggestion (19 September 1875 [MH]), Howells wrote to George H. Warner on 22 October 1875 (Mark Twain Memorial, Hartford): "I shall be just as glad to have Syrian as Egyptian material—so that it is C. D. W.'s, I am content. Please have Mr. Bliss send me some of it at once." The Syrian material appeared in the *Atlantic,* July–November 1876, and was collected as *In the Levant* (1877).

2. The rich man with whom Aldrich traveled in Europe has not been identified.

3. In his letter of 19 September, Warner praised James and expressed his hope that if Howells "wont write the great Novel, . . . Mr James will . . . ."

4. James wrote two letters a month for the New York *Tribune* from October 1875 to August 1876; then he resigned because he couldn't bring himself to write the " 'newsy' and gossipy" letters Reid wanted. See *James Letters,* II, 63–64; L. Edel and I. D. Lind, eds., *Parisian Sketches* (New York: New York University Press, 1957).

5. *The Masque of Pandora and Other Poems* (1875).

6. Richard Watson Gilder (1844–1909) was assistant editor of *Scribner's* (1870–1881) and became editor of its successor, the *Century,* in 1881. The book Howells refers to here is *The New Day: A Poem in Songs and Sonnets* (1875).

7. *Gabriel Conroy* was serialized in *Scribner's,* November 1875–August 1876.

8. Howells' signature and the complimentary close have been excised.

8 NOVEMBER 1875, CAMBRIDGE, TO WILLIAM WETMORE STORY

> *. . . The Atlantic Monthly. . . .*
> *Cambridge, Mass.* Nov. 8, 1875.

My dear Sir:[1]

I am glad you have sent your poem to me rather than to Blackwood, for I believe The Atlantic will bring it before the public to which your fame is dearest, and to which the allegory will be most intelligible.[2] I like the whole poem, but I think the passage beginning

"What matters it when I am turned to dust"

is particularly true and fine: it gave even my jaded editorial sense a thrill.

The magazine shall be sent as you desire. It's of course a great pleasure to me that you think well of it, and I hope it wont disappoint you when you come to see it regularly. How and where shall I send pay for the poem when it's printed? (In the February number—*my* next, as to copy.)

I should like indeed to see you in Rome, but Italy gets farther from me every day.

> Very truly yours
> W. D. Howells.

W. W. Story, Esq.

1. William Wetmore Story (1819–1895) had begun a career as a lawyer. He published a book of poems, but soon turned to sculpture; in 1856 he settled in Rome, where his studio became a center for European and American artists.

2. "Phidias to Pericles," *Atlantic*, February 1876. Story sent Howells the MS. in a letter of 17 September 1875 (MH), which explained that the poem had already been set in type for publication in *Blackwood's Edinburgh Magazine*, but was subsequently withdrawn by Story for publication in America. The poem is about Phidias' defense of his probity, which has been attacked by the rabble. Howells' reference to an allegorical meaning suggests that Story used the poem to justify himself against certain critics.

14 NOVEMBER 1875, CAMBRIDGE, TO HJALMAR H. BOYESEN

...The Atlantic Monthly....
Cambridge, Mass. Nov. 14, 1875.

My dear Boyesen:

Forgive my long neglect. I have been very much pre-occupied.

"Novalis" you will find in the December number, and I'll work the third article in as soon as ever I can.[1]

I'm glad to hear that you're getting on with your novel,[2] which I shall want to see. Since you read me those passages I've thought with pleasure of the design and characters, but have felt more and more that you ought to strive for greater brevity—of words, sentences, paragraphs, chapters. I believe you have the genius of Björnsen.[3] But think of that rogue's slyness!—he gives you in five words what most men want a hundred for.

Yours sincerely
W. D. Howells.

1. See Howells to Boyesen, 30 November 1874, n. 1.

2. The novel Boyesen was writing at this time was probably *Falconberg* (1879), the MS. of which Howells criticized in some detail in his letter of 19 September 1876.

3. Bjornstjerne Bjornson (1832–1910), Norwegian author, achieved fame from his first play in 1856 and in 1903 received the Nobel Prize. Howells' review of *The Happy Boy* and *The Fisher Maiden*, *Atlantic*, April 1870, and frequent writing on him thereafter suggest Bjornson's importance as an influence. Bjornson's visit to the United States in 1880–1881 was a lively event, with theological skirmishes between him and orthodox Lutherans of the midwest.

21 NOVEMBER 1875, CAMBRIDGE, TO SAMUEL L. CLEMENS

> ... *The Atlantic Monthly*. . . .
> *Cambridge, Mass.* Nov. 21, 1875.

Dear Clemens:

Here is the Literary Nightmare, which I'm going to put into the January,[1] and want back by the return mail. I couldn't give it up.

—I finished reading Tom Sawyer a week ago, sitting up till one A.M., to get to the end, simply because it was impossible to leave off. It's altogether the best boy's story I ever read. It will be an immense success. But I think you ought to treat it explicitly *as* a boy's story. Grown-ups will enjoy it just as much if you do; and if you should put it forth as a study of boy character from the grown-up point of view, you'd give the wrong key to it.[2]—I have made some corrections and suggestions in faltering pencil, which you'll have to look for. They're almost all in the first third. When you fairly swing off, you had better be let alone.—The adventures are enchanting. I wish *I* had been on that island. The treasure-hunting, the loss in the cave—it's all exciting and splendid. I shouldn't think of publishing this story serially.[3] Give me a hint when it's to be out, and I'll start the sheep to jumping in the right places.

—I don't seem to think I like the last chapter. I believe I would cut that.[4]

—Mrs. H. has Mrs. C.'s letter to answer. In the meantime she sends love, and I will send the Ms. of my notice some time this week—it's at the printers'.[5] How shall I return the book MS?

> Yours ever
> W. D. Howells.

Took down Roughing It, last night, and made a fool of myself over it, as usual.

---

1. Howells apparently sent with this letter the proof sheets of "A Literary Nightmare," which did not appear in the *Atlantic* until February 1876. See *Twain-Howells*, p. 105.

2. Howells and Clemens had been discussing and corresponding about *The Adventures of Tom Sawyer* since June. One question that concerned them was whether the novel should be aimed at an adult or a juvenile audience. This consideration apparently had an important bearing on another question: whether Clemens should trace Tom's life into adulthood or end the book with the hero still a boy. But on 5 July 1875 (NN) Clemens wrote: "I have finished the story & didn't take the chap beyond boyhood. I believe it would be fatal to do it in any shape but autobiographically—like Gil Blas. I perhaps made a mistake in not writing it in the first person. If I went on, now, & took him into manhood, he would just be like all the one-horse men in literature & the reader would conceive a hearty contempt for him." See *Twain-Howells*, pp. 91–92, 110–12.

3. Howells at first was eager to serialize *Tom Sawyer* in the *Atlantic*, but Clemens

thought that the magazine could not afford to pay him the $6,500 he would have to ask for it. Nevertheless he wanted Howells to read and edit the MS. Howells did so during the second week of November, after having received an amanuensis copy earlier that month or late in October. This copy, with Howells' marginal notes, is now located in the state capitol of Missouri, Jefferson City. See *Twain-Howells*, pp. 90, 92, 110–12; and, for an example of a revision made by Howells, ibid., p. 124.

4. In his letter of 23 November 1875 (NN; *Twain-Howells*, pp. 112–13), Clemens replied: "As to that last chapter, I think of just leaving it off & adding nothing in its place. Something told me that the book was done when I got to that point—& so the strong temptation to put Huck's life at the widow's into detail instead of generalizing it in a paragraph, was resisted."

5. Howells is here referring to his review of *Mark Twain's Sketches, New and Old*, *Atlantic*, December 1875.

22 NOVEMBER 1875, CAMBRIDGE, TO JAMES T. FIELDS

> ...*The Atlantic Monthly*. ...
> *Cambridge, Mass.* Nov. 22, 1875.

Dear Mr. Fields:

I'm exceedingly pleased that you like my story,[1] and I thank you for thinking to say so. It's more of an experiment upon my public than I've ever ventured before, and I shall not consider it successful till I have their approval of it in book-form. But it's immensely heartening to have a shake of the hand like yours.

—I supposed the Harpers had been corrupting you, but I didn't blame you—I would hail corruption, myself, with open arms. Besides, it was a great advantage to have the papers so nicely illustrated.[2]

I will send this to Boston, and I hope Mrs. Fields will look into it and see that we send ever so much love to both of you.[3]

> Ever sincerely yours
> W. D. Howells.

1. "Private Theatricals." Fields praised its first installment in his letter of 20 November 1875 (MH): "...I cannot wait to tell you how your new story delights the very cockles of my heart. It seems to be, so far, the author's best as regards a good many points of excellence." On the same day Fanny Kemble also wrote of her appreciation of the new novel (MH; *Life in Letters*, I, 205): "Your Mrs Farrell is terrific—do for pity's sake give her the Small-Pox—she deserves it...." Constance F. Woolson added her praise on 11 December 1875 (MH): "...I think them [the first two installments] better than anything you have published yet. The little touches in the second number, where a woman describes a woman, are delightfully real, and I suspect Mrs Howells aided you there; for no man, unaided, knows such things." J. G. Whittier was also pleased, as he wrote on 19 December 1875 (MH): " 'Private Theatricals' is equal to anything thee have written. Mrs Farrell is wonderfully well done. I have seen several of her kind, but she seems to combine the characteristics of all. I like thy tender, half-relenting way of showing her up, like Izaak Walton's putting the frog on the hook 'as if you loved him.' " A week earlier C. D. Warner, writing from Munich on 12 December 1875 (MH), joined the general acclaim: "You've

hit the hill farmer between wind and water. I know him. If he ever reads your description, which is not likely, he will murder you. Of course you never expect to go into the country again after this. Nor into any summer boarding house. How dare you make it so true? How dare you paint a woman as she is? You will ruin our whole social fabric." Howells decided not to publish the novel in book form probably because of his dissatisfaction with the ending. Almost a year later, on 16 August 1876 (MH), J. R. Osgood wrote that he was very disappointed about the decision to put off book publication: "The book will have a good sale if published this Autumn, and will certainly suffer by postponement. I should be willing to make you a proposition for a guaranty of a certain am[oun]t if this would have any effect on your mind."

2. *Harper's Monthly* had made a "royal offer" (as Fields called it in his letter to Howells) for an article on the English poet Bryan Waller Procter. It appeared in the November 1875 number under the title, " 'Barry Cornwall' and Some of His Friends," and was richly illustrated, mostly with portraits of famous nineteenth-century English poets.

3. Fields had sent his letter from Philadelphia, and he did not expect to return to Boston "for many a day yet."

27 NOVEMBER 1875, CAMBRIDGE, TO WILLIAM C. HOWELLS

Cambridge, Nov. 27, 1875.

Dear father:

I don't know whether Elinor has told the girls of my having a typewriter, but here you have evidence of the fact. It belonged to Mark Twain, who got so tired of it that he was glad to trade it off for an old saddle; the man who owned the saddle preferred to give it up while still sane enough to have legal authority for such an act of surrender, and so Clemens sent it on to me.[1] The principal trouble with it seems to be that the keys have to be struck so hard as to make your fingers sore; but this difficulty might be got over, I should think, by having some sort of strength-gaining leverage for the key-board. Or perhaps a softer cylinder to strike the types against would serve the purpose. One becomes sufficiently unconscious of the mechanism with a little practice, to be able to use it with comfort, and great speed is certainly possible. I wonder whether Mr. Ross[2] is still as much enamored of his machine as at first?

On Friday evening I dined at Henry Adams's with Lord Houghton, whom I found a very agreeable man, with plenty of delightful talk about people that I wanted to hear of.[3] He had known Heine, and spoke of him a good deal. Also of other Jews he had known—Disraeli amongst the rest. He said D. had always been perfectly consistent in two things: He had always been a stedfast Jew and a stedfast Republican. Wasn't that news about the Queen's Prime Minister? Houghton looks somewhat like the portraits of Washington, chiefly on account of the bulge given to his lips by a very badly made set of false teeth, which dropped down from time to time, and had to be put back with the tongue or finger. He is an elderly man, and quite bald. This was the third time I had been asked to meet him.

With our joint love to all,

Your aff'te son,
Will.

1. In the correspondence between Clemens and Howells the typewriter is mentioned and used for the first time in Clemens' letter of 9 December 1874 (NN). But the new invention being rather imperfect, Clemens decided to get rid of it and consequently wrote Howells on 21 June 1875 (MH): "I don't think Bliss wants that type-writer, because he don't send for it. I'll sell it to you for the twelve dollars I've got to pay him for his saddle—or I'll gladly send it to you for nothing if you choose (for, to be honest, I think $12 *is* too much for it.) Anyway, I'll send it." However, there were so many mix-ups in the trade with Elisha Bliss that Howells did not get the typewriter until 3 November. See *Twain-Howells*, pp. 51, 88–90, 109.

2. The Ross family has not been identified, except that they appear to have been residents of Quebec. Howells saw them briefly again in 1882, when he and his family were on their way to Europe. See Howells to W. C. Howells, 22 July 1882 (MH).

3. Henry Adams had invited Howells on 21 November 1875 (MH) for a "man's dinner" in honor of Richard Monckton Milnes, Lord Houghton (1809–1885), the English politician, poet, and patron of letters.

18 December 1875, Cambridge, to John Hay

The Atlantic Monthly,
Cambridge, Mass., Dec. 18, 1875.

My dear Hay:

You need not fear but I shall be kind to Mr. Astor in spite of his millions;[1] I once believed that rich men were to be blamed for their wealth, but now I think they are to be pitied and I shall be very compassionate to your friend, who, by the way, I think called on me with his mother for my consular verification of their signatures, in Venice. At any rate I shall accuse him of having done so and try to found some claim upon his beneficence through that service.

It's well that you can plead a suffering family at Warsaw, for on hearing that you had visited Boston without letting me know,[2] I renounced you with the self-devotion that we feel in giving up unworthy friends, and thought very poorly of you for a long time. But this rigid mood melts before your excuse; only don't do it again. If ever I come to Ashtabula county, single or doubly, you may depend upon seeing us both in Cleveland. We have a great desire to see Mrs. Hay, of whose willingness to see us it gives us ever so much pleasure to know. Until I got your letter, I was not quite certain whether you had left New York or not: I heard conflicting rumors about the fact. I don't know whether or not you're glad to be out of the turmoil of newspaper life;[3] if you're not I'll take leave to be glad for you; you owe a debt to literature which you've made everybody believe you can pay handsomely, and I wish you would begin to reimburse the needy muse through the *Atlantic*. (I knew the editor couldn't be kept out much longer—forgive his vulgar insistene!) Why shouldn't you be able to send me something now, at last? Many a year have I tried to get you to do it.

I try to imagine your occupations and associations, but fail to do so through ignorance of Cleveland. I suppose you see David Gray of Buffalo,[4] now and then. I think him a lovely fellow, and I was so sorry to hear from Mark Twain that he was not prospering in a worldly way. Clemens I see four or five times a year. Harry James is gone abroad again not to return, I fancy, even for visits. Aldrich has got home and is living quietly at Ponkapog—which sounds like a joke, but isn't. He and his wife paid us a visit last week.

I'm greatly pleased that you liked my *F. Conclusion*. The present story in the *Atlantic* is a much slighter affair, and lacks a strong motive such as that had.[5]

Mrs. Howells joins me in regard to Mrs. Hay, the *Töchterlein*[6] and yourself.

Yours cordially,
W. D. Howells.

1. Hay had provided William Waldorf Astor (1848–1919), great-grandson of John Jacob Astor and recent graduate of the Columbia University Law School, with a letter of introduction, as he explained in his letter to Howells of 10 December 1875 (MH): "You know of course that he is the heir—only son of J. J. Astor II—to more money than you can think of in a summer vacation. But do not sit down on him for that, for he is a very fine young fellow. He has a decided taste for art, has made two creditable statues, reads a good deal and has just begun practice as a lawyer.... Some of these days, he will probably do a great deal for art and such things in New York."

2. In the same letter, Hay excused himself for not visiting Howells on a recent trip to Boston: "If you could have been present at the wigging I got when I came home last summer from my visit to Boston and told my wife I had not seen you, you would have wished, in mere charity, that I had come to you. But I got through with my business in one day, and was expected by all my brethren at Warsaw in Illinois...."

3. Hay had recently resigned his position on the editorial staff of the New York *Tribune*, which he had joined in 1870.

4. David Gray (1836–1888) was born in Scotland, worked as a reporter for the Buffalo *Courier* (1859–1876), and subsequently assumed the position of editor-in-chief of that paper. Mark Twain became his friend during the year (1870–1871) he spent in Buffalo.

5. In his letter of 10 December, Hay wrote that the priest in *A Foregone Conclusion* "is the best thing of the sort that has been done." The "present story in the *Atlantic*" is, of course, "Private Theatricals."

6. German for "little daughter."

19 DECEMBER 1875, CAMBRIDGE, TO JAMES R. LOWELL

Cambridge, Dec. 19, 1875.

Dear Mr. Lowell:

Your kind note[1] almost brought me to Elmwood in person to say my thanks, and Mrs. Howells thought it finer than anything in the Commemoration Ode.[2] I'm glad exceedingly that you like what I've done, and I don't resent that you should find passages ill-done. In fact the criticism is perfectly just, and is none the less deserved because the sins were committed as much from perversity as ignorance. Having no proof-reader over me, and having so long bowed down to correctness, I did take a wicked pleasure in writing "if there was a hell," but I know that it was foolish, and that I wouldn't have borne it from another. It's too late to bother you with the proof of No IV, but I shall take you at your word, and send you V, when it's in print. What mostly "stumps" me in this English tongue (it's elegance seems a thing of negatives, like the bearing of a gentleman,) is the wills and shalls, and woulds and shouldn'ts. Their true use comes only from being born in one or other of the Englands, I'm quite convinced—though I would see H-gg-ns-n[3] dead before I'd own it.

—Your letter made me think of the old Sacramento street days,[4] and I was happy to have again pleased you.

Yours ever
W. D. Howells.

1. Lowell had written Howells on 17 December 1875 (MH), expressing his pleasure about "Private Theatricals": "your last number (I mean your story) is admirable. You have shown up that fascinating slut terribly well, & Mrs Gilbert is excellent." Then he proceeded to correct a few stylistic infelicities, such as changing "if there *was* a hell" to "if there had been."

2. "Ode Recited at the Harvard Commemoration, July 21, 1865."

3. Thomas Wentworth Higginson, whose relations with the *Atlantic* and its editor were rather strained.

4. In his reply of 21 December 1875 (OFH), Lowell expressed his warm paternal feelings for Howells: "'Old Sacramento Street days,' indeed! I haven't changed my mind about you from the first. I don't change it so easily when once made up. It is as bothersome as repacking a trunk. A mere boy like you would be spoiled if we old fellows kept telling him how nice he was."

21 DECEMBER 1875, CAMBRIDGE, TO JAMES R. LOWELL

> ... *The Atlantic Monthly.*...
> *Cambridge, Mass.* Dec. 21, 1875.

Dear Mr. Lowell:

Cranch shall have all imaginable kindness in the next Atlantic,[1] and if I could, I would have put him among my poets. But I was afraid I might be the least cordial to him, and I judged it best to leave him out. Why *does* he think me ill-disposed? I'm the only editor who prints his verses, the only connoisseur who buys his pictures! And I would be glad to publish something from him every month if I could. I don't blame his grudge, though; and I'll do all I can to remove it.

—I didn't mean to provoke you to greater praise, nor to accuse your constancy. Both have been more precious to me than I know how to say without violating the decorums of our race.

> Yours ever gratefully
> W. D. Howells.

1. In his letter of 21 December 1875 (OFH), Lowell interceded in behalf of Christopher Pearse Cranch, whose second volume of poetry, *The Bird and the Bell* (1875), had recently been published. "He was hurt," Lowell wrote, "by your not mentioning him among your poets & I labored with him in vain to convince him that you had no private grudge against him." In his review of "Four New Books of Poetry," *Atlantic*, January 1876, Howells did not include Cranch's.

26 DECEMBER 1875, CAMBRIDGE, TO WILLIAM C. HOWELLS

> Cambridge, Dec. 26, 1875.

Dear father:

I think it is quite time to resume my letters to you, so long interrupted by correspondence with the more professionally literary members of your family.[1] I return Annie's note from the Galaxy people, & wish I had some consolation to offer her beyond the fact that story-readers are so careless one may make almost any kind of disconnection without disturbing them greatly. If her story is reprinted in book-form she can correct the provoking blunder.—(It is *too* great a bore to use that type-writer, and I come back to pen and ink with joy.)[2] I will send Vic's play back by express. I am glad that she intends to remodel it before offering it anywhere.—Christmas passed off with unusual brilliance for the children. We had a Christmas tree for the first time, and that dear, good little Winny decorated it in the prettiest way; the others were not allowed to see it till yesterday morning after breakfast, when there was a grand tableau in the front parlor. They all had a great many presents from friends whom our well-known contempt of Christmas gifts can't deter; and in the afternoon came a great package from New York: I don't know whether Elinor was more provoked or pleased. One thing only was lacking: Boyesen did not pay his usual Christmas visit to Cambridge.[3] But he will probably be here all next summer, to make up for it.

I don't think of anything in the way of news. Tell Annie that I have written to Mr. Church[4] suggesting that they should pay her with the publication of each number of her story. I doubt if she gets $500.—I am going to write to Uncle Aleck to-day,[5] and Winny will send her poem.— She made a little book for Pillà, as a Christmas present, which has six new poems in it.

All join in love to all.

> Your affectionate son
> Will.

1. In two long letters to Victoria Howells, 12 and 19 December 1875 (MH), Howells criticized a play his sister had written, and he refused to give it to an agent or producer, as she had asked her brother to do. There is no extant correspondence with Annie at this time, but her novel, "Reuben Dale," had just begun to appear in the *Galaxy*.

2. With this parenthetical sentence Howells continues the letter in his own autograph. For the story of the typewriter, see Howells to Clemens, 27 November 1875, n. 1.

3. There was another thing missing: Mr. and Mrs. J. T. Fields, who usually gave a large Christmas party for their friends and friends' children, had canceled the traditional event, at which Howells appeared dressed up as Santa Claus. He wrote to Mrs. Fields on 19 December 1875 (CSmH): "I wont pretend that the children are not opposed to this suspension of festivities; they so fondly remember every party which you've given heretofore. For myself, my noble and candid spirit so much abhors to bear the garb of a slave (even to St Nicholas,) and to wear a mask, that I confess I bear their deprivation patiently—not but what I should very much hate to be left uninvited next year!"

4. Francis P. Church, editor of the *Galaxy*.

5. "Uncle Aleck" was Alec or Alexander Dean, one of the river pilot uncles who so impressed the young Howells.

---

5 JANUARY 1876, CAMBRIDGE, TO CHARLES D. WARNER

> ... *The Atlantic Monthly*....
> *Cambridge, Mass.* Jan. 5, 1876.

My dear Warner:

Imagine my rage when your first installment of MS.[1] came to me the other day so watersoaked as to be almost illegible. In any other handwriting I could not have read it, but yours was rather improved by going down in the Deutschland,[2] and to my surprise I got through it quite comfortably, and my wrath was changed to comparative satisfaction. The second part has now come, and I have read that also.[3] I will carefully keep all the MS., and I will tell you how I propose to use it. We are now packed so full of accepted material, that before July there is no use in my attempting to print you continuously, and in the number for that month, with your connivance and consent I will begin and run you steadily to the end of the year. I shall probably skip about somewhat in my extracts from your Ms., and take such parts as seem capable of the best effect in the magazine. The tone is good,—soberly disgusted I sh'd call it,—and the writing is in an easy unstrained manner. I don't say un*r*estrained manner for I have had a feeling that you ought to let yourself loose upon the subject a little more. Also, I shd say that in preparing this material both for The Atlantic and your book-public, you were writing with a divided mind. If this is so, don't let the Atlantic confuse you: I can get enough for my purpose any way out of what you send, and you ought to keep up the unity of your work.[4] It is too soon, yet, for me judge of your general intention. If I were to venture a criticism of what you've done so far, I should say—especially of your first chapter on Jerusalem,—that you don't give enough personality to your narrative: I would rather have one good Turk or dirty Jew got by heart than a whole generalized population. Your Yankee woman at Jaffa, for example, was excellent.

We are uncommonly gay this winter in Cambridge, and parties and receptions and dinners are popping off in every direction. Think of a sober oldster like me being out four nights this week,—and Mrs. Howells too! In a literary way there is nothing very new. You asked me once about Harte's story.[5] I've read only the first number, which had good things in it but was very cheap in passages, and drew too wildly upon the last reasons of the novelist—starvation, cannibalism, etc. I am leaving the whole thing now till it's finished. It isn't making a great impression, so far as I can observe; but you know this isn't the quarter in which Harte is most admired and his story may be greatly liked elsewhere.—I shall be curious to know how you like mine as it goes on.[6] The hill farmer needed to be done. But of course I know there is ever so much good remaining in his race—chiefly on the spindle side—and this I'm going to recognize.[7] Mrs. Warner must forgive my little freedoms to my great honor and reverence for her sex.[8] Think of a poor simple fearer of female loveliness like myself living to have his "well-known contempt of woman" spoken of in the Springfield Republican.[9] It's ridiculous.

Mrs. Howells joins me in love to both of you.—My wrist is fairly played out.

Yours ever
W. D. Howells.

I'll see to those blunders of yours in Chap I.[10]

1. "From Jaffa to Jerusalem," *Atlantic*, July 1876.

2. The S. S. *Deutschland*, bound for New York from Bremen, was wrecked off the English coast on 6 December 1875. Howells' humorous stab at Warner's handwriting can be appreciated by anyone who has had to decipher its almost complete illegibility.

3. "Jerusalem," *Atlantic*, August 1876.

4. On 22 December 1875 (MH) Warner sent the third installment of his travel narrative and wrote in the accompanying letter: "Of course you can make my material suit your monthly wants.... My present division into chapters may or may not be the final arrangement for the book. If you alter it, only take care to have each installment in the magazine end well."

5. *Gabriel Conroy* was serialized in *Scribner's*, November 1875–August 1876.

6. "Private Theatricals."

7. For Warner's comment on the "hill farmer," see Howells to Fields, 22 November 1875, n. 1.

8. Warner, in his letter of 12 December 1875 (MH), wrote that "Mrs Warner has a crow to pick with you. Why shouldn't the ladies as they pass take up the end of the arrested work and talk seriously about it? What makes the beauty of a house, the grace of it, if it is not these pieces of color and femininity? It is in vain I say that you only mentioned a fact; she sees you behind there somewhere with an odd look in your eyes."

9. The Springfield *Republican*, 22 December 1875, does not seem to contain the particular phrase quoted by Howells; however, it comments on his treatment of women in "Private Theatricals": "There is something too much of the mere commonplace,—even though it be brilliant commonplace,—and too little romance and idealism in the story, thus far. Mrs Farrell is a flirt, who goes about her predestined work in life with so much directness and so little conscience, that she robs herself of half the effect she should have, and excites hostility too soon. Then women do not like to see all the foibles and pettinesses of their sex so clearly exposed to view.... It is worth mentioning this, because Mr Howells has hitherto found his most admiring readers among women, and ought not rashly to encounter their disfavor or disappointment."

10. In his letter of 16 December 1875 (MH), Warner asked Howells to make a few minor changes in the MS. he had submitted for publication in the *Atlantic*.

23 JANUARY 1876, CAMBRIDGE, TO WILLIAM C. HOWELLS

Cambridge, Jan. 23, 1876.

Dear father:

Aurelia's long & satisfactory letter to Elinor came the other day, & enlightened us as to your present life; & the diary is, according to Elinor, a very lively record of the past. But Aurelia must consider that it is so much manuscript to me, & excuse me if I haven't read it yet. I hope to do so before long. Vic's play I sent off on Thursday,[1] I think, & I suppose it will have reached you before this does.

I'm sorry whenever I fail to write you on Sunday, but you must know from your own experience what a desperate affair it sometimes looks like, when you sit down & try to conjure up some sort of general intelligence. I am ashamed to repeat the silly gossip of our social life,

& there is very little else to tell. We have both gone out a great deal more this winter than ever before, & though it is all very pleasant, it is distinctly unprofitable. For a social animal it is amusing to observe how little man can see of his fellows without becoming demoralized by it. To us a great deal of society comes now-a-days in the way of invitations which we can't, for one reason or other, refuse. Elinor attributes them all to my growing reputation, & when she doesn't feel like going, "takes it out of" me for being so famous. The worst of it all is for the children, who have a right to more evenings than we spend with them, & who all complain grievously when they find us dressing to go to a dinner or a party. Bua says he does hate to hear the front door close after me when I'm going out; but they are all very good & patient, & it's only a brief outburst of disapproval. Still we both feel the disadvantages of our present uncontrollable way of living so much that we talk very seriously of going into the country for two or three years, now when it w'd do the children so much good, & w'd give us the sort of repose & retirement that we both need. If we c'd get the right kind of tenant for our house, I think we sh'd make up our minds in a day. We c'd of course go abroad for the same money that we sh'd spend here in the country, & merely to live in Europe now w'd be education for the children. But one at my time of life loses a vast deal of an indefinable, essential something, by living out of one's own country, & I'm afraid to risk it. If we leave Cambridge at all, we shall probably go to some such place as Ponkapog, where Aldrich lives, within ten or fifteen miles of Boston. Where we were last summer is rather too far away.[2]

The winter has lagged along towards the end of January, & we have not yet had snow enough to cover the ground. Except for two or three cold snaps the mercury has stood at about an average of fifty degrees. Your talk of sleighing is almost unintelligible. The other day I met an Irishman carrying a willow twig all covered with catkins. Here & there in the yard we find new green leaves of clover. I suppose we're to pay for it somehow, but how it doesn't yet appear. I'm delighted that the Galaxy people have paid Annie something on her story.[3] If she gets three hundred dollars for the whole it will be doing very well. But I advise her to take whatever they send without remonstrance. It's fortunate for her to get a thing published now-a-days when all the magazines are so full.

I hope she is writing something else. She ought to give up society & coffee, & devote herself to literature & oatmeal. I c'd give equally good advice to all of you, but I don't suppose you'd take it, & besides I've still got my own case on my hands. So I send our united love instead.

Your aff'te son,
Will.

1. See Howells to W. C. Howells, 26 December 1875, n. 1.
2. See Howells to Annie A. Fields, 18 July 1875, n. 2.
3. "Reuben Dale."

13 FEBRUARY 1876, CAMBRIDGE, TO WILLIAM C. HOWELLS

...The Atlantic Monthly....
Cambridge, Mass. February 13, 1876.

Dear father:

What you write of the behavior of the thermometer at Quebec is perfectly incomprehensible to me. To-day is a sunny morning such as I should ordinarily be very glad to see late in April. There is no snow, and little or no frost in the ground. In fact the whole week has been very mild.

Yesterday, Bro. Leander of the Shakers was here, to talk with me about the Brick Farm, and Elinor and I expect to go up to Shirley, and arrange with a sub-tenant whom the Shakers have found on Tuesday. If matters are satisfactory, we shall probably spend four or five months there, this year. It will be a saving of time and money to me, and a great luxury to all the rest of the family.

Of course I only wrote of Mrs. Kemble's compliment,[1] to you for family consumption. It was certainly very gratifying. People tell me that I chanced upon one of her amiable moods, and that she can be intensely disagreeable, which I dare say is true. She will publish in The Atlantic the story of her life up to the time of her marriage.[2] "After that," she said, "I will leave my heirs to print it."

I'm glad you take to Miss Marnie Storer and Mr. Warner, for I have a great respect for them both.[3] I've never seen a girl of more character, I think. The girls may be interested to know that Mr. Greenough is writing another play—on a somewhat larger scale than the Queen of Hearts.[4] I made a long call on him yesterday, without Pillà, who thinks his boy Robby Greenough, the most remarkable boy of four years in Cambridge. Nevertheless I had to interfere yesterday and save him from being pummeled with a ten pin in her hands, on account of a difference of opinion. I thought Henry might like to know of this dreadful behavior.

We are all well, except poor old Bua, who has had toothache for the last twenty-four hours. And after being up with him twenty-times last night, I don't feel very lively myself.

United love to all.

Your aff'te son
Will.

1. See Howells to Fields, 22 November 1875, n. 1.
2. "Old Woman's Gossip."
3. Mr. and Mrs. Robert B. Storer are listed in the 1879 Cambridge directory as residing on Garden Street at the corner of Linnaean; Marnie Storer was probably their daughter. "Mr. Warner" was a friend of Miss Storer, and Howells refers to him as "her Warner" in his letter of 18 June 1876 to his father.
4. Howells had seen a private performance of *Queen of Hearts* a year earlier at Longfellow's, and he was preparing a review of the play for the *Atlantic*, May 1876.

22 FEBRUARY 1876, CAMBRIDGE, TO CHARLES D. WARNER

> ... *The Atlantic Monthly....*
> *Cambridge, Mass.* Feb. 22, 1876.

My dear Warner:

I have your letters of the 30th and 25th ult.—and the MS. accompanying the latter.[1] I know nothing of Bliss's plans for the publication of the Syrian book, and if I had at all supposed he was going to get it out this year, I should certainly not thought of delaying your matter till July. The trouble with me was such a glut of old material, which I was anxious to work off before beginning a new series. But you understand. Now I'm conscience stricken at having unwittingly proposed something to your obvious disadvantage, and I will do my best to repair the wrong by beginning to print in June. I will also, if you like, share the material with Scribner, for I can explain to Mr Gilder how the case stands, and he'll be glad to get some of it. I couldn't forgive myself if I had been the avoidable means of loss to you.[2]—Also, you take too dark a color from the vague doubt I expressed about the chapters sent me. In the light of your explained plan, I see the matter differently, and I'm sorry I made any strictures at all. I know the prodigious difficulty of the task, and I know too that you'll come off with honor. I've not yet had time to read the last chapter received.

If you go to Paris, remember that Harry James's address is 29 Rue de Luxembourg.[3] He'll be very glad to see you.

Of course I'm too much of a cormorant to be satisfied with what praises you give my story, though they're very delightful—as far as they go! As to the criticism, a very little of that is much more satisfying.[4] There's a hideous possibility that you're right; the only thing that I have to say in self-defence is that the idea did not occur to me—and I'm making silent criticisms of the thing all the time. But the fault isn't in the size of the canvas—it's in the size of the painter. Think how much shorter is a play of Shakespeare! (with whom I'm now modestly beginning to compare myself.)

—We have had the meekest and mildest of winters known for a

hundred years. Last night six inches of snow fell—the heaviest fall we've had, and now it's thawing under a warm sun. The willows have had catkins out for a month. Not a pound of ice cut, yet.

Elinor joins me in love to you both.

Yours ever
W. D. Howells.

1. This was the fourth installment of Warner's account of his travels in Syria.

2. Warner explained in his letters of 25 and 30 January 1876 (MH) that he had made "a sort of promise" to write a novel and an occasional travel sketch for *Scribner's*, and that E. P. Bliss's delay in publishing the book on Egypt had added to the confusion. Howells' inability or unwillingness to begin the series of travel sketches in the *Atlantic* before July greatly disappointed Warner, especially since he had decided to "let Scribner's go...."

3. Howells had by this time probably received James's letter of 3 February 1876 (MH; *James Letters*, II, 22–23), in which he wrote about "the little *coterie* of the young realists in fiction" he met in Paris.

4. The critical comments about "Private Theatricals" appear in Warner's letter of 30 January: "And if I were to venture a criticism upon the story thus far—it is perhaps only a matter of feeling—it would be this: not that Easton goes so suddenly to his distruction [sic] and that a romance is born and half over in a few pages, but that these two people seem to be introduced of set purpose to make a romance; and are set at once about it. *You* do it; not they. I can see your hand in creating and setting them going. Whereas the other characters live and act of themselves. If this is true, that these people do not develope [sic] themselves, but that you develope [sic] them, I am sure the fault is in your too small canvas."

3 MARCH 1876, CAMBRIDGE, TO THOMAS B. ALDRICH

...*The Atlantic Monthly*....
Cambridge, Mass. March 3, 1876.

My dear Aldrich:

I am very glad to hear that you're writing a story,[1] and of course I want you to offer it to The Atlantic. I am not writing one, and I'm in despair what to do. If a plot doesn't come to me pretty soon, I shall feel as guilty as Belknap about drawing my salary.[2]

Do add all the pages you can to the C. old G.,[3] and take your time about the proof.

My P. T.[4] ends in May. I'm glad you like the quarrel, for I felt rather proud of that. But I know that there are bad breaks in the story. I shall change it greatly in reprinting.

I have no notices of the poem worth sending.[5] What I have are mere inanities. I hope to see you soon.

Yours ever
W. D. Howells.

1. Aldrich wrote Howells two days earlier (MS. not located) that he had begun work on *The Queen of Sheba,* which first appeared in the *Atlantic,* July–December 1877. See F. Greenslet, *The Life of Thomas Bailey Aldrich* (Boston: Houghton Mifflin, 1908), pp. 122–24.

2. William W. Belknap (1829–1890) was secretary of war in the Grant administration. On 2 March 1876 a Congressional committee reported to the House of Representatives that there was evidence of his being guilty of malfeasance in office. He was subsequently impeached and forced to resign.

3. T. B. Aldrich, "A Visit to a Certain Old Gentleman," *Atlantic,* May 1876.

4. "Private Theatricals."

5. T. B. Aldrich, "The Legend of Ara-Coeli," *Atlantic,* March 1876.

19 MARCH 1876, CAMBRIDGE, TO WILLIAM C. HOWELLS

>   *... The Atlantic Monthly. ...*
>   *Cambridge, Mass.* March 19, 1876.

Dear father:

I gave you the slip last Sunday by going down to Hartford to see Mark Twain, who talked to me all day, so that I got no chance to write. I took John with me, and as his mother had prepared his mind for the splendors of the Twain mansion, he came to everything with the most exalted fairy-palace expectations. He found some red soap in the bathroom. "Why, they've even got their soap painted!" says he; and the next morning when he found the black-serving-man getting ready for breakfast, he came and woke me. "Better get up, papa. The *slave* is setting the table." I suppose he thought Clemens could have that darkey's head off whenever he liked. He was delightful through the whole visit.[1] The Shepards of New York have been visiting us ever since Thursday, and we have had a very good time with them.[2] Shepard would like very much to have a recent foto of you, and a copy of that one of Annie putting on her snow-shoes. I send one of mine for that French critic, with my compliments. He ought to distinguish between an attack on his church, and the portrayal of an unhappy priest, but I suppose this is hard for a Catholic to do.[3]—We went this morning to church at the College Chapel, when, after service, I spoke with Mrs. Storer's sister, Miss Hoar of Concord,[4] who expressed great gratitude for the kindness of the Howellses to her relatives at Quebec.—I hope the girls are both well again. We were both very sorry to hear of their sickness. For the rest of the festive season they should take "Go slow," for a motto. It must have made a terrible time for you with Henry, and it was distressing to have him affected by it as he was. The Shepards join us in love to all of you.

>   Your aff'te son
>   Will.

Glad to hear that Annie's story is to be reprinted.[5]

1. Howells and Bua visited the Clemenses on 11 and 12 March; upon his return to Cambridge on 13 March (CU; *Twain-Howells*, p. 127) Howells wrote Mark Twain that "Bua and I did have a *good* time, and he has flourished your princely hospitality and orient pearl over Winny at a pitiless rate."

2. Augustus D. Shepard and his wife Joanna Mead Shepard, Elinor Howells' sister.

3. The "French critic" has not been identified, but the difficulties Howells encountered with some Catholic readers of *A Foregone Conclusion* are indicated in his letter to J. B. O'Reilly, 24 September 1874.

4. See Howells to W. C. Howells, 13 February 1876, n. 3. Elizabeth Hoar was the sister of Sarah (Mrs. Robert B.) Storer; they were probably the daughters of Samuel Hoar (1788–1856), a prominent lawyer and Whig politician.

5. "Reuben Dale" was at that time running as a serial in the *Galaxy*, and after Howells had read some unfavorable reviews of it he urged, in a letter to his father of 24 March 1876 (MH), that book publication not be considered: "We all know how innocently she has written it, but I never approved of the subject, and I'm afraid now that if it is republished her name will be connected for a long time with disagreeable associations in many people's minds and her literary career—to speak of nothing else—retarded." That Howells may also have been concerned about his own reputation is suggested by the closing sentence: "Both these papers are friendly to me, and I am afraid they take the friendliest view of the *morale* of the story that will be taken."

2 APRIL 1876, CAMBRIDGE, TO THOMAS B. ALDRICH

> *...The Atlantic Monthly....*
> *Cambridge, Mass.* April 2, 1876.

My dear Aldrich:

Here is a proof of your poem,[1] which I think lovely. I found Bua reading the first stanza this morning, and he asked me to read him the rest. Then he asked who made it. I told him Mr. Aldrich. "Why," said he, "it's just the way he talks!"

I send also a scheme of Mark Twain's, which we shall carry out if we can get any one to help. That is he and I will write a story on the proposed basis, if you and two or three others will do so.[2] Tell me what you think of the plan.

If convenient to you, I may run down to Ponk.[3] some day this week, and bring the comedy—or farce.[4]

> Yours ever
> W. D. H.

1. Probably "Unsung," *Atlantic*, June 1876.

2. The idea, apparently discussed during Howells' visit to Hartford, 11–12 March, was for a dozen authors to write a story with the same plot, without knowing what the others had written. Mark Twain wrote his "blindfold novelette" by 26 April and gave it the title, "A Murder, a Mystery, and a Marriage." See *Twain-Howells*, pp. 129–36 and passim.

3. Ponkapog, Massachusetts.

4. *The Parlor Car*, about which Howells wrote Aldrich on 11 March 1876 (MH): "I have just written a little farce, which at this moment seems to me—flown with

the Muse—bright enough to have been *talked* by you. I call it The Parlor Car. Managers are already (in my imagination) competing for it. But I wish to sell it outright."

9 APRIL 1876, CAMBRIDGE, TO WILLIAM C. HOWELLS

> ... *The Atlantic Monthly....*
> *Cambridge, Mass.* April 9, 1876.

Dear father:

We have been through another brief winter since I last wrote, and have come out into spring again. The season is almost as backward as it was three weeks ago, and I don't think we shall soon have warm weather. Mr. Storer,[1] who called last Sunday night, told me of the enormous snow-drifts in Quebec, which your photographs afterwards showed. If you're continued in office I must sometime see Quebec in the winter. Winny, as she wrote you, is delighted with her hat which is certainly beautiful. I didn't suppose the *sauvage* was at all capable of such work. Winny will wear the hat this summer with due pride in it, though probably she'll never say so. I can now begin to realize in her silence how unsatisfactory you must have found me on that journey up the Ohio[2] when the most you could get out of me in regard to anything was "Yes, indeed." I suppose we all grow more demonstrative as we grow older.

This week, I have been twice to see Uncle Tom's Cabin, as played by the Howards,[3] who brought it out in 1852. Howard has long been an acquaintance of mine—he lives in Cambridge—and Wednesday afternoon he took me behind the scenes and introduced me to his wife, Topsy. She had her black paint on, and as she was going to play again in the evening, she said it was no use to wash up. Her two little boys came into the dressing-room, and she put her arms round them, and it was a very pretty, domestic effect. She was very sensible, well-mannered and lady-like.—I went again yesterday, and took John and Winny and Winny's little friend, Lilly Guild. They were delighted, of course, though Winny still prefers Romeo and Juliet. One thing struck me: how, slavery being gone, the life had gone out of the tragedies it produced. The sorrows of people 2000 years ago, would have affected me more than those of people so lately slaves.

When we got home in the evening, I found waiting me a copy of *Voreilige Schlüsse*, a German translation of A Foregone Conclusion, which Auerbach, the novelist's son, has just published in Stuttgart.[4] With love to all,

> Your affectionate son
> Will.

Mr. Storer spoke with great cordiality of you, and the kindness you had shown his family.

1. See Howells to W. C. Howells, 13 February 1876, n. 3.
2. See Howells to W. C. Howells, 7 May 1871, n. 1.
3. After an early unsuccessful run of only a few nights in New York, *Uncle Tom's Cabin* was produced by G. C. Howard, then manager of the Museum at Troy, New York. At his request the novel was dramatized by George L. Aiken, and the play then became a great success, with Cordelia Howard as little Eva and her mother as Topsy. See A. H. Quinn, *A History of the American Drama*, 2d ed. (New York: F. S. Crofts, 1951), p. 288.
4. *Voreilige Schlüsse*, translated by Minna Wesselhoeft, was published by A. B. Auerbach in Stuttgart (1876).

24 APRIL 1876, CAMBRIDGE, TO JOHN AUGUSTIN DALY

> *...The Atlantic Monthly....*
> *Cambridge, Mass.* April 24, 1876.

My dear Sir:

You have doubtless forgotten a very kind invitation you gave me something more than a year since to send you anything I might write in the way of a play; and it's with no purpose of trying to create a sense of obligation in you that I recall a fact so gratifying to myself.

Here is a little comedy which I have pleased myself in writing.[1] It was meant to be printed in The Atlantic, (and so the stage-direction, for the reader's intelligence, was made very full); but I read it to an actor the other day, and he said it would *play*: I myself had fancied that a drawing-room car on the stage would be a pretty novelty, and that some amusing effects could be produced by an imitation of the motion of a train, and the collision.

However, here is the thing. I feel so diffident about it, that I have scarcely the courage to ask you to read it. But if you will do so, I shall be very glad.

If by any chance it should please you, and you should feel like bringing it out on some off-night when nobody will be there, pray tell me whether it will hurt or help it for your purpose to be published in The Atlantic.[2]

> Yours truly
> W. D. Howells.

Mr. Daly.

1. *The Parlor Car*, *Atlantic*, September 1876.
2. Daly replied on 6 May 1876 (MH), suggesting the possibility to "try" the

play "at some special benefit performance . . . ." He felt that "this bright & original little play of yours is a good step towards that perfect play of American life or incidents which I look to you to produce . . . ."

13 MAY 1876, CAMBRIDGE, TO OLIVER W. HOLMES

> . . . *The Atlantic Monthly. . . .*
> *Cambridge, Mass.* May 13, 1876.

Dear Dr. Holmes:

I think this poem most delightful,[1] and I shall be very glad indeed to have it. If you give it me at once—as I hope you will—please send it to Mr. Garrison at the Riverside Press, marked "copy for July Atlantic." I'm going to Philadelphia for a week.[2]

What will you think of my taste, I wonder, when I tell you that I think Mark Twain's last, one of his very best? In spite of certain inequalities, I think it in some points his very best; it seems to me to go deeper than anything else he has written, and it strongly moved me from its serious side.[3]

I felt obliged by my conscience to so much candor, but if what I say impeaches my judgment of your poem, pray believe me joking: I want that poem at any cost.

> Yours sincerely
> W. D. Howells.

1. "How the Old Horse Won the Bet," *Atlantic*, July 1876. Holmes sent the poem and a letter on 12 May (MH), asking Howells to "run your eye over a poem I read last evening at the Harvard Advocate Editors dinner and send it back to me for revision etc and a title. If you think it can be shaped into an available poem for the Atlantic you will tell me so—if otherwise promise that you will not trouble yourself with fair words to save any apprehended bruising of my sensibilities. I am getting fast into the Archbishop's period of production and if you play the part of Gil Blas to me you shall not experience the ingratitude which was his reward."

2. See Howells to W. C. Howells, 15 May 1876.

3. "Facts Concerning the Recent Carnival of Crime in Connecticut," *Atlantic*, June 1876. Howells referred again to Mark Twain's sketch in his letter to T. B. Aldrich, also of 13 May 1876 (MH): "I think with you that the Twain sketch is uneven, but it is altogether the strongest thing he's done, with a pulse of the deepest feeling in it. It made me resolve never to take crackers again when I had praised turn-overs."

15 MAY 1876, CAMBRIDGE, TO WILLIAM C. HOWELLS

> *. . . The Atlantic Monthly. . . .*
> *Cambridge, Mass.* May 15, 1876.

Dear father—

Annie's letter had to do duty for both of you last Sunday; but her letters are always fully equal to any extra requirement, they are so good. Tell her that Elinor was fairly shopped up getting ready for the Centennial,[1] but that I'm going into Boston for some final purchases tomorrow, and that I'm going to look up her écru patterns for her. I'm quite an adept in ladies' shopping, in spite of my hating it so.

We expect to start Tuesday morning at 10, and to pass the night in Jersey City at the Taylor House, near the depot, and then push on to Philadelphia by an early train next day. Our letter and telegraph address will be, till May 24, "Bryn Mawr, (Rosemont) Pa," though you had better send your letters to Cmbdge as usual.

I am to write something about the Exhibition for The Atlantic,[2] and I suppose I shall come home a few days before Elinor to finish up my article.

Yesterday we drove out to Waverley, where you saw the great oaks, and where we saw a most beautiful little fall on Beaver Brook. There is a pretty cottage near by, which in our present longing for the cheapness and seclusion of the country, seems the very place where we ought to go to live. We haven't the least idea, however, that the owner would sell it!

There is a desperate dearth of news of all kinds. I haven't hit on any plot yet for a new story, and in the meantime I'm tragically toiling away at a comedy, which may never make anybody laugh.[3]

We all unite in love to you all.

> Your affectionate son
> Will.

1. The Centennial Exhibition at Philadelphia, which opened 10 May 1876.

2. The Centennial Exhibition was the subject of Howells' "A Sennight of the Centennial," *Atlantic*, July 1876. On 27 May 1876 (MH) Howells wrote his father from Cambridge: "We enjoyed and admired it immensely; it far surpassed in interest any expectation I had formed of it. With the Longfellows we were charmingly situated at Rosemont, in a country that rolled in fatness. I had forgotten in this bare New England what a more southerly climate can do for the landscape, and the denseness of the foliage and the herbage astonished me. There, the woods were full of redbud and dogwood blossoms; I heard the meadowlarks and the red-birds sing; even the *feel* of the soft air was full of the past. But when last Monday came, with its terrible heat, I was glad that my lines were cast nearer the Northpole. I'm content here."

3. See Howells to Daly, 8 June 1876, n. 3.

8 JUNE 1876, CAMBRIDGE, TO JOHN AUGUSTIN DALY

> *...The Atlantic Monthly....*
> Cambridge, Mass. June 8, 1876.

My dear Mr. Daly:

I perceive you have not yet found it convenient to produce my play, and I hope the Parlor Car has not turned into an elephant on your hands.[1]

If it has not, and you still think of giving it, sometime, don't you think it would be well when I publish it (in the Atlantic for August) to have it announced that the piece is to be given at your theatre?[2] This would forestall any other manager's possible fancy for it, and save bother.

I am writing a comedy in four acts, two of which are done. If it should seem worth showing to you, on what basis would you care to treat for it? If I have luck, I shall finish it in a month.[3]

> Very truly yours,
> W. D. Howells.

1. In his reply of 10 June 1876 (MH), Daly indicated that he had decided against presenting *The Parlor Car* at a New York benefit on 24 May solely because Howells was unable to attend on that date. But he then continued: "I will present it next season—in the way I formerly suggested...." Even though he announced the play for 1876–1877, Daly never produced it. See W. J. Meserve, *The Complete Plays of W. D. Howells* (New York: New York University Press, 1960), pp. 23–24.

2. The play appeared in the September issue of the *Atlantic*.

3. Howells was already working on *Out of the Question* although it was not published in the *Atlantic* until February 1877, and had five rather than four acts when it was completed. He finished it in September, after having written the campaign biography of Rutherford B. Hayes. See Howells to Daly, 15 September 1876 (DFo). Daly's letter of 10 June suggests his continued interest in Howells' dramatic projects; it also explains the financial rewards that could be reaped by writing a successful play: "I look with interest for your larger play[.] I hope you will be able to complete it. [¶] I give $5. pr act for all new plays: i.e. for a 4 act play $20. per night—as long as it runs—& the pay is the same out of the city. [¶] A successful play ought to bring you $5,000 a year, at *least*."

10 JUNE 1876, CAMBRIDGE, TO SARAH ORNE JEWETT

> *...The Atlantic Monthly....*
> Cambridge, Mass. June 10, 1876.

Dear Miss Jewett:

I am sorry to find that you were right in your misgiving about this story.[1] It's very "brightly" written—that is to say, you wrote it—but there is no climax beyond the éclaircissement of Tom, which somehow isn't a climax; and then it appears to me impossible that you should do successfully what you've undertaken in it: assume a young man's character in the supposed narrator. It seems possible for fictionists to create characters of the opposite sex—though I suspect that men's women and women's men are a good deal alike—but when it comes to casting the whole autobiographical being in a character of the alien sex, the line is drawn distinctly.

I think your proposed Deephaven finish is capital, and I shall look forward to reading it with great pleasure.[2]

I'm sorry you distress yourself about what you said of your Mrs. F., for Mrs. Howells and I both understood, and never attributed unkindness to you.[3]—We are just on the eve of going into the country, (that is, we're going next Wednesday) and York seems a great way off to everything but our longing.[4] The fact is we spent all our money on the Centennial,[5] and we're expecting to "pinch" for months to come. But we feel grateful to you all the same, and Mrs. Howells wishes to be cordially remembered to your sister and yourself.

Yours truly
W. D. Howells.

1. "Hallowell's Pretty Sister," first appeared in *Good Company* 5, no. 9 (1880), and is reprinted in R. Cary, ed., *The Uncollected Short Stories of Sarah Orne Jewett* (Waterville, Me.: Colby College Press, 1971), pp. 45–52.

2. "Deephaven Excursions," *Atlantic*, September 1876, was the third of the stories in the Deephaven series that appeared in the *Atlantic* before the collection was published by Osgood & Co. in book form as *Deephaven* (1877). The first two stories had appeared in 1873 and 1875 respectively. In a letter of 20 October 1876 (OOxM) to a Mr. Niles (probably Thomas Niles of the publishing firm of Roberts Brothers, Boston), Howells recommended book publication of the stories: "...I commend them to your consideration as material for a most delightful book. I could not praise their literary character too highly."

3. The meaning of this passage is obscure although "Mrs. F." may refer to Annie A. Fields.

4. Jewett lived in South Berwick, near York, Maine.

5. See Howells to W. C. Howells, 15 May 1876.

18 JUNE 1876, SHIRLEY VILLAGE, MASSACHUSETTS, TO WILLIAM C. HOWELLS

Shirley Village, June 18, 1876.

Dear father:

I arrived here with the children Friday, and Elinor came last night. So here we all are again, with the promise of a very pleasant summer before us. Our tenant-landlord is a seven or eight foot Vermonter, very good-natured, but better versed in horses than in authors and their families, and the care of us falls chiefly to "the woman" as he calls his wife. We have to teach her our ideas of cooking, but she's very willing to learn, and so far all goes well. The moral atmosphere is a great improvement over that of last summer, when those unhappy Robinsons were here.[1]—Last Tuesday we met Miss Marnie Storer and her Warner at dinner at the Longfellows', and I had a long talk with her about Quebec.[2] She was full of praises of you all, which were very grateful to me as I have a singularly high respect for her. I told her that *you* were rather a favorite of mine, and she said you were a darling—or words to that effect.—Elinor and I are both highly excited about the nomination of Hayes,[3] and have our office picked out—minister to Switzerland. It makes me feel very easy about you for another four years, for I haven't the least doubt of his election, whereas I don't believe they could have elected Blaine.[4]

I went to Shaker meeting this morning, and every thing is in train.— Here is a pert picture of a very pert young person.[5] But in spite of the pertness, ask the girls if there isn't a curious likeness both to mother and yourself in it.

Elinor and the children join me in love to all.

Your affectionate son
Will.

1. See Howells to Garrison, 2 August 1875.
2. See Howells to W. C. Howells, 13 February 1876, n. 3.
3. Rutherford B. Hayes (1822–1893), then governor of Ohio, was a relative of Elinor Howells; he was nominated for president at the National Republican convention in Cincinnati on 14 June 1876. Howells wrote Hayes on 18 June (OFH), congratulating him upon his nomination: "we are most glad and happy in it, and are aware of a very distinct growth of the family affections." Hayes replied on 27 June (MH): "I am glad the family affections have a boost—we Smiths are so proud of our family, that I know, unfortunate outside people like you ... must feel at a disadvantage in being so mated. ... you don't know how fond we are of managing to let folks know in a casual way that the editor of the Atlantic, the author of &c &c is our Cousin."
4. James G. Blaine (1830–1891), a congressman from Maine, was Hayes' chief opponent at the National Republican convention.
5. Probably a photograph of either Winifred or Mildred.

20 JULY 1876, CAMBRIDGE, TO RUTHERFORD B. HAYES

... The Atlantic Monthly. ...
Cambridge, Mass. July 20, 1876.

Dear General:

I have just received this letter from my "owner,"[1] proposing something that I confess I felt tempted to propose to him the instant you were nominated. The objection is "nepotism," not to say "Caesarism." I desire your election far more than any profit the book would bring me; but if you think a biography from my pen would help, and not hurt the good cause, I will gladly go on and write it. Perhaps, in this connection, it might be well to consult with some such mutual friend as Comly. In case the matter strikes you favorably, will you kindly get Mitchell to cause somebody to send me the materials of your life? I should want every scrap that could be raked up, whether seemingly unimportant or not. I should think Laura might interview herself and Mrs. Hayes for personal matters, which of course I should use so as not to cause you loathing.[2] Whoever gets together the materials would be paid for his pains (or pleasures,) and I should want him to indicate any works on the war in which your career was mentioned. My book could not be long, and I should try to make it good otherwise.—If you have any reluctance about this, pray deal frankly with me. Heaven knows I would not give any dirty rogue grounds to bespatter a reputation for highmindedness which the nation will be proud of in you, whether you're elected or not.

—I had hoped to have a paper in the magazine from Carl Schurz, but to my great grief, he's going too actively into the campaign to be able to write[3]

> Yours sincerely
> W. D. Howells.

1. The letter from H. O. Houghton is dated 18 July 1876 (OFH); in it Houghton proposes that Howells write a campaign biography of Hayes: "Who is better fitted to write it than the 'accomplished scholar & able critic,' W. D. Howells? ... [¶] ... Could it be ready and printed by Sept 1st.?"

2. Laura Platt Mitchell, the wife of John G. Mitchell, was related both to the Hayes family and, through Elinor, to the Howellses. See Howells to Anne T. Howells, 19 December 1861, n. 2.

3. Carl Schurz (1829–1906), a participant in the German revolution of 1848, came to the United States in 1852, where he distinguished himself as a general in the Union army, as U. S. senator from Missouri (1869–1875), and as an active member of the Republican party. He was appointed secretary of the interior by President Hayes in 1877 and began the civil service reform movement.

30 JULY 1876, TOWNSEND HARBOR, MASSACHUSETTS,
    TO WILLIAM C. HOWELLS

> Townsend Harbor, Mass. July 30, 1876.

Dear father:

I don't know whether we gave you any warning of our extreme discontent with our landlord-tenant and his family at the Brick Farm.[1] He had gradually turned out a surly ruffian, and his wife a slut. Everything on the table was sour, dirty, or rancid, and the discomfort of our whole life intolerable. We had constantly complained to the Shakers, and in their slow way they had prepared to put Vorse out. But he was going to settle down at the next neighbors, and in that lonely place he could have offered us annoyances that wd have spoiled our whole summer. Besides we did not want to take the whole responsibility of putting him to shame before his shabby friends. Our miserable quarrel with him had become our whole life, and after my sunstroke the worry was more than I could bear.[2] So Monday afternoon, we suddenly packed and left for this place—a farmhouse we had seen the Saturday before—where we find ourselves in quite incredible peace. We pay less, and fare better, and though we miss the vast commodiousness of the Brick, and the open plain on which it stands, we are unspeakably glad to be away.—My address is at the head of this letter. When you come to visit us, you will find us at Mr. Taylor's on the road from Townsend Harbor to Pepperell.— Houghton has asked me to write a life of Hayes, and I'm much inclined to do it. I have Hayes's decided consent, and if Houghton can get the book adopted by some of the committees, I think he'll want to go right on with it. I've written for material to Columbus.[3] We should expect to have the life out about Sept. 15, and I should leave the family here, and go down to Cambridge to write it. I suppose that it would sell.—I must answer Annie's letter another time. Love to her and all the rest.

> Your aff'te son
> Will.

1. The farmhouse at Shirley Village, where the Howellses spent part of the summers of 1875 and 1876. They arrived at Townsend Harbor on 24 July. When Howells wrote to C. D. Warner, 1 August 1876 (CtHT), about the Shirley experience, he referred to "a most squalid and harassing quarrel with the dogs and pigs of people with whom we were boarding . . . ." The descriptive part of this sentence was silently omitted by Mildred Howells in *Life in Letters*, I, 224.

2. On 18 July, as Howells took a relative to the railroad station, he was overcome by the heat, as he wrote his father on 23 July (MH): ". . . I had another seizure from the heat, such as I had in New York five years ago, and had to remain at the doctor's, and be carried home in his buggy. My nerves have not yet recovered their tone, and I feel considerably shaken."

3. Hayes expressed his pleasure in Howells' proposed biography even though another one, by J. Q. Howard, was already near completion. "No doubt a half barrell of stuff—letters, speeches, mem, Diaries &c &c can be sent you, out of which you would get up a romance that would be taking." See Hayes to Howells, 23 July 1876 (MH). Howells enlisted the services of his old friend J. M. Comly to act as adviser and to recommend a person who would collect materials. See Howells to Comly, 28 July 1876 (OHi).

8 AUGUST 1876, TOWNSEND HARBOR, MASSACHUSETTS, TO JAMES R. LOWELL

Townsend Harbor, Mass. August 8, 1876.

Dear Mr. Lowell:

Mr. Houghton has sent me your poem for which I thank you, and which I like greatly.[1] Do you know of many children's albums in which you have written such verses? They have a faintly melancholy grace that pleases me more than I can say, and I think they come of one of your best moods. I shall keep them, if you please, for the first place in the November number. Let me be perfectly frank and tell you what I should like to do. I am going to have each month next year a piece of music by Paine, and other maestri of Boston and Cambridge, and I should like extremely if you thought the words appropriate for music to have Paine set them to some grave, simple music for the January number.[2] They have deeper meaning than lyrics generally, (always the fault one must find with you!) but they're very lyrical for all that in their flow, and they have a shadowy ballad-form. What do you think? Is it an absurd idea?

—I am going on to write a life of Hayes, which will be brief, and I hope, good—brief, at all events. I think I shall enjoy doing it, and if it doesn't help elect Tilden I shall be very glad.[3] It has been terribly hot here for the last three days, and one might as well have been in Cambridge. However, I'm delighted with every day in the New England country: the whole time is full of pleasure and instruction for me. This region is fairer and outwardly far more prosperous than I thought it at first. The neatness and perfect repair of everything is wonderful after the tumbledown of Jaffrey, Princeton and North Lancaster.

Yours faithfully
W. D. Howells.

1. "Birthday Verses," *Atlantic*, January 1877.

2. In his reply of 9 August 1876 (MH), Lowell explained that he wrote the poem in 1856 for his niece, "then a girl not much older than Winnie"; but he felt that the verses "are better for print than music." Although Lowell's poem was not set to music, Howells realized his plan of printing such songs in the *Atlantic*, with music by John Knowles Paine, Julius Eichberg, and George L. Osgood.

3. Samuel J. Tilden (1814–1886), then governor of New York, had been nominated for president at the National Democratic convention in St. Louis in June.

20 AUGUST 1876, TOWNSEND HARBOR, MASSACHUSETTS,
TO EDMUND C. STEDMAN

Townsend Harbor, Aug. 20, 1876.

My dear Stedman:

You have told the lovely legend most beautifully, with every grace of heart and art: the poem has just that pensive music and movement which the story asks, and I shall give it the first place in the January number.[1] I kiss my hand to you for the exquisite kindness (only too great) in the second stanza. I shall let it go in, against my risk, for nobody knows now that I ever was or could have been a poet.[2]

The poem is better without the French version, which is only less lovely.[3]

—I'm writing a book—the life of Hayes—in three weeks, and must send you a scanter letter than I like to get from you.

Yours ever
W. D. Howells.

1. "Sister Beatrice," *Atlantic*, January 1877, begins on p. 69 rather than in "the first place."

2. In the second stanza of the poem, which tells the legend of an abbess who becomes a prostitute but is eventually pardoned and restored to her office, the poet asks why chance has brought this legend to him rather than to others. Without naming any of the other poets, Stedman describes Howells, John Hay, and Bayard Taylor. Of Howells he writes:

Why not to one who, with a steadfast eye,
Ingathering her shadow and her sheen,
Saw Venice as she is, and, standing nigh,
Drew from the life that old, dismantled queen?

3. In Stedman's collected *Poems* (1908) the poem is subtitled: "A Legend from the 'Sermones Discipuli' of Jean Herolt, the Dominican, A. D. 1518."

23 AUGUST 1876, TOWNSEND HARBOR, MASSACHUSETTS, TO WEBB C. HAYES

Townsend Harbor, August 23, 1876.

My dear Mr. Hayes:[1]

Thanks for the package of letters which I shall have the pleasure of reading, and some of which I may use, though it's rather the purpose of my book to show what your father is than to tell what people have said to him. He may trust my discretion about their use, and please tell him not to be appalled by anything he finds in the proofs sent Mr. Rogers— if he cares to read them.[2] I am *always* absurd in my first proofs. Still I'd be glad to have him note any very brazen lies or particularly tinkling follies.

One thing I should like to give him his choice about: after he is wounded at South Mountain, does he prefer to lie twenty feet *before* or twenty feet *behind* his men, who continue fighting? His diary says *behind*; his short hand statement says *before*. I'd have made it behind, for a Presidential candidate is always corrupt and unreliable; still, if I'm wrong, perhaps he'd better telegraph me. I'm now writing up his battles, and the work interests me immensely.—Elinor's mother lies at the point of death in New Jersey. We shall probably go on to-morrow night to see her. But my address will be here.

> Yours truly
> W. D. Howells.

1. Webb C. Hayes (1856–1934) was the son of R. B. Hayes; as his father's secretary he helped Howells assemble the materials for the campaign biography. He later distinguished himself as an industrialist and soldier, and was chiefly responsible for the construction of the Hayes Memorial Library in Fremont, Ohio.

2. William K. Rogers (1828–1893), of Columbus, Ohio, was first suggested by Hayes as a trustworthy assistant, who would provide Howells with letters and other documents for the biography, because Webb Hayes was incapacitated by illness. See R. B. Hayes to Howells, 5 August 1876 (MH). Hayes' reaction to reading the proofs was one of extreme caution: "*No quoting* [from early diaries] of anything on political or semi political topics capable of being turned to account by the adversary. For instance Mr Howard [author of another campaign life] mentions that I was a member of the Sons of Temperance. This should have been omitted. That subject is not safe. Prohibitionists and liquor men are alike crotchetty [sic] and sensitive....*I am a liberal* on that subject, but it is not to be blabbed....Be careful not to commit me on religion, temperance, or free trade. Silence is the only safety." See Hayes to Howells, 24 August 1876 (MH).

LATE AUGUST OR EARLY SEPTEMBER 1876, CAMBRIDGE[?], TO FRANCIS J. GARRISON

Dear Garrison:

I send the last of the copy and the Preface.[1] I can't make the editorial slip till I have the whole book in sheets or proofs before me. I enclose a letter from Whitelaw Reid.[2] Dowse him, shower him, deluge him with advance sheets—it's very important. Don't forget Eggleston of the N. Y. Post.[3] Send copies to G. W. Curtis at Ashfield Mass., and Harper's, N. York. St! St! Chew-chew! Hoot, hoot! Cling-cling! Good-bye!

> W. D. H.

P. S. I'm going to drive out to Lexington to-morrow. Be back at noon.[4]

1. Howells is here referring to the Hayes biography.
2. The letter from Reid, editor of the New York *Tribune*, has apparently been lost.
3. George C. Eggleston was literary editor of the *Post*.
4. The morning round trip to Lexington suggests that this letter was written

while Howells was in Cambridge on one of his frequent interruptions of his summer residence at Townsend Harbor. The enthusiasm with which he supported Hayes' candidacy was partly due to the family relationship; even Elinor became involved in her cousin's biography. She acted as a critic of the portrait of Hayes that was to be included in the volume. See her note to Garrison, dated "Wednesday noon" (NjP).

7 SEPTEMBER 1876, CAMBRIDGE, TO RUTHERFORD B. HAYES

Cambridge, Sept. 7, 1876.

Dear General Hayes:

I have this afternoon finished my book, and am a free man once more. As soon as it's printed and bound, of course copies will go to you and Mr. Rogers. What it's fate or mission will be, heaven knows; but I can't help believing that it will receive vastly more notice than the other lives.[1]

In the two final chapters I have quoted a great deal from your messages and speeches, and made the book more fully representative of you in that respect than I had expected to do. It's horribly crude, I feel; and the haste with which I worked was subversive of all my literary principles and habits. I've done the work in twenty-eight days, and have made a thorough use of the material.

I don't wonder you and Mr. Rogers have been dismayed at the typographical errors. You have had the proofs before they received any correction whatever; but in the book you'll find no blunders but mine.— Well, we have Adams nominated for governor by the Democrats.[2] Of course he will be defeated, and perhaps by a larger majority than any other man they could have named. The Irish will go against him—which in ordinary circumstances would make me go for him[3]—and he will run altogether behind his ticket.—What *do* you make of the Arkansas election?[4] Not a conundrum and requires no answer.

Yours very truly
W. D. Howells.

1. *Sketch of the Life and Character of Rutherford B. Hayes* was published by Hurd & Houghton at the Riverside Press on 15 September 1876. Although the book's sales were disappointing (see *Twain-Howells*, pp. 149, 155), it earned Howells Hayes' lasting friendship and entrée to the White House. At least two other campaign biographies were published: Russell H. Conwell, *Life and Public Services of Gov. Rutherford B. Hayes* and James Q. Howard, *The Life, Public Services and Select Speeches of Rutherford B. Hayes*.

2. Charles Francis Adams (1807–1886) had been associated with the Liberal Republicans, but was persuaded to accept the Democratic nomination for governor of Massachusetts. He lost the election to Alexander H. Rice. See K. I. Polakoff, *The Politics of Inertia* (Baton Rouge, La.: Louisiana State University Press, 1973), pp. 172–73.

3. The Irish opposed Adams because of his position on the Fenian raids against Canada in 1866, when he was American minister to Great Britain. See Polakoff,

p. 172. For other expressions of Howells' anti-Irish bias, see his letters to Henry James, 26 June–24 July 1869, and to C. E. Norton, 7–21 November 1869.

4. Howells and Hayes may have considered the gubernatorial election in Arkansas as a significant indicator of the fortunes of the Republican party nationally. The hitherto firmly entrenched Republicans in Arkansas were severely weakened by intraparty strife (the Brooks–Baxter war), and as a result William R. Smith, a Democrat, won the governorship. See Garland Bayliss, "Public Affairs in Arkansas, 1874–1896" (Ph.D. diss., University of Texas, 1972).

17 SEPTEMBER 1876, TOWNSEND HARBOR, MASSACHUSETTS,
   TO BAYARD TAYLOR

Townsend Harbor, Mass. Sept. 17, 1876.

Dear Taylor:

I'm sorry for you. Piatt is the kindest and dearest fellow in the world, but he's perfectly merciless. He ought to know as well as you or I that a book of verses w'd now fall from the press with a deadness that there is no comparison for. Its mortality would infect a whole literature, and we should all perish. As for my talking with Osgood, I can't, for I'm still 40 miles away from him, and if I saw him it would come at once to his asking me, "Do you think it would pay?" And what could I say? It's a serious matter to urge a publisher to make a loss he can't afford.[1]

—Can you send me something in the way of song-poetry? We are to have a piece of music by Paine, Buck, Osgood, Boott, and others in each number next year, with words by our best poets.[2]

Yours ever
W. D. Howells.

1. J. J. Piatt, with whom Howells had coauthored his first book almost seventeen years earlier, persisted in using Howells to advance his own literary fortunes, not always in the most tactful manner. See Howells to W. C. Howells, 11 December 1870.

2. See Howells to Lowell, 8 August 1876, n. 2. Dudley Buck (1838–1909) had composed the cantata sung at the opening of the Centennial Exhibition at Philadelphia; Francis Boott (1813–1904) was well known for his secular and spiritual songs.

19 SEPTEMBER 1876, CAMBRIDGE, TO HJALMAR H. BOYESEN

... The Atlantic Monthly....
Cambridge, Mass. Sept. 19, 1876.

My dear Boyesen:

I read your story last night,[1] after an unavoidable delay for which I'm very sorry.

The last half strikes me as the best; the closing chapters, from the time of Einar's exposure are extremely interesting, and the nobility and sweetness of Helga are beautifully brought out. I felt,—but felt that you had not vividly enough expressed or enforced,—the fact, that her love absolutely supported and saved him from ruin: that was a novel and high thought, and gave me a joyful thrill. She is a fine creature, and Einar is capitally done. So is Nordened; I don't know whether the doctor is so good, artistically. The story is a great advance on the Norseman's Pilgrimage, but falls below Gunnar in sweetness and unity. I should be glad to take it for next year, but for one thing: *it is too long.* Too long not only for the magazine, but for the reader. The first hundred pages ought to be told in twenty. Whole chapters could profitably disappear after you get Einar to America. Even after his exposure when everything should march swiftly, you are deliberate and expansive beyond endurance. What struck me was that it was chiefly a prolixity of statement; not poetic vagary as in Gunnar. Now of course you can get this story published as it is, but I can't help urging you not to print it till you've reduced it almost one half. Your freshness—surprise—as a Norwegian writer of English is gone, and now you must be judged like the rest of us. It rests with yourself to be a writer of tame, pleasant-enough spun-out fiction, or to take your place with such concise dramatic poets as Tourgueneff and Björnson. I'll return the MS. by express.—I'm ever so sorry not to have seen you this summer. I *was* frightfully busy, but could have given you a day.

Yours ever
W. D. Howells.

1. *Falconberg* was published by Scribner in 1879.

24 SEPTEMBER 1876, TOWNSEND HARBOR, MASSACHUSETTS,
   TO CHARLES E. NORTON

Townsend Harbor, Mass. Sept. 24, 1876.

Dear friend:

I'm exceedingly glad you have read my book with a good opinion of Hayes, who merited a better book than I could make in three weeks.[1] My work does not at all represent the richness and beauty of the material put into my hands; but if I'd had six months for it, I could have given it the color I wanted. However, if you've got from it the notion of a very brave, single-hearted, firm-willed, humorous, unpretentiously self-reliant man, I haven't quite failed. As I studied the material, I had to check myself in the claims I wished to make for him; I had to remind myself that if I praised him so much, I should inflict a real discomfort upon the man personally, which I had no right to do. Some lines of Lowell's from the Elm-Tree Ode[2]—

> "Soldier and Statesman, rarest unison,
> High-poised example of great duties done
> Simply as breathing"—

embodied my conception of him better than anything I could have said (of course!), but I took them out of my title-page where I had them, because I felt that it was better to understate than to overstate such a man.

The summer indeed has gone, and we are going after it to-morrow, when we all set out for Cambridge. It has been a most voluminous season, and the odd experiences are almost a match for those of last summer. But I'm getting tired of odd experiences, and long for a little respectable commonplace.—In addition to the Hayes book, I've written a long story in dramatic form (an invention of my own)[3] and have begun that "New Medea" I once told you of.[4] With our best regards to all the ladies,

Yours ever

W. D. Howells.

1. Norton's praise, conveyed in a letter of 21 September 1876 (MH), seems to be rather extravagant in view of the obvious flaws in the hastily written campaign biography: "Your little volume is something more than the best of campaign documents. It will have a longer lease of life than the canvass, and will long be read as an excellent story of the life of one of those Americans who in this generation justify our faith in American principles in politics & in society."

2. J. R. Lowell, "Under the Old Elm," *Atlantic*, August 1875.

3. *Out of the Question.*

4. In 1862 Howells appears to have read a German translation of Euripides' *Medea* (see Howells to W. C. Howells, 7 March 1862); and in 1875 he saw a performance probably of an English version of Franz Grillparzer's *Medea* that suggested to him the similarity between the play and an Indiana divorce case. Whatever Howells may have written at this time of what eventually became *A Modern Instance* has not survived, and he did not return to the project until 1881. See George N. Bennett's introduction to *A Modern Instance*, HE, pp. xi–xiii.

11 OCTOBER 1876, CAMBRIDGE, TO THOMAS B. ALDRICH

... The Atlantic Monthly. ...

Cambridge, Mass. Oct. 11, 1876.

My dear Aldrich:

We are starting in January our new department, the Contributor's Club, the plan of which I've heretofore explained to you; and I wish you would for love or money's sake send me a ¶ or two. Vent your spleen as freely as if you were writing somebody else a letter about me; and take any topic under the sun. We like to have the ¶¶ about a quarter or half a page long, but if you get going nicely, don't stop till you've done. Do try, that's a good fellow; I suppose we shall have plenty of material after a month, but now the thing must be factitious.[1]

Yours ever
W. D. Howells.

1. "The Contributors' Club" was inaugurated in the January 1877 number of the *Atlantic*. At this time Howells solicited contributions from many of his friends and regular contributors. To H. H. Boyesen he wrote on 6 October 1876 (ViU): "There's another department which I wish you'd write for—our Contributor's Club; a place where you can briefly say anything you like on any sort of subject. See Atlantic prospectus for 1877! You can attack, defend, praise, or blame any body you like in the C. C. All we require is that you shall be lively." Mark Twain was also invited to contribute something: "Do send me at least a ¶, spitting your spite at somebody or something. Write it as if it were a passage from a private letter." (10 October 1876 [CU]; *Twain-Howells*, pp. 156–57.) The most detailed statement of Howells' plans for the new department is contained in his letter to E. C. Stedman of 12 December 1876 (NNC): "You have the right idea of the Club: those things *are* intended to provoke comment and question. I mean it also to be a place where a gentleman and scholar like yourself can make haut tony memoranda of an [sic] catholic nature, for after-use or not, as he likes; and I want to keep the tone high. . . . by and by I expect to interest cultivated people everywhere, and accumulate a mass of correspondence . . . . The names of all contributors to the Club will be kept strictly secret. . . . if you know any bright women who are disposed to write in the Club, invite them for me. I much desire the discussion of social matter."

12 NOVEMBER 1876, CAMBRIDGE, TO WILLIAM C. HOWELLS

. . . The Atlantic Monthly. . . .
Cambridge, Mass. Nov. 12, 1876.

Dear Father:

You will know from your own state better than I can tell you what an awful week this has been to me. I hardly dare hope yet that we have carried the election, but unless we are cheated in Florida or Louisiana, it seems probable we have.[1] Grant's having sent troops to both States is applauded by all, and will insure a fair count. We may not know what the result is till the end of the week; but we have the bitter reflection that whatever the count shows, not half of the Republican vote was cast at the South.[2] There is no use trying to write about it—I get perfectly frantic. Last night when I went to bed I felt sore from head to foot, as if the conflicting reports had all taken effect on my body like blows. I can't speak of the Tilden-republicans: the subject is too nauseous.[3] Pah!—Of course Elinor and I talk a great deal of you and of the effect on your prospects, but we are so bewildered by our new hopes that we don't think very clearly. You may be sure, though, that we share every moment of your anxiety.—If Tilden comes in and makes Adams his Secretary of State, Adams may refuse for shame's sake to allow any sweeping change in the service:[4] it would then be a question for you to decide whether you could hold office, gagged, under such a President. But it is the thousandth part of a chance that you would be allowed to remain.—If you go back to Ohio, why couldn't you "scoop" both Ashtabula and Jefferson by settling in the former place, and letting Joe stay in the latter?

> Your affectionate son
> Will.

1. The results of the election remained in doubt for almost four months, during which Democrats and Republicans charged each other with vote fraud, especially in Florida, Louisiana, and South Carolina. Hayes was eventually declared the winner on 2 March 1877.

2. The Republicans charged that many of their supporters in the South, particularly blacks, had been kept from the polls by intimidation and acts of violence.

3. As governor of New York, Tilden had established a reputation as a reformer and consequently attracted some Republicans into his camp.

4. See Howells to Hayes, 7 September 1876, n. 2.

30 NOVEMBER 1876, CAMBRIDGE, TO SAMUEL L. CLEMENS

> ... *The Atlantic Monthly....*
> *Cambridge, Mass.* Nov. 30, 1876.

My dear Clemens:

Here is Millet's letter, received to-day.[1] His terms are reasonable, certainly; but he seems bound to go. I don't know when he means to come back. Perhaps you may think worth while to write him.—There are two pictures for sale by that painter—Eugene Benson—who did the oriental scene over Appleton's mantelpiece.[2] I'll see them, and write you of them.

—You ought to write something better than that about Helen's Babbies. You use expressions there that would lose us all our book-club circulation. Do attack the folly systematically and analytically—write what you said at dinner the other day about it.[3]

—I am still looking up the spot-ivy business. I'm going to see Dr. Gray about it,[4] and get a bit of true spot to send you—I doubt *both* the present specimens.

Your visit was a perfect ovation for us: we *never* enjoy anything so much as those visits of yours. The smoke and the Scotch and the late hours almost kill us; but we look each other in the eye when you are gone, and say what a glorious time it was, and air the library, and begin sleeping and dieting, and longing to have you back again. I hope the play[5] didn't suffer any hurt from your absence. Mrs. Howells, whom you talked to most about it, thinks it's going to be tremendously funny, and I liked all you told me of it.

Yours ever
W. D. Howells.

1. Francis D. Millet (1846–1912), an artist and journalist, painted a portrait of Mark Twain; in 1877 he left the United States to report on the Russo-Turkish War for the New York *Herald*.

2. Eugene Benson (1839–1908), a minor American painter, lived, after 1873, mostly in France and Italy. Appleton is most likely Thomas G. Appleton.

3. Mark Twain had apparently reviewed John Habberton's sentimental novel, *Helen's Babies*, for the *Atlantic*, but the review remained unpublished.

4. Asa Gray.

5. *Ah Sin*, by Mark Twain and Bret Harte. The latter was staying with the Clemenses at Hartford to work on the play; Clemens went for a few days to Boston for some public readings.

4 DECEMBER 1876, CAMBRIDGE, TO JAMES R. LOWELL

. . . *The Atlantic Monthly*. . . .
Cambridge, Mass. Dec. 4, 1876.

Dear Mr. Lowell:

I think it right that you should see this dispatch,[1] which I have answered as follows: "I have heard no such rumors here as those you have referred to, and do not believe anything of the kind. Don't connect my name with the matter." I added the last sentence because Mr. Smith is a newspaper man, and might make a public use of my despatch referring to me as final authority in a matter about which I know nothing except that the whole thing seems utterly impossible.

Yours ever
W. D. Howells

1. Howells had received a telegram from William H. Smith, a fellow Ohio journalist of former years, who was at this time manager of the Western Associated Press in Chicago. The dispatch, dated 4 December 1876 (Smith's draft at OHi; Western Union's transmitted text at MH), inquired whether a recent article ("A Disputed Election or a Failure to Elect," *Nation*, 30 November 1876) "advising Hayes Elector to vote for some one not candidate late election and thus throw election into house . . ." was written by Lowell. On behalf of his fellow Republicans of the Northwest, Smith expressed deep dismay about such a proposition, but promised that they "will not condemn [Lowell] until they have the facts." A few days later Lowell assured Howells in person that he was committed to Hayes and that "Godkin had lost his head, for once, in writing" the *Nation* article. See

Howells to W. C. Howells, 10 December 1876 (MH). The author of the controversial piece was, in fact, Charles Francis Adams; however, he never acknowledged his authorship.

18 DECEMBER 1876, CAMBRIDGE, TO CHARLES D. WARNER

> ... *The Atlantic Monthly.* ...
> Cambridge, Mass. Dec. 18, 1876.

My dear Warner:

Your criticism of the Club is most sensible in all respects.[1] I too feel the necessity of keeping the tone high, and when I find that I cannot, I shall give the thing up. Of course, I expect it to be brighter and better than it now is; and I needn't say that I shall be humbly grateful for any help you can give me with it.

—I'm glad you liked Lathrop's story.[2] I think it a very uncommonly fine piece of work, and wonderfully mature.

—The review which I wrote of your book was insufficient.[3] I have learned to do those things with great difficulty and very unsatisfactorily— as far as I'm concerned. You are very kind to say you liked it. I often blush, as a book-noticer, at the poorness, the wretched meagreness of my work. But as magazines are now made, I can't help it.

I'm coming to Hartford one of these days. Mrs Howells has suggested the Warners' coming to Cambridge. Why not?

> Yours ever
> W. D. Howells.

1. With reference to the new department in the *Atlantic*, "The Contributors' Club," Warner wrote Howells on 17 December 1876 (MH): "Perhaps the danger of such a thing is too little formality rather than too much. Whatever the fun or the license of it, the highest literary level attainable ought to be kept .... I don't believe you can afford to put in anecdotes ...."

2. G. P. Lathrop, "Left Out," *Atlantic*, January 1877.

3. Howells reviewed *In the Levant* in the *Atlantic*, January 1877.

31 DECEMBER 1876, CAMBRIDGE, TO WILLIAM C. HOWELLS

> ... *The Atlantic Monthly.* ...
> Cambridge, Mass. Dec. 31, 1876.

Dear father:

I telegraphed you on Friday that I had given up the Swiss scheme,[1] because when I saw what the situation was in regard to you I could not do otherwise. Before I heard from you I had made up my mind not to *ask* for the place either under Grant or Hayes, for I did not see how I could decently do so; but I thought that if my willingness to take it were known, it *might* be offered and then I should accept it. Of course all this was counting unhatched chickens, for Hayes may not be declared President and there are many other contingencies. As it is, I shall do nothing more in this matter or any other till the question of your promotion is settled.[2] You can make your mind entirely easy in regard to it. I know your reluctance to have me relinquish any apparent advancement, but in this case—which is so very conditional at the best—I am not at all dependent on the place.—I'm sorry to hear that your arm is so seriously bruised, and I hope you are able to favor it as much as you need. I am so proud of the handwriting of Winny's last letter that I feel like advising you to take her for a consular clerk. For the first time since she has been with you in her last letter she writes that she is homesick and that she wishes she were at home. This may be because she was not well; but I remember so distinctly my own sufferings in that way that I am not willing she should endure them unnecessarily. I wish you would find out whether she really wishes to return, and if she does, to look up some chance of sending her. I should want her to come by way of Montreal and down the Vermont Central R. R. You could telegraph me, and if you had not found people bound for Boston, but had been able to send her with a New York party, I could go to meet her at Springfield or some other points on the route. But give me ample notice. If Winny were at home now she could begin the half year at the Williston school.[3] We don't desire her to come unless she is really homesick.—I am glad you all liked the presents. Tell Annie that it was Elinor first thought of sending that check. With love to all

> Your affectionate son
> Will.

1. Howells had earlier (letter to W. C. Howells, 18 June 1876) expressed his interest in getting a foreign service appointment in Switzerland; and on 24 December 1876 (MH) he wrote his father: "I have just now a temptation offered me. The U. S. Minister to Switzerland is the friend of a particular friend of mine who last night asked me to meet him at dinner. Mr. Ruble has come home to resign, and their joint suggestion was that I should apply for the place, which they believe I could easily get from Grant, if my appointment were known to be agreeable to Hayes, by whom of course it would be in effect made...." Horace Rublee (1829–1896) was American minister to Switzerland (1869–1877).

2. W. C. Howells was interested in becoming American consul general at Montreal.

3. Williston Seminary in Easthampton, Massachusetts, was founded by Samuel Williston, a philanthropist who had made his fortune in the manufacture of buttons and suspenders.

II

Emerging Novelist and Busy Editor

1 8 7 7 – 1 8 8 1

Introduction

HOWELLS wrote to his father on 22 August 1880, explaining that he had just declined an invitation from President Hayes to accompany him on a trip out West. "Of course I miss a great deal," he reflected, "but in this life you can't do everything." Despite his disclaimer, there seemed to be very little in the years 1877–1881 that Howells missed: the *Atlantic* continued to flourish under his editorship; plays and books of an achieved maturity appeared regularly; he felt himself able to speak with more assured critical authority than at any earlier point in his career; he grew even happier in his friendships and family life than he had been before; and, adding a final touch to the whole, he found himself on friendly personal terms with the president of the United States (a relative of Elinor's), whom the Howellses visited in the White House. A kind of nemesis ended this period of unalloyed prosperity, however, in the year 1881, which marked the decline of Howells' older daughter Winny into pathetic invalidism and brought to Howells himself an attack of illness, perhaps more physical than neurotic, but still the cause of a five-month delay in the completion of *A Modern Instance.*

Fittingly, the first letter of the 1877–1881 sequence accepts Holmes's amusing poem on the Hayes-Tilden contest. With settlement in Hayes's favor, Howells soon began politicking for his father's advancement as consul, in effect trading off his own chance for the Swiss mission. As he wrote to Hayes's secretary William K. Rogers on 7 April 1877: "My father, now Consul at Quebec, is looking to promotion in the service to Toronto or Montreal when there shall be a vacancy—and I am very solicitous that no supposed desire for office on my part should interfere with his legitimate hopes." Although the desired appointment was some time in coming, Howells' efforts on behalf of his father proved finally successful. His support for James Russell Lowell, however, turned out to be a more difficult problem: not because Howells was reluctant to advance his literary mentor or because the president had any reservations, but because of Lowell's unwillingness to accept a proffered appointment as American minister to Austria. At one point Howells could only apologize to Hayes about Lowell's lack of interest: "That is his affair, and of course I have nothing to say.... I am now only sorry to have troubled you for nothing" (28 May 1877). Eventually Hayes appointed Lowell as minister to Spain; and a little more than two years later, in full concurrence with Howells' suggesting Lowell for the English mission, Hayes offered Lowell an appointment that proved even more attractive.

Hayes also consulted Howells about other appointments. As a result of a cautious endorsement (9 April 1878), Bret Harte received first a minor and then a more desirable consular appointment. But if this pleased one of Howells' literary friends, it markedly upset another. Either guessing Howells' support or having learned of it, Mark Twain exclaimed in a letter to Howells of 27 June 1878: "If he had only been made a home official, I think I could stand it; but to send this nasty creature to puke upon the American name in a foreign land is too much." And as for Clarence King, though he had other friends to promote his interests, Howells' letter of introduction to Hayes un-doubtedly helped in King's appointment as director of the U. S. Geo-logical Survey.

Howells' involvement in governmental affairs extended beyond making recommendations for political appointments; during these years he also made numerous personal contacts with statesmen and politicians. At the Harvard and Newport festivities for Hayes in 1877, he met Carl Schurz and William M. Evarts; during the week-long visit to the White House in 1880, he saw and talked with many notables; and on the occasion of the Grant dinner in Garfield's presidential campaign, he wined and dined with the leading Republicans of the day. The election of Garfield, a friend of Howells' father, promised four more years of closeness to the chief executive—both the Swiss mission and the Montreal consulship emerged again as soon as Garfield took office—but the attempted assassination of Garfield in July, followed by his death in September, mostly put an end to Howells' presidential intimacies.

Yet authorship was Howells' profession, and the period of the late 1870s was full of projected and completed plays and novels. Some time in the spring of 1877 he finished *A Counterfeit Presentment*, though he continued to revise it after its appearance in the *Atlantic* and through its opening by Lawrence Barrett on 11 October. In sending a new act to Barrett on 14 November 1877 he observed: "What pleases me about all the praise the play gets, both on your account and my own is that people seem honestly *glad* of an American comedy that makes its way without farcical or melodramatic effects." At the same time he was beginning his translation of the Spanish play *Un drama nuevo* and finished it in September 1878 for its premiere on 25 October. Though *A Counterfeit Presentment* was given up by Barrett after the 1877–1878 season, *Yorick's Love*, as the Spanish play came to be known, was much more successful, and Barrett presented it frequently until his death in 1891.

In his plays and dramatic translations Howells appears to have been experimenting with a new form. As he explained to John Hay, on 22 February 1877, referring to *Out of the Question*, a play that never found a producer, "there is a middle form between narrative and drama, which may be developed into something very pleasant to the reader, and convenient to the fictionist." But whatever literary importance he may have attached to his plays, Howells, like so many of his novelist contemporaries, felt even more the glamor and longed for the elusive profits of the stage. When *A Counterfeit Presentment* appeared in Boston, he remarked to his father (3 April 1878), "I never had my popularity at arm's length before, and it was very pleasant."

In 1877 Howells wrote the introductions to six volumes of "Choice Autobiographies." Although he and James R. Osgood had at one time envisioned the publication of fifty or seventy-five volumes, the series ended with these six. His major efforts seem to have been devoted to the writing of *The Lady of the Aroostook*, which he may well have begun before 1877 and certainly continued later, for this was the first novel that he partly wrote during its serialization in the *Atlantic*, November 1878–March 1879. That he considered his book "unthe-atricable," as he told Ellen Hutchinson on 19 February 1879, also suggests his thinking about ways for connecting fiction and the stage. But whether for the theater or not, Howells' latest novel brought from Henry James the comment that "It is the most brilliant thing you have done, & I don't see how your own manner can go farther." Still, James added the advice that Howells "attack the great field of American life" on still more sides, "& you will do even better things than this" (7 April 1879).

Long before publishing *The Lady of the Aroostook*, Howells had begun *The Undiscovered Country*, of which he reported on 6 January 1878 that "I try to paint that hopeless sophistication into which the sincerest spiritualists fall." With this novel begins his treatment of "serious matters," as he remarked retrospectively to his father (1 February 1880) soon after the serialization had begun.

While Howells thought that he had nearly finished this novel by the end of June 1879, completion was at least another six months off, perhaps because ideas for other books interfered. Soon after beginning *The Undiscovered Country* he started *A Woman's Reason*, which was thoroughly plotted when, on 14 March 1878, he described it to Boyesen as "the history of a young girl brought up in good society who is sud-denly thrown upon her own resources for a livelihood." But by September, after six hundred pages, he had decided to put the novel aside as a failure, not to take it up again until 1882. On 4 January 1880 he wrote C. E. Norton that he had "broken ground" on *Doctor Breen's Practice* and apparently wrote it most of that year, though in July he was "alternately taking [it] up and throwing [it] away." Perhaps at the same time he was working on *A Fearful Responsibility*, which could have had its beginning as early as July 1879. Although the exact chronology remains unclear, Howells had finished that short novel by April 1881; and it seems likely that at least by that time he had also completed *Doctor Breen's Practice*.

Only a month or two earlier, on 18 February 1881, Howells presented his ideas for *A Modern Instance* to Osgood, with whom he had just made a new contract. He proposed to deal with the most serious subject he had yet explored: "as the question of spiritualism was the moving principle in The Undiscovered Country, so the question of divorce will be that of The New Medea." Then he continued: "I intend to treat it tragically, though of course the story is not to be wholly tragical; and I feel that I have a theme only less intense and pathetic than slavery." Howells had hoped to come close to completion by Thanksgiving, when he proposed to visit his father, but with the onset of his illness in mid-November, he did not finish *A Modern Instance* until May or June 1882, though it began its serialization in the *Century* in December of the preceding year.

The author who in 1876 had wondered whether he could think of new plots had disciplined himself by the end of the decade to offer completed novels at yearly intervals. He had moved toward a deeper penetration into American life, from comedy in an international setting, to spiritualism, to problems of professional women, and to divorce. It is no wonder that at the beginning of 1881 he could make a contract with Osgood that stipulated a novel a year for each of three years, since two were close to completion and the third about to be outlined.

Meanwhile Howells continued guiding the fortunes of the *Atlantic*, until he resigned in early January 1881. At that time he told Houghton he had lost interest in the magazine and hinted at past disagreements over editorial policy: "I have been making a magazine that is neither your ideal nor mine . . . ." Still, in his later editorship, he thought the magazine was "chirking up," to use a phrase from a letter to his father of 22 December 1877; and at the beginning of 1878 he or his publisher secured the subscription list of the *Galaxy*, thus expanding the readership. Also, his editorial correspondence appears as frequent and thoughtful as ever.

Yet he made no important innovations such as the "Contributors'

Club" of earlier years. Rather, he appears to have prided himself on his authors and on his working with them to produce better contributions, as some of his letters to William H. Bishop, Arthur G. Sedgwick, and Charles Dudley Warner show. On 11 September 1877 he suggested to Bishop his concept for a monthly letter from New York: "Imagine yourself still a cultivated and amiable inhabitant of Milwaukee; imagine yourself also the New York friend of your Milwaukee self. Such accounts of New York matters as you would write your Milwaukee self are probably what I should want for the magazine. Do you see?" Howells also showed himself an alert editor in proposing new articles, as to Samuel P. Langley on 18 May 1879: "I wish you had time and inclination to write out for The Atlantic an account of your two months on Mt. Etna." Langley did, and an essay of July 1880, "Wintering on Aetna," was the result. Or on 31 March 1879 Howells asked Samuel A. Green for a more sensational article on "Mysterious Disappearances," suggested by the recent murder of a girl at Lynn.

On a quite different level, he continued to show his abiding interest in obtaining contributions from Mark Twain and Henry James. Though as always unable to secure Clemens' "subscription books," he began the period with the four-number sketch of a Bermuda journey, "Some Rambling Notes of an Idle Excursion," and regularly through the subsequent years published shorter pieces with equal delight. "Have you come home with your pockets full of Atlanticable papers?" he asked him on his return from Europe. Though Clemens had apparently not many to offer, Howells was soon inviting him to speak at the Holmes breakfast of December 1879, probably to show his faith in the man who had made the "hideous mistake" at the Whittier Birthday Dinner two years before.

The relation to James remains somewhat obscure, since though there are two dozen extant letters from James to Howells in the 1877–1881 period, not a single letter from Howells has survived. The *Atlantic* did publish James's two great novels of the period, *The American* (June 1876–May 1877) and *The Portrait of a Lady* (November 1880–December 1881). It also brought out the charming *Europeans* in July–October 1878, but it missed out on *Daisy Miller* and *Washington Square*. James's letters to Howells give little ground for speculating about the reason for the losses. Howells had wished that *The American* end with the marriage of Newman and Mme. de Cintré, a criticism to which James replied vigorously on 30 March 1877, though in the same letter he promised *The Europeans*; and Howells' review of James's *Hawthorne* brought a strong defense from James on 31 January 1880, though by this time arrangements for publication of *The Portrait* were well advanced. Whatever the reasons for Howells' not getting *Daisy Miller* and

Washington Square, James liked what Howells was writing, though usually with strong qualification. *The Undiscovered Country* he thought "the least *entertaining* of your books," but he admitted that the subject was "larger & heavier" than Howells had yet tried, and it was carried off "with great ease" (20 July 1880). Shortly before he embarked for America in 1881 James had read *Doctor Breen's Practice*; he called it "barring perhaps the *Foregone Conclusion*," Howells' "best thing.... full of vivacity, of reality, of the feeling of life & human nature, of happy touches of all sorts." Perhaps *Daisy Miller* and *Washington Square* were not offered to the *Atlantic* because they lacked happy endings; but if they were withheld, the friendship between the two authors continued.

Occasionally prudishness overtook Howells, as when on 16 April 1878 he rejected a manuscript from an unknown contributor sent by that sturdy enemy of vulgarity, his friend C. E. Norton: "I no longer wish to be put in pain about a woman's virtue, or to ask that suffering from others. It's odious; all the tragedy went out of that situation long ago, and only the displeasures remain." Curiously, after Howells left the *Atlantic* he submitted for publication one of his closest approaches to "French realism," the sketch "Police Report," over which he showed amusing hesitation. If anything distinguishes the *Atlantic* after 1876 from Howells' earlier editorship, it would seem to be its ventures into more radical social and political subjects, as demonstrated by the Harrison series (though a conservative diagnosis), the debate over the Single Tax, and the acceptance just before Howells resigned of H. D. Lloyd's attack on the Standard Oil trust.

Also, more subtly, the magazine exhibited the development of Howells' literary standards, which were frequently reflected in letters to contributors. Thus on 1 April 1877 he wrote to Warner on the novel, observing, among many other things, that "What one really needs is a strong *motive*; then he [the novelist] enlarges his territory in his reader's mind." However, as his 17 September 1879 letter to Higginson makes plain, such a motive was humanistic rather than didactic. While Howells would "feel degraded merely to amuse people," he was "very often puzzled to know what is the truth, and that may account for the 'stopping-short' which you notice." Later, on 21 March 1880, Howells advised Bishop: "My hope is that you will be very serious about your work, and not deal in any of those pitiful winks to the reader, with which that bad artist Thackeray has undermined most of our constitutions." Finally, in a kind of Homeric boast he wrote to his father on 11 September 1881, "I think that I know rather more about the business of writing novels than any critic living...." We may smile at his arrogance, we may wish for a qualifying "*almost* any critic," but the passionate defense of his accomplishments still has to be reckoned with.

If as a literary critic Howells here exhibited a kind of hubris, as a human being during these years he retained the serenity of the earlier 1870s. The move to nearby Belmont in mid-1878 brought a desirable escape from the obligatory parties of Cambridge and Boston, though as Howells insisted, Belmont was not very far from Cambridge, pointing out to Norton on 16 April 1878 that in his new home he would be "much nearer Shady Hill than I am now." Designed by McKim, Mead, & Bigelow, Redtop, as the Belmont house was called, had a dignity and repose that sharply differentiated it from the clutter of 37 Concord Avenue. As Howells told his father on 31 March 1878, when the new house was being built, it "is blossoming out into a very quaint and peculiar beauty. It is going to be something really exquisite, and, what is better, convenient." Also, quite apart from the building was its magnificent site on Belmont Hill, with a view over Boston that extended to the ocean beyond.

Though at Belmont Howells could choose his outside engagements, he could not always choose his guests, for to his consternation the new house became a magnet for "swarms of friends and semi-friends." But between visits the family drew closer together than ever, and expressions of delight and love for the children abound. After Winny's illness developed at the end of 1880, there came moments when she re-emerged into her charming poise and social grace, and there remained always the hope that she might completely recover. Still, the parents' concern was real: "I see these days of her beautiful youth slipping away, in this sort of dull painful dream, and I grieve over her." The family were to leave Belmont at the end of 1881, but the reason for the departure was Howells' own sickness rather than Winny's. After two months it left him feeling as if he had aged five years, but he seldom doubted the future; as he told Mark Twain early in 1882, "I may young up again . . . ."

G. A.

9 JANUARY 1877, CAMBRIDGE, TO OLIVER W. HOLMES

> *The Riverside Press,...*
> *Cambridge, Mass.* Jan. 9, *1877.*

Dear Doctor Holmes:

I had supposed it quite impossible to get your poem[1] into the February number, but such is the enterprise of our people that they said it must go in, somehow, and although the magazine was in the bindery, they have sent the poem to the printers, and you will get a proof of it with this to-day. The bearer will wait, and I need not urge upon you the necessity of returning the proof by him at once; of course we cannot give you a revise. The poem will be placed the last thing in the magazine, and attention will be specially called to it on the cover and in the papers. We all like it exceedingly, and are ready to believe that it will prove a solution of the whole political difficulty.[2] Certainly no one can read it without being recalled to his senses—if he has any.

> Yours faithfully
> W. D. Howells.

1. "How Not to Settle It," *Atlantic*, February 1877. A few days earlier, 6 January (DLC), Howells had written Holmes accepting the poem for the March issue, since the February number was "impenetrably stereotyped." At the same time he commented: "It developed and grew upon me, as I read it, in the most delightful fashion ... the greatest—in fact the only—good that has come out of the present political misery."
2. The penultimate stanza suggests the solution best:

> I say once more, as I have said before,
>> If voting for our Tildens and our Hayses
> Means only fight, then, Liberty, good night!
>> Pack up your ballot-box and go to blazes!

18 FEBRUARY 1877, CAMBRIDGE, TO ANNE T. HOWELLS

> *...The Atlantic Monthly....*
> *Cambridge, Mass.* Feb'y 18, *1877.*

Dear Annie:

Elinor is going to church, and leaves me on duty at the family letters. She is very grateful for your thinking of her in connection with the silks, but returns these as being all too light; besides, we don't see how we could get the pattern into the States without payment of heavy duty. Elinor will get your waists for you in town to-morrow.—Thanks for the recipe for the water-bouquet: if ever we do society again, I shall try it; I should think it would be very pretty.—I didn't know that the Lanes had not been to see Winny. As they have not, she can use her pleasure about calling on them. I wanted her to go because I hated to seem to drop them, when we had once been so friendly with them.[1]—We would rather Winny would not read such excruciating novels as Jane Eyre.[2] If you could get her Jane Austen's stories, or Miss Mulock's[3] out of the library, we should be very glad. And for my own part, I wish she would read biography, history and poetry, rather than any sort of novels.—We were at Newport two days last week, and enjoyed it greatly, Elinor having never been there before. The weather was quite mild. You can have the MS. of A Foregone Conclusion, if you like. It's in a good state, and it's the best book I ever did or ever shall write. Tell me just when—if you can—is to be your wedding. I'm glad to hear of your success as a *cantatrice*, but will Père Fréchette be glad?[4] I should want you to be a good and firm Protestant, but not an obnoxious one. But of course you know the ground better than I. How do you get on remodeling your story for Harper?[5]

All send love to all with special kisses for Winny.

> Your aff'te brother
> Will.

1. See Howells' letter to his father, 9 July 1874, n. 1.

2. Howells first read *Jane Eyre* when in Dayton, Ohio, at about age twelve and later recalled only his association of it with the "Rochester Knockings." See *My Literary Passions* (1895), p. 35. On rereading it fifty years later he praised it for "the frank recognition of the rights of love as love," yet along with *Wuthering Heights*, Howells thought that it "established the bullied heroine in a supremacy which she held till the sinuous heroine began softly but effectually to displace her." See *Heroines of Fiction* (1901), I, 221–29.

3. Dinah Maria Mulock (1826–1887) began publishing novels in 1850. Her most famous is *John Halifax, Gentleman* (1857). Howells did not mention her in his criticisms of women writers.

4. Louis Fréchette, a contractor, was father of Antoine Léonard Achille and Louis Honoré Fréchette, the writer. See also Howells to Warner, 1 April 1877, n. 3.

5. "The Chances of War, and How One Was Missed," *Harper's Monthly*, September 1881. The first piece *Harper's Monthly* published by Annie was an article on Rideau Hall, which appeared in July 1881.

22 FEBRUARY 1877, CAMBRIDGE, TO JOHN HAY

> The Atlantic Monthly,
> Cambridge, Mass., February 22, 1877.

Dear Hay:

Many thanks for your capital ¶ for the Club[1]—what you said needed saying—and more yet for your letter. My wife and I had just been talking of you, and wondering when and how you would reappear in literature, for that you must, we held for certain. I wish that it were to be in a story for the *Atlantic.*—I am glad you like *The American*.[2] The fact that Harry James could write likingly of such a fellow-countryman as Newman is the most hopeful thing in his literary history, since *Gabrielle de Bergerac*.[3] I put my joy at your liking my comedy last, but you'll easily believe it's first in my mind.[4] The play is too short to have any strong effect, I suppose, but it seems to me to prove that there is a middle form between narrative and drama, which may be developed into something very pleasant to the reader, and convenient to the fictionist. At any rate my story wouldn't take any other shape.

It does really seem as if we should have Hayes at last. Of course I pin my faith to him, and I believe he will do all that a very wise and just man can do to help us. But we can't be helped against our will, and there lies the danger. Some day I hope to come to Cleveland; your asking me is the main inducement; but I don't yet see the hour, as the Italians say. In the meantime, why shouldn't we exchange fotografs, all round? I am very curious to see your family, and don't like to wait till I meet them. Mrs. Howells joins me in cordial regard.

Yours ever,
W. D. Howells.

1. "Corrupting Influences of the 'Postal Card,' " the title assigned in the semi-annual table of contents, appeared in "The Contributors' Club," *Atlantic*, June 1877. In his letter of 20 February 1877 (MH), Hay refers to a rumor that Howells is to write a "No Name" story and says, "Your name is too valuable to veil. If you do, let me know, in strict confidence. I cannot afford to lose anything you write...." The "No Name Series" volumes were published anonymously by Roberts Brothers, beginning in 1876.

2. Henry James, *The American*, *Atlantic*, June 1876–May 1877. The novel had first been accepted as a serial by the *Galaxy*, but Howells secured it for the *Atlantic*. See Howells to F. P. Church, 29 February 1876 (NN); also *James Letters*. II, 31, 35.

3. Henry James, "Gabrielle de Bergerac," *Atlantic*, July–September 1869.

4. *Out of the Question*, *Atlantic*, February–April 1877. Howells' next sentence refers to his experimentation in that work with the combination of dramatic and narrative form.

18 MARCH 1877, CAMBRIDGE, TO JAMES R. OSGOOD

...The Atlantic Monthly....
Cambridge, Mass. March 18, 1877.

My dear Osgood:

I told Ticknor[1] last night that the Riverside Press people would have the plates of Out of the Question ready by All Fools' Day,—which ought to be lucky for me—and he spoke of sending the paper right out and having the book printed as fast as each signature was cast. I think this a good plan. The pages will be leaded like those of Baddeck,[2] and will be from 225 to 250 in number. So you mustn't ask less than $1.25 for the book, and I wish you could advertise the others of the series at $1.50.[3]

—If I had given the proper thought to your kind offer, the other night, to bring my name forward in connection with the Swiss mission, I should have asked you not to do it. I didn't think much about it—and not at all seriously. But I beg you now to do nothing. I am not going *to ask* nor *to be asked for*. I couldn't stomach it. Besides there are reasons which I can't give here, for my reluctance to have my name suggested.

Yours ever
W. D. Howells.

1. Benjamin Holt Ticknor (b. 1843?), the second son of William D. Ticknor, was a partner in James R. Osgood & Co. (1871–1878; 1881–1885).

2. *Baddeck and That Sort of Thing*, by C. D. Warner.

3. *Out of the Question* was published by James R. Osgood & Co. during the week of April 21, and was priced at $1.25. It ran to 183 pages, "much less than I expected," as Howells wrote Osgood on 29 March 1877 (MH). In the same letter he proposed that Osgood pay for the plates, saying, "I want to get all I can from the book as soon as I can." The series alluded to is a group of novels designated as "Little Classics." On 5 April (MH) Osgood wrote Howells: "We accept your proposal and will pay for the plates and publish on the usual terms of ten per cent on the sales."

25 MARCH 1877, CAMBRIDGE, TO MARIANNE W. BATCHELDER

Cambridge, March 25, 1877.

Dear Mrs. Batchelder:[1]

Will you let me intrude a moment upon the sorrow which we all share to say how truly dear and reverend your father's memory is to me? I can never forget the prompt kindness with which he sought us out in our first little house on Sacramento street, and helped in greater degree than he ever knew to make Cambridge home to us; and neither my wife nor I ever met him without feeling the sight of his friendly face a real benediction. He bore a very striking resemblance to her father which we always liked to note, and he had the same cheerful and kindly voice.

It has been our misfortune not to have seen so much of him as we might, but for pressing cares and other preoccupations; and it deeply grieves me to think that during his last illness I let a shyness about adding to the many inquiries, with which I feared he might be disturbed, prevent me from asking at his own door after his health, but we constantly heard of him, and I was on my way at last to offer my congratulations on his recovery, when I heard the sad final news.

Every one's life is poorer for such a loss as his, and we shall all miss his gracious presence with a regret which is the measure of our sympathy for you whose bereavement is so great.

We hear that your mother is not well, and this is partly my excuse for addressing to you a letter which ought perhaps to have been sent to her. Will you kindly remember us to her with most affectionate and respectful sympathy? With Mrs. Howells's and my own sincere condolence,

Yours truly
W. D. Howells.

1. Marianne Washburn Batchelder was the daughter of Emory Washburn (1800–1877), an eminent Massachusetts lawyer, legislator, and judge, who served as governor for two terms (1854–1856) and was Bussy Professor of Law at Harvard (1856–1876). She was married to Samuel Batchelder (1830–1888), a Cambridge lawyer.

1 APRIL 1877, CAMBRIDGE, TO CHARLES D. WARNER

Cambridge, April 1, 1877.

My dear Warner:

One of few drawbacks of my visit to Hartford[1] was that I had really no long talk with you on the many points I should have liked to discuss with you: for example, novels, what they are, and what they are for. I still don't agree with you that a novel need be long in order to be great. I believe I grow more and more contrary-minded on this point, and it seems to me that the people of the next age will look with as much amaze upon our big novels, as we do upon Richardson's. The man who has set the standard for the novel of the future is Tourguénef, whom certainly you can't blame for want of a vast outlook, or side-light, or world. And only consider a play of Shakespeare, which is of such limitless suggestion, how short it is! No, I can't believe that I should be greater with more room, or Black smaller with less.[2] (I don't propose to speak of him, however, for I've never yet read one of his book; such parts of chapters as I've read, seemed to me somewhat strained and cumbrous in expression.) What one really needs is a strong *motive*; then he enlarges his territory in his reader's mind. The great art is to make your reader recur to your book with the impression that certain passages are much longer than they really are. But perhaps I'm really without desire for the sort of success you believe in for me. Very likely I don't want much world, or effect of it, in my fictions. Not that I could compel it if I did want it; but I find that on taking stock, at forty-year, of my experiences, and likes and dislikes, that I don't care for society, and that I do care intensely for people. I suppose therefore my tendency would always be to get my characters away from their belongings, and let four or five people act upon each other. I hate to read stories in which I have to drop the thread of one person's fate and take up that of another; so I suppose I shall always have my people so few that their fates can be interwoven and kept constantly in common before the reader. This is merely opening the subject; some day we must talk it all out.

But I'm afraid that day is not to be this spring, unless you and Mrs. Warner can come here. We are going away for the summer early in June, and before we go, I must see my sister married at Quebec,[3] and that will take all the time I shall have for junketing. Mrs. Howells is to have Winny home in a fortnight, and then opens a grand campaign of summer's sewing. Perhaps during the summer we can contrive a meeting; but as for the apple blossoms, I despair of seeing them in Hartford.—It was a real joy to meet you and your wife again. I had to give a very full report of what you said, and how you looked, when I got home, for Mrs. Howells and I will never be divorced on account of the Warners. It's our united love that we send them now.

Yours ever
W. D. Howells

1. Howells visited Hartford some time in March.

2. William Black (1841–1894), the Scottish novelist. In *Heroines of Fiction* (II, 214) Howells observes that Black sometimes wrote insipidly or emotionally, but that for a time, as in *MacLeod of Dare* (1879), he wrote "naturalistic fiction of the old-fashioned English kind." In reply to Howells' comments Warner wrote, 3 April 1877 (MH): "You may write novels an inch long if you like, and I will swear by 'em. You may write like Shakespeare, as you suggest you are going to, and I wont move a muscle." ,

3. Annie married Antoine Léonard Achille Fréchette on 20 June 1877. Then translator in the Canadian House of Commons, he later became Translator of Laws and chief of the Translation Bench of the House of Commons.

7 APRIL 1877, CAMBRIDGE, TO WILLIAM K. ROGERS

... The Atlantic Monthly....
Cambridge, Mass. April 7, 1877.

Dear Mr. Rogers:

Thanks for your kind note in regard to the Ticknor matter.[1] I am still a little anxious to know whether you received a note of mine begging you to destroy Mr. H. S. Noyes's[2] memorandum asking that I should be "remembered in the distribution of the minor foreign appointments."[3] My father, now Consul at Quebec, is looking to promotion in the service to Toronto or Montreal when there shall be a vacancy—and I am very solicitous that no supposed desire for office on my part should interfere with his legitimate hopes. I venture to trouble you therefore again, and if you have not already removed the memorandum from your files, to ask you to do so. To reduce your trouble to a minimum I enclose a card which you need only post after granting my request.

Mrs. Howells joins me in cordial regards. We often talk of your pleasant visit last summer. This year we go to Conanicut, near Newport, for our outing.

Yours sincerely
W. D. Howells.

1. According to a letter from B. H. Ticknor to Howells of 2 February 1877 (MH), Howard M. Ticknor had applied for a foreign service appointment at Rome; Howells was asked to support the application by a private letter to President Hayes.

2. Horatio S. Noyes (1814?–1883), Elinor Howells' uncle and cousin of R. B. Hayes, was a businessman in Springfield, Massachusetts, Chicago, and Newtonville, Massachusetts. He had been editor of the Boston *Daily News* (1873–1874). An obituary by Howells appeared in the Newton *Journal*, 18 August 1883.

3. The minor foreign appointment for Howells had developed into consideration of him as minister to Switzerland. See Howells to his father, 31 December 1876, n. 1, and 8 April and 22 April 1877; also *Twain-Howells*, p. 174. As for the senior Howells' promotion, Rogers replied to Howells, 10 April 1877 (MH), recommending that formal application and recommendations be made by friends "according to the new regulations governing the Civil Service of the Government." Nearly a year later, 31 March 1878 (MH), Howells was still cautioning his father about entertaining hopes for the new appointment, but a few days later, 3 April 1878 (MH; *Life in Letters*, I, 250–51), Howells congratulated his father on the appointment having been made. In late May or early June 1878 the elder Howells took up his new post at Toronto. Rogers was at this time Hayes' private secretary.

8 APRIL 1877, CAMBRIDGE, TO WILLIAM C. HOWELLS

...The Atlantic Monthly....
Cambridge, Mass. April 8, 1877.

Dear father:

I telegraphed you yesterday of Winny's safe arrival, and I suppose she is writing her aunties of her experience in getting here. The lady with her was very kind, and it seemed a most fortunate arrangement for Winny. Now that we have her back, we realize how much we have missed her. She seems larger, and much more mature in her manners, and we both think her greatly improved. Of course she is still rather languid and tired, but she promises us red cheeks as soon as she is rested. John and Pillà are in raptures over her, and we are a very happy and united family.—We have got Annie's spoons and silk in the house, but I shall not send them till I have explicit instructions from you how to do it. Winny's things came through without being opened, and she could have brought Elinor's dress as well as not, but I am glad you did not send it if you felt it to be any risk to you. I wish you would not give any more of those letters to travellers for inspectors: I'm afraid it may sometime get you into trouble, for people are very unscrupulous, and if the bearer of a letter from you *were* found to be smuggling, it would be your disgrace. Let me earnestly beg you to refuse absolutely all applications for such letters. It wont hurt people to have their trunks opened if they've nothing dutiable in them. Do think of this.—Tell me what sort of document to send with the silver and silk, to be shown to the Canadian customs.—Toronto, by your showing, seems quite as desirable as Montreal, but is it vacant, and is there any real prospect of your advancement to the post? I hope you wont be annoyed by the newspaper mention of my name for the Swiss mission.[1] No intimation has reached me from Washington that I was considered for the place; and I should of course decline it if your promotion to the first vacancy were not promised. But it isn't likely to be offered, and I don't know how any talk of it got into the papers.—I believe there is no other news. We all send love.

Your affectionate son
Will.

1. See Howells to Rogers, 7 April 1877, n. 3.

9 April 1877, Cambridge, to Rutherford B. Hayes

Cambridge, April 9, 1877.

Dear Mr. President:

Your kind note brought me a greater regret than I like to tell, for I had hoped that I was at least not too late in naming Mr. Lowell to you.[1]

I now enclose a letter from my friend and his, Mr. Norton, in regard to the matter of Lowell's appointment to another place. If England is also filled or spoken for, I am still anxious that your administration should be connected with so great and honored a name as Lowell's, and I suggest that he be remembered in connection with the Hague or with Brussels. I mention these places, but I wont limit you to them! Indeed, I feel more strongly than I write in regard to this matter. You know Lowell as our first literary man, but without his acquantance, you cannot know how much more of a man than that he is. I don't urge him; that isn't fit for him or you; but you can be sure that there is no man in the country, who by social, legal and literary training could do us half so much honor abroad as Lowell.

—Elinor opened your letter, and read it aloud. The children were all for starting at once to Washington.[2] In the meantime we thank you cordially for your kind invitation, and hope some time to profit by it. With our united regards to all,

> Yours ever
> W. D. Howells.

1. On 4 April 1877 (draft at MH; *Life in Letters*, I, 234) Howells had written Hayes that Lowell "would accept the mission to Spain." On 7 April 1877 (MH) Hayes replied: "I am sorry we did not know the fact you mention. Mr Evarts recommended an app't for Spain a few days ago, and I assented. I am not sure that Mr E. would have desired your friend, but &c &c." On the same day (OFH) Norton wrote Howells that Lowell would not be disinclined to go to England or anywhere else. This is the letter referred to in the next sentence.

2. In his letter of the seventh Hayes invited the Howellses to visit "at our new home," the White House.

22 APRIL 1877, CAMBRIDGE, TO WILLIAM C. HOWELLS

> ... *The Atlantic Monthly*....
> *Cambridge, Mass.* April 22, 1877.

Dear father:

I wrote to Annie on Friday, but had only one thing to say. I hope that the paper which she thought obligatory turns out not to be so. In any case I don't see how it could have any legal force, though she ought not to refuse any the less on that account to sign it.[1] We are both very glad that Annie is pleased with the spoons, which we thought extremely pretty. I thought, as Aurelia does, that the marking was quite like that on grandmother's spoons.

You see the Swiss mission has been given to a Mr. Schneider of Chicago.[2] I suppose I might have had it if I had tried for it, but I don't regret that the faint annoying hope that it might be offered in such a way as to make acceptance possible, is gone.—I am going to edit for Osgood a library of autobiography.[3] That has always been my favorite reading, and I shall have both pleasure and profit in the work I hope. It may run to fifty volumes like Chance Acq.

—Did you see that disgusting ¶ in the Tribune in which poor Winny and her sonnet were dragged out before the public?[4] I don't know when any-thing has vexed me more. We were especially trying not to have any publicity about it, and we shall not let her see the silly notice.

We are all well and unite in love to all of you.

> Your affectionate son
> Will.

1. Perhaps a prenuptial declaration that her children would be baptized and nurtured as Catholics.

2. George Schneider (1823–1905), president of the National Bank of Illinois (1871–1897), declined the appointment. See Howells to Rogers, 7 April 1877, n. 3.

3. See Howells to T. W. Higginson, 2 July 1877, for the series of "Choice Autobiographies."

4. The paragraph in the New York *Tribune* has not been located.

25 APRIL 1877, CAMBRIDGE, TO FRANCIS J. GARRISON

Memorandum. . . . H. O. Houghton & Co. . . .
Cambridge, Mass. April 25, 1877
To Mr. Garrison

I thought the close of the S. Carolinian's[1] paper just right. his painting that picture of Southern luxury, and then with one dash recognizing the fact that it was not at its best worth what it cost, seemed to me to say much more than could otherwise have been said.[2]

W. D. H.

1. Belton O. Townsend; see Howells to Townsend, 19 December 1874, n. 1. In a letter to Warner, 4 February 1877 (CtHT), Howells described Townsend as "a young fellow who has never been out of South Carolina, but who, as he wrote me, had 'read himself out of all sympathy with his section and its political and social theories.' "

2. Howells is writing of "South Carolina Society," *Atlantic*, June 1877, of which the closing sentence reads: "It often strikes me, as I think of the intense enjoyment of the olden time, that perhaps just as the strongest force in physics is evolved from the greatest consumption of material, so it is ordained in human affairs that the most exquisite happiness shall be founded on the intensest misery of others."

28 MAY 1877, CAMBRIDGE, TO RUTHERFORD B. HAYES

. . . The Atlantic Monthly. . . .
Cambridge, Mass. May 28, 1877

Dear Mr. President:

Mr Lowell came on Saturday to tell me that he had declined the Austrian mission. That is his affair, and of course I have nothing to say, but as to my part in applying to you it seems due to myself, as well as to you, that I should assure you that I never should have written to you as I did if I could have expected this result. I could not consult him directly, but I had every reason to believe that he would accept. I am now only sorry to have troubled you for nothing.[1]

If you are coming to Boston on the 17ᵗʰ of June will you kindly let me know? It would make Elinor and me very happy if you would stay with us while you are hereabouts, and we should be doubly happy if you brought Mrs Hayes with you.—We hear it rumored also, that you may be in Cambridge on the 27th at the Commencement. Can you let me know if this is true?

Very truly yours
W. D. Howells.

1. Beginning with a letter from Howells to Hayes of 4 April (draft at MH; *Life in Letters*, I, 234), a number of letters (MH, OFH) give some of the particulars of the negotiations with Howells as intermediary. In *Literary Friends and Acquaintance*, HE, pp. 200–201, Howells gives a simplified account, but he adds the detail that after Lowell called on him and refused the Austrian appointment, they talked for a while of other things; upon leaving, Lowell "said with a sigh of vague reluctance, 'I *should* like to see a play of Calderon'...."

5 JUNE 1877, CAMBRIDGE, TO MONCURE D. CONWAY

...The Atlantic Monthly....
Cambridge, Mass. June 5, 1877.

Dear Conway:

Having at once accepted your article,[1] I felt that you must somehow be at peace about it, and so treated myself easily as to announcing the fact. Just when I can print it, I can't now say, but I will let you know so that you can "simultane", and I will send you a duplicate proof for that purpose.[2] I shall be glad to see your name in the Atlantic again, and I wish that when now and then a book of peculiar interest, and not likely to be reprinted here, comes out in London, you would make a paper, with extracts, on it. They would not pay a great deal for that kind of work, but then it would not be very hard to do.

—I hope that by this time Mrs. Conway is nearly well again. There is nothing like moving into a new house to bring on impending disasters, and the only advantage is that you have greater comforts and alleviations about you. We are just leaving ours, to go and batten on the seaside near Newport for three months. I dare say you know Conanicut Island; we go into a farmhouse, there.—Fiske is to employ the summer in building a new house (for *his* wife to break down in,) on the same street where he now lives.[3] He talked at one time of buying mine, which I should have been willing to sell in order to place myself in the country near Cambridge.—Our Winifred spent the winter in Quebec with her grandfather, for the sake of the French, and came home in April, curiously grown and quieted. John announced the other day that he was going to hurry up and perfect himself in base-ball, so as to be able to enter Harvard! You see how high our standard is.

Elinor joins me in best love to you and Mrs. Conway.

Yours ever
W. D. Howells.

1. "The Romance of a Family," *Atlantic*, July 1878, drawn largely from Joseph L. Chester, *Some Account of the Taylor Family* (1875).

2. No British publication has been located.

3. John Fiske, who was living at 4 Berkeley Street, planned to build a new house at 22 Berkeley Street. See John S. Clark, *Life and Letters of John Fiske* (Boston: Houghton Mifflin, 1917), II, 79–81.

19 June 1877, Montreal, to Elinor M. Howells

Steamboat Montreal,
Montreal, June 19, 1877.

Dear Elinor:

I arrived at 9 this morning after a very prosperous and comfortable journey.[1] But I dreamed as much as if I were at Conanicut, and all night long it was the children, the children, the children. (My *waking* thoughts are for *you!*) I was so tired that I got a fair amount of sleep, and had a capital breakfast at St. Alban's.—All the people on the boat here are the same, and I am hand and glove with the porter. It is a lovely day, and though hot in the sun, there is a delicious breeze from the river. Montreal *is* a beautiful place.—At the book store, where I asked *incognito*, they told me that the Canadian edition of my books had an *immense* sale. They don't keep Osgood's any more! Isn't it too bad?[2]

I telegraphed father that I should be at Quebec by the boat to-morrow morning. I'm going to *dress* on the boat, for I don't suppose they've house-room. I saw by the "Sentinel" that Sam, Joe and Eliza started for Q. last week.[3]—Everything here seems so like other summer days that I fancy you and the chicks are somewhere about the boat; and I feel like jumping to look if Bua's in danger. Dear Boy! I hope he's well and *good*. I *know* the rest are well. Those two girls are models, and so is John. Love to them all, and to you. I'll write to-morrow after the wedding.

Your
W. D. H.

I send some *oars* to the boys from Newport. But Bua must wait till I get back. I'll enclose a scrap from the Boston Herald.[4]

1. Howells took the route via Rutland and Burlington, a trip of about eleven hours.

2. Belford Brothers of Toronto published pirated editions of *Their Wedding Journey* and *A Chance Acquaintance* in 1876.

3. A brief note appeared in the Ashtabula *Sentinel*, 14 June 1877.
4. The clipping is no longer extant and has not been identified.

2 JULY 1877, CAMBRIDGE, TO WILLIAM C. HOWELLS

> *. . . The Atlantic Monthly. . . .*
> *Cambridge, Mass.* July 2, 1877.

Dear father:

I am back at Conanicut again after a most exciting week. Tuesday morning I went down to meet the President 25 miles below Boston, and breakfasted with him, and afterwards rode with his son in the procession. Elinor came up at noon, and we went with the Hayes party to the concert that night. Elinor attended the Commencement exercises with them Wednesday, and I dined with the President at the Mayor's[1] dinner in the evening. He invited us to go with their party to Providence and Newport, but we couldn't. So on Friday we went in to meet them at the Governor's[2] in Newport, and presented Bua and Mil. They were most cordial at all times. I was also introduced to Schurz and Evarts.[3]— You can't imagine the cordiality with which Hayes has been received. I never saw so popular a man, and I greatly admired the perfect taste and sense of all that he said and did.—Probably we shall go to visit at the White House this winter or fall. There was no chance to allude to you during this reception; but I've no doubt that with what has been already done, you are in the way of succeeding to any vacancy above you.[4]

—Willy Mead[5] is with us here for a few days, and we are all very well. We are glad to hear that Annie is so comfortably settled, and long to have a letter from her. I know you must miss her at Quebec.

Elinor and all the children send love to all of you.

> Your affectionate son
> **Will.**

1. Frederick O. Prince (1818–1899), lawyer, graduated from Harvard in 1836. An active Democrat, he was elected mayor of Boston for several terms beginning in 1876.

2. Charles C. Van Zandt (1830–1894), lawyer, was active in state politics from 1855 and served as chairman of the state delegation to the convention that nominated Hayes. He was the Republican governor of Rhode Island (1877–1880).

3. Carl Schurz and William M. Evarts (1818–1901), secretary of state under Hayes (1877–1881).

4. See Howells to Rogers, 7 April 1877, n. 3.

5. William R. Mead, Elinor Howells' brother.

2 July 1877, Cambridge, to Thomas W. Higginson

> ... *The Atlantic Monthly*. ...
> *Cambridge, Mass.* July 2, 1877.

Dear Col. Higginson:

I am very greatly obliged by your kindness, and thank you for the offer of your own books as well as for the access to the Redwood Library.[1] I have Mme La Rochejacquelin, and Cellini (an old friend); the Montpensier I already know of through your delightful papers.[2] I have prepared the "shrill Wilhelmina," as Carlyle calls her,[3] for the first set of four autos. which I shall publish. Her of Anspach I've not seen (though I've sent to England for the book) nor Mme. Roland nor Burroughs.[4]

—I find that I shall have to make a distinction between autos. and memoirs, and perhaps reject the latter, though this is a point upon which I sh'd like to talk with you. The richness of the field is immense in autos. alone. I get so much interested in the characters that I'm afraid I shall make my essays (which include a sequel to each auto.) perhaps too full. On Goldoni the essay ran to 117 of these pages.[5] I try to include collateral matter throwing light on the autobiographer and his time and place.

The first four volumes will be published early in October: 2 of M. of Bairaith, 1 of Goldoni, 1 of Lord Herbert and Thomas Ellwood, the Quaker.[6] I shall try to give in each issue a variety of character, calling and nationality.

> Yours truly
> **W. D. Howells.**

1. The Redwood Library in Newport was founded in 1730 as a philosophical society and later named after the philanthropist Abraham Redwood (1709–1788). Howells wanted to use it while vacationing in Conanicut and working on a series of "Choice Autobiographies."

2. The Marquise de Larochejaquelein (1772–1857) published her *Mémoires* in 1815; Benvenuto Cellini's (1500–1571) autobiography appeared in 1730; Duchesse Louise d'Orléans Montpensier (1627–1693), "la Grande Madamoiselle," wrote *Mémoires* published in 1815. Higginson's essay on her first appeared in the *Atlantic*, July 1858, and then in his *Atlantic Papers* (1871) under the title "Madamoiselle's Campaigns."

3. In chapter 1, book 4, of the *History of Friedrich II. of Prussia* (1858–1865), Carlyle refers to the *Mémoires* (1812) of Frederica Sophia Wilhelmina (1709–1758): "Among these Books, touching on Friedrich's childhood, and treating of his Father's Court, there is hardly above one that we can characterise as fairly human: the Book written by his little Sister Wilhelmina, when she grew to size and knowledge of good and evil;—and this, of what flighty uncertain nature it is, the world partly knows." He speaks of its author as "a most shrill female soul busy with intense earnestness here....[The book] exaggerates dreadfully, in its shrill female way...."

4. The *Mémoires* of Elizabeth Craven, Margravine of Anspach-Baireuth (1720–1828) appeared in 1826; Madame Manon-Jeanne Philipon Roland (1754–1793) wrote

Mémoires, published in 1864. Howells is probably referring to the *Memoir of Stephen Burroughs* (1798–1804), an American criminal autobiography.

5. The Goldoni essay took thirteen pages in the *Atlantic* and twenty-six in the book.

6. For the actual publication dates of the "Choice Autobiographies" and the appearance of some of the introductory essays in the *Atlantic,* see Gibson-Arms, *Bibliography,* pp. 104–5.

4 AUGUST 1877, CAMBRIDGE, TO WILLIAM C. HOWELLS

> ... *The Atlantic Monthly. . . .*
> *Cambridge, Mass.* Aug. 4, 1877.

Dear father:

I sent you last Tuesday a letter from Mr. Rogers, the President's private secretary, which I hope you got, and which was no doubt highly satisfactory. It seems to me a pretty good indication that you will get the place when Gen. Dart resigns.[1] I shall write Mr. Rogers, to-day, thanking him for his friendly interest in the matter.—We are at last at an end of our foggy weather, and have come out in the most brilliant air imaginable. It is really delicious. Yesterday we went for the first time to see the famous game of Polo, a sort of croquet or *shinny,* played by men mounted on ponies. I enjoyed it much more than I expected, and the sight of all the rich and handsome spectators in their carriages was something very impressive in its way. Newport is quite a revelation, and if I had plenty of money I should like nothing better than to see it thoroughly for one season—and then never see it again. A great and cheap delight of the place is the boat-sailing, in the Bay, and out on the ocean. The boats are very broad, and rigged with one enormous sail, which is simply and easily managed. If I lived here, I should certainly own a boat.—I enclose a sheet of the September Atlantic, with a notice of the count's book.[2] It's a pity he shouldn't make a thorough work on proverbs. This notice must not be reprinted or publicly used in any way before the 20th of August, when the number is published. Don't let the count forget the play I asked about.[3]

All join me in love to all.

> Your aff'te son
> **Will.**

1. William A. Dart had been consul general at Montreal since 16 April 1869. The difference in salary was large: in 1874, $4,000 for the Montreal post and $1,500 for Quebec and Toronto. See Howells to Rogers, 7 April 1877, n. 3.

2. In his review (*Atlantic,* September 1877) of *Popular Sayings from Old Iberia* (2d ed.) by Fieldat [Count Premio Real] and Aitiaiche [Anne Howells Fréchette] Howells uses the phrase "it is a pity" that the book is not longer, and he notes that "one of the editors is a Spaniard (*Fieldat* is the armorial legend of an ancient Andalusian house)." Count Premio Real (José Antonio de Lavelle y Romero) was the

Spanish consul general in Quebec and a close friend of Howells' father and sisters. On 14 February 1879 (MH) he wrote to Howells: "I would like your writings & magazine to act as carrier pigeons of literature between the old and new worlds, and thus widen their field of usefulness."

3. *Un drama nuevo* (1867), which Howells translated as *Yorick's Love*. It is generally regarded as the masterpiece of Manuel Tamayo y Baus (1829–1898), who wrote more than fifty plays during his lifetime.

28 AUGUST 1877, CAMBRIDGE, TO BELTON O. TOWNSEND

> *...The Atlantic Monthly....*
> *Cambridge, Mass.* August 28, 1877.

My dear friend:

You must forgive me for letting your letter go so long unanswered: it was not an easy letter to answer, especially when I must return your lines. They express, or rather intimate a deep and true feeling, but they are not poetry. That is final with me, against them; you would not yourself have me appeal from that perception to my regard for you.[1] I have no doubt that your destiny is literature, but that it is poetry I am not all sure; in fact I do doubt that. You have already made an impression in the magazine which few men of your age have done,[2] and you have but to go on in the course you have taken. I hope still to use one or two more of your papers. Do you know that they have been made the subject of wide editorial comment in the press?[3]

Why not try something in the way of a very realistic short story of South Carolinian life?[4] I am sure that you have the material for it.— Beware of forsaking yourself on expression: the simplest word is the best.—I earnestly hope that no harm may come to you from your Atlantic papers, which several Southerners have praised to me for their truth.

May I beg you to make my respectful compliments to your mother?

> Very cordially yours
> W. D. Howells.

1. See Howells to Townsend, 19 December 1874, n. 1.
2. See Howells to Garrison, 25 April 1877.
3. An early, rather negative, comment on the first article on South Carolina by Townsend appeared in the *Nation*, 15 February 1877. Howells may be referring to later ones that have not been identified.
4. No such story has been located.

2 SEPTEMBER 1877, CAMBRIDGE, TO JOHN HAY

> The Atlantic Monthly,
> Cambridge, Mass., Sept. 2, 1877.

My dear Hay:

Some day I shall make myself very happy by visiting you, but it will not be on the *premiere* of my play.[1] Suppose the thing failed upon the stage? What would you do with my remains? No, no! I wouldn't see the play till its success was assured, even for the pleasure of seeing you—and I can't say more than that. But you and Mrs. Hay be in the claque—I am sure that if you smile upon it it *must* prosper,—and if I am called out, you speak for me. If it *does* succeed, and you keep it in Cleveland a fortnight, why I may ac—— But this is folly.

I thank you with all my heart for the kind things you say and feel, and I present Mrs. Hay with my grateful duty. Mrs. Howells will be most glad to come with me when I come. She is now on an island near Newport, where we have all been for the summer, since June 6th. I'm afraid your friend the future Bishop[2] may have called and found my house locked up. I shall be glad to see him if he turns up.—I never told you how very much we liked your Astor[3] whom you sent to me. I asked him to lunch,—to Mrs. Howells' despair. "Never mind," I said, "I'll have Smith send the lunch out from Boston." (Smith is the old colored caterer, friend of Sumner;[4] character; sayer of things: "Madam, do you wish me to *do* it, or to *over*do it?" he asked of a lady intending a party.) Smith named over a lot of things for my lunch. "Oh, good gracious, that won't do," said I, beginning to rend my garments and looking round for ashes to strew upon my head. "I'm to have the richest man in America to lunch. Now, what?" "My dear sir," said Smith, "you want the simplest lunch that can be got." It was a success.

> Yours ever,
> W. D. Howells.

1. *A Counterfeit Presentment* was played in Cleveland, opening 22 October. See Howells to Osgood, 28 October 1877, n. 2.

2. Craufurd Tait, M. A. of Christ Church, Oxford, and later a curate, died in 1878.

3. William Waldorf Astor.

4. Joshua B. Smith, lifelong friend and defender of Charles Sumner (1811–1874), the antislavery senator.

2 SEPTEMBER 1877, CAMBRIDGE, TO WILLIAM C. HOWELLS

. . . The Atlantic Monthly. . . .
Cambridge, Mass. Sept. 2, 1877.

Dear father:

I don't now remember how it was I failed to write you last Sunday, but I hope you took it for granted we were well, and did not feel troubled. I left the family at Conanicut yesterday, and came up for a week or ten days preparatory to our final return, which will be about the 20th. I shall be glad, as I usually am, after a season of boarding, and so I think will Elinor, but the children, even Winnie, are much attached to the island, and will be sorry to come away.

I got a letter from Vic about my sending Joe tickets for my play in Cleveland,[1] and not sending them to Sam. I think that on all accounts when there is business of this sort to be written about, it will be best for you hereafter to write the latter. I don't resent it from Vic, but it inevitably leads to unpleasantness, and it seems to me your affair. In this case I thought of sending Joe and not Sam, because I could introduce Joe to the actor[2] and do them both a pleasure; if I sent Sam, I felt that it would be a burden all round. However, I will see that he has a ticket, and some one will have to pay his way to and from Cleveland. It isn't that I don't care for him, but it seems to me that as he is no longer a child we might act without reference to his exaggerated sensitiveness in such a matter.—I hope you are not thinking of taking him into the consulate at Montreal, if you get that place. He has no education to make him useful, and he would load you up with his family and be no end of trouble and expense. Besides, it would be contrary to the spirit of the service for you to employ him. If you wish to help him, it would be far better to pay him $500 or $600 a year outright, and let him stay at home. I speak frankly in your own interest, for I think this would be the worst thing that could happen to you both. You *know* that at his time of life, he cannot form habits of punctuality and industry; you could not depend on him, and he would probably involve you in some trouble. Moreover, he could be of no use to himself. I earnestly trust that you wont let yourself be governed by a mistaken sense of kindness in the matter. With best love to all,

Your aff'te son
Will.

1. See Howells to Hay, 2 September 1877, n. 1.

2. Lawrence Barrett (1838–1891), well-known actor and producer. Besides his frequent appearances in standard plays, he showed a marked interest in new works by young and comparatively unknown authors. Perhaps he met Howells through Edwin Booth, with whom he had played as early as 1857.

11 September 1877, Cambridge, to William H. Bishop

Cambridge, Mass., Sept. 11, 1877.

Dear Mr. Bishop:[1]

I wonder if I can explain to you a project of mine?

I have long wanted to find somebody in New York who could treat the aesthetic interests of that city in a monthly paper in the *Atlantic*. I do not mean that he shall *report* literary, social, dramatic, musical and artistic events, but that he shall somehow express or distil the vital essence of those subjects, and give us that in the casual, touch and go manner of a French *chronique*. Anything in the way of *news* would be stale by the time we could print it, but what is said or thought about the news is more durable, and can be enjoyed long after the news is old. Imagine yourself still a cultivated and amiable inhabitant of Milwaukee; imagine yourself also the New York friend of your Milwaukee self. Such accounts of New York matters as you would write your Milwaukee self are probably what I should want for the magazine. Do you see?

Several have tried this, but they have all been put to death for their failure: it is one of those fabled emulations in which the penalty for failure is necessarily death, with confiscation; but if you would like to try it, I should be glad. I know it makes a man heavy to charge him to be light, but your success will largely depend upon your volatility. Cut as close to the quick as you like, but no drop of blood, mind; no hacking; and for the most, be good-natured. Also, for your own sake, be unknown;[2] that alone can render you free. Let me hear from you.

Very truly yours,
W. D. Howells.

1. William H. Bishop (1847–1928) had already secured serialization of *Detmold: A Romance*, which was to begin in the *Atlantic*, December 1877. Author of many novels, he also taught modern languages at Yale (1893–1902) and served as a U. S. consul at Genoa (1903–1904) and Palermo (1905–1910).
2. "Open Letters from New York," under the pseudonym "Raymond Westbrook," appeared in the *Atlantic*, January–July 1878.

14 October 1877, Cambridge, to A. W. Whelpley

. . . The Atlantic Monthly. . . .
Cambridge, Mass. Oct. 14, 1877.

Dear Mr. Whelpley:[1]

A thousand thanks for your very kind note, which was most welcome; though I had heard from Mr. Barrett of the non-failure of the piece, I was extremely glad of a word from an outsider.[2] Mr. Barrett has telegraphed Osgood that every seat for last night was sold. I don't see that I could ask anything better, except that the play should be better.

Thank all my good friends for me. I can't tell you what a pleasure it is to me that this pleasant thing should have happened in the metropolis of my own State. Once Ohioan, always Ohioan—without prejudice to Boston.

Will you do me a favor? I should like a play-bill of the first night, if you can find one.[3]

Yours sincerely
W. D. Howells.

1. A. W. Whelpley (1831–1900), a native of New York City, went to Cincinnati in the 1850s, where he was employed in the printing and publishing business. In 1886 he was made librarian of the Cincinnati Public Library, a position he held until his death. See C. T. Greve, *Centennial History of Cincinnati and Representative Citizens* (Chicago: Biographical Publishing Co., 1904), II, 440–41.

2. Whelpley wrote Howells twice on 11 October 1877 (MH), the first letter commenting on the favorable critical reception of *A Counterfeit Presentment* in Cincinnati, and the second enclosing a review by J. J. Piatt. Howells replied on 17 October (OHi), in part commenting: "Certainly no one was ever more kindly treated than I by my Cincinnati critics." The same day Whelpley wrote once again, this time to apologize for the adverse review in the Cincinnati *Times*: "I expressed my *regrets* so louldy [sic], that I had an interview with the writer, who disclaimed any intention of disparaging the play—etc....I have ascertained through my reporter friends, on comparing notes, that the article was penned without the play being witnessed—He never *saw* it, & I am confident never *read* it...." Besides Piatt's notice in the *Commercial*, there appeared a review of Howells' play by his Ohio friend Samuel Reed in the *Gazette*. See also Piatt to Howells, 17 October 1877 (MH) and Reed to Howells, 20 October 1877 (MH).

3. A scrapbook of playbills is in the Howells Collection (MH).

21 OCTOBER 1877, CAMBRIDGE, TO CHARLES D. WARNER

...The Atlantic Monthly....
Cambridge, Mass. Oct. 21, 1877.

My dear Warner:

The bear-story is amazing good and I want awfully to have your name to it. But I can understand just why you don't want to put it. Can't we get over the difficulty by saying at the start "My friend said," and then go on and give the fable, which we would call "Killing a Bear"? Or still better, can't you go on and tell three or four more Adirondack lies about as long as this, which we could use as the first of the series?[1] The region is the home of falsehood, and the whole subject richly susceptible of burlesque. You could do Shooting a Loon, Striking a Trout, Lost in the Woods, etc.—*all* lies.[2] I see a great opening for a book that would tickle everybody, and run like My Summer in a Garden.[3] Do think of it.

We may be kept a day or two over our time. Friends seem to be impending, who may detain us here, though probably they will blow over. I'll let you know promptly.[4]

Mrs. Howells has Mrs. Warner's very kind letter, and will answer it in person very soon.

Do you know that "Being a Boy" is one of the best names I ever heard of? I long to see the book.[5]—I hope to read my essay on Gibbon in Hartford as a lecture, if Mr. Gage can appoint an early date for me.[6] I've found him very interesting, and I admire him no end.

Yours ever
W. D. Howells.

P. S. Aldrich's story will tell better as a book than in numbers.[7] Knowing the end from the beginning as I did, I couldn't feel it as you did, bit by bit. But I agree with you that the first part was deliciously fresh.

1. The problem was that Warner did not wish to put his name to a first-person story that was not true. It was solved by an editorial note at the beginning of "How I Killed a Bear," *Atlantic*, January 1878, the first of "The Adirondacks Verified" series. The note explains that former explorers had made the region "tame and commonplace," but that these sketches treat it "as in some degree the home of romance and adventure." Each article in the series carries Warner's name.

2. "Shooting a Loon" was not published. Among the six essays of the series were "A Fight with a Trout," March 1878, and "Lost in the Woods," February 1878. The six printed sketches, along with two new ones, were published as *In the Wilderness* (1878).

3. *My Summer in a Garden* (1870), by C. D. Warner, was so popular that by 1895 it would go to 44 printings.

4. Howells first suggested visiting Warner in the latter part of October, remarking that "till my taxes are paid (Oct. 10) I could not come unless I came on a public subscription." See Howells to Warner, 30 September 1877 (CtHT). The day after the present letter, he asked Osgood (MH) for $50 "to keep my house from burning up uninsured." The visit finally took place on 26 October.

5. Howells reviewed Warner's *Being a Boy* (1878) in the *Atlantic*, December 1877—"as something which is as good in quality as it is new in kind."

6. The Edward Gibbon lecture was given 12 December, and the essay first appeared in the *Atlantic*, January 1878. William Leonard Gage (1832–1889) was a Unitarian clergyman in Hartford (1868–1884).

7. *The Queen of Sheba* (1878) appeared in the *Atlantic*, July–November 1877. Howells reviewed it there January 1878, praising it as a "romance" with "singular freshness and interest...."

28 OCTOBER 1877, CAMBRIDGE, TO JAMES R. OSGOOD

> *... The Atlantic Monthly. . . .*
> *Cambridge, Mass.* Oct. 28, 1877.

Dear Osgood:

I shall be glad to come to the lunch. When (what hour) and where is it to be?—I got your letter[1] yesterday at Hartford, and referred it to Warner and Clemens. Warner, I think, will come; but Clemens, who said you were the best publisher who ever breathed, and that you could have everything he owned, declared that he could *not.*

I return Mr. Rhodes's letter, whom please give my cordial thanks and regards. I have glowing letters from Hay, Mason and Barrett, which I'll show you.[2]

> Yours ever
> W. D. Howells.

I have got the Alfieris. *Could* you hold back Goldoni till Dec. 1st, and Gibbon till Jan. 1st? I don't see how I'm to get Marmomtel ready, with the corrections to my play, for another month yet.[3]

1. Osgood's letter has not been found.
2. On 23 October 1877 (MH) John Hay wrote to Howells from Cleveland with some pleasure about *A Counterfeit Presentment.* "It seemed to me almost too good to act—but I see my mistake now—it is an admirable acting piece...." Hay also mentions Frank Mason's editorial in the Cleveland *Leader* of 23 October. On 26 October (MH) Mason himself wrote to Howells more enthusiastically than Hay, but he noted the defect in the abruptness of the revulsion of feeling shown by Constance jn the final scene which Barrett was revising. Barrett wrote frequently to Howells; the letter referred to here may be that of 24 October (MH) in which he said, "the occasion was a brilliant one.... The applause... only disturbed by the laughter." Rhodes, whose letter has not been found, remains unidentified.
3. See Howells to Higginson, 2 July 1877, on the series of "Choice Autobiographies."

14 NOVEMBER 1877, CAMBRIDGE, TO LAWRENCE BARRETT

> *... The Atlantic Monthly. . . .*
> *Cambridge, Mass.* Nov. 14, 1877.

Dear Mr. Barrett:

I mail you herewith the new act.[1] I need not lecture upon it. You will see what it is. Understand that I don't hold you bound to like it, and above all that I don't expect you, or desire you to accept it if you don't like it.

I have worked with the idea of telling the story more fully and of developing Bartlett's character by certain situations in which I leave almost everything to your acting. You will see what I mean when you come to the love-making which must be made love-making, as concerns the audience, and kept from seeming love-making, to Constance.[2] I think that in these scenes you have the opportunity for some of the finest effects in the play.

Of course I want all the suggestion and criticism you can give.

We had a lovely visit from the Hays, and much more talk about the comedy in Cleveland than I can report.[3] They spoke with unqualified praise of your acting, which they said interpreted the most delicate shades of character, while it gave the broad effects with force and vigor. They spoke of uncommon *quality* in the audiences drawn by the comedy and yet of the capability the play has of pleasing the popular element.— Mrs. Hay says the applause often started from the galleries. I asked particularly about the song,[4] and Hay said you did it charmingly, and with the prettiest effect.—In a letter recently received from Miss Constance Fennimore Woolson[5] (the writer,) she says: "Letters from Cleveland speak of your play with enthusiasm: it was greatly admired by the best people they have out there. 'I don't know when I've seen anything better or brighter,' writes a lady whom I consider an excellent and fastidious judge."

—What pleases me about all the praise the play gets, both on your account and my own is that people seem honestly *glad* of an American comedy that makes its way without farcical or melodramatic effects. Does n't this indicate a great field before us? You have your finger on the patient's pulse and can tell how much of his joy is real & how much is affected.

The Hays were full of kind words about you, and after listening to them, I almost felt that I had seen you act. They had not a word of adverse criticism. I have broken ground on the Spanish play.[6]

—I infer from all the notices that the play succeeds as a comedy of *character*. In this direction I have worked in the new act.

Can you do me the favor to send me a play bill from each place? I want to make a collection.[7] I shouldn't care for them with a second play.

Yours truly
W. D. Howells.

Sorry for your lame knee. Hope it's all right now.

Postscript.

The canvas on which Constance proposes to paint must be portentously large—say three or four feet by five. In drawing she must use a mahl-stick in her left hand to support her right.

The easel should stand so as to bring the canvas almost edgewise to the audience, and interpose it like a screen between her and Bartlett, where they stand before it, and General Wyatt where he sits beside his small table. This is mere suggestion—the way I imagined the scene.

I feel anxious about the General's *snore*. Pray have it a snore of the utmost possible refinement. If a sufficiently comical effect could be produced by his simply being discovered asleep when his paper drops, the snore might be omitted.[8] I may think of some better device to make Bartlett laugh and Constance angry if the act pleases you otherwise.

1. The new third act of *A Counterfeit Presentment* appears in the second issue of the 1877 edition. See W. J. Meserve, *The Complete Plays of W. D. Howells* (New York: New York University Press, 1960), pp. 90–99.

2. This scene occurs at the end of the third act, as a preparation for her acceptance of Bartlett. Barrett hesitated to use the new act in Indianapolis, but introduced it into the play in Detroit in December.

3. See Howells to Osgood, 28 October 1877, n. 2.

4. "Romance," a three-stanza song, is sung in the final act of *A Counterfeit Presentment*.

5. Constance Fenimore Woolson (1840–1894), novelist and close friend of Henry James. She had published *Castle Nowhere* (1875) and contributed to the *Atlantic*. Howells slightly misquotes her letter of 5 November 1877 (MH).

6. *Yorick's Love*.

7. See Howells to Whelpley, 14 October 1877, n. 3.

8. In the printed version the General's snore is described as "a loud, prolonged, and very stertorous respiration." See Meserve, *Complete Plays*, p. 97.

24 NOVEMBER 1877, CAMBRIDGE, TO WILLIAM C. HOWELLS

...The Atlantic Monthly....
Cambridge, Mass. Nov. 24, 1877.

Dear father:

I believe we have had no letter from you this week, but it is such a busy, bewildering time that I hardly know. Eight days ago, Will Dean's daughter Carol,[1] who has been going to school at Wellesley College, wrote that she had been sick, and would like to come to us for a few days change. She came, and we found that she had had facial paralysis from overstudy, I suppose; and Monday she was to go back, when she met a schoolmate at the station who told her that scarlet fever had broken out in the college, and so she came back to us. She had to have her clothes brought to our house, and you can imagine with what terror we received such a guest, and how anxious we still feel. Fortunately she had not met lately any of the girls who were taken. We don't know how long she will stay, but we hope she will go shortly after Thanksgiving, as we are then to have other company. She is a very heavy and frivolous girl, though well meaning enough, and the visit is of course a burden, especially when one thinks with what scanty welcome her people would receive one of us under the same circumstances. We feared a breaking-up of our family holidays when she came to school in the neighborhood, but the present case passes our wildest fears. I suppose it is right we should grin and bear it, or at least bear it.—Except for this, our life goes on as usual. We are extremely busy; and in my own case every year seems to increase my work: I used to hope that I could set some limit to it. The children are all getting on nicely in school, and but for the usual colds are well.

I enclose a proof of your little paper about the Indians.[2] I had expected to get it into the January number, but now I'm afraid it must go over till February. I suppose Elinor wrote Aurelia that the President had asked us to visit at the White House. We could not have afforded the visit and were obliged to decline.—I sent a package for Annie to your care, the other day. I hope it came safely. Did you get the Goldoni autobiography? If I were not so harassed with work, I should immensely enjoy doing those books. As it is they're a pleasure.[3]

We all send love to all of you.

Your aff'te son
Will.

I feel sorry to have written so grudgingly about poor Carol. But our lives are devoured by people we don't care for.

1. Caroline Dean, the daughter of Howells' cousin who lived in St. Paul, attended Wellesley College (1877–1879).
2. William C. Howells' paper on Indians appeared unsigned in "The Contributors' Club," *Atlantic*, March 1878. This essay (impatient with Canadian treatment of Indians as a model and scornful of Indians generally) may have resulted from Howells' asking the Fréchettes to write one in his letter to his father of 9 September 1877 (MH).
3. See Howells to Higginson, 2 July 1877.

27 NOVEMBER 1877, BOSTON, TO JAMES R. OSGOOD

... *James R Osgood & Co* ....
Boston, Nov. 27, *1877*

Dear Osgood:

On getting your long letter this morning,[1] I felt like instantly withdrawing all my copyrights from you, but the reflection that you were probably losing money on them restrained me. I have now no resource, but to write out to Barrett and request his mediation. I consider every thing you say about art-criticism as personal,[2] and I am very bitter about that stab at *plays* which their authors try to get written into public favor. That took me under the fifth rib.

However—and here my magnanimity walks in and floors you—I had after writing to you written a handsome notice of the River Path, the illustrations of which I greatly admire, though you may despise me for it.[3] —I'm sorry I can't see you for I had several exasperating things to say.—I am contriving a book on art criticism which I hope to fob upon you when you're in your cups, and simply ruin you.

Yours cordially ever
W. D. H.

1. Osgood's letter has not been found, nor his note about Barrett which Howells received later that day. This is mentioned in a second letter to Osgood, dated 27 November 1877 (NjP), characterizing the present letter as "a note intended to be of a humorous character."

2. The reference to Barrett is unclear, but apparently Osgood had been critical of Howells' venturing into the field of art criticism when he commented, in a letter to Osgood of 23 November 1877 (MH), on the "undertakerish sentimentality" of Miss Jessie Curtis's illustrations of Aldrich's *A Midnight Fantasy, and The Little Violinist.*

3. Howells reviewed Whittier's illustrated *The River Path*, published by J. R. Osgood & Co., in the *Atlantic*, January 1878: "the only unpleasing pictures in the book are Mr. Waud's helpless literalisms and Miss Curtis's extremely black eyelashed angels and cherubs."

2 DECEMBER 1877, CAMBRIDGE, TO EDMUND C. STEDMAN

... *The Atlantic Monthly.* ...
Cambridge, Mass. December 2, 1877.

My dear Stedman:

I send back your poem with great reluctance; it is one of the lightest, brightest, gracefullest, most musical things you have done; but I dare not publish it in The Atlantic, because thousands of people who never heard of Aucassin and Nicolette, and want a hell for their enemies, stand ready to attaint us of wickedness, and would treat your pretty poem as an attack on the trinity.[1] Print it in Scribner, or some orthodox paper, and it will be all right.

By all means let me have your tropical pieces.[2] Unless they fall strangely below your mark, I shall want them all.

Yours ever
W. D. Howells.

1. "Provençal Lovers: Aucassin and Nicolette" did not have magazine publication and first appeared in *Lyrics and Idylls with Other Poems* (1879). In the poem Aucassin argues that purgatory provides more delightful company than heaven.

2. The *Atlantic* published "Jamaica," February 1878, and "The Rose and the Jasmine," April 1878, two of the fifteen poems that were first grouped as "The Carib Sea" in *Poems Now First Collected* (1897). Another poem in the group, "The Creole Lover's Song," had already appeared in the *Atlantic*, April 1877.

19 DECEMBER 1877, CAMBRIDGE, TO CHARLES E. NORTON

...The Atlantic Monthly....
Cambridge, Mass. Dec. 19, 1877.

Dear Mr. Norton:

I send your proof,[1] which I have read through with the freshest pleasure in your narration, familiar as the facts largely were. It is lovely. And what a sweet and graceful and gracious speech you made the other night!—All sense of that and of other things was long blotted out for me by that hideous mistake of poor Clemens's.[2] As you have more than once expressed a kindness for him, you will like to know that before he had fairly touched his point, he felt the awfulness of what he was doing, but was fatally helpless to stop. He was completely crushed by it, and though it killed the joy of the time for me, I pitied him; for he *has* a good and reverent nature for good things, and his performance was like an effect of demonical possession. The worst of it was, I couldn't see any retrieval for him.

Yours truly
W. D. Howells.

1. "Venice and St. Mark's," *Atlantic*, February 1878.
2. Clemens' Whittier Birthday speech was delivered 17 December 1877, in honor of Whittier's seventieth birthday. Emerson, Longfellow, Holmes, Howells, and Whittier himself, sat at the head table. Clemens' idea had been to show three thirsty tramps, deadbeats, presenting themselves to a California miner as Emerson, Longfellow, and Holmes, before admitting to being impostors. The response of the public and of Clemens and Howells is fully described by Henry Nash Smith, " 'That Hideous Mistake of Poor Clemens's'," *Harvard Library Bulletin* 9 (1955), 145–80. See also *My Mark Twain*, in *Literary Friends and Acquaintance*, HE, pp. 293–97, and Howells to Clemens, 6 January 1878.

22 DECEMBER 1877, CAMBRIDGE, TO WILLIAM C. HOWELLS

...The Atlantic Monthly....
Cambridge, Mass. Dec. 22, 1877.

Dear father:

I would gladly do what you ask me in the way of writing to Mr. Rogers, but I know from Burchard Hayes's talk last summer that R. is held in no sort of esteem, and would not know anything about the probabilities in the case of Smith.[1] And there is nobody else at Washington to whom I could write. Please tell Aurelia that I think the publication of her notices may have been delayed in the Literary World by their devoting so great part of the last number to Whittier.[2] She certainly would be entitled by common usage to have the paper sent to her regularly, and she should write to request it. When Mr. Blanchette[3] comes I will do my best to put him in the way of seeing Mr. Parkman, but I don't see how I can do more than give him a letter, for I go so rarely to pay visits in Boston. We have very little family news, and I can scarcely rake up anything to say.—My lecture at Hartford was very well received, I'm told, and I certainly enjoyed giving it.[4] I shall send you soon the volume of Gibbon on which it was based. The series has not yet had a rapid sale, but Osgood is hopeful about it, and expects to make a good thing of it. Matters with the book trade are still, however, in a very discouraging state. The magazine, on the other hand is "chirking up," decidedly.

The children have got ready, as usual, for Christmas, and I am beginning to feel my customary sinking of heart at the approach of what Pil aptly calls the hollow-days. There should be no anniversaries for a man past thirty.—Joe sent me a scrap from some old diary of mine, the other day, written on New Years eve of 1853.[5] It was like my dead self speaking to me. Do you remember how you and I used to walk to and from that first house out of Jefferson, and I used to talk of writing a life of Cervantes?[6] It's all immensely melancholy to think about, but no doubt there is a meaning in all this business which we shall yet find out. —I like your lecture on printing very much.[7] It's capitally written.

All join me in dearest love.

Your aff'te son
Will.

1. Rutherford B. Hayes had offered the collectorship for the port of Chicago to William H. Smith in June 1877, but the incumbent in the post refused to resign. However, Smith apparently received the post about March 1878 and held it until 1883. Birchard Hayes (1853–1926), the president's son, graduated from Harvard Law School in 1877; later, as a lawyer, he specialized in real estate and taxes.

2. No signed notices by Aurelia appear in the *Literary World*, although each number contains several unsigned pieces, some of which may be hers.

3. Probably Joseph Goderic Blanchet (1829–1890), a member of the Canadian House of Commons (1867–1883).

4. See Howells to Warner, 21 October 1877, n. 6. The *Courant* noted the following day that the audience maintained a "breathless silence" throughout. See also *Twain-Howells*, p. 210.

5. The scrap, dated 1 January 1853, is inserted in "Diary and Spanish Exercises, 1850–1859" (MH) and reads in part: "The past—oh! thou dark mysterious realm of perished hopes and fears, how dear thou art! But I will not now lift the veil that palls thy solemn face, rather let me bend my knee at the shrine of futurity, and, fixing my eye on the day-star of hope, begin this year with new resolves and higher motives."

6. See *Impressions and Experiences* (1896), p. 9: "I had taught myself to read Spanish, in my passion for Don Quixote, and I was then, at the age of fifteen, preparing to write a life of Cervantes."

7. The elder Howells' lecture has not been identified; it was not printed in the Ashtabula *Sentinel*.

25 DECEMBER 1877, CAMBRIDGE, TO SAMUEL L. CLEMENS

> ...*The Atlantic Monthly*....
> *Cambridge, Mass*. Dec. 25, 1877.

My dear Clemens:

I was just about to ask you to let me postpone your story a month, because I found the Feb'y number overfull, and your paper had come last to hand. But I have no idea of dropping you out of the Atlantic, and Mr. Houghton has still less, if possible.[1] You are going to help and not hurt us many a year yet, if you will. Every one with whom I have talked about your speech regards it as a fatality—one of those sorrows into which a man walks with his eyes wide open, no one knows why. I believe that Emerson, Longfellow and Holmes themselves can easily conceive of it in that light, and while I think your regret does you honor and does you good, I don't want you to dwell too morbidly on the matter. Mr. Norton left a note on my table the other day, expressing just the right feeling towards you about it.[2] One of the most fastidious men here, who *read* the speech, saw no offense in it.[3] But I don't pretend not to agree with you about it. All I want you to do is not to exaggerate the damage. You are not going to be floored by it; there is more justice than that even in *this* world. And especially as regards *me,* just call the sore spot well. I could say more and with better heart in praise of your good-feeling (which was what I always liked in you) since this thing happened than I could before.

—A man isn't hurt by any honest effort at reparation. Why shouldn't you write to each of those men and say frankly that at such and such an hour on the 17th of December you did so and so? They would take it in the right spirit, I'm sure.[4] If they didn't the right would be yours.

Mrs. Howells joins me in cordial regards to Mrs Clemens and yourself.

> Ever yours
> W. D. Howells.

1. "The Loves of Alonzo Fitz Clarence and Rosannah Ethelton," *Atlantic*, March 1878. Because of the Whittier Birthday speech, Mark Twain had asked Howells on 23 December 1877 (MH), not to print the story. On 25 December 1877 (CtHT) Howells wrote to Warner: "This morning I got a letter from poor Clemens that almost breaks my heart. I hope I shall be able to answer it in just the right way."

2. See Howells to Norton, 19 December 1877. Norton's reply has not been found.

3. The editors of *Twain-Howells* (p. 214, n. 3) identify Howells' reference as probably Francis J. Child, since Howells later refers to him as one "who had read the newspaper report" and praised "Clemens's burlesque as the richest piece of humor in the world" (*My Mark Twain*, in *Literary Friends and Acquaintance*, HE, p. 296).

4. For comment regarding the letter of apology and the replies from Longfellow, Holmes, and Emerson's daughter, see *Twain-Howells*, p. 215.

6 JANUARY 1878, CAMBRIDGE, TO SAMUEL L. CLEMENS

. . . The Atlantic Monthly. . . .
Cambridge, Mass. Jan. 6, 1877.[1]

My dear Clemens:

Your letter about the play gave me great joy, and so did Warner's most kindly criticism in the Courant.[2] I am very happy in your liking for it. We shall yet write a play together; but you must not expect any profit out of it if we do. I am the champion prosperity-extinguisher. To tell you the truth, I'm awfully discouraged at the failure of the comedy to draw houses in New England. I don't suppose it paid expenses in either Worcester, Providence, Springfield or Hartford, and I shall not blame Barrett if he withdraws it. I wonder if you had any talk with him about it?

—I was with Mr. Longfellow the morning he got your letter. He spoke of it as "most pathetic," and said everyone seemed to care more for that affair than he did.[3] I know you had the right sort of answer from him.— I couldn't help reading to Mr. Norton, the other day, what you had said of him, and it gave him the greatest pleasure.[4]

Winny will send her name. She now sends her love to your tribe with all of us.

Yours ever
W. D. Howells.

1. Howells mistakenly dated this letter 1877.

2. Clemens' letter to Howells, 4 January 1878 (MH; *Twain-Howells*, p. 216), began: "The play is enchanting. I laughed & cried all the way through it." In an unsigned review of *A Counterfeit Presentment* in the Hartford *Courant* of 3 January 1878, Warner compared Howells' writing with Goldoni's "pure comedy of unexaggerated real life." But he found the third act slow, though often amusing.

3. Referring to his performance at the Whittier Birthday dinner, Clemens had written in his letter to Emerson, Longfellow, and Holmes, dated 27 December 1877 (MH; Smith, *Harvard Library Bulletin* 9 [1955], 164): "But I do not ask you to forgive what I did that night, for it is not forgivable; I simply had it at heart to ask you to believe that I am only heedlessly a savage, not premeditatedly; & that I am under as severe punishment as even you could adjudge to me if you were required to appoint my penalty. I do not ask you to say one word in answer to this; it is not needful, & would of course be distasteful & difficult. I beg you to consider that in letting me unbosom myself you will do me an act of grace that will be

sufficient in itself." Longfellow answered on 6 January: "I am a little troubled, that you should be so much troubled about a matter of such slight importance. The newspapers have made all the mischief.... [¶] I do not believe that anybody was much hurt. Certainly I was not, and Holmes tells me he was not.... [¶] It was a very pleasant dinner, and I think Whittier enjoyed it very much" (p. 167).

4. In an undated letter, presumably written late in December 1877 (MH; *Twain-Howells*, p. 214), Clemens told Howells: "It is curious, but I pitched early upon Mr. Norton as the very man who would think some generous thing about that matter, whether he said it or not. It is splendid to be a man like that—but it is given to few to be."

6 JANUARY 1878, CAMBRIDGE, TO WILLIAM C. HOWELLS

... The Atlantic Monthly....
Cambridge, Mass. Jan. 6, 1878.

Dear father:

I will try after this not to let my weekly letters be interrupted by anything, but I am not sure if I can always help it. We have simply a storm of visitors, and when we are not ourselves invaded, we go and invade somebody else. It is the most foolish existence possible, and we do all we can, short of positive rudeness and unkindness, to escape it. Sometimes I feel almost distracted, to see my time and substance so terribly wasted, as they are, upon people and things for which I care nothing. We hope that when we get to Belmont we shall be more neglected by our friends.[1]

You have read of the union of The Galaxy with The Atlantic.[2] This will not alter my place at all, and we expect that it will help The Atlantic. We shall at any rate have The Galaxy subscribers for one year.

I don't know whether I've written you that I saw my play. It was given at Worcester,[3] and it seemed to me very good. Some places in it were slight for the stage, as those matters go, but on the whole, I didn't see why it should not do. It has not drawn so good houses in New England as in the West, for some reason. It will be played this week in Washington.

I hope you have received Gibbon's life and like it as well as the others.[4] The study of his character interested me a great deal.

I am sorry to hear that Henry seems not very well. It was most kind of the count[5] (who is apparently a sort of fairy prince) to give him those presents. Henry ought by all means to wear cuffs at the request of so good a friend; perhaps a moustache would be too great a sacrifice.—Pilla now gives me memorandums when I go down. Yesterday's read: "A book in lig print." L-i-g spells *large*. Tell Henry that she has a Japanese doll, which we have named Hop Sing (after a Chinese washerman in Boston.) It squeaks (in Japanese) and is a high favorite. Yesterday Winny tried her snow shoes on the small drifts hereabouts. I believe it was a very successful performance, but I had to go away before it began.—I have got started on a new story:[6] the persons whom I've so far developed, are an old theoretical doctor who takes up spiritualism, after having long been a mesmerist, and tries to make a medium of his daughter, insisting that she shall eke out her natural power of supernaturalism by tricks, which in his craze, he intends as models or suggestions that the spirits shall use for their communications. I try to paint that hopeless sophistication into which the sincerest spiritualists fall.

When do you expect little Mary Howells?[7] It seems to me an excellent idea for her to pass the winter with you.

All join me in love to all

Your aff'te son
Will

1. Construction of the new house at Belmont, which was designed by McKim, Mead & Bigelow, had begun in 1877. On 13 January 1878 (MH) Howells was able to report to his father that "I suppose they have got the brick-work all up, and are ready to frame, though the cold snap was an interruption. You must remember the place—it is a little more than two miles west of Cambridge, on the Fitchburg road. Our hill-top commands the most magnificent prospect, including the whole vast valley in which Boston and its suburbs lie, and a light-house far out at sea.— At present our project is not to sell, but to let our Cambridge house. The rent will much more than pay that at Belmont, and enable us to keep a horse besides." Although built according to Howells' and Elinor's taste and specifications, the house was to be the property of Charles Fairchild, from whom they rented it. See Howells to Fairchild, 6 October 1881.

2. The *Galaxy* subscription list was sold to the *Atlantic* in 1878; though rivals, the two magazines had many contributors in common. See F. L. Mott, *A History of American Magazines, 1865–1885* (Cambridge, Mass.: Harvard University Press, 1938), pp. 361–81.

3. *A Counterfeit Presentment* played in Worcester on 26 December 1877.

4. *Memoirs of Edward Gibbon*, one in a series of "Choice Autobiographies," was published 20 December 1877. See also Howells to Warner, 21 October 1877, n. 6.

5. Count Premio Real. See Howells to W. C. Howells, 4 August 1877, n. 2.

6. *The Undiscovered Country.*

7. Mary Elizabeth Howells.

12 JANUARY 1878, CAMBRIDGE, TO CHARLES D. WARNER

... *The Atlantic Monthly.* ...
Cambridge, Mass. Jan. 12, 1878.

My dear Warner:

I don't think the whole delightfulness of this fun reached me in the MS. it's *wunderbar*! I never saw more delicate satire; and I am fool enough to be just as excited over the adventure as if it were fact, or possible.[1]

—I want to thank you cordially for that kind notice of my play.[2] I was of course glad of the praise, and I was glad that you put your finger on the weak point of the third (new act) which *is* over-literary, and which I shall make less so—for, in spite of his discouraging season in New England, Barrett isn't going to withdraw the play.

I don't know whether I'd rather or not that you said those kind things out of tenderness for the playwright. I love you the same, anyway.

Yours ever
W. D. Howells

1. Evidently Howells was returning proof of Warner's "A Fight with a Trout," *Atlantic*, March 1878.
2. For Warner's review of *A Counterfeit Presentment*, see Howells to Clemens, 6 January 1878, n. 2.

19 JANUARY 1878, CAMBRIDGE, TO WILLIAM C. HOWELLS

...The Atlantic Monthly....
Cambridge, Mass. Jan. 19, 1878.

Dear father:

I walked down to Fresh Pond with the children this evening, (which was mild and spring-like,) and found the ice very thin and unhopeful looking. In fact, I believe they have cut none yet, and it looks as if this were to be one of the winters in which they secure a crop by sliding one field of ice on top of another, and letting the successive layers freeze till they have a sufficient thickness. The unnatural continuance of the mild weather is making talk of the approach of the Gulf Stream to this coast; but I dare say next winter will find it far enough away.

I made a long call on James, this morning, and had as usual, much edifying talk with him. He is about publishing another book on Swedenborgianism, in the form of letters to a friend.[1] I believe it is mainly to account for the present condition of the church and the world, the latter of which he thinks much the most respectable, and destined to absorb the former, which was evolved from it in the fall of man. (When we go to Belmont, by the way, it is quite likely that we shall send the children to the New Church school at Waltham. We wrote to Dr. Worcester[2] the other day for the school circular, and in replying he said it was "a long time since he had heard from his old friend from Ashtabula.") James is physically feebler from the paralytic shock which he had summer before last, but his mind seems as quick and active as ever. I will send you his book when it comes out.—I feel that somehow my visit to you last summer was very unsatisfactory. When shall we have one that will be tranquil and fulfilling? I wish you could come here in May, after we have moved, and spend your quarterly fortnight with us in our new quarters. It's a lovely country all about Belmont, and we expect to have a horse, and could make you have a pleasant time.—I'm so glad you're going to take another house, and that it's going to be near the Esplanade, for that was always a favorite part of the town with me. I shall be curious to know just where it is.—Why do we never hear from Vic any more? Do we owe her a letter? She is such a large part of the family life that it is strange to have her silent.—Yesterday, I was asked to meet Mr. Bristow at lunch, in Boston.[3] The Bostonians are disposed to take him up, and it is to be hoped their favor will not spoil his chances for the next Presidency. He seems a very agreeable man, and I had a pleasant chat with him. He is very frank and (if I may whisper it) Hayes did not seem so. But Hayes struck me as the abler man of the two—that is broader. Bristow is like a great *force.*

Give my love to all.

Your aff'te son
Will.

1. *Society the Redeemed Form of Man* (1879).
2. Dr. Thomas Worcester.
3. Benjamin Helm Bristow (1832–1896), as secretary of the treasury (1874–1876) was responsible for dismantling the "Whiskey Ring," a corrupt association of distillers and Internal Revenue Service agents. Bristow unsuccessfully sought the Republican presidential nomination in 1876.

30 JANUARY 1878, CAMBRIDGE, TO JAMES A. GARFIELD

. . . The Atlantic Monthly. . . .
Cambridge, Mass. Jan. 30, 1878.

Dear General Garfield:

I am back on your hands again for that powerful political article which all magazine people are now seeking for their public. I have tried in vain both Senator Hoar and Senator Edmunds[1] on the Presidential-elections question,[2] and the silver business is so stale that I cannot touch that. Can you suggest any body else for any other question? I some-times think that a vividly written anonymous paper would perhaps be the best thing; but I have not the range of political writers, and don't know just where to turn. Aid me, I beseech you, with any merciful suggestions that occur to you.—I hate to go to the enemy, but how would it do to ask Thurman[3] to write on the Pr.-elections question? It is n't a political, or party matter.—Should you object to writing anonymously (I suppose you wouldn't like to write over your own name) a paper treating of the administrational reforms under Hayes, and telling just what has been done and what machinery and hope exists for reform?[4] I would guard your incognito.

Yours very cordially,
W. D. Howells

1. George Frisbie Hoar (1826–1904) was Republican senator from Massachusetts (1877–1904). While a member of the House of Representatives (1869–1877), he served on the Electoral Commission which resolved the Hayes-Tilden election controversy. George Franklin Edmunds (1828–1919) was Republican senator from Vermont (1866–1891). As chairman of the Committee on the Judiciary (1872–1879 and 1881–1891), he helped secure passage of the Electoral Count Act of 1877.

2. In the presidential election of 1876 Tilden received 184 uncontested Electoral College votes, Hayes 165, and a total of 20 disputed votes were claimed by both parties. After Congress failed to resolve the issue, even after voting itself such decision-making powers, the specially established Electoral Commission of five senators, five representatives, and five Supreme Court justices eventually voted by a single vote margin in favor of the Republican ticket.

3. Allan Granberry Thurman (1813–1895) was Democratic senator from Ohio (1867–1881). As a member of the Electoral Commission, he cast one of the seven votes to seat Tilden.

4. An unsigned article titled "Presidential Elections," *Atlantic*, November 1878, addresses this issue, although it seems somewhat late to be the result of Howells' request in this letter.

25 FEBRUARY 1878, CAMBRIDGE, TO WILLIAM BIGELOW

... The Atlantic Monthly....
Cambridge, Mass. February 25, 1878.

Dear Mr. Bigelow:[1]

Mr. Myers will write you for such details as he needs.[2] We went out to the house today, and found it happily progressing. We shall enlarge the conservatory according to Mr McKim's suggestion, so as to include the piazza, and shall have a snow-box at the front door, and not two doors there (in the front hall). In the façade, Winny's short window will be changed back to the left gable, as first planned. The stairs which are now anatomically up are lovely in design. I still bewail the red roof of which the redwood shingles threaten to deprive me. The red roof (pray Say to Mr. McKim) is the most colonial feature of all, having been suggested first by the appearance of a scalped settler. He cannot reject it without a violation of what Mrs. Howells calls, McKimism. By the way, Myers is waiting for the redwood shingles.

Yours truly
W. D. Howells.

I'm afraid Willy will find the Hayeses hopelessly incorruptible.[3]

1. William Bigelow (b. 1853) was a partner in the firm of McKim, Mead & Bigelow, which designed the new Howells residence at Belmont in a modernized Colonial style. Charles F. McKim (1847–1909) had studied architecture at Harvard and in Paris; William R. Mead was Elinor Howells' brother. In a letter from Howells to Mead, 25 March 1878 (MA), we learn about some of the details of the interior design: "even with the third window added by Mr. McKim, the library will

be too dark if paneled in redwood. Can you think of some other wood? But we should like all the mantels in the house of redwood." Further information on this particular point and many others regarding the house plans is contained in some thirty letters from Elinor Howells to her brother William, all at the Amherst College Library. For instance, on 15 June 1878, she wrote: "The library we *really* do not want white." But on 3 July she reversed herself, writing: "Mr. McKim's letter was delightful. The vellum suggestion seemed to throw light. *White* it shall be." The Belmont house is now owned by Mr. and Mrs. Edward W. Merrill, who are in the process of restoring it.

2. George Myers was the contractor.

3. William R. Mead, who was related to the family of Rutherford B. Hayes, apparently was involved in some business matter with the president.

14 MARCH 1878, CAMBRIDGE, TO HJALMAR H. BOYESEN

> ... *The Atlantic Monthly....*
> *Cambridge, Mass.* March 14, 1878.

My dear Boyesen:

The wish to write you a longer letter than I now have time for must not keep me from writing at once to congratulate you on the joyful fact you have imparted to me. I am ready to believe all that you tell me of the young lady,[1] and shall only be too glad some day to verify it. In the meantime present the lovely unknown the respectful compliments of your friend, and tell her that literature expects a great deal of her in the way of inspiration and encouragement to you. She is to naturalize you in the supreme degree, to make known to you the soul of American womanhood, and to give you that hold upon our life which you have already shown yourself to have upon our letters.

I wish with all my heart I *could* write you such letters as I used; but of all the time that we have not, the time that we have once lived, is the most unattainable. In other words, I am now forty-one, and then I was thirty-four. It has touched and gratified me that you should attribute any part of your success to me. At least I can own to a wish to be useful to you.—Just now, I am beginning what I think will be my longest story—twice or three times as long as any I've hitherto written.[2] It is the history of a young girl brought up in good society who is suddenly thrown upon her own resources for a livelihood. If you'll consider the subject a moment you'll see how rich it is, in the variety of experience and adventure it suggests. I mean to treat it very realistically, and study in it the callings to which women devote them-selves. It ought to be immensely pathetic.—Mr. Barrett, who has been playing my comedy[3] in the South and West has come to Boston, at last, and will give it here early in April.—Mrs. Howells is in New York, and can't join me in wishing you happiness. But I know she will be glad to hear the news you tell me, for we are both great friends of marriage. Winny sends her love and good wishes. Did you know that the children called their boat last summer at Conanicut, The Boyesen?—I should be delighted to come to the wedding, and at least wont put myself out of the question yet by declining. But you know that New York is rather sun-stroky in July, and that I can't bear the heat.—Belmont is the first station beyond Cambridge on the Fitchburg road: we shall be on a hill that overlooks Boston as far as the coast of Spain.[4]

> With cordial regards,
> W. D. Howells.

1. Elizabeth M. Keen, of "an old Philadelphia family," though her father owned a Chicago bookstore. See C. A. Glasrud, *Hjalmar Hjorth Boyesen* (Northfield, Minn.: Norwegian-American Historical Association, 1963), pp. 49–50.

2. *A Woman's Reason* (1883). Howells first mentioned the novel in a letter to T. S. Collier, 25 February 1878 (RPB; Arms, *Journal of Rutgers University Library* 8 [1944], 10–11), asking how he could get the fiancé out of the country for three years.

3. *A Counterfeit Presentment.*

4. See Howells to W. C. Howells, 6 January 1878, n. 1.

19 MARCH 1878, CAMBRIDGE, TO LAWRENCE BARRETT

> ... *The Atlantic Monthly....*
> *Cambridge, Mass.* March 19, 1878.

Dear Mr. Barrett:

Since seeing you I have thought over the cast for the comedy,[1] and very much wish that you could get Mrs. Vincent to take the landlady's part, and give Mrs. Wyatt's part say to the lady who played Duchatelet's mother last Saturday afternoon in The Marble Heart.[2] Mrs. Vincent has so much of the *Vis comica*, that I don't see how she is to restrain herself within the bounds of the somewhat subdued anxiety of Mrs. Wyatt. That is a part which might be acted neutrally, colorlessly, and no harm done; but people are so used to laughing at everything Mrs. Vincent does, that I'm afraid that with the best ideas of what it should be, she would find it taken in a comic sense. I owe her too much gratitude for pleasure in times past to say anything that should seem to slight her powers; I know what a delightful artist she is, and if she would only take the landlady's part, she would really add another character to the play, and contribute vastly to its success. We could restore much that we cut out of the opening scenes of the new act,[3] and the part would not be so slight as it now is.

Madame Duchatelet (I don't remember her name) would make a good

enough Mrs. Wyatt. If you think fit, please show this letter to Mr Field.[4]
I forgot to ask who does the general. Mr. Clannin?[5]

Yours sincerely
W. D. Howells.

1. *A Counterfeit Presentment.*

2. Mary Ann Farlow Vincent (1818–1887) came to the Boston Museum in 1852 and was a member of the stock company for more than 34 years, in which time she played hundreds of parts on the Boston stage as the Museum's leading comedienne. Barrett replied to Howells' suggestion in a letter dated only "Thursday" (21 March 1878; MH): "It would be fatal to put the lady you speak of in Mrs. Vincent's part. The audience will accept the latter lady in any part, however unfitted she may be." Thus Mrs. Vincent played Mrs. General Wyatt, and Mrs. Laura Phillips played the landlady at the Boston performance. *The Marble Heart; or, the Sculptor's Dream*, a translation by Charles Selby of Théodore Barrière's *Les Filles de Marbre* (1853), appears to have had its first stage presentation in 1854 at the Royal Adelphi Theatre, London. Raphael Duchatelet is the name of the central character, a young French sculptor.

3. On 14 November 1877 Howells sent Barrett a new act "with the idea of telling the story more fully and of developing Bartlett's character by certain situations" (NjP; Meserve, *The Complete Plays of W. D. Howells* [New York: New York University Press, 1960], p. 71).

4. Roswell Martin Field (1851–1919) was an author, journalist, and manager of the Boston Museum.

5. R. F. McClannin (1832–1899) was a very popular actor who began his career in Providence, Rhode Island; following engagements in Chicago and New Orleans, he settled in Boston after the Civil War. He was a member of the Boston Museum company.

31 MARCH 1878, CAMBRIDGE, TO WILLIAM C. HOWELLS

. . . The Atlantic Monthly. . . .
Cambridge, Mass. March 31, 1878.

Dear father:

I am very glad of the gleam of hope you have in regard to Toronto,[1] but I think, after your experience, that you are quite right to treat it as a gleam only. For my own part, I shall be sorry to have you leave Quebec, and I doubt if you'll find Toronto any great advantage, pecuniarily: it must be a much more expensive place. But of course you have looked carefully into the matter.—You lost nothing by my not writing last Sunday, for there was no news, and to day there is scarcely anything but the excitement of my play,[2] which is to be brought out at the Boston Museum to-morrow night. There is a full house in prospect, and I can't help feeling some hope that it will go off well.[3] I have been at two rehearsals,—very strange and amusing experiences to me. A rehearsal is the bare bones merely of playing; the actors only walk through their parts, with hardly any show of action or elocution.

Mr. Longfellow and his old friend Greene[4] came in to the second rehearsal, and sat it all through.—I'm more and more impressed with the hardness of an actor's life. It's an extremely serious affair, with the least possible fun about it. What struck me most in regard to my own share in the business was the inexorable fashion in which what I had so lightly and vaguely described had to be *realized* on the stage. A hat—just what kind of hat? A chair—precisely what sort of chair?

We were out at Belmont yesterday looking at the house, which is blossoming out into a very quaint and peculiar beauty. It is going to be something really exquisite, and, what is better, convenient. We shall be very impatient to see you after we get into it. All are well and join me in love to all,

> Your affectionate son
> Will.

1. Howells had written his father on 17 March 1878 (MH) about the possibility of securing a consular position in Toronto, sharing his "disappointment in regard to the place at Toronto, which I certainly think you had reason to expect after what was said to Mr. Garfield." But in a letter of 3 April 1878 (MH; *Life in Letters,* I, 250–51) he notes that the morning paper reports "the President has sent in your name for Toronto . . . ."

2. *A Counterfeit Presentment.*

3. On 2 April 1878 (MH; *Life in Letters,* I, 250) Aldrich wrote: "It is an awful thing to see another man so successful as you were last night. . . . Wasn't it all delightful?" On the following day (MH) F. J. Garrison wrote in a memorandum to Howells: "If you are not tired of congratulations, please accept mine on the brilliant success of Monday evening. I have rarely enjoyed a performance so thoroughly . . . ." Howells wrote his father in his letter of 3 April: "The first night was a superb ovation[,] a gurgle of laughter from beginning to end, and a constant clapping of hands. . . . I never had my popularity at arm's length before, and it was very pleasant."

4. George Washington Greene.

9 APRIL 1878, NEW YORK, TO RUTHERFORD B. HAYES

New York, April 9, 1878.

Dear Mr. President:

Elinor has sent me your note from Cambridge.

I am reluctant to say anything about the matter you refer to me, but I will do so at your request. Personally, I have a great affection for the man,[1] and personally I know nothing to his disadvantage. He spent a week with us at Cambridge when he first came East,[2] and we all liked him. He was lax about appointments, but that is a common fault. After he went away, he began to contract debts, and was arrested for debt in Boston.[3] (I saw this.) He is notorious for borrowing and *was* notorious for drinking. This is *report.* He never borrowed of *me,* nor drank more than I, (in my presence) and yesterday I saw his doctor who says his habits are good, now; and I have heard the same thing from others. From what I hear he is really making an effort to reform. It would be a godsend to him, if he could get such a place; for he is poor, and he writes with difficulty and very little. He has had the worst reputation as regards punctuality, solvency and sobriety; but he has had a terrible lesson in falling from the highest prosperity to the lowest adversity in literature, and—you are good enough judge of men to know whether he will profit by it or not.[4]

Personally, I should be glad of his appointment, and I should have great hopes of him—and fears. It would be easy to recall him, if he misbehaved, and a hint of such a fate would be useful to him.

—I must beg that you will not show this letter to anyone whatever, but will kindly return it to me at Cambridge.

Very respectfully yours
W. D. Howells.

1. Bret Harte. On 5 April 1878 (MH) Hayes wrote Howells seeking "for personal & private use" Howells' opinion on the "appointment of Bret Harte [as] consul at Nice." Apparently Hayes had "heard sinister things about him from Mark Twain."

2. On the Hartes' visit to the Howellses in 1871, see Howells to W. C. Howells, 5 March 1871.

3. "Throughout much of his life he was embarrassed by debt, never more so than during his stay in the East.... During this period...he lived generally from hand to mouth" (*Dictionary of American Biography* [New York: C. Scribner's Sons, 1932], VIII, 364). But so far nothing has been located to verify Howells' report that he was arrested for debt.

4. Hayes was apparently undaunted by the reports and rumors he had heard of Harte, because shortly after this letter he appointed him to the U. S. consulate at Crefeld, Germany. Harte served at this post until 1880, when in July he became consul in Glasgow, Scotland, where he served until 1885.

14 APRIL 1878, BOSTON, TO WILLIAM C. HOWELLS

...The Atlantic Monthly....
Boston. April 14, 1878.

Dear father:

I got home from New York yesterday morning after ten days' stay, all of which was taken up with continuous junketing. It began the night of the 4th with the Taylor dinner at Delmonico's.[1] Next night Harper made a dinner party for me; next night Church of the late Galaxy dined me;[2] Sunday I spent with Charley Mead's family; Monday morning I breakfasted with Sedgwick at the Union Club, and went out to Shepards for the night.[3] Tuesday I lunched with Quincy Ward, and dined with Whitelaw Reid, at whose house I spent three days. Wednesday night, I dined at the Union League Club, meeting all the New York sages in politics, literature and finance, including Tilden, Bryant and John Jacob Astor (the last said, "Mr Howells, nobody has enjoyed your Doorstep Acquaintance more than I"—which amused me, coming from a man of his millions). Next day Reid made a dinner party for me; Friday morning I breakfasted at Ward's, and then ran out to Henry Howells's at Flushing, and got back in time to take the boat. So you see what a round it was. I enjoyed it all, for the novelty and excitement, and was glad to have it over. I met and made up all old sorrows with Dr. Holland, which I was glad to do.[4]

I don't see what makes you think the Senate hasn't confirmed you.[5] It seems to me I've seen the announcement of your confirmation. At any rate there can't be any doubt about the matter.—I found the family all well on my return. I bought Pil a new doll, with long yellow hair, and she said she should call it *Ophelia*, because its hair was like a *field* of wheat. Apropos of Bible readings, she asked Winny the other day, what *was* an altar to burn *insects* on? She is very odd, and makes every scrap of knowledge go as far as it will stretch.—Shall you start for Toronto as soon as you are confirmed?

All join me in love to all of you.

Your aff'te son
Will.

1. The dinner was given in recognition of Bayard Taylor's appointment as U. S. minister in Berlin; William Cullen Bryant presided. See M. Hansen-Taylor and H. E. Scudder, eds., *Life and Letters of Bayard Taylor* (Boston: Houghton Mifflin, 1884), II, 729.

2. Probably Francis P. Church and Joseph Henry Harper, though Church's brother William C. and another Harper are possible.

3. Arthur G. Sedgwick, Charles L. Mead (Elinor Howells' brother), and Augustus D. Shepard (Elinor's brother-in-law).

4. Howells reviewed J. G. Holland's *Plain Talks on Familiar Subjects* in the *Nation*, 23 November 1865. The essay, entitled "Concerning Timothy Titcomb," labels the work of Holland "heavy and trite." Howells also reviewed Holland's *Kathrina*, *Atlantic*, December 1867. In this review he wrote that a parable "teaches only so far as it is true to life; and in a tale professing to deal with persons of our own day and country, we have a right to expect some fidelity to our contemporaries and neighbors. But we find nothing of this in 'Kathrina'...."

5. W. C. Howells was confirmed as U. S. consul at Toronto on 24 April 1878.

16 APRIL 1878, BOSTON, TO CHARLES E. NORTON

> *. . . The Atlantic Monthly. . . .*
> *Boston.* April 16, 1878.

Dear Mr. Norton:

I was away in New York when your circular came. Of course I wish to subscribe for the Turner pictures,[1] which I should like (if for no other reason) because I liked you—or because you liked them; it makes no difference which. I know they will be very useful to the artistic branches of the family, and I shall look up at them from the inferior levels of literature, and do my best to have some ideas about them.

The little drama you sent me has some very striking qualities. The dialogue is managed with great point and brilliancy: it seems really Louis Quinze Frenchmen speaking. What I can't abide is the matter between Helen and Casanova. I no longer wish to be put in pain about a woman's virtue, or to ask that suffering from others. It's odious; all the tragedy went out of that situation long ago, and only the displeasures remain. There is no reason but this for not printing the bright and shapely play, which I should otherwise be glad to have in The Atlantic.[2] I will bring you the MS. in a few days.

I'm very glad that you will soon let me have a paper of your own.—At Belmont, I shall be much nearer Shady Hill than I am now. It breaks my heart to have people think I'm base enough to make anything but a geographical remove from Cambridge.

> Yours ever
> W. D. Howells.

---

1. The particular pictures, presumably reproductions of paintings by J. M. W. Turner, have not been identified. Norton's nephew, Francis Bullard, later bequeathed a large collection of Turner prints to the Boston Museum of Fine Arts, but whether there is any connection between it and the subscription mentioned here is unknown.

2. The play, which has not been identified, was apparently not by Norton, but transmitted by him to Howells. In a letter two years later to Brander Matthews, 25 August 1880 (NNC), Howells advances editorial caution for what may also be his prudishness. He admits Matthews' article is "new and good," but adds, "I am somewhat anxious for 'the cheek of the young person' who might be pained by the equivocalities necessarily touched upon. She reads the Atlantic a great deal and has to be tenderly regarded." The article is perhaps a part of one of two 1880–1881 books by Matthews on the French stage.

4 MAY 1878, BOSTON, TO THOMAS S. COLLIER

> *... The Atlantic Monthly. ...*
> *Boston.* May 4, 1878.

My dear Mr. Collier:[1]

I beg to turn to you again for use of your naval knowledge.

You may remember that I consulted you about sending off a young hero of mine, (of the U. S. N.) to the China station.[2] Having got him safely there, I now wish to have him try to get back to the young lady whom the sudden death of her father has left more than commonly forlorn. So I want to ask:

I. How are letters best addressed to naval officers? Through the Navy Department?

II. How would an officer telegraph from China? That is, what is the nearest cable-station?

III. How would he go about to get leave of absence? Could he get it in some exigencies from his superior officer, or from the nearest U. S. Minister, or must he wait for leave from Washington?

IV. What are the chances by which an officer wishing to return, and having interest with his superior could get himself sent home on business of the service? Or are there *no* chances?

V Suppose the young man to have started home, how would he come? Are there steamers for California direct from China?

VI: What would be a good accident by which I could delay the steamer, or make her put back; and would it be imaginable that the young man should try to push on by sailing vessel?

VII. On what island, or little visited coast could I have him wrecked, so as to delay his arrival in America for a year or two?[3]

You see I have asked you some hard questions; but I rely on your kindness.

> **Yours sincerely**
> **W. D. Howells.**

1. Thomas S. Collier (1842–1893) was a naval officer, physician, and poet. He served in the navy through the Civil War, retiring in 1883. He published one volume of his own poems under the title *Song Spray.*

2. See Howells to Boyesen, 14 March 1878, n. 2.

3. A summary of the final treatment of these problems in *A Woman's Reason* is given in Arms, "A Novel and Two Letters." *Journal of Rutgers University Library* 8 (1944), 12.

2 June 1878, Boston, to Samuel L. Clemens

> *...The Atlantic Monthly....*
> Boston. June 2, 1878.

My dear Clemens

Ich habe Ihren herzerfreuenden Brief erhalten[1]—or do you prefer English by this time? There is at least one American family whom your absence from the country truly bereaves, and I need not tell you your letter was truly welcome, and duly read aloud at the breakfast table the morning it came.[2] We are still in Cambridge, and we no longer put our faith in joiners. The Belmont house is promised us in a month— and was so a month ago. But the weather remains charmingly cool in Cambridge, and as nobody wants to buy or to hire this house, it costs us nothing to stay in it. Just now we are excited about a horse and phaeton which we are to buy, and I suppose that by the end of a fort- night I shall be the worst sold ass in Massachusetts. But to a literary man all these things are gain: they turn into material, as we all know.[3] The only thing that doesn't is a displeasure with an actor: that's a thing that one likes to keep to one's self.—I am working away steadily at my new story,[4] which promises to be a long one, and I am venturing on some untried paths in it. Think of so domestic a man as I wrecking his hero on a coral island—an uninhabited *atoll*—in the South Pacific! There's courage for you! Till I get this done, I try not even to think of a play, though to tell you the truth I would ten times rather write plays than anything else, and I shall tackle the Steam Generator[5] at the earliest opportunity. I have had a very pleasant letter from your cub-dramatist in Hartford, renouncing—or rather disclaiming—all right and title to Clews.[6]—Osgood goes abroad this month, with Waring.[7] Aldrich spends the summer at Swampscott. John Hay is, I suppose, in Europe by this time: from a short note he sent me before sailing, I'm afraid his health is delicate. Him and O. you would like to see, and will, I dare say. Harte, you know, has got a consular appointment somewhere in Germany.[8] So you see you are likely to be joined by the whole fraternity during the summer. I alone shall stay at home. In fact, I find that I have outlived all longing for Europe: you are now the principal attraction of that elderly enchantress, as far as I'm con- cerned.—I hope you'll find all the hoped-for leisure there, and that you'll not be able to keep from writing for The Atlantic. Otherwise I must begin printing your private letters to satisfy the popular demand. People are constantly asking when you're going to begin. (That's a pleasant thorn to plant in a friend's side.)—When I parted from you, that dismal day in New York, I saw that the weather was capable of anything, and I'm not surprised to hear how it used you; but I hope that by this time

Mrs. Clemens is all well of her cold, and that poor Susie is more recon-
ciled to Rosa's composition.[9] Really, however, I could imagine the
German going harder with you, for you always seemed to me a man
who liked to be understood with the least possible personal inconvenience. The worst thing about any foreign country is its language,
which the natives never can speak with our accent.—What a stupid
letter. But give me another chance, by answering. You know that at
my dullest, my heart is in the right place. Mrs. Howells joins me in
love to both of you.

Affectionately
W. D. Howells.

Tell me about Capt. Wakeman in Heaven,[10] and all your other
enterprises.

1. German for "I have received your heartwarming letter."
2. The letter referred to is dated "May 4. Frankfort on the Main" (MH; *Twain-
Howells*, pp. 227–28). The Clemens family had left Hartford on 27 March and arrived
in Hamburg about a month later.
3. "Buying a Horse," *Atlantic*, June 1879.
4. *A Woman's Reason*.
5. This is the beginning of the plan for a collaborative play, which eventually
became *Colonel Sellers as a Scientist* (1883). See Meserve, *The Complete Plays of
W. D. Howells* (New York: New York University Press, 1960), pp. 205–8.
6. "Clews" is another title for Mark Twain's play "Cap'n Simon Wheeler, the
Amateur Detective"; the "cub-dramatist" has not been identified, but see *Twain-
Howells*, p. 234.
7. George E. Waring, Jr.
8. See Howells to Hayes, 9 April 1878, n. 4.
9. Rosa was the teacher from whom Susy Clemens took German lessons. In his
letter of 4 May, Clemens reported Susy's complaint about Rosa: "Mamma, I wish
Rosa was made in English." Olivia Susan Clemens (1872–1896) was Clemens's oldest
daughter.
10. In his reply to this letter (27 June 1878; MH), Clemens sent Howells an outline
of the story, which eventually became "Extract from Captain Stormfield's Visit to
Heaven," *Harper's Monthly*, January 1908. See *Twain-Howells*, pp. 236, 238.

2 JUNE 1878, BOSTON, TO WILLIAM C. HOWELLS

. . . The Atlantic Monthly. . . .
Boston. June 2, 1878.

Dear father:

I am going to send this letter to Toronto, *any* way, because I think
you certainly have a right to be there, by this time. It was very gratifying
to Elinor and me to see the account of the testimonial to you in Quebec.[1]
It was a fitting close to your life there. I fancy you'll find many agreeable

people also in Toronto. I have given a letter of introduction to a nice young fellow who has just gone from St. John's N. B. to take charge of Belford's Monthly at Toronto. His name is Stewart,[2] and he has a house in the same block with you. I am quite curious to hear from you, and to know what sort of house you have, etc.

We shall probably be in Cambridge till July: the Belmont house finishes up slowly. But we are putting in plants and vines, and the place will have a homelike look at once.

The family are all uncommonly well, and are just now absorbed in the great enterprise of buying a horse and phaeton.[3] The purchase is to be chiefly for Winny, but we shall all expect to ride in it.—I don't know whether we've told you that Winny always takes the highest honors at her school examinations, and that John has "caught up" with a French class ahead of him at school, and sometimes has the best marks of any. This is all the more remarkable in J. (as Pillà calls him,) because he has no love for learning, naturally.—Base ball rages in Cambridge this spring, and the furore extends even to Winny: she came home from a little party exultant last night, because she had had the great honor of playing Thumbs up with the Short Stop of the Freshman Nine. She and John go to all the matches, and our table talk is a jargon of "hot balls," "hot grounders," "second bases," "pitchers," "catches," "licks," and I don't know what else. It amuses me, who never cared a straw for any sort of game, except marbles.

We all unite in love to you all.

Your aff'te son
Will.

1. Howells probably read about the testimonial in the Quebec *Morning Chronicle*, from which the Ashtabula *Sentinel*, 6 June 1878, reprinted an item concerning the occasion of W. C. Howells' move to Toronto.

2. George Stewart (1848–1906) was a journalist and author. In 1867 he founded *Stewart's Literary Quarterly Magazine* and was its editor (1867–1872). He served as editor-in-chief of *Rose-Belford's Canadian Monthly* (1878–1882), and in 1879 he also assumed the editorship of the Quebec *Daily Chronicle* (1879–1896).

3. See Howells to Clemens, 2 June 1878, n. 3.

16 JUNE 1878, BOSTON, TO WILLIAM C. HOWELLS

. . . The Atlantic Monthly. . . .
Boston. June 16, 1878.

Dear father—

I have at last had a letter from you at Toronto, and that newspaper account of your pleasant reception has come to hand.[1] Certainly your public farewells and welcomes have been of the most gratifying kind. I should think you would soon be as comfortable in Toronto as in Quebec.

—The last week has been quite eventless with us, and I really don't know what to write beyond the fact that we are all well. We shall probably be in Cambridge till the end of the month. But fortunately the summer has so far been very cool, and we haven't suffered even from dust. We have now some hopes of selling the house here, but it is only a hope. I think we can let it without much trouble; but I should greatly prefer to sell. If I could sell this, I should have enough to own that at Belmont out and out.

—You must let me know as fully as you can about your life in Toronto. I suppose you will now begin writing full letters in the *Sentinel* again.[2] It was astonishing how long the Quebec material held out.

—Republicans are not feeling very lively about the present state of things, and I see no chance for the party next time except under Grant. At the same, I should feel that his re-election would be almost a confession that popular government was near its end among us: when in time of peace only one man can save us, we're hardly worth saving.—The best men about here still believe in Hayes, but with that lukewarmness which seems to have been the greatest liking he could inspire. In all my disappointment however, when I think of the awful position, the entire isolation of the man, he seems to me the most compassionable character in history. With the best heart to do well, he has been able to command no following among politicians, and he has let die out the greatest popularity that ever a man had. A year ago the people were frantic over him, and now![3]—We all join in love to you all.

> Your aff'te son,
> Will.

1. The Toronto *Globe*, 12 June 1878, carried an account of W. C. Howells' arrival in Toronto on 10 June, and of a reception given in his honor by the New England Society on the following day. This item was reprinted in the Ashtabula *Sentinel*, 20 June 1878.

2. W. C. Howells resumed his "Familiar Letters from the Editor" in the *Sentinel*, 4 July 1878, after a lapse of a month.

3. Hayes' popularity suffered as a result of his conciliatory policies in dealing with the South, his efforts to implement a reform of the civil service, and his hard-money position, which led him to veto the Bland-Allison Act in 1878. See Howells to Hayes, 16 March 1879, especially n. 3.

21 July 1878, Belmont, to William C. Howells

Belmont, July 21, 1878.

Dear father:

This is the first letter I write you from the new house, where we have been living in perfect chaos for the last two weeks. I had let the house in Cambridge to people who wished to move in at once,[1] and so we hurried out here, where we have ever since the 8th had a horde of carpenters and painters. The house is really very lovely, and perfectly unique. Now that we have quiet in it, I think we shall, "humanly speaking," be content.—Winny was greatly gratified with your letter, which made me feel rather ashamed of never speaking, or seldom speaking, to the children as you wrote to her. I must hope for some "remains" of good in them from you. My own life has been too much given to the merely artistic and to worldly ambition. Besides I have not found, as you did in Swedenborg, a philosophic system, to which I could give entire faith. My morality has been a hand to mouth affair.

—I see by your Sentinel letter that you have had the terrible heat at Toronto that has almost consumed us.[2] Even on this hill, which is the coolest place I ever knew, there was one night when we could scarcely sleep, and whenever the wind fell, the days were like flame. The heat was just as great at the seaside.—Elinor says she is going to write very soon. In the meantime she wants me to tell you that the latchstring is out, and she invites you one and all to visit us. We hope to live hereafter more for our friends and families than we did in Cambridge.—The children are very happy here, and we think will be very well. I bought a pony horse, the other day and a pretty second hand phaeton, which they were to drive. We left the pony unhitched before our door, and he caught sight of the barn, and started for it. As he went on he went faster, and extended his tour over the greater part of the farm, and a stone wall four feet high. There he left the smashed up phaeton upside down, and broke for the bottom of the hill.[3] He did not hurt himself, but is ruined for our driving, and I must get rid of him. Luckily I have heard of another pony, the pet of a clergyman's family, who has steadier habits if not better principles. We begin country life in the regular Sparrow grass manner.[4]—I shall be interested in all you can tell me about your life in Toronto.

We all join love to all with you.

Your aff'te son
Will.[5]

---

1. Howells leased the Cambridge house to Justin Winsor, who had become librarian at Harvard in 1877.

2. In "Familiar Letter from the Editor," *Sentinel*, 25 July 1878 (dated Toronto, 19 July), W. C. Howells complained that the weather was *"dieful* hot."

3. In Howells' sketch, "Buying a Horse," the pony Billy runs away in much the same fashion as described here.

4. In a review of the works of Frederick S. Cozzens, *Atlantic*, March 1871, Howells had described *The Sparrowgrass Papers* (1855) as "fantastic sketches of the citizen's life in the country,—fantastic, and yet so truthful that most urban and suburban people can match them out of their own observation."

5. Victoria M. Howells probably gave the letter to her sister Annie; it bears the endorsement: "Please return this to us, as father has not answered it, V. M. H."

23 AUGUST 1878, BOSTON, TO WILLIAM WETMORE STORY

. . . The Atlantic Monthly. . . .
Boston. Aug. 23, 1878.

Dear Mr. Story:

I am glad to have the Excursion again, and the Juliet which I think wonderfully good—I heard all the tribe of Giovannas, Augustas, and Bettinas speaking in it. I shall print it in November.[1]—The Rabbi's Letter[2] I've read with great pleasure, and with a full sense of its philosophic value, as well as its truth to time and place. I had hoped to take it, but on looking more soberly at its length, I must, I find, forego it. Printed in single columns it would make 14 pp.; in double columns, fine type, not less than 6. The publishers object to my tendency to long poetry, and I dare not put this burden upon them.—I have acted upon a supposable wish of yours in not asking them to print the poem in a book unless I could first use it in the magazine.

Frankly, I shall be glad to get the short poems, and the articles that you propose.[3] But shouldn't you think it well to give them (the latter) a name different from that of the Blackwood series?[4]

—I think we all here in America felt personally and nationally glad to see you.[5] If a man is worth being an event, he never knows how great an event he is; and of course you cannot understand how general was the interest in your visit. It suffered us to reclaim you with your great fame, and to enrich a somewhat poverty-stricken period with a name that makes us proud to be your countrymen.

Yours very sincerely
W. D. Howells.

1. "Roba di Roma," *Atlantic*, November 1878, is a two-page poem with the directive below the title: "Julietta appears above at a balcony." "The Excursion" probably is "A Roman Holiday, Twenty Years Ago," *Atlantic*, February–March 1879. The Italian names refer to children's nurses employed by the Howellses during their years in Venice.

2. "The Rabbi's Letter" was apparently never printed.

3. Only one poem appears after this letter, "Do You Remember?" *Atlantic*, January 1880.

4. The first installments of Story's *Conversations in a Studio* (1890) appeared under the title "In a Studio" in *Blackwood's* during 1875 and 1876.

5. Story made one of several visits to America in 1877–1878.

4 SEPTEMBER 1878, BOSTON, TO CHARLES E. NORTON

> *...The Atlantic Monthly....*
> Boston. Sept. 4, 1878.

Dear friend:

I wanted to send a word with the proofs the other day to tell you how greatly I had enjoyed that tranquilly pleasing and satisfactory paper.[1] It was truly refreshing.

I have a second paper from our friend Harrison.[2] It is about the Nationals—results of his talk with thirty different workingmen from three different States. It is astonishing, disheartening and alarming. If those fellows get the upper hand, good-by, Liberty! We shall be ground down by the dullest and stupidest despotism that ever was.

I think Harrison's papers will do great good, and I'm anxious that in this time of high-pressure magazining, their quiet worth should be noticed. Will you call Godkin's attention to them?[3] I can't, I suppose, without seeming to be asking something for the Atlantic.

—We have had a lovely summer in our pretty new house, where I hope some day to welcome you. Mrs Howells joins me in love to all of you.

> Aff'tely yours
> W. D. Howells.

1. "Florence, and St. Mary of the Flower," *Atlantic*, November–December 1878.

2. The first paper by Harrison, "Certain Dangerous Tendencies in American Life," *Atlantic*, October 1878, gave the future book its title. The second paper, "The Nationals, Their Origins and Their Aims," November 1878, concerns the National Party, a radical group opposed to the banking and monetary system of the time and favoring government ownership of transportation and land. Jonathan Baxter Harrison (1835–1907) was an author and Unitarian clergyman of New Hampshire.

3. Whether or not Norton acted on Howells' suggestion is not known; but the *Nation*, 26 September 1878, praised Harrison's first article, calling it a "diagnosis of our moral condition" by "a patriotic, thoughtful, sincere, and observant man." Later Howells wrote Norton, 24 September 1878 (MH), of the success of Harrison's first paper: "It has notice by the column, everywhere." In the same letter he also regards it as likely that Osgood will publish Harrison's series as a book, which he did in 1880 under the title *Certain Dangerous Tendencies in American Life, and Other Papers*. The book contained eight essays, all of which appeared in the *Atlantic* between October 1878 and October 1879.

8 September 1878, Belmont, to William C. Howells

Belmont, Sept. 8, 1878.

Dear father:

I confess that I am somewhat puzzled how to begin a letter this morning, for of all newsless times, this seems the dryest. We have had company all week, and are weary to death of it. People have swarmed upon us this summer, and the business of life has had to go on subordinately to this so-called pleasure. Our only way will be to refuse all invitations to go any where ourselves, if we hope to cut down our own visitors. I suppose, however, you know all about the matter.—We have got our dear old John back after his two weeks' absence at Scotch Plains,¹ and he and Winny will soon resume their schooling. They will go to Cambridge, this winter; and after that we shall see what we shall do.—My play of A Counterfeit Presentment is coming out at the Boston Museum sometime in October; and I have got Out of the Question nearly ready for them.² Barrett will produce the Spanish play in Chicago this month.³ I have a story that begins in the November Atlantic.⁴ So you see, I have not been idle. Besides all this, I wrote six hundred pages of a story which I've been obliged to throw aside as a failure.⁵ The autobiographies will be continued very slowly: the series has not succeeded, so far.⁶ But publishers and others are looking for better times this fall, and it may revive and go ahead. There never was anything of the kind so handsomely received, and fully noticed by the press.—We have had a cold northeasterly storm, the past week; but now it has cleared off, and the weather is exquisite. We expect to enjoy the autumn here, particularly—with the fine days, and our open fires for the evening.—I enclose for Annie, $1.25—the difference between a check she sent, and the price Elinor paid for her corsets.—With best love to all,

Your aff'te son
Will.

1. To visit his aunt and uncle, the Augustus D. Shepards.

2. *A Counterfeit Presentment*, which opened at the Boston Museum on 1 April 1878, did not return there in October; the other play was apparently never performed in Boston because on 4 November 1878 (MH) R. M. Field, the manager of the Boston Museum, wrote Howells: "I have given very careful perusal and consideration to your rearrangement of 'Out of the Question,' and regret most sincerely my inability to give a favorable reply in regard thereto. . . . 'Out of the Question' requires greater alteration than has yet been made to render it an effective *acting* play. . . . It seems to me, however, that further invention and elaboration are required with respect to the plot . . . ."

3. Barrett postponed the Chicago performance of *Yorick's Love* because of dissatisfaction with the script. In Barrett's letter of 9 October 1878 (MH) the substance of his dissatisfaction is revealed: "the last act has reached me at so late an hour,

and the rehearsals have so exhibited its defects that I fear I must withdraw the announcements, and take it into my work room for a couple of weeks more. As there were no directions in your Mss for the disposition of characters in any scene or on exits or on entrance[s], I was put to great trouble in working all those things out, and I shall have much more trouble yet in completing the work." The play had its premiere in Cleveland later in the month, however. See Howells to Hay, 29 October 1878, n. 1.

4. *The Lady of the Aroostook, Atlantic,* November 1878–March 1879.
5. Probably *A Woman's Reason.*
6. See Howells to Higginson, 2 July 1877.

18 SEPTEMBER 1878, BOSTON, TO HORATIO S. NOYES

... The Atlantic Monthly....
Boston. Sept. 18—1878.

Dear Mr. Noyes,

Could you lend me the journal you kept of your voyage to Europe? I am sending a party to sea (in fiction) on the same line of travel, and wish them to leave an intelligent record.[1] Do bring it to Belmont, or if you can't, send it to me.

We all join in love to your family.

Very sincerely yours,
W. D. Howells.

1. *The Lady of the Aroostook, Atlantic,* November 1878–March 1879. Howells would have had until about 1 October for final touches on the first installment, though later installments also describe the voyage.

23 SEPTEMBER 1878, BOSTON, TO WILLIAM C. HOWELLS

... The Atlantic Monthly....
Boston. Sept. 23, 1878.

Dear father:

Yesterday I finished the Spanish play,[1] and in the afternoon Piatt came out from Boston, where he is staying a few days with the usual load of MS. You can imagine that I had little chance to write my Sunday letter. I drove Piatt over to Lexington, that he might see the battle ground, and then after tea walked him towards the horsecars in Arlington. He was a little more cheerful than usual, and made many affectionate inquiries after you. He is a good soul.—Fancy our rapture at getting, the other day, a note from Carol Dean, telling us that she had come back to Wellesley for the winter. It is hard to have so much company as we do, at any rate, but C. D. is a burden on the mind as well as the purse which I can hardly make up my temper to stand: she is on the whole the least agreeable young girl I know—thoroughly selfish, obtuse and vain. But I suppose we shall do what is right, by her.[2]

The weather is divinely lovely, and the country all about is looking its best. I wish you were here to drive over these hills with me. We have not had any frost yet; the leaves are scarcely tinged, and the fields are as green as in June.

The oil fever at Jefferson seems to have burnt out.[3] I searched the last Sentinel in vain for anything about it.

If you will give me the name of that book again, which you'd like to have, I'll gladly send it. I've mislaid your letter.

Tell Annie it's all right about that dollar.

> "Tis better to be paid and paid,
> Than never to be paid at all."[4]

We shall have in December, a highly appreciative review of Louis Frechette's poems.[5] I wish to be particularly remembered to A. Fréchette.

We have no news, and so send love to all.

Your aff'te son
Will.

Tell Henry that the horse stood up on his hind feet the other day when the train came in; and that he stops to scrape flies off with his big toes. I'm glad Henry still models himself on Budda Will. We sent you a package for Annie last week.

1. Howells apparently made revisions in *Yorick's Love* because Barrett had expressed his dissatisfaction with the play. See Howells to W. C. Howells, 8 September 1878, n. 3.

2. See Howells to W. C. Howells, 24 November 1877, n. 1.

3. The Ashtabula *Sentinel*, 12 September 1878, carried the following item: "Quite a little excitement was produced last Thursday morning by the discovery of oil on the surface of the water in the town well, which is being deepened. After more or less speculation as to the probable result of the find, it leaked out that a couple of bad boys, old ones, had poured a pint or so of Mecca oil, into the well, just for fun. Before the *fraud* was discovered, the news had been telegraphed to the morning papers at Cleveland."

4. The lines are a parody of Tennyson's: " 'Tis better to have loved and lost/ Than never to have loved at all" (*In Memoriam*, XXVII, 15–16).

5. The review of *Pêle-Mêle: Fantaisies et Souvenirs Poétiques* did not appear until January 1879. The reviewer (probably Howells, though the cumulative *Atlantic* index notes no author) praises Fréchette's poetical writing for its variety, and in this volume finds, "a real addition to literature of the lighter sort." Louis Honoré Fréchette (1839–1908), the brother of Achille, was active in both politics and journalism as well as in writing poetry; he became president of the Royal Society of Canada in 1900.

6 OCTOBER 1878, BOSTON, TO WILLIAM C. HOWELLS

> ... *The Atlantic Monthly*. ...
> Boston. Oct. 6, 1878.

Dear father:

I believe there is nothing to interest you greatly in the history of the past week. We are at last alone. Mary Mead—whom I like so much—went away on Thursday. That day we had five people to dinner,—Mary, her brother Willy and McKim the other architect,[1] and the two Aldriches. We ardently hope for a cessation of all this, with the coming of cold weather, but heaven only knows. The beauty and oddity of the new house have proved a great cross to the inhabitants, in bringing swarms of friends and semi-friends to see it.

You must be feeling very lonely without the Annie-folks. I wish dearly that *they* could come to visit us; but the guests that one would choose are mostly obliged to stay at home. (I don't reflect on our Thursday company.) And this reminds me to ask if you are not coming sometime soon. When you were here last, you spoke of having a pass on the Grand Trunk road that would enable you to travel freely, and I hoped it would bring you to us oftener.—We have a fire in the library this morning, and the children are making it a family room. John is putting away his butterfly collection for the winter, and Winny is drawing, and Pil circulating about generally. John has had a fearful tug in reading through a chapter of the Testament. Unless Sam had less love of literature, I don't know of any Howells who has less than John.—Before breakfast I went and got into John's bed, with Pil, and presently Winny followed, and we had a good time joking and telling stories just as we used when they were little things. I wish Henry could hear some of the stories. Politics as you must notice, are going somewhat crazily everywhere, this fall. Butler, however, hardly stands a chance for being governor, though he would certainly have been elected if the Democrats had nominated him.[2] In this district Banks failed of a nomination and so is finally shelved, I suppose.[3]—I wonder if you read the first article in the October Atlantic, and what you think of it. We shall have a paper by the same hand in November on the origin and aims of the Workingmen's party.[4]

All join me in love to all.

> Your aff'te son
> Will

---

1. See Howells to Bigelow, 25 February 1878, n. 1.

2. Benjamin Franklin Butler (1818–1893) was elected to Congress as a Republican in 1866 and served until he lost his seat in the Democratic wave in 1875. After

several unsuccessful attempts in the 1870s, he finally was elected governor of Massachusetts in 1882.

3. Nathaniel P. Banks, a Massachusetts congressman (1865–1873, 1875–1879, 1889–1891), was a U. S. marshal (1879–1888); in his many political campaigns he occasionally ran as a Democrat. See also Howells to Conway, 16 and 22 May 1864.

4. See Howells to Norton, 4 September 1878, n. 2.

29 OCTOBER 1878, BOSTON, TO JOHN HAY

The Atlantic Monthly,
Boston, October 29, 1878.

My dear Hay:

I thank you with all my heart for your thoughtful kindness in writing me about *A New Play*.[1] But I ought, in justice to the absent Señor Estébanez, to disclaim a good three-fourths of your praise. The trouble with Mr. Daly's version was that it was not Estébanez, but the tradition of the stage.[2] I blank-versified the more touching and noble speeches, and here and there I helped the Spaniard out a little; but that Hawthornian grip of the subject is his own. He is a *great* man, if he has done nothing but this.

I haven't the least idea how far Mr. Barrett has let my work alone. He wrote me from Chicago three weeks ago, in quite a panic, that it was all bad, and that he should have to "take it into his workshop" and do it over.[3] Since then I have not heard from him.

I see the fault (for long runs) that you speak of, and I thank you for putting your finger on it. I could remedy it with ease, by bringing Woodford, the author of the supposed play, into greater prominence as a comic element. Do tell me one thing: Is there a second part of the last act, in which Yorick loses himself in the character of Count Octavio? And does the play close with a speech of Yorick's?—I'm glad Shakespeare was kept out. I urged that fervently, but Mr. Barrett made no sign as to his intention in regard to it.[4]—I do hope he will succeed with the play,[5] for his own sake. My own stake in it is small.

It is worth while to write a story to have such praise you give *The L. of the A.*[6] Present my regards and gratitude to Mrs. Hay.

Yours cordially,
W. D. Howells.

This seems a stupid and complaining response to your letter. But let me say that I am most deeply touched and gratified, and I love you more than I could tell. What you have done is what I never could have done. I don't even know how to acknowledge it properly!

1. Under this title *Yorick's Love* had its premiere in Cleveland on 25 October 1878. In a letter dated 26 October 1878 (MH; *Life in Letters*, I, 257–58), Hay told Howells: "It was a great tragedy, nobly played, in short ... an honest and legitimate success. The success was yours too, for it was a very different play from the one I saw at the Fifth Avenue Theatre some years ago, improved almost beyond recognition. It was the best written play I have heard for a long time."

2. Augustin Daly's version, first produced 5 December 1874 in New York, had failed. See Meserve, *The Complete Plays of W. D. Howells* (New York: New York University Press, 1960), p. 111. Estébanez, the pseudonym of Manuel Tamayo y Baus. See Howells to W. C. Howells, 4 August 1877, n. 3.

3. See Howells to W. C. Howells, 8 September 1878, n. 2; also Barrett to Howells, 18 October 1878 (MH).

4. See Meserve, *Complete Plays*, pp. 110–14, for a description of the revisions and several manuscripts. The text Meserve prints is Barrett's manuscript version from the Lord Chamberlain's office in London (1884).

5. Barrett presented the play until his death in 1891.

6. *The Lady of the Aroostook*. Hay concluded his 26 October letter with praise of the first installment.

30 OCTOBER 1878, BOSTON, TO HORACE E. SCUDDER

... The Atlantic Monthly....
Boston. Oct. 30, 1878.

My dear Scudder:

It seems to me that this notice[1] will be grievous to the already aggrieved publishers because it faintly recognizes in a general way the good side of the book and painfully particularizes its fault, to the extent of three or four fourths of your review. Can't you spread the poultice over more surface, and confine the new raw a little?

Your corrupt friend
W. D. H.

1. Scudder had written a review of the second volume of *A Popular History of the United States*, by William Cullen Bryant and Sydney Howard Gay (1878). Probably because Bryant died on 12 June 1878, just a few days before the publication of his history, Howells thought it unbecoming to publish a severely critical review. The tone of Scudder's unpublished "notice" is suggested by his comment on the first volume of Bryant's history: "We cannot get over the feeling that we are reading careful notes made for a history rather than history itself ..." (*Atlantic*, September 1876).

11 NOVEMBER 1878, BOSTON, TO HENRY W. LONGFELLOW

... The Atlantic Monthly. ...
Boston. November 11, 1878.

Dear Mr. Longfellow:

I sent your letter out to Hay himself, who has doubtless answered your questions before this.[1]

I don't know of any better source than Coggeshall's Poets and Poetry of the West (College library) to send you to for local Western poems. There are more poets and poetry in the book.[2]

I am very proud and glad to have you include Avery in your collection[3]

Yours very truly
W. D. Howells

1. Longfellow's letter has not been found.

2. Six of Howells' poems along with several biographical notices appeared in this 1860 anthology edited by William T. Coggeshall. See Howells to Victoria Howells, 26 December 1858, n. 7.

3. "Avery" first appeared in *Their Wedding Journey* (1872) and again in *Poems* (1873). *Poems of Places*, edited by Longfellow, appeared in nearly 30 volumes (1876–1879); the one to which Howells refers is subtitled "America: Western States" (1879).

21 NOVEMBER 1878, BELMONT, TO HJALMAR H. BOYESEN

... The Atlantic Monthly. ...
Boston. Nov. 21, 1878.

My dear Boyesen:

I have received your letter from Berlin and your cards from Berlin and Munich; and I am to make you what must seem the ungracious return of owning that I liked your story so little that I let Scribners have it, though I was exceedingly anxious to have your name in The Atlantic again.[1] Do forgive me, and send me something else. It seemed to me that the subject of your story was not treated with your characteristic delicacy, and that your effort to vernacularize the Tyrolese patois in English was not successful. I would not venture to say this if you did not know how much I prize and admire your genius.—I am extremely obliged to you for your notes about Schmidt and Heyse.[2] I would rather have Tourgueneff think well of me than any other living man. I hope that some day I shall have the great happiness of meeting him.[3]—Who is Heinrich Homberger, who writes about Private Theatricals in Das Magazin für die Literatur des Auslandes, and who wrote of A Foregone Conclusion in the Rundschau?[4] If one may say it of a critic who praises one, he is uncommonly subtle and profound. I did not know till I saw his review that the former novel had been translated. I have never been able to satisfy myself with any revision I could make of it, and I had rather my unknown oversetter had waited my motion. But these things can't be helped.—I hope you will enjoy Italy; that you are happy I know, and I offer my respectful homage to the cause of your bliss. I heartily wish I could see you a married man.—We are richly content with our new home in Belmont, where we have the prettiest house I ever saw, on the crest of a hill overlooking all the vast plain in which Boston lies, and commanding five light-houses at night. You shall see them all, and Mrs. Boyesen shall look at them from Mrs. Howells's balcony, while you and I smoke our cigarettes on the northeast piazza. Louis Dyer, who is now *tuting* in Greek at Harvard, often rides horseback out to see us, and great part of Cambridge has called. But we shall soon be snowed in and left alone on our hilltop.—The Lathrops have left Cambridge, and have a lodging in Boston. Lathrop, you know, is now editor of the Boston Courier.[5]—I have not seen Mr. Longfellow for a great while, but I hear that he is very well this winter. The Fieldses were out here the other day to dinner.—Every Wednesday I spend at the Atlantic office in Boston, and I see numbers of people.—I hear from Stedman that poor Taylor is in a bad way. I am exceedingly sorry for it; he is a lovable and good man.—Whitelaw Reid has asked me to his house for the monthly meeting of the Century Club, Dec. 7. John Hay is to be my fellow guest.—Mrs. Howells thinks with me that your Scribner story is very profound and powerful.[6] All of us join in regards.

Yours ever
W. D. Howells.

1. "Ilka on the Hill-Top," *Scribner's*, November 1880.
2. Reviews of J. Heinrich Schmidt, *An Introduction to the Rhythmic and Metric of the Classical Languages* (1878; translated by John William White) and Paul Heyse, *Das Ding an sich und andere Novellen* (1879) appeared in the *Atlantic*, February and April 1879, respectively.
3. For Boyesen's role in introducing Turgenev to Howells' works, see Howells to Boyesen, 10 June 1874.
4. Homberger (1838–1890) wrote "William Dean Howells," *Deutsche Rundschau*, June 1877, and a review of the German translation of "Private Theatricals" in the Berlin weekly, *Magazin für die Literatur des Auslandes* (12 October 1878). The latter is a lengthy and perceptive discussion of Howells' particular brand of realism, which Homberger considered superior to that of Bret Harte, Turgenev, and Flaubert. The review concludes with the statement that "Howells' book is not only artistically successful and psychologically true, but is conducive to morality as well." According to a letter Howells wrote to T. S. Perry, 29 August 1877 (InU),

Perry sent the earlier Homberger piece to Howells, who then commented: "Homberger is a man to be cherished. But I am more Caviar fürs Volk, please the pigs, than he thinks. His compliment in that respect, reminded me of cruel praise received the other day from a would-be contributoress. 'I am delighted to find *one* person at last, who enjoys your books.' Imagine how quickly *her* contribution went back. [¶]...Homberger says many of the things that I could myself have said of the book if it had been decent to do so. Can I more fully express my content?" Much later, in 1892, Howells referred to Homberger as "a famous critic who has reviewed my books in Germany." See Franklin Smith, "An Hour with Mr. Howells," in U. Halfmann, ed., *Interviews with William Dean Howells* (Arlington, Texas: University of Texas, 1973), pp. 16–19.

5. Dissatisfied with his position at the *Atlantic*, George P. Lathrop resigned on 1 September 1877. In a letter of 4 July 1877 (MH) Lathrop wrote: "I have been disappointed in my relations with The Atlantic since I became your assistant, because I have never been able to throw into the work the tremendous ardor wh. I felt about it....I could not help feeling that in a good many ways there was a tendency to make me an outsider, a merely mechanical clerk...." On 29 August 1877 (MH) Lathrop once again wrote: "Your note of the 28th., signifying your willingness that my resignation from The Atlantic should go into effect on Sept. 1st., is received."

6. "Annunciata," *Scribner's*, October 1879.

24 NOVEMBER 1878, BOSTON, TO EDMUND C. STEDMAN

> ...*The Atlantic Monthly*....
> Boston. Nov. 24, 1878.

My dear Stedman:

I am truly grieved to hear what you tell me of poor dear old Taylor.[1] It seems too bad. I don't know what to say of so sad a thing.—Of course I shall print your review[2] as editorial: I haven't read it yet, but I know it's good, and I shall be glad of all the kind things you say of it.

—I hope to see you in a week or two. Meantime thank you for liking my story.[3] But I am not the special-reporter you think. Of course, one *materializes* as the spiritualists say, from all his experience and observation, but every shred of what you've read in those chapters (except the woman's stopping the hearse) is pure invention. I am devotedly a realist, but I hope I keep always a heart of ideality in my realism. Nothing is worth doing without that.

> Yours ever
> **W. D. Howells.**

1. As Howells wrote Boyesen on 21 November, "I hear from Stedman that poor Taylor is in a bad way." Stedman's letter to Howells, 15 November 1878 (in part, L. Stedman and G. M. Gould, eds., *Life and Letters of Edmund Clarence Stedman* [New York: Moffat, Yard, 1910], II, 338), makes no reference to Taylor's illness, although this is probably the letter Howells is referring to. Howells wrote Stedman on 19 December (NNC), having just heard of Taylor's death on the same day, "it was what we all dreaded, of course."

2. It is possible that Stedman wrote the review of Taylor's *Prince Deukalion: A Lyric Drama* (1878), *Atlantic*, January 1879, though it is attributed to G. P. Lathrop in the *Atlantic Index*. In his letter of 19 December, Howells asked Stedman for "a paper of personal reminiscence and of literary analysis," which he could print in the next (February 1879) issue if he might have it by the end of the next week. Apparently Stedman refused, since "Reminiscences of Bayard Taylor" in the February number is signed by R. H. Stoddard.

3. The first installment of *The Lady of the Aroostook*, *Atlantic*, November 1878. In the opening scene Lydia's aunt goes out to the gate to ask the hearse driver whom he has been burying. When she learns, she says, " 'Why, I thought the funeral wa' n't to be till to-morrow! Well, I declare . . . .' "

4 DECEMBER 1878, BOSTON, TO THOMAS B. ALDRICH

. . . The Atlantic Monthly. . . .
Boston. Dec. 4, 1878.

My dear Aldrich:

I sent you a postal in answer to your letter, meaning to write more at large, before this. I *had* written in answer to your first note about the proof, and then tore up my letter, which was of the tenor of that I sent you finally, not reflecting that you were meanwhile left in the dark, but trusting to my own sense of rectitude for your information.—What afflicted me was your seeming to treat me as an editor who was attempting to be arbitrary with you whereas I had always shown you the interest and consideration of a friend. It's all right, and we wont misunderstand each other again.[1]

I'm glad to hear the story's getting forward,[2] and I've no doubt that it's all your domestic tyrant thinks it. After *my* stories pass a similar tribunal, I feel like defying fate with 'em. Why don't you come up some Wednesday, so we can lunch together?

I'm going to New York on Saturday, for the monthly meeting of the Century Club, and expect to be home again Tuesday morning.

Could you send me a few roots of water-cress out of your brook? I want to try it in my conservatory fountain.

Yours ever
W. D. Howells.

1. Neither Howells' postal to Aldrich nor Aldrich's "first note" (or other Aldrich letters on this imbroglio) have been found. However, on 26 November (MH) Howells wrote that he would include certain late additions if possible and explained that "The piece was marked for the Club without my authority by the foreman . . . ." At the same time Howells complained that he thought Aldrich had been "needlessly peremptory." "Our New Neighbors at Ponkapog" appeared in the *Atlantic*, January 1879.

2. Aldrich was beginning *The Stillwater Tragedy*, *Atlantic*, April–September 1880.

1 JANUARY 1879, BOSTON, TO ARTHUR G. SEDGWICK

> *. . . The Atlantic Monthly. . . .*
> *Boston.* Jan. 1, 1878.[1]

My dear Sedgwick:

I think the paper on New York Theatres is very good, and I shall use it as an article,[2] and shall be glad if you can go on with the other New York topics we talked of, though in the *articulary* as opposed to the *epistolary* form.

About the Washington letters I feel more doubtful. This one comes too late for the February number, and so I send it back, suggesting that you charge a little more heavily in the direction of Congressional president-making, and let me have it back under the title of Electioneering for 1880 in Congress. That will give me my desired political article for March.[3] Perhaps you could enlarge upon the different men and their chances. I can squeeze the "pisen" out of your opinions.

—Wallack is considering as to the production of Counterfeit Presentment at his theatre.[4] Could you not assemble a mob of large, rich, and personally impressive Club men, and go round, and send up your compliments, and beg to know *when* Mr. Howells's charming comedy is to be given?

> Yours ever
> **W. D. Howells.**

1. Though Howells dated the letter 1878, the articles of which he writes show this as a slip for 1879.
2. "New York Theatres," *Atlantic*, April 1879.
3. Sedgwick probably wrote the unsigned "Presidential Electioneering in the Senate," *Atlantic*, March 1879. He had contributed an unsigned paper on "Washington Society" in December 1877, and in 1878 had published three signed political articles, with a fourth on copyright in February 1879.
4. Barrett presented *A Counterfeit Presentment* in 1877–1878, though not in New York; Lester Wallack's interest in the play did not result in its production at Wallack's Theatre.

4 JANUARY 1879, BOSTON, TO RUTHERFORD B. HAYES

> *. . . The Atlantic Monthly. . . .*
> *Boston.* Jan. 4, 1879.

Dear Mr. President:

I have the honor and pleasure of introducing Mr. Clarence King,[1] whose name in science and literature we are all so proud of. He knows everything about California especially, from supposititious diamond mines in Arizona to the last graces of the Pike dialect, and he is, as you see a charming and most civilized New Englander. If you know his book, "Mountaineering in the Sierra Nevadas," as well as I do,[2] you must share my sole grief against him, namely, that a man who can give us such literature, should be content to be merely a great scientist.

Elinor is giving him a letter to Mrs Hayes,[3] and we both particularly recommend him.

Yours very truly
W. D. Howells.

P. S You will be interested to know that Mr. King began his Mountaineering, as a boy, on Round Mountain at West Brattleboro.[4]

1. Clarence King (1842–1901), geologist and mining engineer, was the first director of the U. S. Geological Survey (May 1879–March 1881). See T. Wilkins, *Clarence King* (New York: Macmillan, 1958), pp. 238–63. In a letter to S. Weir Mitchell, 1 January 1902 (PU), Howells wrote: "I was at poor Clarence King's funeral today.... He was a man who could have done great things in literature if it had not been for envious science."

2. Howells reviewed *Mountaineering in the Sierra Nevada* in the *Atlantic*, April 1872, where it had appeared as a serial, May–August 1871. King was also a regular contributor of geological and demographic articles from 1871 to 1875.

3. Elinor M. Howells to Lucy Hayes, undated (OFH).

4. According to *Life in Letters*, I, 261, Hayes' grandfather had a tavern in West Brattleboro.

19 FEBRUARY 1879, BOSTON, TO ELLEN HUTCHINSON

. . . The Atlantic Monthly. . . .
Boston. Feb. 19, 1879.

Dear Miss Hutchinson:[1]

I should have been greatly the loser if you *hadn't* written me that kind and lovely letter.[2] One thing you say *particularly* pleases me: that about the ideality *in* my realism. That's what I always strive for, and I should be untrue to realism itself if I didn't strive for it.

I wish I could dramatize the story, but nothing seems so untheatricable. Mrs. Phelps shall dramatize it, and I will come to the *première!*[3]

Thanking you again and again,

Very sincerely yours,
W. D. Howells.

1. Ellen Hutchinson (d. 1933) helped E. C. Stedman edit his *Library of American Literature* (1888–1890). She also was at one time art editor of the New York *Tribune* and was succeeded in that post by Royal Cortissoz, whom she married in 1897.

2. Probably in appreciation of *The Lady of the Aroostook*, which had just concluded in the March *Atlantic* and which appeared as a book on 27 February 1879.

3. Mrs. Phelps has not been identified; it is unlikely that Howells may be referring to Elizabeth Stuart Phelps, who did not marry until 1888.

19 FEBRUARY 1879, BOSTON, TO CHARLES D. WARNER

. . . The Atlantic Monthly. . . .
Boston. Feb. 19, 1879.

My dear Warner:

You may be all right about the story, but I am *sure* of your kindness, and I thank you for that with all my might.[1] You say the things that I *hoped* were true, and since you say them, I will believe them. Of course I did my best; there were *gasps* when I felt the whole thing slipping through my fingers. But I hung on, somehow.—This is the first story that I ever began to print before I had finished it; so that I may claim now to be a regular-built novelist, I suppose.

—It's too bad to hear of your only *looking* our way. I see that I shall be obliged to come to see *you*. Mrs. Howells joins me in love to both of you. Since your letter came she has really plucked up some respect for me.

Yours affectionately
W. D. Howells.

"I haven't said at all what I wanted to say. There was a great deal I ought to say. I can't seem to recollect it."[2]

1. See Howells to Hutchinson, 19 February 1879, n. 2.
2. Spoken by Lydia in *The Lady of the Aroostook* (1879), p. 314.

7 MARCH 1879, BOSTON, TO RICHARD G. WHITE

. . . The Atlantic Monthly. . . .
Boston. March 7, 1879.

Dear Mr. White:[1]

I put my pencil through that paragraph because I thought it took from the dignity of your paper, and because I feared that it might vex a man whom you meant to please. As I heard the saying, it was about a fashionable person who drove too much with a Mrs. Hearn—also fashionable—and it touched a local scandal.[2]

Living in London is delightful.[3] I enjoyed every bit of it, and long for more. And I wish to say again how much I should prefer such papers hereafter to those on Americanisms.[4] I feel that there is a vast and spreading discontent with that topic, which may any day burst into a murderous tumult in which we shall both perish. The papers murmur, the publishers groan. Be persuaded, my dear Sir, to leave it—at least for three or four months, and write of travel, art, music, society. Where are those papers on New York society, of which we talked?[5]

Forgive my plain speech, and send me anything but Americanisms.

Yours sincerely
W. D. Howells.

1. Richard Grant White (1821–1885), New York critic and author, was like his friend C. E. Norton a well-known man of letters and arbiter of taste.

2. Howells may be referring to the earlier removal of a passage from "London Streets," *Atlantic*, February 1879. The sketch ends with a conversation with an unmarried girl who tells the narrator she recently gave birth to a child. White comments approvingly that "there was not a word of reproach, and no talk of betrayal or of ruin."

3. "Living in London," *Atlantic*, April 1879. Quite possibly this may be the essay referred to in the first paragraph.

4. Eight papers on "Americanisms" appeared in the *Atlantic*, April 1878–May 1879. Two later ones had slightly variant titles: "Assorted Americanisms," November 1879, and "British Americanisms," May 1880.

5. The papers on New York society did not appear.

10 MARCH 1879, BOSTON, TO HORACE E. SCUDDER

...*The Atlantic Monthly*....
Boston. March 10, 1879.

Dear Scudder:

Here is the proof—work your will with it. You might insinuate that Dr. Eliot reports too often.[1]

John (we are glad that you liked him and found him funny, which I was *not*, at his age) has come home simply frantic on insects. He is a perfect bug-fiend, in fact, and bores us to death with thoraxes and antennae of every sort.

Thank *you*, dear Mrs. Scudder, for turning aside the stab aimed at my skeleton. I'm sure I should have felt it through all the padding that forty-two years have laid upon my bones. That little thrust, by the way, postpones *a certain story* by a *certain person* for another *eighteen months*.[2] (And he can't help himself, for he's paid for it.)

As soon as the softening weather makes it safe to visit the Arctic slopes of the Reservoir, I'm coming to board with you.[3]

Yours ever
W. D. Howells.

What a heaven-born day! Blue birds every where. As if the sky had fallen.

1. Scudder did not follow Howells' suggestion in his review of Charles W. Eliot, *Thirty-Fourth and Thirty-Fifth Semi-Annual Report of the Superintendent of Public Schools, Atlantic,* July 1879.

2. What critical "stab" Scudder had contemplated is unclear, but Howells' humorous threat to revenge himself by postponing the publication of one of Scudder's stories probably refers to "Accidentally Overheard," *Atlantic,* March 1880.

3. The 1879 Cambridge directory gives Scudder's residence as 9 Highland Street, about a mile west of the Harvard yard; the reservoir, abutting Reservoir and Highland streets, no longer exists.

16 MARCH 1879, BOSTON, TO RUTHERFORD B. HAYES

... *The Atlantic Monthly*....
Boston. March 16, 1879.

Dear Mr. President:

Even before your kind letter came, we had read the fate of the California trip in the certainty of an extra session, and were prepared for the worst.[1] At least it was a splendid prospect, while it lasted, and I think you would have liked my book about it—if I had written it.

—The Chinese veto-message was everything your friends could have wished in dignity, humanity and common sense of justice.[2] In that and the silver veto and the New York Custom House business and your good will to the irreclaimable South,[3] you have made history of the best kind.

Elinor sends her love to all.

Yours very truly
W. D. Howells.

1. Hayes had written Howells on 9 March 1879 (MH) that "We lose our California trip. This extra Session compels us to give it up." He had called a special session of the Forty-sixth Congress for the purpose of making the requisite appropriations for the three branches of the government.

2. Hayes vetoed an 1879 act of Congress which restricted Chinese immigration. The move to restrict Chinese immigration was spearheaded by Dennis Kearney, president of the Workingman's Party. Hayes regarded the act as a violation of the Burlingame Treaty.

3. The Bland-Allison Act, requiring governmental purchase of silver between $2 and $4 million a month, was passed over presidential veto, 1 March 1878. On 11 July 1878 Hayes suspended Chester A. Arthur and other favorites of Roscoe Conkling and the Republican stalwarts from the New York Custom House; and in early 1879 his own appointments were confirmed. On the South, see Howells to W. C. Howells, 17 May 1880, n. 6.

17 MARCH 1879, BOSTON, TO JAMES P. STABLER

The Atlantic Monthly
March 17, 1879.

Dear Sir:[1]

I'm afraid that I can't explain or excuse my heroine's name, which seemed to me from the first an essential part of her.

I still think I am right on the point you allege against me.[2] Women worth thinking and writing about are never blinded by romance, though they are often blinded by affection.[3]

---

1. James P. Stabler (1839–1925), electrician and inventor, was chief clerk in the statistical division of the U. S. Department of Agriculture at the time this letter was written. A nephew of Stabler, the Howells scholar Rudolf Kirk, described his uncle as "one of the most brilliant men I have ever known.... Of course he was a country cuss, was dead honest, couldn't make money, was cheated out of a large sum that another man made on one of his inventions. He was a great skeptic in matters of religion and probably got to Heaven ahead of the righteous."

2. In his letter to Howells of 14 March, Stabler had spoken of "inflicting such a name as Lydia Blood upon such a lovely character as the heroine." Evidently Stabler retained a copy of his own letter; it appears in full in Clara M. and Rudolf Kirk, eds., *William Dean Howells; Representative Selections* (New York: Hill and Wang, 1950; reprint ed., 1961), p. cxxxv, n. 347. Stabler's letter mainly concerned itself with Howells' remark, "Women are never blinded by romance, however much they like it in the abstract" (*The Lady of the Aroostook* [1879], p. 317; *Atlantic*, March 1879). Stabler commented: "The statement made thus broadly cannot be true it seems to me, whether applied to man or woman, and it occurred to me that it was probably intended especially for Lydia, & was through an oversight put in the form of a generality." Stabler's comment on Howells' response is written on the verso of the holograph, according to the Kirks, and reads as follows: "Mr. Howells begs the question by limiting the application of a broad statement which included all women to 'women worth thinking or writing about.' He attempts to justify himself by qualifying the phrase without admitting that he was in error—I do not think that candid or very manly & will always think less of Howells for it. J. P. S."

3. Complimentary close and signature have been omitted in the Kirks' edition.

---

31 MARCH 1879, BOSTON, TO SAMUEL A. GREEN

... *The Atlantic Monthly*. . . .
Boston. March 31, 1879.

Dear Sir:[1]

At the suggestion of Mr. James M. Bugbee,[2] I beg to apply to you for an article on "mysterious disappearances" which I wish to have for The Atlantic.[3] The matter has been brought very freshly to my mind by the numerous "identifications" of the body of the murdered girl at Lynn, with other young women whose friends have lost sight of them. The fact seems to be that the number of missing people is far greater than the public supposes.

If your leisure and inclinations would permit you to undertake this, I should be extremely glad. In case you consent, Mr. Bugbee would like to be of service to you with facts.

Yours truly
W. D. Howells.

Dr. Green.

1. Samuel A. Green (1830–1918), a graduate of Harvard, served as city physician (1871–1880) and was elected mayor of Boston in 1882. From 1868 until his death he was librarian of the Massachusetts Historical Society.

2. James McKellar Bugbee (1837–1913) appears to have been a member of the first Boston Police Commission, which was established in 1878. He was the author of "Boston Under the Mayors, 1822–1880," in Justin Winsor, ed., *The Memorial History of Boston* (1881), III, 217–92, and a frequent contributor to the *Atlantic*.

3. "Mysterious Disappearances" appeared unsigned in the *Atlantic*, November 1879, but the cumulative index gives J. M. Bugbee as the author. The "Lynn Mystery" is treated in a paragraph, with the observation that before her identification in late March "no fewer than fifty girls of about the same age had mysteriously disappeared within a short time...."

31 MARCH 1879, BOSTON, TO ANNIE A. FIELDS

...The Atlantic Monthly....
Boston. March 31, 1879.

Dear Mrs. Fields:

I venture to trouble you about a matter about which I should trouble Mr. Fields if I were sure of his being at home, and I should trouble him, only because I haven't "got nowhar to go," besides. You know Mr. Warner is condemned to read for the benefit of the Gloucester sufferers, at Tremont Temple next Saturday night,[1] and he wants some sort of slide-up-and-downable reading desk, so that he can have his MS. just under his chin when he reads. Will you kindly refer this want to Mr. Fields when he is at home? And I wish, speaking with the most bated breath that somehow Warner could be paid his expenses out of the proceeds. Of course, he doesn't dream of my mentioning this.

I am to read a poem, which Heaven is yet to send me.[2] Do,—if you have any printed account of that shipwreck—send it me: I am beginning to hate those 145 widows. Not that they are to blame.

—And dear Mrs. Fields let me thank you most cordially for those kind words you sent me about my book.[3] My pleasure in its success would have lacked a great deal without them.

Yours sincerely
W. D. Howells.

1. The Saturday mentioned by Howells was 5 April; no account of the event has been located.

2. On 3 April 1879 (CSmH) Howells wrote Mrs. Fields again about his poem and thanked her for the information he requested: "I have done a little poem which my wife calls—perhaps too flatteringly—atrocious, and which she would not hear read on any account...."

3. *The Lady of the Aroostook*, published in late February.

12 APRIL 1879, BOSTON, TO WILLIAM H. BISHOP

The Atlantic Monthly,
Boston, April 12, 1879.

My dear Mr. Bishop:

I have never had two minds about *Detmold*: I have thought it always a story strongly moved and with movement enough to the end; the heroine is sweet and novel; the hero a good type of good fellow; their love-making is charming; all the accessories pleased me. I have urged all this more than once; but I knew nothing of the selling qualities of the book, and I could only tell Mr. Osgood that I believed it would sell. I knew what he wrote you, and if I were you, I should make the plates and take the risk. If it sells a thousand you more than save yourself. I assure you that it shall not lack help in the *Atlantic*:[1] I admire and like it as much as I ever did, and whatever I *don't* know of pictures, I *do* know of books.

I have had one great disappointment in your paper on the exhibition,[2] namely, that you said nothing of Fuller's paintings: *The Romany Girl* and *She Was a Witch*. I like his work far better than that of any other American; it seems to me beautiful and interesting, with a soul as well as a body. These two pictures especially charmed me. Didn't you think them good; or do you object to his methods, or did you merely pass them in carelessness or weariness? If you like them well enough to send me a page of manuscript about them, I should be glad. Fuller is one of the painters who feel and think; and most of them seem to do neither.[3]

Yours ever,
W. D. Howells.

1. In his August 1879 *Atlantic* review Howells wrote of *Detmold* that "The story is well balanced, and is most conscientiously wrought out to the end with care that never falters and never visibly becomes anxiety.... [¶] It is fine without being superfine, and it is delicate without weakness.... It is in fine a finished achievement of a high sort in fiction...."

2. In "Two New York Exhibitions," *Atlantic*, June 1879, Bishop complied with Howells' request by giving a long paragraph to Fuller, though somewhat restrained in enthusiasm.

3. Howells contributed a fifty-page "Sketch of George Fuller's Life" to J. B. Millet, ed., *George Fuller: His Life and Works* (1886). George Fuller (1822–1884), after painting somewhat sporadically in his earlier career, moved to Boston in 1876 and immediately became a highly regarded artist.

22 APRIL 1879, BOSTON, TO LAWRENCE BARRETT

> ... *The Atlantic Monthly.* ...
> Boston. April 22, 1879.

Dear Mr. Barrett:

Here is the new act amended, as nearly as I could mend it after your wishes.[1] I *could not* put that talk of Gregory's into dialogue for Yorick and Alice, and that is the only point at which I have wholly failed. I give you here seventeen pages of fresh matter, and I have got you several new turns that work out Yorick as a humorist. There is also *click* at the close of the act, which it wanted before. I now suggest that the second act (old first,) begin with the enclosed lines spoken in soliloquy by Heywood while he briefly waits Yorick's entry.

—Of course, the diction of the act is not yet as I should *print* it; but its very roughness is a merit, in some respects. I want you in acting to make note of any little turns that will improve it, and we will fight over them in the summer.

You are kind enough to say that you feel bound to make me extra payment for this new work. *I shall not receive it.* If you can on receipt of this MS. send me $300—making up the $5.00 royalties which you were to have paid by the 21st—I shall be very glad indeed. But I want finally no more, all told, than the $2000 royalties originally agreed on.[2] That is enough. And I mean to make this play just what you want it if I can.

> Yours sincerely
> **W. D. Howells.**

1. On the continuing revisions of *Yorick's Love*, see Meserve, *The Complete Plays of W. D. Howells* (New York: New York University Press, 1960), pp. 110–14, and Howells to Hay, 29 October 1878.

2. On 1 October 1880 (CU; *Twain-Howells*, p. 329) Howells reported to Clemens that Barrett "has paid up in full the $2500 promised me for Yorick." On 12 April 1879 (MH) Barrett told Howells in sending $100 that he held himself "bound to make extra compensation for *this* work."

23 APRIL 1879, BOSTON, TO GEORGE W. CURTIS

> ... *The Atlantic Monthly.* ...
> Boston. April 23, 1879.

Dear Mr. Curtis:

I am glad that the paper of Mr Brown pleased you. He is a young man whose present address is Divinity Hall, Cambridge, but who has lived much abroad,—in England and Germany.[1] Morley had taken a paper of his on Socialism in Germany, for The Fortnightly,[2] but after it was in type a pre-engaged paper on the same subject came to hand,[3] and he was forced to return Brown's. I have told him that if he could not place his paper entire in some review, I would take it in reduced form. But I wish it could be printed as it is.

I know nothing more about him, except that he is a young man of exceptionally refined and delicate presence—much like the Harry James of twelve years ago—and that he is a little threadbare.

Yours sincerely
W. D. Howells.

1. George Willard Brown (1853–1910) graduated from Harvard in 1875, was a student at Leipzig (1877–1878), and attended Harvard Law School (1878–1879). After 1881 he practiced law with the New York firm of Brown & Wells. Brown had just published "English Civil Service Reform," *Atlantic*, May 1879, and from March 1880 to July 1882 published three articles and two reviews there.

2. Probably "Socialism in Germany and the United States," *Fortnightly Review*, November 1878; John Morley (1838–1923), Viscount Morley of Blackburn, statesman and man of letters, was its editor (1867–1882); he also edited the *Pall Mall Gazette* (1880–1883).

3. "Socialism and Germany," *Atlantic*, October 1879.

2 MAY 1879, BOSTON, TO JOHN HAY

The Atlantic Monthly,
Boston, May 2, 1879.

My dear Hay:

I am your debtor for a letter that touched me,[1] and for a speech so good, so just and so manly that I felt personally obliged to you for it.[2] How well you put the case of those wretched blacks—I wish it had been your purpose to put that of those who are black inside.

I hope you have good news of your mother, still. All sorrows but those which befall us through our parents, seem reparable. One night at eleven I got a dispatch saying, "Mother very sick—come first train." I got home three hours after her death. She had languished all summer; but because the journey was expensive and I was busy and poor, she had continually sent me word, "Tell Willy that I'm not sick—only just miserable." What tenderness was in her—what inexpressible love for her children!—I could feel for you in what you had been through at your mother's bedside and I could realize the type of character in her. It's wonderful.

My visit to my father in Toronto is postponed till the autumn. Will your sunsets keep so long? I hope so, for I want very much to see them. We shall be able then to appear in our smuggled finery—for Mrs. Howells means to buy clothes in Canada.—How very different it is when they propose to print one's book in Canada, and smuggle *that* across. It makes me feel terribly. You see they are threatening to get out a twenty-cent edition in Toronto of *The Lady of the Aroostook*.[3] I am so glad you liked the end of the book as well as the beginning, for I thought that I had rightly philosophized the situation. Of course, South Bradfield must have the last word. As to the dialect, I am only sure that I have got the conscientiously-cunningly-reluctant, arbitrarily emphatic Yankee *manner*. Your praise does my heart good.—I have it on my soul to tell you that Barrett has paid Taylor's estate the remaining $1000, and that I judged him hastily from the delay. He is to try the play in S. Francisco.[4] He is stale, just now with the Spanish play,[5] which upon my word, I think the most beautiful tragedy I ever saw. I speak of the action and design.—Mrs. Hay's album has cost me no appreciable sum.[6] Take back thy gift. Did I tell you Whittier had written her an original poem in it?

With our love to both of you,

Yours ever,
W. D. Howells.

1. On 4 April 1879 (MH) Hay wrote Howells of his mother breaking her hip a month ago; though he had expected her death, he now thought she would live. "They are no longer made, it seems to me—those wonderful women of her date."

2. The New York *Tribune* reprinted Hay's speech from the Cleveland *Leader* on 24 April 1879 under the title, "Col. John Hay on Negro Exodus. An Eloquent Speech at a Cleveland Meeting in Aid of Colored Immigrants." Hay urged his audience to be charitable and generous in their treatment of former slaves who were beginning to migrate in large numbers to northern cities.

3. See Howells to W. C. Howells, 4 May 1879, n. 2.

4. Bayard Taylor translated Schiller's *Don Carlos* with the intention to have Barrett produce it; but there is no evidence that Barrett ever did, or that Howells is here referring to that play.

5. *Yorick's Love*, which Barrett had been producing in Cincinnati; in his letter to Howells of 12 April 1879 (MH) he wrote of his plan to stage it in San Francisco. See also Meserve, *The Complete Plays of W. D. Howells* (New York: New York University Press, 1960), p. 113.

6. The album has not been identified.

4 MAY 1879, BOSTON, TO WILLIAM C. HOWELLS

...The Atlantic Monthly....
Boston. May 4, 1879.

Dear father:

Since I wrote you I have undergone the old affliction of a boil. It came on my right temple, and has given me a week of misery, but it is now over. The day when it was worst, Mr. Lefaivre,[1] who is on his way to France, came out from Boston, and read me in French a great part of his article on American poetry: I was blind of one eye, and followed him with the other. He staid six hours! Imagine my suffering.—I am greatly obliged by your writing me of the Canadian editions.[2] Osgood will put a stop to the Belford business in Detroit. I have not yet received the copy of the other edition which you sent me. But I don't flatter myself with the notion of "advertising" benefits from it. It is robbery, pure and simple, and is none the less so because for fifty years *our* thieves have plundered English authors. It is a shame and an outrage that the only property which is absolutely created by a man should not be protected by law. It is useless to fret about it, however.

Mr Dyer is here spending the Sunday. He wishes to be remembered, and says he greatly enjoyed a lecture of yours on correspondences, which Mr. Worcester of Waltham gave him.[3]

Mr. Lefaivre also wished to be remembered, and spoke very fondly of you. He had his son Alfred with him, who formed such an attachment to Belmont that he wished never to leave it.

I am glad to hear that Vic is better, though it is not so much better as I hoped. She has had a terrible time.—We all join in love to all.

Your aff'te son
Will.

1. Albert Alexis Lefaivre (b. 1830) was a Quebec literary critic.

2. Howells' concern over the continued Canadian pirating of his books focused on the recently published *The Lady of the Aroostook*, which was soon to be issued in Toronto by Belfords, Clarke & Co. in a format imitating the authorized American edition. On 11 May (MH; see also *Life in Letters*, I, 268) he wrote his father: "The worst of the Belford reprints is that they imitate the American covers, so that the wayfaring man who was intent upon the $2 edition might buy this for $1 by mistake." His knowledge of that practice was based on the unauthorized publication of *Their Wedding Journey* and *A Chance Acquaintance* by Belford Brothers in 1876.

3. W. C. Howells' lecture was delivered in the New Jerusalem Temple, Toronto, on 25 November 1878; it was published as *The Science of Correspondences* (1879). The persons to whom Howells refers are Louis Dyer and the Reverend Thomas Worcester.

18 MAY 1879, BOSTON, TO SAMUEL P. LANGLEY

... *The Atlantic Monthly.* . . .
Boston. May 18, 1879.

Dear Mr. Langley:[1]

I should have answered your note from London sooner, but I was not sure when you were to be at home, and I now write without knowing that you *are* at home.

I could imagine your uncertainty in reading my story, which it was my care to keep from being *your* story—as you will have seen if you have since had patience to hold out to the end. The fact is that having at first seen only the ludicrous side of such an adventure,—and I have heard of several of the kind—I began to be charmed with its poetic possibilities, and as I had never known Miss x x x's name, place, or occupation, I felt able to idylize and idealize to any extent.[2]

Come to see us at our new house in Belmont, and let me at least delude myself while you stay with the notion that I am going on with you to the Maine woods.[3]

Mrs. Howells joins me in cordial regards.

Yours sincerely

W. D. Howells.

P. S. We are neighbors here in Belmont to some cousins of yours, the Robbinses—very charming people.[4] The father has but one defect, his deafness; but I think I never knew anyone who could carry on a one-sided conversation so well. If possible, give us notice of the time you will be here in the summer, so that we many be sure not to miss you. If you bring your best telescope along, you can see Europe from our hill-top.—I wish you had time and inclination to write out for The Atlantic an account of your two months on Mt Etna.[5]

1. Samuel P. Langley (1834–1906) was a pioneer investigator of solar radiation and airplanes. With his brother he had gone to Venice in 1864–1865 and told Howells of their voyage with a single woman passenger on the ship, thus suggesting the story of *The Lady of the Aroostook*. See *Life in Letters*, I, 265.

2. On 23 March (MH; *Life in Letters*, I, 265–66) Langley wrote Howells recalling the voyage and commenting on the first chapters of the novel. From the aunt of the prototype of Lydia Blood he had learned that the young lady was still a schoolteacher and unmarried.

3. In his letter Langley invited Howells on a canoe trip in Maine.

4. The sons and daughters of the Reverend Samuel Dowse Robbins, second cousins of Langley. S. D. Robbins (1812–1884) graduated from the Cambridge Divinity School in 1833 and ministered to several parishes in Massachusetts. He and some of his children had homes about a quarter of a mile from Redtop, Howells' residence at Belmont.

5. "Wintering on Aetna," *Atlantic*, July 1880.

18 MAY 1879, BOSTON, TO EDMUND C. STEDMAN

...The Atlantic Monthly....

Boston. May 18, 1879.

My dear Stedman:

I am glad you are going to have a vacation at last,[1] and I should be proud and happy to join my name with yours in letters of introduction if I knew any Englishman. But I know literally none. I know of course Harry James and M. D. Conway, but you also know them. I met Lord

Houghton, but you met him, too. I am acquainted with Trübner,[2] but he has an arrangement for scooping the author's half of half profits, which afterwards reacts unfavorably on his opinion of the author, and I could not send you to him: besides, he is a German.

I wish you all possible joy and profit of your voyage.

> Yours cordially,
> W. D. Howells.

1. Stedman spent the summer of 1879 in England. On 15 May he wrote in his diary: "In a little over five months have made $11,000. *above my living. Was* ever poet so trusted before. . . . I am *worn down,* and *must* go abroad." See Stedman and Gould, eds., *Life and Letters of Edmund Clarence Stedman* (New York: Moffat, Yard, 1910), I, 575.

2. Nicholaus Trübner (1817–1884), publisher and author, was said to be an intimate friend of Bret Harte. On Howells' relation with Trübner & Co. as publishers of *Venetian Life,* see also *Literary Friends and Acquaintance,* HE, pp. 88–89.

20 JUNE 1879, BOSTON, TO CHARLES D. WARNER

> . . . *The Atlantic Monthly.* . . .
> Boston. June 20, 1879.

My dear Warner:

"My pain and my surprise you might learn from the expression of my eyes"[1] if you had seen them when I caught sight, among other letters on my desk, of yours unanswered. It was plainly a thing to be answered at once that I had considered it done.[2]

—Now as to the business of it: if you like Irving there is no one so fit as you in the country to do the work that your correspondents require. That is for once an honest opinion. And I think the work is worth while. Irving has fallen into abeyance, but what a sweet and lovely spirit he was, and how much we owe him! When I think what he was to me in my young days, my heart goes out to his memory. Do it, by all means.[3]

Equality I have in mind and will place soon.[4] When do you go to the Adirondacks?

> Yours ever
> W. D. Howells

Have you seen my scalp as taken by the war-chief Linton?[5]—Of course I shall be glad to use in the Atlantic anything you write about Irving.

1. The source of Howells' quotation has not been identified.

2. Warner's reply to Howells' letter of 2 June (CtHT) has not been located.

3. Presumably G. P. Putnam's Sons, publishers of *Studies of Irving* (1880), to which Warner contributed an essay. A cut version was published as "Washington Irving," *Atlantic,* March 1880. See also 31 December 1879 and 12 March 1880 to Warner.

4. "Equality," by Warner, *Atlantic,* January 1880.

5. William J. Linton (1812–1897), wood engraver, poet, and printer, illustrated books by such authors as Whittier and Longfellow. In his review of Linton's illustration of Bryant's "Thanatopsis" in the *Atlantic*, January 1878, Howells had found a few faults but many virtues. In the June 1879 *Atlantic*, Linton published "Art Engraving on Wood," and then, dissatisfied by alterations made in the proof of that article, he issued *Editorial Right: A Question of Honesty and Plain Speech*, an eight-page pamphlet containing two letters by Howells of 18 April and 14 May 1879.

22 JUNE 1879, BOSTON, TO JAMES R. LOWELL

...The Atlantic Monthly....
Boston. June 22, 1879.

Dear Mr. Lowell:

Your letter made me so happy that for a while at least I felt that I must have merited so much kindness, to have got it.[1] I have a clearer mind now, but I am happy in your letter, all the same. You are of course the largest part of that public of which I am conscious when I write, and if my book had not pleased you, I should not have thought it successful.— You not only praise that, but you forgive me, apparently for leaving Cambridge. Do you know that at the bottom of my guilty heart, I had all along felt that my going was a sort of disloyalty to you? This grieved me, and secretly embittered Belmont. But now that you don't reproach me, I shall like the new home without a pang. We have an extremely pretty house, to which we have already welcomed most of our Cambridge friends, and we have the landscape that you know. Back of our house, are lovely hill-tops, and gardened slopes, and our road frays off into the most delightful country lane to be found anywhere within a hundred miles of Boston. I hope some day to walk over it all with you. The children—especially Winny—have still keen regrets for Cambridge; but we have continued her and John in their schools there, and they are not unhappy here. They both love the country, and Bua goes in for it with all a boy's relish. His passion is for insects, and he is very mortal to moths and butterflies, which he knows how to "spread", after chloroform, in a manner that moves my admiration. His sole reading is natural history. But Winny! Imagine her reading from the fact that she has kept along with me in Froude's Caesar,[2] and that Shakespear is her favorite. She is grown up a tall girl, and is very good-looking—if I say so. Better still, she is *good.*—This leaves me little space to brag of the youngest, and perhaps that is just as well. But I am not ashamed of her.

I liked particularly what you said about our consciousness of England. But the matter is less serious than it may seem at a distance. Harry James waked up all the women with his Daisy Miller, the intention of which they misconceived, and there has been a vast discussion in which nobody felt very deeply, and everybody talked very loudly. The thing went so far that society almost divided itself in Daisy Millerites and anti-Daisy Millerites.[3] I was glad of it, for I hoped that in making James so thoroughly known, it would call attention in as wide degree to the beautiful work he had been doing so long for very few readers and still fewer lovers. Besides, I felt that he had got his best touch in that little study. His art is an honor to us, and his patriotism—which was duly questioned—is of the wholesome kind that doesn't blink our little foibles. At the end of the ends, however, I must confess that while I think our present consciousness is a fashion, we certainly are more conscious than we used to be, and are less dignified. I have come to understand fully what Hawthorne meant when he said to me that he would like to see some part of America on which the shadow of Europe had not fallen.[4] But it's no deeper than a shadow. In the meantime it seems to me that we are in a fair way to have a pretty school of really native American fiction. There are three or four younger fellows than myself writing, and there are several extremely clever, but not too clever, young women.

You may care to know that my latest theatrical venture is a translation from the Spanish—a modern play, and an extraordinarily good one. My comedy was played some thirty times, but is now in abeyance—not to use a harsher expression. They played it charmingly at the Museum, to packed houses, and I in my simple soul, thought it beautiful.[5] There is no delight like seeing one's play acted. Now I have another story nearly finished.[6]—You see I still come to you with my fond egotism. You are lucky to be beyond earshot, for you might otherwise have the story read to you.—I have sometimes wondered if you would think it quite indecorous for an Excellency like yourself to print anything. It vexes me to have you so long absent from The Atlantic. If you can, pray stretch a point in favor of the first inspiration.—I will do my best for the *wills* and *shalls*. You know I am not native to the right use of them; but Heaven has befriended me in much grammar hitherto, and I don't despair.—We have some hope that Dr. Holmes will begin to write largely again.[7] I saw him the other day, and never was man on the brink of seventy more vivid.—I am glad that you still think well of the President. His action during the last three months has restored him to a favor solider if not so noisy as that which hailed his first declarations of policy.[8] The children all send their love, and Mrs. Howells joins me in best regards to Mrs Lowell and yourself.

Yours ever
W. D. Howells.

1. Lowell wrote to Howells on 2 May (MH), saying of *The Lady of the Aroostook*: "I read it as it came out in the Atlantic & was always as impatient for more as the

French ladies used to be for more Arabian Nights. . . . I am quite in love with your heroine & am grateful to you accordingly, for whenever I come across an imaginary woman that charms me I feel new sap stirring in the roots of my love for the best of women . . . ." Depreciating the "poor little notice" (by G. E. Woodberry) of the novel in the *Nation*, 20 March, James wrote Howells with almost equal enthusiasm on 7 April (MH; *James Letters*, II, 226–27): "It is the most brilliant thing you have done, & I don't see how your own manner can go farther." Though James wished for more "*ventilation*" in the manner, he went on to say: "But apply it largely & freely—attack the great field of American life on as many sides as you can. Plunge into it, don't be afraid, & you will do even better things than this."

2. *Caesar*, by J. A. Froude, was reviewed in the *Atlantic*, September 1879, by J. W. De Forest.

3. Two interesting defenses of *Daisy Miller* are in "The Contributors' Club," *Atlantic*, February (by Constance Fenimore Woolson) and March (by John Hay) 1879. For attribution and discussion of them, see Monteiro, *Papers of the Bibliographical Society of America* 56 (1962), 254–57.

4. See *Literary Friends and Acquaintance*, HE, p. 49.

5. *Yorick's Love* and *A Counterfeit Presentment*. For the Boston Museum performance of the latter, see Howells to his father, 31 March 1878, n. 3.

6. *The Undiscovered Country*, *Atlantic*, January–July 1880.

7. Holmes continued to contribute infrequent poems, but an extended prose essay, "The New Portfolio," did not appear until 1885–1886. Lowell did not contribute between 1877 and 1887.

8. Probably Howells refers to Hayes' vigorous opposition to Congressional attempts to revoke the Force Acts of 1865 and 1874 that had authorized the president to use federal troops in national elections.

29 JUNE 1879, BELMONT, TO ANNIE A. FIELDS

Belmont, June 29, 1879.

Dear Mrs. Fields:

I did not know until the other day when I met Aldrich how very tedious Mr. Fields's sickness had been.[1] Mrs. Howells and I had heard of the nose-bleeding, but did not realize that it could be such a trying thing. Please give our love to Mr. Fields, and believe in our very cordial sympathy.

When he is able to laugh you must tell him of the majestic figure that Aldrich and I cut in the procession on Commencement Day. Of course we failed to get into line where we belonged among the guests and honorary degrees,[2] and a young and very frightened marshal ran us up and down the ranks with no final notions in regard to us, till at last I said, "Oh, tuck us in anywhere. Here's Dr. Peabody[3]—he wont object to our going in front of him." So we took our place in the class of 1701, and marched all round the college grounds, sharing the applause of these veterans, and going in for a full half of the honors bestowed on Dr. Peabody by the 'rahing students. Whom or what they thought us, heaven knows.—Aldrich has come home very much funnier and very much fatter than ever. He is humiliated to find that he weighs a pound more than I do, and he talks violently of reducing his flesh. He says it was all the chocolate in Spain.[4]—We have all been reading with delight Mr. Fields's witty poem on the Owl-Critic.[5] It is capital, and as pat a criticism on criticism as could be. Aldrich, Longfellow, and Osgood were praising it, that day.

—Don't trouble yourself, amidst your many cares, to answer this letter. We merely wished you to know that we knew of Mr. Fields's sickness and were sorry for it. With Mrs. Howells's love,

Yours sincerely
W. D. Howells.

P. S Mrs. Howells wants me to tell you that the seeds have come up nicely—all but the Mourning Bride. That *wont*—being a woman.

1. Sometime in May Fields suffered the first of what his wife described as a "violent hemorrhage from the head." He remained an invalid until his death on 24 April 1881.
2. Howells had received an honorary M. A. degree from Harvard in 1867.
3. Andrew P. Peabody.
4. The Aldriches made a second European tour from January to June 1879. Ferris Greenslet, *The Life of Thomas Bailey Aldrich* (Boston: Houghton Mifflin, 1908), p. 137, remarks that "the happiest memories of this European visit were of his weeks in Spain."
5. "The Owl-Critic," in J. T. Fields, *Ballads and Other Poems* (1881), is a witty poem about a young man who loudly and severely criticizes the unnatural posture and looks of a stuffed owl in a barbershop; at the end the bird turns out to be alive.

20 JULY 1879, BOSTON, TO WILLIAM C. HOWELLS

. . . The Atlantic Monthly. . . .
Boston. July 20, 1879.

Dear father:

I don't know of any pleasanter thing to begin my letter with than the little visit we had, the other evening, from Tom Watkins.[1] He came out about seven, and staid till the ten o'clock train in, and he talked, to our great delight, the whole time. Except Mark Twain I think he is the most amusing talker I know: his humor is incessant, and he is genuinely witty. He told us much about you in Toronto, and of his drives there with Charley, who has not apparently grown more industrious with lapse of time. I hope you all like Watkins as well as we do. He kept Elinor and Mary Mead shrieking the whole evening. He seems very fond of you all, and he thinks Annie has the brightest baby in the world; he has made us very curious to see it.

I suppose our visit will be sometime late in September, if that will be convenient to you, though it may be a little later still. I am drawing my story to a close,[2] and when that is done, I shall loaf a little, I hope.

—I met Goldwin Smith some ten years ago,[3] when he first came to Cambridge, though he would hardly remember the fact. He had then the effect of a man spoiling for a fight—or mad just after one; and gave me a painful idea of the bitterness of the struggle in England. I have a very high respect for his work and his opinions, and I should like extremely to meet him again.

We have just built Pillà a little playhouse at the foot of our first hill, and I wish you could be here to see her delight. She is like Annie in being willing to play all day by herself. Just now, however, whilst her house is new, she has a riot of company. She came down to breakfast the morning they began work on it and said it was to be called Buttercup Cottage. This was entirely her own notion, and the name is partly in honor of the flower, and partly for Little Buttercup in Pinafore.[4] So she explained.

With our united love to all,

> Your aff'te son
> Will.

1. See Howells to A. H. Howells, 29 April 1900, n. 4.
2. *The Undiscovered Country, Atlantic*, January–July 1880.
3. See Howells to W. C. Howells, 18 April 1869, n. 1. Smith contributed "Is Universal Suffrage a Failure?" to the *Atlantic*, January 1879, and "Pessimism," February 1880.
4. "Little Buttercup" is a character in *H. M. S. Pinafore*, by W. S. Gilbert.

24 JULY 1879, BOSTON, TO WILLIAM WETMORE STORY

> ... *The Atlantic Monthly*. ...
> Boston. July 24, 1879.

My dear Mr. Story:

I learn from the publishers that they paid $150 for the two numbers of the Roman Holiday to Mr. Eldridge,[1] your kinsman (?) and that they sent $30 for the poem[2] to your own address at Palazzo Barberini. Herewith I enclose the second of exchange for the latter sum.

The poem on Hillard I could not use because of that too purely local character which those in the seat of the scornful are only too glad to turn against a Boston magazine.[3] I sent it to Mr. Rice of the North American, and I supposed he had communicated with you.[4]

I am sorry that the paper on your design for the monument seemed to you so unjust. I can only say that the gentleman who wrote it, a skilful architect and one of the most conscientious critics, is an admirer of your genius, and is incapable of wittingly doing you wrong.[5] I had to rely upon his judgment in a matter of which I know very little, and I did so, knowing him to be thoroughly fair-minded.

I should be very glad indeed to have something more from you either in poetry or in prose. Are there not some extractable portions of your report on the exhibition, which you could put in magazine form pending the publication of the whole?[6]

—As to my own writing, you know perhaps that I have lately published a novel which has had large acceptance on this darker side of the globe.[7] At present I am well towards the end of another story which I shall first print serially in the magazine. I shall, by the way, see that the Atlantic is hereafter sent regularly to your Roman address.

> Yours sincerely
> W. D. Howells.

P. S. I have had from you only Roba di Roma (Atlantic for November 1878) and the Hillard poem in the way of verse. This draft is for the former.

1. "A Roman Holiday Twenty Years Ago," *Atlantic*, February–March 1879. Eldredge was probably the brother of Story's wife, Emilyn Eldredge Story.

2. "Roba di Roma," *Atlantic*, November 1878. Some such word as "bill" or "draft" has apparently been omitted after "second" in the next sentence.

3. George S. Hillard (1808–1879), lawyer and man of letters, is today known principally as a friend of Hawthorne. Among his literary works is *Six Months in Italy* (1853).

4. Story's reply to Howells, 7 October 1879 (MH), indicates he had not heard from Rice, and the poem was not published in the *North American Review*. Allan Thorndike Rice (1851–1889), a graduate of Oxford (though an American), bought the *North American Review* in 1876 and edited it with great success until his death.

5. "The Washington Monument, and Mr. Story's Design," *Atlantic*, April 1879, signed "An Architect," was by William Pitt Preble Longfellow. Here as elsewhere in the letter Howells is replying to Story's questions and comments in a letter of 5 July (MH).

6. In his letter of 7 October Story responded that he would be happy to have parts of his report on the Paris Exposition printed, if permission could be obtained; but they did not appear in the *Atlantic*. Story had been one of the U. S. commissioners on the fine arts to the Exposition.

7. *The Lady of the Aroostook*; the "other story," mentioned in the next sentence, is *The Undiscovered Country*, *Atlantic*, January–July 1880.

7 AUGUST 1879, BELMONT, TO RUTHERFORD B. HAYES

Belmont, Aug. 7, 1879.

Dear Mr. President:

At the time of the conquest of Granada there was an honest hidalgo who captured one of the Moorish kings. They called him the king-catcher, and when he attempted to seize his next prince, the Moors took *him*![1]

If I write you a second time in regard to a diplomatic appointment, do not let me suffer an analogous ignominy, and be sent abroad myself. I am anxious out of my love and admiration for Mr. Lowell, no less than from my regard for the national advantage, to know whether you have ever thought of him for the English mission. I believe—I don't know from him—that he would be very glad to have it offered him.[2]

—Laura Mitchell and Lilly come to us today for a week's visit.[3]

> Very respectfully yours
> W. D. Howells.

1. See Washington Irving, *Conquest of Granada* (1829), chapter 32, "How the Count de Cabra Attempted to Capture Another King, and How He Fared in His Attempt." Either Howells did not remember the story as Irving tells it or he revised it for the purpose of this letter.

2. Hayes replied on 8 August 1879 (MH): "Yes—I think well of it, and thought so before you suggested it." Lowell's nomination as minister to the Court of St. James came in January 1880, and he served until 1885. Howells wrote Hayes on 23 January 1880 (OFH; Richardson, *New England Quarterly* 15 [1942], 123): "I want to thank you,—as if it were a personal favor to me,—for Lowell's appointment to England. It is one of those things that I have wished so much that I feel that I have a sort of success in it."

3. Lilly was the daughter of Mrs. Laura (John G.) Mitchell, related to both Hayes and Elinor M. Howells. See *Years of My Youth*, HE, p. 202.

20 AUGUST 1879, BOSTON, TO ACHILLE FRÉCHETTE

> *... The Atlantic Monthly. ...*
> *Boston.* Aug. 20, 1879.

My dear Fréchette:

Here is a letter from Dr. Holmes telling his copyright experience.[1] Perhaps it would be well to show this to any lawyer whom you consult— and I should like you to consult one if you do not think the charge will be *very* great, after you have heard from the Minister of Agriculture. I should go to the best lawyer. But I am afraid that a two or three weeks' sojourner would hardly be regarded as "domiciled" in Canada.[2]

With our best love to Annie, the babies and all,

> Your aff'te brother,
> W. D. Howells.

1. Holmes' letter has not been located. To Fréchette's request to keep it, Howells gave assent in a letter to his father, 29 August 1879 (MH).

2. In a letter to his father, 10 August 1879 (MH), Howells had requested information from Fréchette about the requirements for obtaining Canadian copyrights. On

22 August 1879 (MH) Osgood wrote Howells that he was returning a pamphlet on Canadian copyright laws, agreeing with Fréchette that the main question was the meaning of "domicile"; Osgood advised that it probably implied an intent to stay, as did "resident" in this country.

9 SEPTEMBER 1879, BOSTON, TO SAMUEL L. CLEMENS

> ... *The Atlantic Monthly*....
> *Boston*. September 9, 1879.

My dear Clemens:

Sleepeth is the matter—the sleep of a torpid conscience. I will feign that I didn't know where to write you; but I love you and all yours, and I am tremendously glad that you are at home again.[1] When and where shall we meet? I want to see you and talk with you. Have you come home with your pockets full of Atlanticable papers? How about the two books?[2] How about all the family in the flesh and the MS.?

Thanks to your generous interest in the matter, Tauchnitz is putting some of my books into his library. He has already put F. Conclusion in, and the L. of the Aroostook goes next.[3] He has sent me $70 for the first—and the Canadian villains, who have got out *five* editions of the Aroostook, never a cent.[4]

Mrs. Howells unconsciously joins me in love to you all. We go to Toronto the first week in October to see my father. Till then we are at home, and we shall be at home about the 20th of October on our return. When do you get back to Hartford?

> Yours ever
> **W. D. Howells.**

1. Five days after his return from Europe Clemens wrote Howells: "Are you *dead*—or only sleepeth?" (MH; *Twain-Howells*, p. 268).

2. In his reply of 15 September (MH; *Twain-Howells*, p. 269) Clemens wrote: "I think maybe I've got some Atlanticable stuff in my head, but there's none in MS I believe." The two books were probably *A Tramp Abroad* (1880) and *The Stolen White Elephant Etc.* (1882).

3. Clemens had called Christian Bernhard Tauchnitz's attention to Howells. See *Twain-Howells*, p. 369. In letters of 14 May, 24 July, 20 October, and 10 December 1879 (MH) Tauchnitz corresponded with Howells on the novels. For *The Lady of the Aroostook* he paid about $100.

4. See Howells to W. C. Howells, 4 May 1879, n. 2; and Howells to Fréchette, 20 August 1879.

17 September 1879, Boston, to Thomas W. Higginson

...The Atlantic Monthly....
Boston. Sept. 17, 1879.

My dear Higginson:

I ought before now to have acknowledged my indebtedness for the sincere and sober attention you gave me in the World.[1] I am sure that your criticism is that of conviction, and I value your praise the more because I know that you have not always liked my things. I see no errors of statement, though I have made two marginal notes that may be worth considering. As to the positions of the criticism, you have not asked me to speak, and I could not if you had; for I could not express in words the here-and-there differing literary ideal of which I am conscious. It may or may not surprise you if I say that while I despise the *Tendenzromanz* as much as anybody, I should be ashamed and sorry if my novels did not unmistakably teach a lenient, generous, and liberal life: that is, I should feel degraded merely to amuse people. But I am very often puzzled to know what is the truth, and that may account for the "stopping-short" which you notice. It is, however, also a matter of artistic preference.

—Thanks for Mrs. MacKaye's MS. I will read it very soon and report.[2]

Yours sincerely
W. D. Howells.

1. "Howells," *Literary World,* 2 August 1879; reprinted in *Short Studies of American Authors* (1879). Higginson wrote Howells, 13 September 1879 (MH), asking him for corrections of fact before book publication and hinting that Howells might not "keep the track of your critics." This may allude to the opening of the article which suggests that as editor of the *Atlantic* Howells "has inevitably been shielded from much of that healthful discussion which is usually needed for the making of a good author." But Higginson goes on to say: "He has now in *The Lady of the Aroostook* allowed himself a bolder sweep of arm, a more generous handling of full-sized humanity; and with this work begins, we may fain believe, the maturity of his genius."

2. Possibly Maria Ellery McKaye (b. 1830). Howells apparently rejected her manuscript.

17 SEPTEMBER 1879, BOSTON, TO SAMUEL L. CLEMENS

> *...The Atlantic Monthly....*
> Boston. Sept. 17, 1879.
> (Belmont is my P. O.)

My dear Clemens:

We have projected a journey northward and westward, which we expect to set out on, either the first of October, or the first of November. But the date will be decided soon, and then I will make appointments for meeting, accordingly.

—More than once I've taken out the skeleton of that comedy of ours, and viewed it with tears. You know I hate to say or do anything definitive; but I really have a compunction or two about helping to put your brother into drama.[1] You can say that he is your brother, to do what you like with him; but the alien hand might inflict an incurable hurt to his tender heart. That's the way I have felt since your enclosure of his letter to me. I might think differently,—and probably should, as soon as the chance of cooperating with you was gone. I would prefer to talk with you about the matter. As usual my old complaint troubles me—want of time. I am just finishing a longer story than I've written before,[2] and I'm tempted to jump into another, as soon as that is done, by the fact that the editor of Cornhill is ready to simultane.[3]—By the way, why don't your publishers put an injunction on the sale of the Canadian ed. of *Piloting on the M'ppi*?[4] I have seen it for sale at the Albany depot here? Harpers stopped a reprint of a book of theirs by suing every man that sold it.—I have just seen Waring,[5] who had met you since your return. That bro't us very near.

> Yours ever
> W. D. Howells

1. For the play about Orion, see Clemens to Howells, 15 September 1879 (MH; *Twain-Howells*, pp. 269–70): "Orion is a field which grows richer & richer the more he manures it with each top-dressing of religion or other guano."
2. *The Undiscovered Country.*
3. On 10 December 1879 (MH) Leslie Stephen, editor of *Cornhill*, wrote Howells that he would like to begin *Doctor Breen's Practice* as soon as convenient to Howells, but in three later letters of 14 April, 11 November 1880, and 4 January 1881 (MH) he withdrew his offer because Howells could not provide the manuscript as early as Stephen expected.
4. Belford Brothers had pirated *Old Times on the Mississippi* from its *Atlantic* appearance, and sold it in the United States as well as in Canada.
5. George E. Waring, Jr.

16 NOVEMBER 1879, BOSTON, TO WILLIAM C. HOWELLS

> ...*The Atlantic Monthly.*...
> *Boston.* Nov. 16, 1879.

Dear father:

This mid-November day is very like the beginning of September; and how I wish you were here to walk in our lovely woods with the children and me after I finish this letter! John, by the way, was greatly flattered to be written to by you, and he is going to reply to-day. Please tell Aurelia that the numbers of the illustrated butterflies which she sent him are 62 and 72. Elinor wishes me to ask what it was that she promised to get or to do for Vic: there was something, but she has quite forgotten it. I send back Annie's letter, which has duly excited us. It was a most remarkable experience, and Annie has told it with the greatest vividness. She ought to console herself with the reflection that everything of that sort is literary material. The scene of her searching Josephine's trunks was fit for the stage.

We have had a delightful little visit from Joe, which he seemed to enjoy as much as we did. He had no dyspepsia, and I think he was particularly happy because you and he had come to a settlement at last. I don't quite understand, though, what this settlement is. He said it was a complete account, showing income and balance on each side; but Vic says it is no account at all, and you say it is a basis for talk. Do tell me what it is. After you were credited $2.50 a week for your letters and Joe $12.50 for his work, did you divide the income of the office equally? If you did, or if you agreed on any other division, and the charges against each were clearly made, I don't see why the settlement isn't complete.[1]

I am glad you enjoyed your Ohio visit so thoroughly: that was a very happy letter you printed in the Sentinel about it.[2] Now I want you to pay us a visit here, next summer; and we will show you the prettiest country you have seen yet, though the soil produces little except landscape. As a bit of Ohio news indirectly interesting to you, I may tell you that John Hay has been appointed Assistant Sec'y of State in Fred. Seward's place.[3] The appointment is not to be known till it is announced from Washington. He knew the place was to be offered him when I was in Cleveland.

I have not yet finished my story, though I am nearly at the end of it.[4] I have found unusual difficulty in bringing it to a close, and in reconciling the psychological and romantic interests in it. I can scarcely hope that it will be so popular as the last; and yet it may happen to strike just the right chord of the public mind. When it is done, I am going to turn to something very light as a sort of rest.—This is a dry letter; and yet I thought I had a great deal to say. You must always speak of me to Henry. Tell him that I went with Pillà and John into the woods yesterday, and we saw four squirrels on one tree. John wanted to shoot them so badly that I had to take aim at them with my cane; but the cane wouldn't go off and the squirrels escaped unhurt. This morning when John got up, he found four yellow-hammers on the roof outside his window. The weather is so mild that I heard blue-birds. Perhaps Hen will like to hear that when the big dog Rab goes out with us driving, and runs ahead, it excites the horse Blobby very much, and she keeps bobbing her head down, and making bites at him.

Elinor is to write soon. With our united love to all,

Your aff'te son,
Will.

1. As frequently, the family business arrangements are ambiguous. In the previous extant letter to his father, 26 September (MH), Howells is about to visit in Toronto, where these matters may have been discussed. In the two following letters of 23 November and 14 December (MH), no reference is made to the transaction. But a letter to Victoria may belatedly follow up the subject; see 22 May 1881, n. 2.

2. The *Sentinel*, 29 October 1879, carried one of W. C. Howells' "Familiar Letters from the Editor," in which he commented on his recent visit to Ohio. He remarked especially the pleasant weather, the progress evident in the Jefferson-Ashtabula area, and the pleasures of seeing old friends.

3. Frederick W. Seward served under Hayes as assistant secretary of state, 21 March 1877–31 October 1879. John Hay held the office until 1881.

4. *The Undiscovered Country*, about which Howells wrote his father on 14 December 1879 (MH): "My story begins in January, and I have my usual anxieties about it. I still have the very last chapter to write . . . ."

26 DECEMBER 1879, BOSTON, TO RUTHERFORD B. HAYES

. . . The Atlantic Monthly. . . .
Boston. Dec. 26, 1879.

Dear Mr. President:

Your kind note came to glorify our Christmas evening,[1] and make Tourguénief's praise still more precious to me. I shall never think of what he said without thinking that the President took the trouble to write it. With Elinor's love, and happiness which I can't express,

Very gratefully yours,
W. D. Howells.

1. Hayes had written Howells, 22 December 1879 (MH; *Life in Letters*, I, 280) that a German friend of Carl Schurz had heard Turgenev "speak of your writings as superior to those of any one now living, and that he enjoyed them more than the works of any body else."

31 December 1879, Boston, to Charles D. Warner

> ...*Houghton, Osgood & Co....*
> *Boston, Dec.* 31, *1879*

My dear Warner:

Two years ago I was indirectly asked to do Irving for Morley's series, and neither refused nor consented, but of course, didn't do. Our friend Norton of Cambridge asked me; and I have just written, telling him of your essay, and asking his leave to telegraph Morley in his name, to know whether he wants it.[1] He will (if Mr. Norton consents,) reply to me. You will have to stand the cost of cabling. I don't think it would hurt the essay for Morley to use it first in The Atlantic.[2] I will write you again as soon as I hear from Norton.

Your essay is about two thirds the required length, and is just right otherwise. You can easily swell it to the proper size with extracts.

Neither the publishers nor I suffered loss; and I have not even suffered inconvenience by the fire.[3]

> Yours ever
> W. D. Howells.

1. Howells' letter to Norton, 31 December 1879 (CSmH), recalls that Norton once spoke to him about doing the Irving volume for Morley's "English Men of Letters" series, which began to appear in 1878.

2. "Washington Irving," *Atlantic*, March 1880. The present letter replies to Warner's of 30 December (MH), in which he already asked for details of offering the essay to Morley. Also on 2 January 1880 (MH) Warner wrote Howells that he was withdrawing his offer to sell his article to G. P. Putnam.

3. A fire during the night of 28–29 December had led to the total destruction of the Boston office of Houghton, Osgood & Co. Howells' understatement about the severe loss appears to be part of the firm's deliberate effort to reassure its customers. See E. Ballou, *The Building of the House* (Boston: Houghton Mifflin, 1970), pp. 269–70.

8 January 1880, Boston, to Erastus Brainerd

> ...*The Atlantic Monthly....*
> *Boston.* Jan. 8, 1880.

Dear Sir:[1]

I thank you for letting me see your very kind notices of "Yoricks Love," and I am sorry that I cannot make you an adequate return in the way of information about the author. I believe Estabanez is a pseudonym, and I do not know his real name. The play was got for me from Spain by Count Premio-Real, Consul General for Spain at Quebec,[2] and I translated it with such changes and additions in the way of adaptation as Mr. Barrett and I agreed upon. But the conception and structure of the piece are so very essentially the Spaniard's that I always feel free to speak of his noble and impassioned tragedy as it deserves. It seems to me one of the finest I know and I particularly liked the delicacy with which the intrigue was managed. The lovers are innocent in everything but having confessed their love to each other: this forms the strength and unique quality of the drama; and the situation is treated with Northern conscience and Southern passion. Hawthorne or George Eliot could not have managed the plot more profoundly; while no one that I can think of could have touched it with such force and fire as this Spaniard.[3] Beside his work in the play my own is not worthy to be spoken of. If you should mention it again, I wish you would say that I have not palliated the intrigue between Alice and Edmund at all. Estebanez had the genius to imagine it as it stands, and thus to distinguish it from all the vulgar intrigues of that kind in which the drama abounds.[4]

Yours very truly
W. D. Howells

Mr. Brainerd.

1. Erastus Brainerd (1855–1925), a graduate of Harvard, did editorial work at James R. Osgood & Co. (1874–1878) and then became a newspaperman. At this time he appears to have been on the editorial staff of the Philadelphia *Press*. Lawrence Barrett was playing *Yorick's Love* in Philadelphia, preparing for an opening at the Park Theatre in Boston on 20 January.

2. Estébanez, the pseudonym of Manuel Tamayo y Baus. Howells could not have known the "real name" of the author until at least 1884, when a Spanish critic established the identification. See Gerard Flynn, *Manuel Tamayo y Baus* (New York: Twayne Publishers, 1973), pp. 22–23, and Howells to W. C. Howells, 4 August 1877, n. 2 and 3. As late as 6 July 1916 (NN), in a letter to H. E. Krebiehl, Howells still referred to the play as "by Estebanez."

3. On 25 January 1880 (NjP) Howells wrote Barrett that a Harvard tutor "has told his class of students to go to it [the play] as the best illustration they could have of what he had been saying to them about Greek tragedy." The tutor may have been Louis Dyer.

4. See Howells to A. G. Sedgwick, 27 December 1880 (ViU; *Life in Letters*, I, 291–92).

29 JANUARY 1880, BOSTON, TO WILLIAM H. BISHOP

. . . The Atlantic Monthly. . . .
Boston. Jan. 29, 1880.

My dear Mr. Bishop:

I think your story is extremely well done in all respects, and I wish that it "ended well." But I'm glad of it as it is; and I am glad of the reviews, too. I don't know that I care to dip into the Linton puddle again; but I can tell better after I get you into proof.[1]

I am amused at your efforts to bring me to the consciousness of travelling Englishmen.[2] The English do not know me or my works; and if your kindness were proportional to their ignorance, you would weary them. The best way is not to mind them.

Yours ever
W. D. Howells.

P. S. I hope to print your story in the April number.

1. Bishop probably sent Howells the MS. of a story—either "McIntyre's False Face" or "Deodand," *Atlantic*, May and October 1880, respectively—and several reviews of books about painting and medieval church architecture. On the "Linton puddle," see Howells to Warner, 20 June 1879, n. 5.

2. Since Howells did not save Bishop's letter to which this one replies, the allusion remains obscure.

29 FEBRUARY 1880, BOSTON, TO WILLIAM C. HOWELLS

...The Atlantic Monthly....
Boston. Feb. 29, 1880.

Dear father:

I forget whether I wrote you last Sunday, but I believe the children did. They take a great interest in hearing from you, and are very proud of your letters. John has been getting complimented on his good literature at school; and I send you one of his compositions, which we think most amusingly imagined. We asked him why he didn't think women would ever be Presidents of the U. S., and he said, with perfect simplicity, because they hadn't intellect enough. His mother rather disputed this, and he said, "Well, then they would have hysterics." He reads Scott, and knows parts of Ivanhoe by heart.—Pil is amusing in *her* way. Her temper is rather bob-tailed, and she let go her hold of it, the other night, and struck John. I brought her to book for this crime, and she said, "Well, he put me in a *terrible* rage." Please return John's essay.—We are all interested to hear of your move, which I know must be for the better. The other house had so much waste room in it, and was so poorly adapted to your wants.—You can't understand how much pleasure it gives me that you should like my story so well,[1] as you all seem to do. We live so little in the world, that I only hear from it vaguely, but I fancy it is making quite the impression I could wish. From time to time I get letters from people. Here, for instance, is one that may interest you.[2] Please send it back again. I don't know that there is any news to tell you. Elinor is getting well again, though now and then she over-shops herself, and suffers for it.—Winny has her triumphs at school, of course, and comes out first in all her examinations. I think she is growing up a strong, tranquil nature.

All join me in love to all of you.

> Your affte son
> Will.

1. *The Undiscovered Country* began to appear in the January *Atlantic*. On 1 February 1880 (MH) Howells had written to his father: "I particularly hope you will like it, for I have put serious work into it, and it treats of serious matters."

2. The enclosed letter might be from E. E. Hale to Howells, 28 February 1880 (MH): "You have silenced those of us who begged you to write a genuine American story." Another possibility is T. G. Appleton to Howells, 23 February 1880 (MH): "Yours is the kind of realism I like; but Zola would give us Ann Street."

12 MARCH 1880, BOSTON, TO CHARLES D. WARNER

> *...The Atlantic Monthly....*
> *Boston.* March 12, 1880.

My dear Warner:

I am more disgusted than I know how to say at Morley's behavior. His telegram gave us every reason to expect a favorable decision, and I am deeply mortified that I ever suggested the matter to you.[1] Of course, if you had cut Irving up, and ridiculed America generally, your book would have been accepted with acclaim.[2] To think how dull and stupid the greatest number of that series are,[3] and then to think of his rejecting a book that he ought to have gone on his knees to get! I can't express myself. But I humbly beg your pardon for my share in the business, and I want the explicit assurance of your forgiveness. I will never try to do another service to anybody.[4]

> Yours ever
> W. D. Howells.

1. See Howells to Warner, 31 December 1879. They had both been encouraged when Morley cabled Howells in January that he would consider Warner's biography of Irving. But on 11 March (MH) Warner informed Howells: "Mr Morley has rejected the Irving MS. [¶] Well, I ought to have adhered to my general practice—never to submit any thing to an Englishman."

2. Howells probably had in mind James's *Hawthorne*, which on this point he upbraided in his *Atlantic* review, February 1880.

3. Morley's "English Men of Letters."

4. Warner published *Washington Irving* (1881) in the "American Men of Letters" series, which he founded. In his reply to this letter, 15 March (MH), Warner wrote, "I really do not see what you have done to be forgiven."

21 MARCH 1880, BOSTON, TO WILLIAM H. BISHOP

The Atlantic Monthly,
Boston, March 21, 1880.

Dear Mr. Bishop:

I have been greatly interested by the inkling you have given me of your story; and I like it.[1] You take hold of the metropolitan life at its most picturesque and characteristic point: that Fifth Avenue Sunday procession *is* New York. Your underground attachment is what gives me pause. It would be attractive and I think popular; but it might be Wilkie Collinsy or Charles Readesy. If you have grip enough on *society* to get on without it, I would, in your place. The thing is a little too far out of the common. Still, if you *like* to do it—if you would find a pleasure in it,—then you would do it well, and that would be your reason for doing it. This is a little oracular, but it is also true. Your great advantage in this New York affair is that you have the field to yourself. No one can say that you are working up the tracts of those badly assorted Siamese twins, J. and H., who happened to treat intercontinental passion (or bi-continental passion) before you,[2] and so defrauded *Detmold* of his just sales. My hope is that you will be very serious about your work, and not deal in any of those pitiful winks to the reader, with which that bad artist Thackeray has undermined most of our constitutions. You ought to treat it all as if it were history, or something truer. For heaven's sake, don't be sprightly. I am now striking all the witty things out of my work: it bolts the manuscript fearfully; but it is the right thing to do. There oughtn't be a quotable passage in a novel, unless it is dialogue. We have spoilt our readers.

My notion was not to explain anything in my story. It does not end in April (the newspapers to the contrary notwithstanding) but in July; and you will see that there are two reports of the occurrences at the tavern. I'm glad you liked that part of it. The night-walk seemed to me new and right.[3]

Of course I knew that you did me no wrong with Gilbert.[4]

Yours sincerely,
W. D. Howells.

1. *The House of the Merchant Prince*, *Atlantic*, February–December 1882.

2. James and Howells, probably with primary reference to *Daisy Miller* (1879) and *The Lady of the Aroostook*.

3. The major episode at the tavern, ending with a psychic manifestation, occurs in chapter 11 of *The Undiscovered Country*, the "night-walk" in chapter 9. With the *Atlantic*, March 1880, the novel had been printed through chapter 11.

4. Probably Josiah Gilbert Holland, with whom by this time Howells had "made up all old sorrows" (letter to W. C. Howells, 14 April 1878) and who had written two friendly letters on 5 April and 9 December 1879 (MH).

22 MARCH 1880, BOSTON, TO SAMUEL L. CLEMENS

...*The Atlantic Monthly*....
Boston. March 22, 1880.

My dear Clemens:

I have been feebly trying to give the Atlantic readers some notion of
the charm and the solid delightfulness of your book;[1] and now I
must tell you privately what a joy it has been to Mrs. Howells and
me. Since I have read it, I feel sorry for I shall not be able to read it
again for a week, and in what else shall I lose myself so wholly? Mrs.
Howells declares it the wittiest book she ever read, and I say there is
sense enough in it for ten books. That is the idea which my review will
try to fracture the average numbscull with.[2] Well, you are a blessing.
You ought to believe in God's goodness, since he has bestowed upon
the world such a delightful genius as yours to lighten its troubles.

Love from both of us to Mrs. Clemens. We wish we could come to
see you, but we are many promises deep to the Warners, and our first
visit must be to them. We shall hope for you here by mid-April.

Yours ever
W. D. Howells.

1. Review of *A Tramp Abroad*, *Atlantic*, May 1880, reprinted in *My Mark
Twain* (1910).
2. Howells concluded his review: "in this delightful work of a man of most
original and characteristic genius 'the average American' will find much to enlighten
as well as amuse him, much to comfort and stay him in such Americanism as is
worth having, and nothing to flatter him in a mistaken national vanity or a stupid
national prejudice."

17 APRIL 1880, BOSTON, TO WILLIAM C. HOWELLS

...*The Atlantic Monthly*....
Boston. April 17, 1880.

Dear father:

I was glad to get your letter saying that you were in your new house,
and that Henry was better. It must have been a great comfort to you
in every way to have Sam with you. If he is still in Toronto, give him our
love, and tell him that we have been sending out a box to Florence,[1]
with some things in it that may come into play.

We have had rather a society week. The Clemenses were in Boston,
and we had them out a day and night with us.[2] Then on Friday, I went
with Winny to the Fieldses' to meet Ole Bull.[3] We had a sit-down lunch,

and uproarious, story-telling gayety, and after lunch Ole Bull made his fiddle sing to us. It was wonderful: the fiddle did everything but walk round the room. Ole Bull is very white haired, and it was fine to see him as well as hear him playing. His wife was with him—an American, half his age—who accompanied him on the piano: a very gentle and charming person. This was Winny's first grown-up lunch, and might almost be said to have been made for her. She had been at a young girls' dancing party in Cambridge, the night before; and she thinks her life is very full of contrasts.—We are digging our hill-top into shape, and putting in a lot of trees this spring, especially evergreens, for which I've a great fondness. Do you know that there is an American holly, which is perfectly hardy, and keeps its leaves all winter? I'm getting that, and mountain laurel and rhododendrons.—When you come here, I expect you to take a great interest in these things. We are eager to hear about the new house, and whether you find it pleasant.—I had a note from Goldwin Smith, the other day.[4] Do you see anything of him?—I suppose Belford is on the watch for my new book.[5] I'm in hopes he'll find it too long to publish at the cheap rate he gets out the others.

With best love to all from all,

Your aff'te son
Will.

1. Florence Howells was Samuel's wife.

2. In a letter of 19–20 April (MH; *Twain-Howells*, p. 299) Clemens speaks of the "most elegant good time" he and his wife had had. He also mentions hearing Ole Bull at the Fieldses.

3. Ole Bull (1810–1880), Norwegian violinist and composer, made five appearances in the United States. Married to an American wife in 1870, in 1879–1880 they lived at J. R. Lowell's Elmwood in Cambridge.

4. Probably Smith's letter of 6 April 1880 (MH), which recommended W. D. Le Sueur, who proposed to write a paper on the French philosopher Edgar Quinet. Of Le Sueur (1840–1917), civil servant, essayist, and historian, Smith wrote he was "decidedly the best [writer] in Canada.... Agnostic in his tendencies, but perfectly reverent." The paper did not appear in the *Atlantic* or, as far as is known, elsewhere.

5. *The Undiscovered Country* was issued in an unauthorized edition in Toronto by Rose-Belford Publishing Co. in 1880. See Howells to W. C. Howells, 4 May 1879, n. 2.

22 APRIL 1880, BOSTON, TO HENRY W. LONGFELLOW

> ... *The Atlantic Monthly.* ...
> Boston. April 22, 1880.

Dear Mr. Longfellow:

Thank you for the lovely poem,[1] which could not have come but in good time. Once it seemed to me too that I felt in my incomparably smaller way the poet's spring-impulses![2] But much proof-reading and MSS. have left me fit for nothing but prose.

> Yours gratefully
> W. D. Howells.

1. "The Poet and His Songs," *Atlantic*, June 1880. The penultimate stanza reads:

> His, and not his, are the lays
> He sings;—and their fame
> Is his, and not his;—and the praise
> And the pride of a name.

2. Howells refers primarily to the first line: "As the birds come in the Spring ...."

25 APRIL 1880, BOSTON, TO SAMUEL L. CLEMENS

> ... *The Atlantic Monthly.* ...
> Boston. April 25, 1880.

My dear Clemens:

I sent the Conversation by Telephone[1] to the printers at once, with orders to set it and send you proofs instantly. It is one of the best things you have done, and we both think it shows great skill in the treatment of female character. It's delicious. And we've been laughing over the way Twichell takes Mrs. Clemens's conversation—that's cruel good.—The obituary eloquence will go into the next month's Club—July's.[2]

Mrs. Howells has written to Mrs. Clemens and I hope has told her how much we all enjoyed the visit you made us. It was a noble time, but as you found, it left something over for eternity.[3] The incompleteness—the unfinishable incompleteness—of everything in life, ought to point to something, as Dr. Boynton[4] would have said. Well, we can hitch on again at Hartford, either next week or week after—a Maypole dancing-party of the children has to decide for us. But we will let you know in good time for the rightful earl.—I think you've only to ask Ole Bull, if you want him to visit you. What a beautiful old man he is! I suppose neither of us will ever look so, though we might together. We can do anything together.

> Yours ever
> W. D. Howells

1. "A Telephone Conversation," *Atlantic*, June 1880, records a woman's conversation over the telephone.

2. Clemens' piece did not appear until Aldrich had become the *Atlantic* editor; "The Contributors' Club," *Atlantic*, November 1881. However, Howells probably sent Clemens proof on 30 April 1880 (CU; *Twain-Howells*, p. 305).

3. See Howells to W. C. Howells, 17 April 1880, n. 2.

4. The spiritualist in *The Undiscovered Country*.

29 APRIL 1880, BOSTON, TO EDMUND C. STEDMAN

> ... *The Atlantic Monthly*. . . .
> *Boston.* April 29, 1880.

My dear Stedman:

How extraordinary that my old friend should address me as the Editor of the Atlantic Monthly, and not even write me in his own hand! I ought to answer you in kind:

The Editor of the Atlantic Monthly presents his compliments to Mr. Stedman, and begs to state that he has no recollection of ever declining or receiving any poem from Mr. Whitman.[1]

> Yours ever,
> W. D. Howells

P. S. Do you care to print your paper in the Atlantic?[2]

1. Stedman's letter of 26 April 1880 (MH) is a form letter addressed to the editors of several magazines (probably such as *Atlantic*, *Scribner's*, and *Harper's Monthly*), asking them a series of questions about their earlier disposition of poems submitted by Walt Whitman. Stedman felt that allegations which had appeared several years before in the *West Jersey Press* stating that these magazines were boycotting Whitman's poetry were probably exaggerated.

2. Stedman replied on 8 May 1880 (MH; Stedman and Gould, eds., *Life and Letters of Edmund Clarence Stedman* [New York: Moffat, Yard, 1910], II, 106, in part) that the Whitman article was contracted for *Scribner's*, where it appeared in November 1880. He acknowledged encountering difficulties in convincing J. G. Holland to include it and offered it to Howells in case of rejection.

2 MAY 1880, BOSTON, TO WILLIAM C. HOWELLS

> ... *The Atlantic Monthly*. . . .
> *Boston.* May 2, 1880.

Dear father:

I hope you are all feeling well to-day, and are comfortably settled in the new house. Your letter, and one from Vic which Annie enclosed gave us an account of poor Henry's tramp which greatly interested us. It was a strange adventure, which you must be glad to have over. I wish it were possible to have entered into his darkened mind, and known what his ideas and feelings were during his absence from you. Don't you think that if he is quieter, it will be well to supply him with all the exercise you can? His chafing so, is of course greatly in the way of his walking, but I should think you might get him to use some sort of gymnastic apparatus. There is now a contrivance by which one *pulls*, in a sitting posture, and gets the same effect as from rowing: have you seen it? Or better still, couldn't you get a boat put into shoal water somewhere, and have him amuse himself by rowing it round and round? If he fell into a fit, there, he could be got out without danger. I suggest these in default of his refusing to saw wood, or do any wholesome work. Of course, a thousand difficulties present themselves to any plan. Could you get him to use a three-wheeled velocipede? I should be glad to make him a present of one, or send the money for it. That sort does not require any lessons in balancing. Have you a riding school in Toronto, where he could get horse-back exercise? That is very good, and reduces the fat in a healthy way.—Elinor and I start to-morrow to New York, and expect to continue on to Washington. The President has asked us five or six times to visit him and has just repeated the invitation on the occasion of sending Elinor a magnificently bound set of my books, which were done to his order at Riverside. It was a very well imagined and acceptable gift, for now we have a set which we shall be unable to give away: we have never before been able to keep my books. Coming as this invitation does at a time when we were going to New York, any way, we can't refuse it. We expect to stay Tuesday at Scotch Plains,[1] and reach Washington Wednesday night, and start back on Monday.—My story has all gone to press,[2] and this, if ever, seems the time for our visit.—Houghton & Osgood amicably dissolve partnership this week.[3] The Atlantic and all the copyrights remain with Houghton; Osgood takes the heliotyping, and will build up a publishing business of his own. I am exceedingly sorry to be parted from him. He has been for fifteen years my publisher and employer, and my very good and constant friend.—We went last night to a party at Mrs. Storers in Cambridge,[4] and she and all her family made cordial enquiries about you all, and sent love. She said she should have no heart now in going to Quebec, since you were no longer there.—I return the old letters, which Elinor has copied. They are most interesting relics, and I wish we could claim them. What character, and what a dim, far-off life they conjure up! That phrase about "plunging the dagger of disappointment into a mother's heart" must be a tint from the great-grand mother's novel-reading.[5] We come honestly by our fine language.

  Love to all from all

Your aff'te son
Will.

1. The Augustus D. Shepards lived at Scotch Plains, New Jersey.

2. *The Undiscovered Country.*

3. Houghton, Osgood & Co. split up into Houghton, Mifflin & Co. and James R. Osgood & Co. See E. Ballou, *The Building of the House* (Boston: Houghton Mifflin, 1970), pp. 276–78.

4. See Howells to W. C. Howells, 13 February 1876, n. 3.

5. No copies of these letters—as very few by other members of the Howells family—are extant. In *Years of My Youth*, HE, pp. 5–6, Howells mentions the letter as one from his great-grandmother (Susan Beesley Howells [d. 1820] wife of Thomas Howells, 1750–1824) to a daughter "who had made a runaway match and fled to America."

3 MAY 1880, BOSTON, TO THOMAS W. HIGGINSON

...The Atlantic Monthly....
Boston. May 3, 1880.

My dear Higginson:

Our June number is printed, and I am afraid that the July number would come out after the dinner—and the newspapers. Besides, I avoid local-society verse as much as possible. If you could disembarrass this poem of allusion to the Club, I should be glad to print it, for I like it.[1] Can you? I don't see why you can't. If yes, please send it to me at Washington, (Executive Mansion) where I expect to be next week.

—We had heard of your building. What religion will you be of, with that "environment"?[2]

—I have never thanked you for the essays on American authors which you so kindly sent me.[3] Its chief fault was that there wasn't more of it. Of course I don't agree with you in your opinions on several points; but there can't be two minds about your literature. Somebody is yet to have a shy at you in the magazine.

Yours sincerely
W. D. Howells.

1. On 2 May 1880 (MH) Higginson sent Howells a poem he had written for the Papyrus Club. It appeared as "The Reed Immortal," *Atlantic*, August 1880, without an allusion to the club except that an epigraphic note explains that the Egyptians regarded papyrus as an emblem of immortality.

2. In his note of 2 May, Higginson mentioned that he was building a house on Buckingham Street in Cambridge "between Father O'Brien's & Dr. Wharton's." Higginson was a Unitarian, O'Brien (otherwise unidentified) a Roman Catholic, and Francis Wharton a professor at the Protestant Episcopal School.

3. *Short Studies of American Authors* was not reviewed in the *Atlantic*. See Howells to Higginson, 17 September 1879, n. 1.

17 MAY 1880, BOSTON, TO WILLIAM C. HOWELLS

...The Atlantic Monthly....
Boston. May 17, 1880.

Dear father:

Elinor and I returned from our Washington visit on Saturday, after six charming days at the White House. We arrived Friday afternoon of week before last, and next day the President went with us to Mt. Vernon. Monday we visited the Capitol, and drove out with him to Arlington; Tuesday we drove round the city with him; Wednesday we went down the Potomac in a steam yacht with Mrs. Hayes, accompanied by Gen. Myers of the Weather Bureau,[1] and Bancroft the historian;[2] Thursday I went by Mr. Evarts's[3] invitation to Mt Vernon with the diplomatic corps: Elinor was asked, but could not go. There could not have been kinder or more attentive hosts than the Hayeses; and we saw them as constantly as if they were private persons. He is by all odds the weightiest man I met; and after him I liked the Shermans the best. John Sherman remembered and asked after you.[4] Garfield, whom I saw twice with Mrs. Ga, was full of kind inquiries and messages.—We met nearly all the distinguished people, for although Mrs. Hayes had just lost her brother,[5] it was understood that friends would be received, and they came every night.—I can't begin to give you a full account of the visit. Of course we heard a great deal of political talk, but met no reliable prophets. I should myself greatly prefer Sherman as a candidate, and I believe his chances for the nomination are good. —Every morning before breakfast I took a long walk with the President and he talked very fully and freely with me, especially about the South. He said the Southerners had kept their word faithfully with him, and that all the trouble had come from the leadership of the Northern Democrats.[6]

On our return we found the children all well and happy. We had a most successful visit, but how glad we are to be at home!—Tell Henry that Mrs. Garfield asked particularly after him; and so she did after the girls.

With best love from all to all,

Your aff'te son
Will.

1. Albert J. Myer (1829–1880) served in the Civil War, when he established the Signal Corps. In 1870 he became first director of the U.S. Weather Bureau, a position he held until his death.

2. George Bancroft (1800–1891) is most famous for his ten-volume *History of the United States* (1834–1874). After 1874 he made his winter home in Washington, where he had ties as both an historian and diplomat.

3. William M. Evarts.

4. John Sherman (1823–1900) held elective and appointive offices in Washington for nearly fifty years. During Hayes's administration he was secretary of treasury. Immediately before and after he served as U. S. senator from Ohio (1861–1877 and 1881–1897). In 1880 he tried to get the Republican presidential nomination, but it eventually went to J. A. Garfield.

5. Joseph T. Webb (1827–1880), a physician, had been in poor health for several years and died of a stroke.

6. Kenneth E. Davison, *The Presidency of Rutherford B. Hayes* (Westport, Conn.: Greenwood Press, 1972), pp. 136–43, defends Hayes's "so-called withdrawal of the troops" from the South, but on the whole regards his Southern policy as a failure (p. 236). On the problems with the Northern Democrats, Davison observes that Hayes had "a hostile Congress with a Democratic majority in both houses" for most of his term (p. 235).

17 MAY 1880, BOSTON, TO RUTHERFORD B. HAYES

... The Atlantic Monthly. ...
Boston. May 17, 1880.

Dear Mr. President:

Elinor and I reached home on Saturday morning, and are trying our best to sober down to the realities of workday life, and to reduce our respective dimensions to the scale of our domestic architecture. You can imagine which has the greater difficulty.

We recall our visit at the White House with unalloyed delight, and we fancy ourselves a little wiser and better for the experience; though this is probably an error, and it remains our fault that we are not so. There is only one regret with us, and that is that the visit is over. Elinor joins me in thanks for all your kindness, and joins me in the hope also that we are soon to have Webb with us.[1] The tidal wave of apple-blossoms has just struck our hilltop, and the prospect is inexpressible: he could never come in a lovelier season.

With Elinor's love to Mrs. Hayes, Miss Cook, Miss Fanny and yourself,[2] and my own best regards,

Yours gratefully and sincerely
W. D. Howells.

1. Webb C. Hayes, the president's son.

2. Lucy Cook was a cousin of Mrs. Hayes; Fanny Hayes (1867–1950) was the only daughter of the Hayeses.

10 JUNE 1880, BOSTON, TO SYLVESTER BAXTER

> ... *The Atlantic Monthly*. . . .
> *Boston*. June 10, 1880.

Dear Mr. Baxter:[1]

Can you let me see what you have written about Warner and Clemens before it goes into print?[2] They are particularly sensitive, and as you went from me to them, I am anxious to know what report you give.[3]

> Yours sincerely
> W. D. Howells.

1. Sylvester Baxter (1850–1927) was on the editorial staffs of several newspapers and magazines during his lifetime, and author of a half-dozen books.

2. Boston *Herald*, 20 June 1880.

3. On 2 June 1880 (CtHT) Howells wrote Warner introducing Baxter as an interviewer, whom Warner might trust "to respect your mental infirmities and moral obliquities." On 9 June (MH; *Twain-Howells*, pp. 311–12), after excoriating Baxter for his dullness, Mark Twain asked Howells to look at his article before printing; Howells replied on 12 June (CU; *Twain-Howells*, p. 314) that "B. has really written a most blameless and pretty account of you, with appreciation which he got out of my review [of *A Tramp Abroad*]." Baxter's piece, which mentions Warner only in passing, relates details of Clemens' writing habits, home surroundings, and biography, as well as offering passing comments on his works.

14 JUNE 1880, BOSTON, TO SAMUEL L. CLEMENS

> ... *The Atlantic Monthly*. . . .
> *Boston*. June 14, 1880.

My dear Clemens:

I have read the autobiography with close and painful interest. It wrung my heart, and I felt haggard after I had finished it. There is no doubt about its interest to *me*; but I got to questioning whether this interest was not mostly from my knowledge of you and your brother—whether the reader would not need some sort of "inside track" for its appreciation. The best touches in it are those which make us acquainted with *you*; and they will be valuable material hereafter. But the writer's soul is laid *too* bare: it is shocking. I can't risk the paper in the Atlantic; and if you print it anywhere, I hope you wont let your love of the naked truth prevent you from striking out some of the most intimate pages. *Don't* let any one else even see those passages about the autopsy.[1]

The light on your father's character is most pathetic.

> Yours ever
> W. D. Howells.

1. Although the autobiographical piece by Mark Twain is no longer extant, there is some evidence that it contained the account of a traumatic experience at age twelve: the boy appears to have secretly witnessed his father's autopsy. See *Twain-Howells*, p. 315, and Dixon Wecter, *Sam Clemens of Hannibal* (Boston: Houghton Mifflin, 1952), pp. 116–17.

14 JUNE 1880, BOSTON, TO HJALMAR H. BOYESEN

> *...The Atlantic Monthly....*
> *Boston.* June 14, 1880.

My dear Boyesen:

You must use a double forgiveness towards me: I have neglected you a long time, and I send back your poem at last.[1] It doesn't seem to me rooted in anything but a classic mood; and you know I want your genuinest Boyesenian.

I had your news the other day from your fellow-Norseman, Jansen,[2] whom I met at dinner, at the Childs', as ten years before I had met you. It made me melancholy on the whole to go back to that time in which I had so much pleasure: I found that I was no longer thirty-three for example. I don't live any the less in literature; I don't love it less; but it is not a fresh passion, now. That's all. I'm *forty*-three.

Your letter touched me.[3] I wished we could see each other, and that I could know more of your present happiness.

With best regards to Mrs Boyesen, and a kiss to the boy,[4]

> Yours ever
> W. D. Howells.

1. Boyesen had sent Howells a poem "on Hellas" with his letter of 2 April 1880 (MH; Ratner, *New England Quarterly* 35 [1962], 383–84, in part). Though Boyesen did not publish "The Lost Hellas" in a magazine, he printed it as the first poem in his *Idyls of Norway and Other Poems* (1882).

2. Kristofer Janson (1841–1917), writer and clergyman, was educated for the Lutheran ministry in Norway but became a Unitarian, coming to the United States in 1879–1880 and 1881–1893 to serve in the Unitarian Church. Beginning in 1878, his fiction is frequently anti-Lutheran in theme.

3. In the 2 April letter Boyesen had written: "I cannot tell [whether he should have amounted to anything without Howells' influence]; but my heart warms toward you, when I recall those glorious summer evenings we spent together & the noble enthusiasm which your talk & your whole personality aroused in me."

4. Hjalmar Hjorth Boyesen, Jr. (b. 1879).

20 JUNE 1880, BELMONT, TO WILLIAM C. HOWELLS

Belmont, June 20, 1880.

Dear father:

I think you have exactly expressed the meaning of the Garfield nomination in recognizing that it is the success of the goodness and good sense of the country. My first thought was of you when I heard of it, and I truly and silently rejoiced in what I knew would give you such intense pleasure.[1] I should have liked to see you when you got the news. When I was in Washington I called on the Garfields with Elinor, and next evening they came walking over to see us. I met them at the White House gate, and afterwards he said that he had remarked to his wife on my very great resemblance to you, especially in a certain movement of the body when we encountered. This he had often observed in you, and had interpreted to mean the pleasure you felt in your friendliness to him. Then he went on to expatiate to Hayes on this inherited trait, and to wonder from what remote ancestor it had come.

—You will have received my book[2] before this reaches you, and you will like to know that the first edition of 5000 was sold before its publication. It bids fair to be my most popular book. I suppose the reduction of the price has something to do with the greater sale.—Winny and I went down to Magnolia, on the coast, yesterday, where I left her for a fortnight's stay, with our friends the Shalers.[3] She had not been away from home for a great while, and was rather fagged from her school. The rest of us are at home and well.—Have you seen Goldwin Smith's little book on Cowper?[4] It is very simply and sympathetically written, and I think you would like it.—Did Henry's medicine arrive safely? I sent it last Monday by express.—I'm glad to know from Vic's letter that your new house is so pleasant.—With love from all to all,

Your aff'te son
Will.

1. Upon being informed that Garfield had received the Republican presidential nomination at Chicago, Howells had telegraphed, 8 June 1880 (DLC), from Arlington, Massachusetts: "Cordial Congratulations from this part of Ohio."

2. *The Undiscovered Country.*

3. Nathaniel S. Shaler (1841–1906), geologist, who directed the Kentucky State Survey (1873–1878) and established the Harvard summer school in geology. His *Autobiography* (1909) does not mention a summer place at Magnolia.

4. In his review of Goldwin Smith's *Cowper, Atlantic*, September 1880, Howells emphasized Cowper's humanitarianism: "Cowper was the prophet of the new impulse, and he long dictated the morality of that simple and now rather old-fashioned world, in which it was conceded that the feeble and inferior had paramount claims, that it was wrong to give pain, and that selfishness was wicked."

4 JULY 1880, BELMONT, TO CHARLES E. NORTON

Belmont, July 4, 1880.

Dear friend:

I will not betray you to Professors Cook and Trowbridge, even though you cannot stand chemists in fiction.[1] All that you said of my book gave me very great pleasure. Whether you like it or not, you are always one of the half score readers I have in mind when I write: I don't write *at* you, but *for* you; and no doubt you sometimes save me from myself. I would like very much, if I could, to talk over with you the story I'm now alternately taking up and throwing away, till I've come to feel that there's something fatal about it. Perhaps I'll bring what I've done, when I come in August.[2]

I saw Warner, the other day, and I know that he does not go to the Adirondacks, this summer. I hope that he and Clemens will both come.—Of course I should like very much to bring Winny, and I am very glad you asked her, but I am not sure that I can do so.[3]

Please tell Miss Grace that I am going to send her letter to the inimical reviewer of the Nation as a model of all that is dreadful to say of my book.[4]

Yours ever
W. D. Howells.

1. Norton had warmly praised *The Undiscovered Country* in a letter to Howells, 24 June 1880 (MH), especially for the characterization of Boynton. But he added that he could not like Ford much, writing vertically in the margin: "A chemist too, is an abomination!" Josiah Parsons Cooke (1827–1894) was Erving Professor of Chemistry and Mineralogy at Harvard (1851–1894). John Trowbridge (1843–1923), physicist, taught at Harvard (1870–1910), and was appointed Rumford Professor of Physical Science and director of the Jefferson Physical Laboratory in 1888.

2. Most likely *Doctor Breen's Practice*, serialized in the *Atlantic*, August–December 1881, even though "A Fearful Responsibility" was published earlier, *Scribner's*, June–July 1881. The "story" with which Howells struggled all summer is identified by a comment in Henry James's letter to Howells, 11 September 1880 (MH): "G. N. [Grace Norton] also speaks of your writing a story about a 'lady-doctor'! I applaud you that subject—it is rich in actuality—though I cannot, I think, on the whole, say I envy you it."

3. Norton had invited Howells and Winifred on 24 June 1880 (MH) to come to Ashfield. See Howells to W. C. Howells, 22 August 1880.

4. Norton does not mention Grace Norton's response to *The Undiscovered Country* in his letter of 24 June; perhaps she enclosed a note now lost. On 13 August (MH) Howells wrote Norton that he was glad Norton was baffled by W. C. Brownell's review in the *Nation*, 15 July 1880, "for I had begun to be afraid that there was something wrong in me, and that I could not understand criticism when it was set before me." Entitled "The Novels of Mr. Howells," the essay raises the usual questions about realism in Howells' fiction. The reviewer regrets that in *The Undiscovered Country* the author has turned from his lighter earlier novels to a more serious subject. "As it is, the merits of the book remind us of Johnson's remark about

women's preaching: 'It is like a dog's walking on his hind legs. It is not well done, but you are surprised to find it done at all.'" See also Howells to Aldrich, 28 July 1880, n. 1.

8 JULY 1880, BOSTON, TO JAMES MAURICE THOMPSON

>   ... *The Atlantic Monthly.* ...
>   *Boston.* July 8, 1880.

Dear Mr. Thompson:

I have gone over your poems and picked out twenty-four pieces, (including all those on archery and mythology, and your Atlantic verses,) which I think will make a lovely and unique little volume of 125 pp., or so.[1]

When you come here, I should like to talk with you about the arrangement. Mr. Osgood goes to Europe the 21st. If you could arrive a few days before, then you could fix the time of publication with him, and the form of the book. He returns in September. I incline to advise him to put you into the old-fashioned brown muslin, in which Ticknor and Fields published so many charming poems.

—My boy sat by me while I was going over your poems, and I read him those on archery; he knew them all very well, and told me just what words you had changed in transferring them from the "Witchery."[2] He's wild to think you're coming.

>   Yours sincerely
>   W. D. Howells.

P. S. Remember that I live at Belmont on the Fitchburg R.R. The trains out are 7, 9, 11.15, a.m.; 2.20, 4, 5, 5.30, 6.15, and 7.35 p.m. The latest in is 10 p.m. Afternoon trains are the best for you.

1. *Songs of Fair Weather* was published by Osgood in 1883.
2. Howells had reviewed Thompson's *Witchery of Archery: A Complete Manual of Archery* (1879) in the *Atlantic*, August 1879.

21 JULY 1880, BOSTON, TO THOMAS W. HIGGINSON

>   ... *The Atlantic Monthly.* ...
>   *Boston.* July 21, 1880.

My dear Higginson:

Your letter gave me so much pleasure that I should be wanting in common decency if I did not try to express my sense of your kindness.[1]

Your notice does not appear in the August Scribner's,[2] but whatever its reticences, I feel sure that they cannot be more generous than the criticisms you have privately made me. Your letter is at Belmont, and I am acknowledging it here in Boston: so I cannot reply by the card. But I wish to say that a man like Hatch would be apt to quote Shakespear and that the passage "James has a salt and sullen rheum offends him," is out of Othello's mouth, almost verbatim—where he demands his handkerchief of Desdemona.[3]—I think I am not mistaken about the crickets: the tree toad's voice, I noticed last night, came in as an undertone.[4] Those things are with me, as with you I suppose, matters of early impression, rather than of ascertained knowledge: I am often astonished to find how seldom they are erroneous.—As to the waterproof, you are right: it *was* lugged in.[5] I ought to have been man enough to let readers suppose that it was returned; but I wasn't. I did the best I could with the thing. Respect this awful secret, and believe me

Very gratefully and sincerely yours
W. D. Howells.

P. S. Finding your letter at home, I see that the only other point in it is about the bobolinks.[6] Quite probably I am rash about them; they are comparatively recent acquaintance.

1. In his letter to Howells of 16 July 1880 (MH), Higginson had raised the questions of detail in *The Undiscovered Country* that Howells takes up here. See also Higginson's reply, 30 July 1880 (MH), in which he confesses missing the Shakespeare allusion and comments on several others.

2. Higginson's review appeared in *Scribner's*, September 1880. In spite of several queries about nature in his letter, Higginson praises the "delicate observation of the habits of plants and animals" in the review. See also Howells to Higginson, 24 August 1880, n. 2.

3. *The Undiscovered Country* (1880), p. 27. The passage in *Othello*, III, iv, 51, reads: "I have a salt and sorry rheum offends me; / Lend me thy handkerchief." Higginson had commented in his letter: "This sounds disagreeably [sic], &, besides, puzzles the reader's eye for an instant; it looks as if there ought to be a comma after 'salt.' "

4. *The Undiscovered Country*, p. 287: "the hollow din in which the notes of the crickets sum themselves under the moon." Higginson had asked: "Don't you mean tree-frogs or hylas, commonly mistaken for crickets?"

5. In *The Undiscovered Country* a schoolteacher has lent a waterproof to the heroine, who in her illness forgets that she had received it. Higginson had thought that the "reappearance" (in a conversation which suggests Egeria stole it) was the only thing in the book that did not come in smoothly: "it seems rather *dragged* in on its second appearance." Though Higginson cites its reappearance on p. 378, mention is also made of it on pp. 381, 383, and 417.

6. Higginson had remarked that the bobolinks (p. 189) "can hardly be called more than exceptional so early, I should say," citing two authorities on the time of their arrival in the spring. Howells did not comment on three other objections: about birds singing after the rain (p. 187), the need for a semicolon after "dusk" (p. 225), and the confusing syntax of "with the public comb and brush" (p. 150).

25 JULY 1880, BOSTON, TO WILLIAM C. HOWELLS

> ... *The Atlantic Monthly*. ...
> *Boston.* July 25, 1880.

Dear father:

It seems a long time since I have heard from Toronto, and I believe that Annie's letter is all that we have had in two weeks or more. I hope it is nothing but prosperity that keeps you silent.—We have a house full of company, and we have been changing girls, for our Katy, who lived with us nearly six years, has gone away to be married. Next week we hope to go to the seaside, on the Old Colony coast, at Duxbury, where Miles Standish lived.—The Cambridge house is now empty, and is in the hands of agents for sale. I shall offer it for three months, and then try to get another tenant for it if it is not sold.—The other night our friend Dyer brought a young Englishman to call—a Mr. Warren,[1] who had just come from Toronto, where he had been offered a professorship in the University. But he had heard so much from Goldwin Smith that was discouraging about Toronto, and all Canada that he had almost made up his mind to refuse.—What do you think of Garfield's letter of acceptance?[2] There is no doubt but it is a damper to the Reform republicans, though Willy Mead, who is here from New York says the independents there will vote for him, and that is the State where they hold the balance of power. I wish the letter had been boldly in favor of Reform; the Chicago platform was already feeble enough.—I think that since I last wrote we have been two days at the Fieldses' in Manchester, one of the loveliest spots on the coast, and delightfully cool. The summer has been intolerably hot—very much like that of 1870, when Elinor and I came out with the children to visit you in Jefferson, and then went on with Annie to Quebec. At last we have rains, and plenty of them, and the landscape is greener than it has been since April.—How is Henry? I hope he is better, and that you are all enjoying your new house. Write me some particulars when you can.—My book continues to go well, and is about the only book that Houghton is selling in this midsummer dullness.[3] The Banner of Light (spiritualist) has come out very scathingly against it,[4] but the other reviews continue most favorable.—Just now there seems at last to be a chance of our getting a copyright treaty with England. I have been moving in the matter, in connection with the Harpers, and getting authors' approval of their plan.[5] It is possible that by another year the Belfords may have to go into the grocery business.[6] I hope so.—Have you read Goldwin Smith's little book on Cowper?[7] It would delight you, for it treats Cowper in the most admirable way, recognizing all those qualities for which you prize him. Another excellent book in the same series is Leslie Stephen's Pope.[8]

All the family join me in love to all with you.

Your aff'te son
Will.

1. Warren, who remains unidentified, evidently declined the professorship, since university archives contain no record of his appointment.

2. In his formal letter accepting the Republican presidential nomination, 12 July 1880, Garfield had indicated a willingness to "seek and receive the information and assistance" of those whose knowledge "best qualifies them to aid in making the wisest choice" (B. A. Hinsdale, ed., *The Works of J. A. Garfield* [Boston: J. R. Osgood & Co., 1882], II, 786). The statement was commonly regarded as condoning the spoils system.

3. See Howells to W. C. Howells, 20 June 1880, n. 1.

4. The review of *The Undiscovered Country* in the *Banner of Light* (Boston), 17 July 1880, reads in part: "The bigots of America...have perhaps agreed to consider Mr. Howells their Moses who, to reverse the figure, is to lead the world in general, by this book, out of all danger of the now imminent spiritual enlightenment concerning human immortality, and back into the old-fashioned Orthodox fold of blind faith...."

5. On 23 May 1880 (CU; *Twain-Howells*, p. 311) Howells wrote Clemens that on his visit to Washington he had spoken about copyright to Hayes, who had replied that the administration would support a joint proposal of authors and publishers. Howells went on to say that he would ask Harper & Brothers to sponsor a proposal which would give Englishmen copyright if they had American publishers and vice versa. On 28 July 1880 (*Life in Letters*, I, 288–89) Howells sent Hay a memorial on copyright, asking Hay to sign it and reminding him of the treaty proposed by Harper, which according to the editors of *Twain-Howells*, p. 311, had been submitted in 1878.

6. See Howells to W. C. Howells, 4 May 1879, n. 2, and 17 April 1880, n. 5.

7. See Howells to W. C. Howells, 20 June 1880, n. 4.

8. Leslie Stephen, *Alexander Pope* (1880), in the "English Men of Letters" series.

28 July 1880, Boston, to Thomas B. Aldrich

...The Atlantic Monthly....
Boston. July 28, 1880.

My dear Aldrich:

I think Wisdom will not die with the Nation's critic—if she makes an effort;[1] though undoubtedly she will feel the blow.

I want you to set against my shabbiness in failing to answer your letter sooner my present magnanimity in writing you just after I have seen the proposed cover and the (butter)fly-leaves of your new book.[2] The whole idea is charming; and I am afraid that under the allurements of that pretty advertisement I shall order a whole set of your books from the publisher. I am glad that you are going to put your lyrics into vellum: would that I had something worthy of it!—The Atlantic must try to do something special for you apropos of The St. Tr.³—If Fawcett, now, were a little safer, or if I could find any other man who could write as well about you as I might!⁴

I am wasting the summer: dogging away at a story that I shall probably never finish, and helpless to turn to anything else.⁵ You know how that is?—We have been once at the Fieldses', and next week we go a while to Duxbury for the bathing and then I expect to run up to Ashfield to see Norton. We have had a house full of company all summer, and Mrs. Howells has been by no means well. If she were here in Boston she would join me in love to Mrs. Aldrich and yourself.

The Clemenses have another daughter.⁶

> Yours ever
> W. D. Howells.

1. The allusion is at least partly to Brownell's review of *The Undiscovered Country* in the *Nation*; see Howells to Norton, 4 July 1880, n. 4. But in the literary "Notes," *Nation*, 22 July 1880, the reviewer, also Brownell, made some mildly critical remarks about Aldrich's *The Stillwater Tragedy* in the August *Atlantic*.

2. Howells probably saw the cover and flyleaves of *The Stillwater Tragedy*, which was published by Houghton, Mifflin & Co. in September 1880. The volume of poetry bound in vellum, to which Howells refers subsequently, was published by the same firm as *XXXVI Lyrics and XII Sonnets Selected from Cloth of Gold and Flower and Thorn.*

3. Howells decided, as he hinted in his letter to Aldrich, 13 August 1880 (MH). to write not only on *The Stillwater Tragedy* but on other works as well. See "Mr. Aldrich's Fiction," *Atlantic*, November 1880.

4. Edgar Fawcett (1847–1904) the author of novels, plays, and poems, is best known for his satires on New York society. A frequent contributor to the *Atlantic* (1867–1881), he reviewed Aldrich's *Cloth of Gold and Other Poems* with almost unqualified praise in a five-page article, *Atlantic*, December 1874.

5. See Howells to Norton, 4 July 1880, n. 2.

6. Jean Clemens (1880–1909).

22 AUGUST 1880, BOSTON, TO WILLIAM C. HOWELLS

> ... *The Atlantic Monthly,*
> Boston. Aug. 22, 1880.

Dear father:

It seems a great while since I had heard from you, but I suppose I should have heard if you were not all well. I have been away again for a little while, spending three or four days with Norton at his summer place in Ashfield. Winny went with me, and visited his girls. The occasion was a fair which they were holding in benefit of the village academy, and in which Norton took a great interest. It ended with a dinner, and then we had speeches, in which Winny thought I bore my part "very nicely."¹ George Wm. Curtis also lives there in summer, and he spoke. He has lately seen Garfield, and gives him a full and cordial support.[2] I should like to know what you feel and think about election matters. It seems to me that the prospect constantly brightens.— Will you tell Mr. Rose, from me that I gratefully appreciate his intention to pay me half profits on his edition of my book,[3] and that meantime I should be very glad if he would send me a copy of it.—The President renewed his invitation to me to go West with him and Sherman, but the ladies were left out of the expedition this time, and 700 miles of staging were included.[4] I have had a very interrupted summer, and on the whole I thought best not to go. Of course I miss a great deal, but in this life you can't do everything.—I got John a sort of playing pipe yesterday, and I've been picking out the old tunes I used to know on the flute. It makes me think of the summer afternoons in that queer little room where I used to study and write, and squeak the flute. What a long time ago it all was!—Do write some of you, and give me your news.—Love of all to all.

Your aff'te son

W. D. H.

1. Norton instituted an annual harvest festival or "dinner" at Ashfield in 1879 for the benefit of the local Academy. By selling tickets at one dollar each, he hoped to raise sufficient funds for providing local children with a good secondary education, thereby preventing further migration from the village. Norton presided at the dinners, to which he invited many prominent men like Howells as speakers. See K. E. Vanderbilt, *Charles Eliot Norton* (Cambridge, Mass.: Harvard University Press, Belknap Press, 1959), p. 196.

2. Garfield visited the Republican stalwarts in New York in early August—a visit opposed by such Republican reformers as Curtis, though Curtis strongly supported Garfield in *Harper's Weekly*.

3. George MacLean Rose (1829–1898), publisher, came from Scotland to Canada in 1851. As president of the Rose-Belford Publishing Company, he had written Howells on 25 July 1879 (MH) that *The Lady of the Aroostook* had not been published by his own firm but by I. Ross Robertson and Belfords, Clarke & Co. It is not clear whether he paid Howells for publishing *The Undiscovered Country*. See Howells to W. C. Howells, 4 May 1879, n. 2.

4. K. E. Davison, *The Presidency of Rutherford B. Hayes* (Westport, Conn.: Greenwood Press, 1972), pp. 213–21, describes the two-month trip in detail. The group of about nineteen included approximately half a dozen women. For Sherman, see Howells to W. C. Howells, 17 May 1880, n. 4.

24 AUGUST 1880, BOSTON, TO THOMAS W. HIGGINSON

... *The Atlantic Monthly,*
Boston. August 24, 1880.

My dear Higginson:

Your delightful paper came while I was away from home, and I have only just now read it.[1] I am sorry that it is too late for the next number;

but it shall go into the November, and you shall shortly have a proof. It took me fairly and squarely into the woods, and I slipped round on those deeply mossed rocks with you.—To-morrow I will ask them to send you a check for the paper.—I have to thank you for the review in Scribner.[2] It is most kind, and I wish I knew how to say just the right thing in return. But the book has brought me no pleasure (except my wife's praise) that has been *more* a pleasure. I am heartily glad and proud of your liking my work.—If I knew where to hit you with a Ms. I should be tempted to send you 200 pp. of a new story I've begun,[3] because I think *you* could give me just the light I want on it. But I shall probably delay and spare you.

Yours sincerely
W D Howells.

This paper of yours has a quality that we have long lacked. I kept saying to myself that it was wonderful how I should be charmed with a rehearsal of natural features, wh. ordinarily fatigues me. But you have put a pulse of enjoyment in it all, which the reader feels.

1. "A Search for the Pleiades," *Atlantic*, November 1880.
2. Higginson concludes his long review of *The Undiscovered Country*, *Scribner's*, September 1880: "In delicacy of handling, in fineness and firmness of touch, in that local coloring to which Mr. James is so provokingly indifferent, this book ranks with the best work of Mr. Howells; and in no previous novel has he so trusted himself to deal with the depths of human character." See also Howells to Higginson, 21 July 1880, n. 2.
3. See Howells to Norton, 4 July 1880, n. 2.

29 AUGUST 1880, BOSTON, TO CHARLES E. NORTON

... *The Atlantic Monthly*,
Boston. Aug. 29, 1880.

Dear friend:

I hope you are quite recovered from the fatigues and enjoyments of the Fair,[1] which has been echoing up and down the newspapers ever since. It was a most delightful and interesting experience to me, and the pleasure of it haunts all my quiet moods. I shall live a year or two longer than my allotted time in the recollection of that berrying party, and that drive over the hills to Harley.—We have had melting weather since we came home, with sudden cool remorses, such as sent the thermometer from 96 to 60 today. But upon the whole it has been very pleasant, and good working weather, so that I've finished the Italian play I was translating,[2] and am ready to recommence the story to-morrow.[3]—Mrs. Howells approves the notion of an American love-idyl: in fact it is something that we had spoken of together.[4]—Harrison made our drive over to Shelburne Falls a short one, and I parted from a man so full of good works feeling like a practical philanthropist myself. I hope I shall see Clark again before he goes.[5] "I heard a mother singing to her child at Marathon." Si figuri![6] What a charming fellow! I should like to live with him. It is not fair that a man should be twenty-five but once, or should be so twice only at the cost of being fifty.—My wife thanks you for a sight of the mobiglie antiche[7]—a precious reminiscence to both of us. With love to all your house,

Yours aff'tely
W D Howells.

1. On the Ashfield fair, see Howells to W. C. Howells, 22 August 1880.

2. The play has not been identified, although in two letters from Lawrence Barrett to Howells, 5 and 8 August 1880 (MH), there are several references to it. The title appears to have been "Civil Death"; the major character in it was named Conrad (at one time played by Tommaso Salvini in a performance that Howells apparently saw); and Barrett had plans to produce the play in Chicago in the fall and thereafter in Boston. On 1 October 1880 (MH) Barrett asked Howells "the favor of a delay in payments...due you on 'Conrad.'"

3. See Howells to Norton, 4 July 1880, n. 2.

4. Probably "A Fearful Responsibility," which Howells did not finish until April 1881. See *Twain-Howells*, pp. 361–62.

5. The journalist Jonathan B. Harrison and probably Joseph Thacher Clarke (ca. 1855–1920), an archaeologist, who headed the excavation at Assos, Greece, for the Archaeological Institute of America in 1881–1883.

6. The quoted sentence has not been identified; "si figuri" is Italian for "never mind" or "don't mention it."

7. Antique furniture.

14 SEPTEMBER 1880, BOSTON, TO MONCURE D. CONWAY

...The Atlantic Monthly,
Boston. Sept. 14, 1880.

My dear Conway:

The Rossetti papers have turned up, and I have read them with delight.[1] They are charming, and I am extremely glad of them. I will print them in the January and February numbers, and the publishers will pay the $250 (£.50) asked of the Harpers. When you are writing Mr. Rossetti, please tell him how much I like his articles. I want you to ask him also how I can get fotografic copies of two wonderful pictures of his brothers: "How they met themselves" and one of which I don't remember the whole legend; but it ended:

"But I am weary of my life,
And feel like flowers that fade."

A scene of riot, where a girl speaks the words, "With voice of neither maid nor wife."[2] I saw the fotografs fifteen years ago in Norton's study, and can never forget them.—You are too good, to say those things about your visit at Redtop.[3] It was a rapture to us, and the most we could hope was that the weather,—proprio d'inferno![4]—hadn't made it misery to you. Come again in November, and try a different tap of New England air. We shall want to know all about Eustace and his destiny.[5] Mrs. Howells joins me in love to Mrs. Conway, and all of you.

Yours ever
W. D. Howells

I sent you some letters care of Judge Hoadley.[6]

1. William M. Rossetti, "The Wives of Poets," *Atlantic*, January–April 1881. Beginning with Euripides and ending with Poe, Rossetti by his own count sketched the thirty-six wives of twenty-nine poets and comments on the relative happiness of each marriage.

2. The two paintings by Dante Gabriel Rossetti are "How They Met Themselves" and "Hesterna Rosa." See Virginia Surtees, *The Paintings and Drawings of Dante Gabriel Rossetti: A Catalogue Raisonné* (Oxford: Clarendon Press, 1971), no. 118, pl. 182 and no. 57, pl. 49, respectively.

3. The Howells residence at Belmont.

4. Italian for "it befits hell."

5. Eustace Conway (1859–1937), son of M. D. Conway. On 12 September 1880 (MH) Howells wrote to his sister Victoria of the Conways: "They have now lived 18 years in England, but they have come home to place their son in some business, for they cannot bear to have him anything but American. He is a nice young fellow, educated to the law."

6. George Hoadley (1826–1902), educated in Cleveland and at the Harvard Law School, was a judge on the Superior Court of Cincinnati (1851–1866), a professor at the Cincinnati Law School (1864–1887), and governor of Ohio (1883–1885).

17 OCTOBER 1880, BELMONT, TO WILLIAM C. HOWELLS

Belmont, Oct. 17, 1880.

Dear father:

I hope that you are satisfied with the result in Ohio and Indiana.[1] It has been a glorious time with us. At first I had no hope, and hardly dared ask, Wednesday morning, what the news was. I suppose that it leaves scarcely a doubt of Garfield's election.—Wednesday night I went to the Grant dinner, which was of course *strictly nonpartizan*; but the way Republican exultation leaked out in all the speeches, was most amusing.[2] Gen. Hawley, of Connecticut,[3] bowed to me from where he sat, twenty feet away, and said, "Indiana!" as he drank. The majority went up to unimaginable figures during the dinner. Fairchild[4] has confidential advices that make him think we shall even carry North Carolina. Grant has done great work for us during the past fortnight.

I hope you had a pleasant visit at Jefferson, and I am eager to hear about it.—We have had rather a lively week of it here, what politics and company. Warner was out here, one day, and Clemens,[5] the next—both hot Republicans, and full of rejoicing. The children are greatly stirred up, and this morning Winny made me tell the difference between the parties so that she might have it at her tongue's end.—Mr. Longfellow wrote, the other day, and said, "Give a kiss to Winny, for me, and tell her that I have read her beautiful poem in the Youth's Companion with uncommon pleasure."[6] Isn't that charming for her? It's beautiful to see how her innocent face lights up at such things. And the best is that they make no difference in her: she is the same simple, good child; only very happy. John pretends a great disgust with such flatteries. He has just gone down to the Sunday School with a basket of our wonderful greenings as a contribution to the Harvest Home which the children are getting up.

All join me in love to all.

Your aff'te son
Will.

1. On 13 October Garfield won the presidential election by large majorities in Ohio and Indiana.

2. The Middlesex Club gave a reception and a banquet in honor of ex-President U. S. Grant at the Brunswick Hotel on 13 October. See Boston *Evening Transcript*, 14 October 1880.

3. Joseph R. Hawley (1826–1905), editor, soldier, politician, served as U. S. representative (1868–1881) and U. S. senator (1881–1905). He was a close friend and newspaper associate of C. D. Warner.

4. Charles Fairchild (1838–1910) graduated from Harvard in 1858, in 1880 became a broker with Lee, Higginson & Co., and in 1895 founded his own brokerage house in New York. He had persuaded Howells to settle in Belmont, financing the house there. He also played a part in Howells' negotiation with Harper & Brothers. See Fairchild to J. W. Harper, Jr., 14 May 1885 (draft at MH), and Harper to Fairchild, 13 and 14 May 1885 (MH).

5. A telegram from Clemens, 15 October 1880 (MH; *Twain-Howells*, p. 330), announced his visit with Edward H. House, correspondent for the New York *Tribune*, who was traveling with the Grant party.

6. The poem by Winifred Howells has not been identified.

22 OCTOBER 1880, BOSTON, TO WHITELAW REID

> ... *The Atlantic Monthly.* ...
> Boston. Oct. 22, 1880.

My dear Reid:

I am very sorry that I can't profit by your kindness. I should like immensely to come to the Lotos Club dinner,[1] and I should like above all to see you; but I am just at that point in a story where I can only afford the most necessary interruptions;[2] and I must forego the pleasure you offer me. Going to New York means so much more than going and coming, to a quiet man like me—excitement and long delay in simmering down! Hold me excused, and believe that I truly grieve to excuse myself.

Do you want a Boston correspondent for The Tribune? Mr. Louis Dyer, a great friend of mine, who went from Harvard with three honors, and won the highest distinctions at Oxford, would be an admirable fellow for you. He is an instructor at Harvard in the Greek department, and he is an accomplished and easy writer as you may see by his review of Mahaffy's Greek Literature in the November Atlantic.[3] Dyer is that compound which you and I know to be the best sort of American: A Westerner (Chicago) with Eastern finish. And he is a thorough gentleman and thorough scholar.

—The Tribune was so generous to my book when it appeared that your personal expression of liking for it makes me feel hopelessly your debtor.[4] But I am glad to be that and

> Your aff'te friend
> W. D. Howells.

1. The Lotos Club, at 149 Fifth Avenue, was organized in 1870, and Reid was its president at this time.

2. *Doctor Breen's Practice.*

3. Dyer wrote an unfavorable review in the *Atlantic* of J. P. Mahaffy's *A History of Greek Literature.* On the previous Sunday, 17 October (DLC), Howells had written Reid proposing the *Tribune* and *Atlantic* share costs of sending J. B. Harrison to the South to write jointly for them on social conditions there. But Reid's invitation of 19 October (MH) ignores the Harrison proposal, and no reply to the present letter is extant.

4. Reid's review of *The Undiscovered Country* appeared in the *Tribune,* 20 June 1880. He wrote in part: "we lay down the book feeling that here is an American novel of the most piquant originality, whose scenes—familiar enough but never so vividly described—are peopled with types so real that we all seem to know them, and yet so fresh that we study them with a pleased surprise. Nor in tracing the intricacies of psychological action has Mr. Howells forgotten his gifts of acute observation, inimitable grace and propriety of expression, and gentle humor, which charmed us years ago in his 'Venetian Life,' and have grown more and more dear to us in his successive volumes."

5 December 1880, Boston, to William C. Howells

> ... *The Atlantic Monthly,*
> *Boston.* Dec. 5, 1880.

Dear father:

I'm glad to hear of Henry's improvement from the Turkish baths. It's a capital idea, I should think. Winny is better than when I wrote you last, and I hope great good from the gymnasium for her.[1] The children are all delighted with the quarters, which are beautiful. How tasteless ours are in comparison!—Just now I am in all the misery of buying a horse again. Blobby, our mare, has been left stiff and useless by the epizootic, and I have to get another horse, trusting to sell her after she gets better.—On Friday we had to lunch here the Norwegian poet Björnson, who is spending the winter at Mrs. Ole Bull's, in Cambridge. I don't know whether you've ever heard me speak of his books; but he is a great genius. Personally he is huge, and very fair; and in appearance is a curious mixture of Henry and Jim Williams.[2] I like him extremely. He is a hot Republican, and just now is in disgrace at home for having spoken disrespectfully of the king: I think he called him a donkey.

All join me in love to you all.

> Your aff'te son
> Will.

1. This is one of the first references to the onset of Winny's long illness; in letters to his father of 28 November (MH) and to R. B. Hayes of 1 December (OFH) Howells had written of her vertigo. The gymnasium is probably one of the schools of physical therapy established by Dr. Dio Lewis. See Howells to Mead, 8 July 1881, n. 3.

2. Jim Williams, Howells' old Ohio friend.

6 December 1880, Boston, to Henry Demarest Lloyd

> ... *The Atlantic Monthly,*
> *Boston.* Dec. 6, 1880.

Dear Sir:[1]

I accept your paper with pleasure, and will give it the first place in the Atlantic for March.[2] What shall I call it?

> Yours very truly,
> W. D. Howells.

H. D. Lloyd, Esq.

1. Henry Demarest Lloyd (1847–1903), after practicing law in New York City, became an editorial writer for the Chicago *Tribune* (1873–1875). His best known

book, *Wealth Against Commonwealth* (1894), developed out of the essay he wrote for the *Atlantic*.

2. "Story of a Great Monopoly," *Atlantic*, March 1881, exposes the misdoings of the Standard Oil Company. On 5 December 1880 (MH) Charles Francis Adams had written Howells, expressing his approval of the manuscript.

13 DECEMBER 1880, BELMONT, TO SAMUEL L. CLEMENS

Belmont, Dec. 13, 1880.

My dear Clemens:

I have read the Two Ps,[1] and I like it immensely. It begins well, and it ends well, but there are things in the middle that are not so good. The whipping-boy's story seemed poor fun;[2] and the accounts of the court ceremonials are too long, unless you *droll* them more than you have done. I think you might have let in a little more of your humor the whole way through, and satirized things more. This would not have hurt the story for the children, and would have helped it for the grownies. As it is, the book is marvellously good. It realizes most vividly the time. All the *picaresque* part—the tramps, outlaws, etc.,—all the infernal clumsiness and cruelties of the law—are incomparable. The whole intention, the allegory, is splendid, and powerfully enforced. The subordinate stories, like that of Hendon, are well assimilated and thoroughly interesting.

I think the book will be a great success unless some marauding ass, who does not snuff his wonted pasturage there should prevail on all the other asses to turn up their noses in pure ignorance. It is such a book as *I* would expect from you, knowing what a bottom of fury there is to your fun; but the public at large ought to be *led* to expect it, and must be.

No white man ought to use a stylographic pen, anyhow.[3] You will be surprised, perhaps, that I have written you at all about the book, but Osgood sent it to me, and it took five good hours out of me on Saturday, and I think I have a right to say something. And I say it is *good*—and only long-winded in places. You ought to look out for those. The interest of the story mounts continually; there are passages that are tremendously moving; and it is full of good things.[4]

Yours ever
W. D. Howells.

Hendon's mock—and growingly real—subordination to the prince is delightful—one of a hundred fine traits of the story.

1. *The Prince and the Pauper.*
2. In an appendix to *Twain-Howells*, pp. 873–74, the editors comment fully on

the removal of the whipping-boy's story. In brief, manuscript pages 315–42 are missing, and p. 314 carries Clemens' comment, "This chapter withdrawn and cancelled." In the published version there is brief reference to the events of the canceled portion at the beginning of chapter 15.

3. At the paragraph break Howells gives up writing with the stylographic pen.

4. Ten months later, when Howells was reading proof and at the same time preparing a review (New York *Tribune*, 25 October 1881), he objected to "such words as devil, and hick (for person) and basting (for beating,)," as well as the form of the ballad "There Was a Woman in Our Town" in a book "for babes." See 12 and 13 October 1881 letters to Clemens, with Clemens' grateful permission of 15 October to make changes (CU; MH; *Twain-Howells*, pp. 375–77).

10 JANUARY 1881, BELMONT, TO HENRY O. HOUGHTON

Belmont, Jan. 10, 1881.

Dear Mr. Houghton:

I have written to Mr. Osgood to say that I withdraw from my proposed engagement with him; and I have done this for the reason that I will not be made the battle-ground between you and him in your differences as to the interpretation of your agreement.[1] I have no more right to question the sincerity of his construction of that contract than I have to question yours. All that I intend is not to be the occasion of trouble between you.

Yours sincerely
W. D. Howells.

P. S. I will send a copy of this to Mr. Osgood.[2]

1. With the dissolution of the partnership between Houghton and Osgood in 1880 (see Howells to W. C. Howells, 2 May 1880, n. 3), Houghton, Mifflin & Co. became the owners of the *Atlantic* and the publishers of Howells' books. The "engagement" proposed by Osgood, however, was an offer to act as Howells' agent and to acquire the rights to his books, a step that Houghton strongly opposed. See E. Ballou, *The Building of the House* (Boston: Houghton Mifflin, 1970), pp. 290–91.

2. The letter of the same date to Osgood (copy by Howells at MH; *Life in Letters*, I, 293) differs somewhat in wording.

14 JANUARY 1881, BELMONT, TO HENRY O. HOUGHTON

Belmont Jan. 14, 1881

Dear Mr Houghton:

I have received your note from New York;[1] and before we meet, tomorrow I wish to make certain points which I fear you may not have clearly in mind.

I   Anything that you may have to propose to me is to refer to my literary production alone; for since I first told you that I desired to give up the Atlantic editorship I have not changed my mind in regard to that matter.[2]

II When you have made me the offer, "such as business would justify,"—if you still wish to make it,—I will faithfully consider it from a business point of view, and if I think it undesirable, I shall feel myself free to make terms with any other publisher. I did not see anyone outside of my own family when I determined Monday night to write you and Mr Osgood as I did, and I came home after meeting you without speaking to him or hearing from him again. My letter to you was not for the purpose of inviting a proposal from you. I have for a long time wished to give up editing, in which I have ceased to be interested, and have planned various ways for relinquishing it; especially since I have felt myself unable to meet your wishes in some features of management. I have been making a magazine that is neither your ideal nor mine; and I had resolved to get out of it as soon as I could see my way to a living without it, when Osgood's offer came.[3]

But it always seemed to me perfectly feasible for me to get out of it and form a new relation peaceably; and when I found myself the occasion of disturbance between your house and his, I determined to forego the best offer I could imagine as to all its conditions; though I was assured that I was in nowise concerned in your contract with him. I gave up his offer in good faith, and I remained, as I saw the situation, without a future with either of you. I had certainly no right ever to hear from him again. But I wish to tell you that I *have* heard from him, in friendly recognition of my motives, and I feel so far bound to him for having made me a generous proposal at a time when I saw no reason to expect one from you, that I wish to end the affair, one way or other, at once.[4] I hope therefore, that our talk tomorrow may be full and final.[5]

Yours sincerely
W D. Howells

1. The "note from New York" has not been located.

2. The exact date on which Howells first told Houghton of resigning as editor is uncertain, but it was before he wrote his letter of 10 January. Upon receiving it, Houghton wrote Aldrich: "I am not without hope that we can still arrange matters, pleasantly all around, so that you can be editor of the Atlantic, and Mr. Howells remain writer for it, and continue to add his new books to our list." See E. Ballou, *The Building of the House* (Boston: Houghton Mifflin, 1970), p. 291.

3. Presumably this was Osgood's offer to publish Howells' books.

4. Osgood to Howells, 11 January 1881 (MH), requested that negotiations remain open. Howells replied noncommittally on 12 January (MH).

5. The matter was evidently settled in the talk; at least no written response from Houghton is extant.

4 February 1881, Belmont, to James R. Osgood

Belmont, Feb. 4, 1881.

My dear Osgood:

This appears all right. I see you leave out the clause by which I renew for five years if I like; and I suggest striking out the words "at least" in the 6th line from bottom of page 1st. I do not expect to furnish *more* than one novel a year, according to our agreement.[1]

I should like to talk with you about clause 8, to which we may want to add a proviso.*

I hope to see you to-morrow.

Yours ever
W. D. Howells.

*Nothing serious, however. You can have the agreement copied and ready.

1. On 2 February 1881 (MH; *Life in Letters*, I, 294) Howells told Osgood of his resignation as editor and proposed that Osgood publish his "writings hereafter." For further details of the contract see Howells to W. C. Howells, 13 February 1881.

8 February 1881, Boston, to Horace E. Scudder

... The Atlantic Monthly....
Boston. Feb. 8, 1881.

My dear Scudder:

You break my heart! And yet I thank you for doing it, with all the pieces.[1] You may be sure that I have enjoyed our relation as fully and thoroughly as you. I need not tell you how much I have respected your work in the magazine, how glad I was to have it there, how happy in all the personal meetings it has led to. Such a one as that of yesterday! It did me good all over. In a word, you know I love you.

But I have grown terribly, inexorably tired of editing. I think my nerves have given way under the fifteen years' fret and substantial unsuccess. At any rate the MSS., the proofs, the books, the letters have become insupportable. Many a time, in the past few years I have been minded to jump out and take the consequences—to throw myself upon the market as you did, *braver Mann!*[2]—rather than continue the work which I was conscious of wishing to slight. The praise the magazine got ceased to give me pleasure, the blame galled me worse than ever. Then to see a good thing go unwelcomed, or sniffed at!—The chance came to *light soft*, and I jumped out.

I dare say I shall often regret the change—I too hate all changes, and this is a very great one—but I shall do my best not to regret it.

I write to you frankly, as you did to me. Dear old contributor, salve et vale.[3]

Yours ever
W. D. Howells.

1. Between 1874 and 1880 Scudder had contributed five articles, two stories, and eighty-three reviews or groups of reviews to the *Atlantic*. This letter replies to one from Scudder, 7 February (MH), regretting Howells' resignation—"...I have an injured feeling, something I fancy as if my second wife had run away from me."

2. German for "worthy man." Howells probably refers to the brief period of Scudder's partnership in Hurd & Houghton (1872–1875). See Howells to Aldrich, 8 January 1875, n. 5.

3. Latin for "Be well and farewell."

13 FEBRUARY 1881, BELMONT, TO WILLIAM C. HOWELLS

Belmont, Feb. 13, 1881.

Dear father:

I have been waiting for the matter to take final shape before writing you of a change in my affairs, of which you may have seen some rumor in the papers. I leave The Atlantic editorship on the 1st of March, and go into the employ of Osgood. I agree (for three years) to write him one novel a year, and he agrees to pay me a weekly salary for it, and to pay me copyright on its republication in book form. He gives me for the story alone as much as I got for a story and all my editorial work, and he leaves me free to live anywhere, and to do any other work I like after the story is finished. The arrangement is ideal, and was his own proposition. I felt entirely free to accept it because though I have every year written more and more in the Atlantic, with a constantly growing reputation, I have remained on the same salary ever since Mr. Houghton had it—eight years.[1] Besides, I have grown fearfully tired of editorial work, and impatient, as I have often told you, to devote myself to authorship.—The new arrangement wont make any change in our plans for the present.

I have been made uneasy by Willy Howells's reports of his father's sickness; but I hope soon to hear that he is quite well again. I wish Joe could get a good long vacation, somehow. He seemed to me very delicate when he was here last.

Winny is very slowly improving. I can't see that she was helped at all by our trip to New York; but she was at least not hurt. She and her mother are now at a hotel in Boston for a week, so that Winny may get if possible, some amusement out of the city. The long cold winter has been very trying to her in Belmont; but now we have had a most tremendous thaw, and I hope the back of the winter is broken.

Pil and John are at home with me. John feels aggrieved at gran'pa's not answering his letter.—I rejoice with you in Henry's improvement. With love to all,

Your aff'te son
Will.

1. From the beginning of his editorship of the *Atlantic* in 1871 Howells received $5,000 a year.

17 FEBRUARY 1881, BOSTON, TO JAMES R. OSGOOD

... *James R. Osgood & Co....*
Boston. Feb'y 17, *1881.*

Dear Osgood:

I have just written a dispatch asking whether you would trust my judgment about accepting Mr. Houghton's dinner independently of you. The persons asked are Aldrich, Warner, Fields, Clemens, and four Boston newspaper men. I told Mr. Houghton at first that I should not come unless you were asked.[1] We had a long talk, and he urged that this was his personal and private affair, by which he meant no reflection upon you whatever. I think I will get him to say this in writing or before Aldrich;[2] and then if you approve, I will accept. I will if possible get him to agree to the transfer of my plates to me, and to the republication of my story where I like.[3] I have not yet decided that I will go to the dinner, but my judgment now is in favor of it. Let me know what your feeling is.[4]

Yours ever
W. D. H.

1. The dinner was to take place on 26 February, and appears to have been a private party, as is suggested in Howells' note of acceptance, 20 February 1881 (ViU), in which he writes of "the very kind invitation of Mr. and Mrs. Houghton ...."

2. No record of this appears in existing correspondence.

3. Since *The Undiscovered Country* had appeared under the Houghton Mifflin imprint, Howells evidently hoped to have it transferred to Osgood.

4. See Textual Apparatus for Osgood's probable reply, written at the end of this letter, to delay a decision until after talking with Howells on Sunday.

18 February 1881, Belmont, to James R. Osgood

Belmont, Feb'y 18, 1881.

My dear Osgood:

The wish of the Scribner management to know the scope of my proposed story is perfectly reasonable, and I should be glad to gratify it even minutely if I could. But I have a difficulty which they will readily understand. The plot is the last thing for which I care. In whatever I do I try to make the faithful study of character and the dramatic treatment of incident my hold upon the reader; and I always find it a disadvantage in this attempt if I speak of my work fully beforehand. It is hard for me to present anything more than the motive of my work in this case; but I can say that just as the question of spiritualism was the moving principle in The Undiscovered Country, so the question of divorce will be that of The New Medea.[1] This subject occurred to me years ago as one of the few which are both great and simple. We all know what an enormous fact it is in American life, and that it has never been treated seriously. I intend to treat it tragically, though of course the story is not to be wholly tragical; and I feel that I have a theme only less intense and pathetic than slavery. I propose to take a couple who are up to a certain point almost equally to blame for their misery; their love marriage falls into ruin through the undisciplined character of both; but the reader's sympathy is chiefly with the wife because she inevitably suffers most. I have told you that the story begins in Northern New England; that much of it is placed in Boston; and that it closes in Indiana, where the wife arrives too late to prevent the clandestine divorce which her husband has sought. It is wronging my material to indicate its nature in this arid fashion, and I do it very reluctantly. But our friends can readily see that the story is on no mean scale geographically! I think they can trust me to treat the theme without *shadiness*, and not to let the moral slip through my fingers. Of course, I don't mean to write a *tendency-romance*; but I should be ashamed to write a novel that did not distinctly mean something, or that did not show that I had felt strongly about it.

I wish I could be more explicit; I see my work clearly to the end, but I could not be more specific without spoiling it for myself.

I believe that I have got a *great* motive; I shall do my best with it, and I must let my past performance promise what that will be.

Yours ever
W. D. Howells.

1. "The New Medea" became *A Modern Instance*, which appeared in the *Century*, the successor to *Scribner's*, December 1881–October 1882. See also Howells to W. C. Howells, 7 March 1862, n. 3.

27 February 1881, Boston, to Rose Terry Cooke

28 Brimmer Street
Feb'y 27, 1881.

Dear Mrs. Cooke:[1]

Thank you for your very kind letter.[2] It has been a pang for me to sever the thousand invisible ties that bound me to my old work; but I had grown very tired of editing, and I hope to keep all the contributors for friends still. You will find Aldrich a sympathetic and appreciative editor, who will be glad of all the good writing he can get.

—We came in town the other day to spend what the Canadians call the back-winter: the two months of mud and sorrow that precede the spring. Mrs. Howells joins me in cordial regards, and thanks for your invitation to Winsted.[3] We shall hail any chance that takes us there, you may be sure.

Yours sincerely
W D Howells.

What a handsome book Osgood has made of the book you made so good![4]

1. Rose Terry Cooke (1827–1892), a writer of mostly local color stories, had contributed to the *Atlantic* since the first number of the first volume. Her best known collection is *Huckleberries Gathered from New England Hills* (1891).
2. A letter of 21 February 1881 (MH) regrets Howells' resignation and thanks him for his consideration and kindness as editor.
3. Winsted is in northwestern Connecticut.
4. *Somebody's Neighbors* was published by Osgood on 5 March 1881.

10 April 1881, Boston, to Victoria M. Howells

28 Brimmer st.,
Boston, April 10, 1881.

Dear Vic:

You will be glad to know that Elinor and I did the necessary swearing to that deed of Aunt Lile's, and that I sent it to Uncle William, registered, on Friday.[1] I suppose it will go safely, and I hope will be found all right.—I have not yet written to Garfield, though I will gladly do so. Please tell me if father has ever written to him, and what he said, and whether he has ever been answered. I wrote to Garfield, as soon as my appointment was rumored,[2] and told him I did not want the place, but would be glad if he could give father promotion; he made no answer, and he has not answered any of my letters since his nomination. I do not care for this; but I wish to know just what father has done before I write. Did you make or have any hint about Montreal while you were at Mentor?—I feel pretty sure that father will get the place, but I hope he wont set his heart too fondly on it. Mr. Mead's disappointment was terrible, and I am anxious that father shouldn't get to brooding upon this matter.[3] After all he has a place, now, and he can afford to be patient.—We are going back to Belmont next week, but please answer me here, as soon as you get this letter.

You must be having a delightful time with Annie and her babes. Give them our love, and tell Annie that we are anxious to have a fotograf of Howells.[4] When is Annie's article to come out in Harper?[5] I know it will be charming. Tell her that her Ottawa letter to me was all right in every respect, and that I will write her one of my dullest and driest letters in return, as soon as I get time.—Winny's cure goes on slowly, but she is unmistakably growing better. I am the only one who has kept entirely well this winter.—That book on the American Consul, was written by a friend of mine.[6] It has made the cold chills run over me, too. But the country that uses its servants so meanly as ours does, has no right to anything but shame abroad.—What has become of the Count?[7] Is he still in Quebec?

With love from all to all,

Your aff'te brother
Will.

1. Presumably Aunt Lile was the wife of William Dean, Howells' uncle. But the nature of the deed has not been discovered.

2. On 21 February 1881 (DLC) Howells wrote Garfield that there were rumors that he had been offered the position of U. S. minister to Switzerland, but that he asked for no office and expected none.

3. Apparently the senior Howells wished for a further advancement, this time to the Montreal consulship. With Vic probably he had called on Garfield at his home in Mentor, a town halfway between Cleveland and Ashtabula. Though Larkin G. Mead, Jr., having served as an acting consul, may be referred to, the use of "Mr. Mead" in context seems to suggest that Larkin G. Mead, Sr., had at some time suffered the disappointment.

4. Howells Fréchette, nicknamed "Mole," was born 13 August 1879.

5. "Life at Rideau Hall," *Harper's Monthly*, July 1881, an article on the "White House" of Canada.

6. *Adventures of an American Consul Abroad, by Samuel Sampleton, Esq.* (1878), by Luigi Monti, is a novel that presents a consul typical in his naiveté and poverty— "a sketch which not only abounds in amiable satire, but is admirably faithful in all its characterizations," as the reviewer (probably Howells) commented in the *Atlantic*, August 1878. Luigi Monti (1836–1914), a naturalized American citizen, served as American consul at Palermo (1861–1873). Author of several works in Italian, he also published three Sicilian sketches in the *Atlantic*, January 1876, February 1877, and August 1880. A letter from Longfellow to Howells, 14 March 1881 (MH), suggests that the two men propose him for another consulship, which however he did not receive. See also Woodress, *Howells & Italy*, p. 107.

7. Count Premio Real. The count was still in Quebec when the Howells family sailed for Europe the following year. See Howells to V. M. Howells, 21 July 1882.

17 April 1881, Boston, to James R. Osgood

Boston, April 17, 1880.[1]

Dear Osgood:

I have no objection to your closing with the Scribner people on the basis of $20.00 a page to me for magazine use of the Signorial Cities, and ten per cent. copyright on a $5 book,[2] conditionally upon my being able to do the work at all. I think, however, that if I should find my travelling expenses great in getting material, there ought to be some consideration of them in any contract we make. But that we can arrange. I authorize you to bargain as aforesaid with the magazine.

Now as to the Library of Humor, I am not so easy in my mind. I ought to keep very fresh for my new story,[3] which I fore-feel is going to be a drain on me; and I do not like to bargain to do work, and then fail. I spoke very confidently about it to Clemens, when I was at Hartford, but I have been "renigging" in my own mind, somewhat, since. He first talked with me about paying me $5000 outright, and then talked of giving me one fourth of the profits. I agreed to both; but I prefer now, if I undertake the work, to do it for an outright sum. Please read him this letter, and get his ideas. As matters stand, I believe that if I have no other work, I can finish my novel by December 31, and sail for Europe; but if I undertake the L. of H. with him, I may find it fagging, and may have to postpone my trip till the summer of '82. Before I decide, I should like to know how big a book he means to make, and so be able to estimate the work.[4]

Yours ever
W. D. Howells.

1. Howells inadvertently wrote "1880" rather than "1881"; the letter is a reply to one from Osgood, 15 April 1881 (MH).
2. "Signorial Cities" eventually appeared as *Tuscan Cities* (1886), with serialization in the *Century*, February–October 1885.
3. *A Modern Instance.*
4. *Mark Twain's Library of Humor* (1888), first mentioned in October 1880, was the subject matter of many letters before its publication on 15 December 1887. See Howells to Clemens, 17 April 1881.

17 April 1881, Boston, to Samuel L. Clemens

Boston, April 17, 1881.

My dear Clemens:

I have written to Osgood to-day about the Library of Humor, and have asked him to read my letter to you;[1] but Mrs. Howells, who has charge of my sense of decency—I wish she didn't brag so about her superior management of it—suggests that *you* ought to hear from me first. Osgood tells me that you and he are about to strike a bargain, and he wants to know if I'm ready to go to work. He also tells me that you would like to push the job through before you go to Elmira. I suppose he doesn't perhaps quite understand; but I could not agree to work at it except in the most leisurely way; you spoke of an hour a day; and I don't see how I could give more time. You see that I have to get ready a novel for Scribner by November 1st, so as to let them have the opening chapters for January; and I wish to finish it by Dec. 31, and cut for Europe. I don't know exactly how hard this work will be; but it wont be very light; and I don't know how big a book you wish to make. With the rashness of youth, I agreed to do anything, when I was at your house; but I now wish you to let me suspend my decision till I see Osgood, and get your latest ideas from him. I think also I should prefer to return to your first idea of paying me a stipulated sum—$5000—and leave the rich possibilities of the venture to you. I believe that I could help you to that extent; but I could not afford to lose my labor if the work failed. I hope this wont seem fickle or unreasonable. The questions with me are: I How many volumes and how large? II Whether I can decently spring the notion of a stipulated sum on you instead of a royalty? III Whether I could undertake the work experimentally, and back out if I found it too hard?[2]

Mrs. Howells is feeling badly at not having written to Mrs. Clemens and thanked her for the good time she made us have at your house.[3] She has been in bed the greater part of the past fortnight; but she is up now, and will start the universe on the right basis again in a few days. She joins me in love to all of you.

Please write me at Belmont: we go back on Thursday.

Yours ever
W. D. Howells.

P. S. My difficulty in finishing the two-number story that I've just ended has given me a scare about loading up with more work till I see my way through the novel.[4] If I were not able to go to Europe in December, then I should have a clear three months before I begin another story, and should be glad and humbly thankful to help you on the L. of H. Or if you and Osgood can agree on terms, and leave the time blank, I can still be your man. What I dread is to enter on work that I can't decently back out from. Why don't you go on with the Etiquette Book,[5] and let the L. of H. rest awhile? I *don't* want to give it up; but I don't want to begin it till the way is clearer to me.

1. See the preceding letter to Osgood.

2. Clemens replied on 19 April (MH) that God (if he took an interest) alone knew the number of volumes; that Clemens would pay $5000; and that Howells could withdraw from the project. See *Twain-Howells*, pp. 363–64.

3. The visit was in the latter part of March, but according to the editors of *Twain-Howells* cannot be precisely dated.

4. *A Fearful Responsibility* was about to appear in *Scribner's*, as Howells continued to work on *A Modern Instance*.

5. On 5 March 1881 (CU; *Twain-Howells*, pp. 359–60) Howells had written Clemens of Mrs. Charles Fairchild's suggestion that Clemens write a burlesque book of etiquette. More than seventy pages survive, with one page published in A. B. Paine, *Mark Twain: A Biography* (New York: Harper & Brothers, 1912), pp. 705–6.

28 APRIL 1881, XENIA, OHIO, TO ELINOR M. HOWELLS

Xenia, Ohio, April 28, '81

Dear Elinor:

I posted a letter to you at Pittsburg this morning, and I expect to write again from Crawfordsville *to-morrow evening*.[1] I have great hopes of my trip; I laid before Smith[2] the skeleton of my plot, and he takes a strong interest, and will be of essential service. Between him and Thompson, I think I shall get all the data I want.[3]—He came here in order to see a preacher whom he wants to send to Rome to "profess" in the Protestant Theological Seminary there.[4] Did you know that the Mr. Clarke, with whom Mary went to Italy, has turned out a very bad fellow?[5]—Smith is going to drive to Eureka with me to-morrow, and perhaps we shall drive all the way to Dayton. We shall go on from there to Indianapolis and Crawfordsville. Love to the chicks.

Your
W. D. H.

This is the town where I was so terribly home sick when I came up to work in the printing office from Eureka.[6]

1. Howells was visiting Crawfordsville, Indiana, ·to witness divorce proceedings in preparation for *A Modern Instance*. The Pittsburgh letter posted on the same day has not been located.

2. Roswell Smith (1829–1892), lawyer and publisher, founded *Scribner's* with J. G. Holland, Charles Scribner, and R. W. Gilder in 1870. In 1881 the name of the magazine was changed to the *Century* when Smith acquired a controlling interest.

3. J. M. Thompson wrote Howells on 29 March 1881 (MH) that he would be glad to have him visit or that he, Thompson, would write a divorce court scene for Howells' rewording. See Fertig, *American Literature* 38 (1966), 104. Howells' letters to Thompson at this time have not been located, but an eight-page undated draft of a letter from Thompson to Howells (GEU), written in response to reading *A Modern Instance* in manuscript, is critical of Howells' treatment of the climactic courtroom scene and of his inaccurate observations of Indiana. Summing up, Thompson states: "Now what I suggest is that you ought to tone down the whole scene to

a more *moral* than a *physical* tragedy. Make your effect with Bartley, the Squire and Marcia, without the aid of consternation and sudden disease, by a play of your fine ability in depicting situations." In making this and other suggestions, Thompson evidently intended to make the novel more realistic, but he repeatedly stressed that Howells is his "master" and that he take these suggestions with a grain of salt.

4. See Howells to Winifred Howells, 1 May 1881.

5. There is no indication of the identity of this Mr. Clarke, but the reference is to Mary Mead's visit to Venice in 1863–1865. According to Elinor Howells' "Venetian Diary," her sister was to make the transatlantic voyage in the company of "the Clarks," and she shared her cabin with "Miss Clark."

6. See *Years of My Youth*, HE, pp. 53–54, 267.

1 MAY 1881, CRAWFORDSVILLE, INDIANA, TO WINIFRED HOWELLS

Crawfordsville, Ind., May 1, 1881.

Dear Winny:

I reached here last night, and found your dear little letter waiting for me, with several letters enclosed by mamma.[1] I thought that I ought not to pass through Richmond without seeing my uncle Joseph, and I staid there Friday night. Clara Howells happened to be at home, and I had a very pleasant little visit: they were all most kind.[2] I went with uncle to see one of his sons-in-law in the court-house, and my coming quite broke up the session of the court for the time. The judge came down from the bench, and all the lawyers crowded, to be introduced. I think I shall get everything I came for, out here. I wish you were with me to see the beautiful country, and the strange life. Indianapolis is a magnificent city.—Tell mamma that we stopped in Xenia to see a Rev. Mr. Morehead, for the Italian Free Church Mission, and he turned out to be a young American whom we met at Dr. Slayton's in Florence.[3] I'm sorry you feel so discouraged about yourself. You mustn't lose courage; it will all go well with you again, you may be sure. With love to all,

Your loving
Papa

Tell John that Maurice Thompson is very nice.

1. Winny's letter is not extant. Other letters to Elinor about the trip are at MH: 29 April (*Life in Letters*, I, 297) on revisiting Xenia; 3 May on probably going to Chicago from Crawfordsville; 4(?) May on leaving Crawfordsville; and two dated 5 May on visiting the mines at Dansville and arriving in Chicago.

2. Joseph Howells (1814–1896), the physician, had evidently moved from Hamilton to Richmond, Indiana. Clara Howells may have been his daughter, though perhaps a niece.

3. Neither the Reverend Mr. Morehead nor Dr. Slayton is mentioned in the letters or journals of Howells' Italian period.

22 MAY 1881, BELMONT, TO VICTORIA M. HOWELLS

Belmont, May 22, 1881.

Dear Vic:

I am just getting over the worst cold I ever had; it has kept me in the house all the week till yesterday, and I have been sorer and sicker than I have for years. I think it was brought on by working hard at tree-planting, the day after I got home, and then getting chilled after a drive to Cambridge.

—I don't quite understand the point you put about the mortgage of the farm. If you buy the farm, and choose to sell it to Sam, he can give you a mortgage on it for the sum unpaid; or if you lend him part of the purchase money, he can mortgage it to you for the amount of the sum loaned; there is no other way to secure you. As to advancing that money for seed potatoes, etc., I do not see how you can get out of that. If Joe advances it now, either in money or in Sentinel accounts, he will have a right to deduct it from the first payment of interest due you on the Sentinel purchase. You see that in putting Sam on a farm father must also furnish him the means to put in crops and to live till he can sell those crops, and trust to getting his loans back then.[1] I think the chance of ever getting them back is very small. But you must realize that Joe has nothing whatever to do with furnishing seed or implements to Sam. Father will tell you this, and he can explain that when Joe has given his notes, and secured father by mortgage or otherwise for the half of the Sentinel which he buys, he will have nothing more to do but pay his interest and notes as they fall due.[2] It is a hardship that father should have to support Sam, but unless Sam can borrow money to live upon for a year, this is what he must do. After all, it will be no worse than giving him the Sentinel store accounts.—But perhaps I haven't exactly understood you.

It is still uncertain whether I shall go to Washington or not. There is no time fixed for the copyright business, and I am not sure that I shall go in any case.[3] I am to have a week's notice of the appointment: as soon as I get that I will telegraph to father. I wish that he would also telegraph me when he expects to be there,—when he gets ready to start, —and how long he means to stay.

I will pack up a dinner plate of the Canton China and send it to you to-morrow, and Elinor and I will enquire the exact cost. You know that I have been so sick as scarcely to be able to move since I got home.

I return the letter of your Hamilton farmer. What a lovely home that must be!—I never have seen a town or region that I liked better.[4]

Winny is taking up the cold I am leaving off. But the rest are well and join me in love to you all.

> Your aff'te brother,
> Will.

1. Setting up Sam as a farmer seems to have been one of the many projects for him that was unrealized. See, for example, Howells to W. C. Howells, 15 May and 12 June 1881 (MH), and 3 July 1881.
2. Joe's buying the *Sentinel* may refer to business matters discussed in Howells to W. C. Howells, 16 November 1879, n. 2. Howells had also visited Toronto on the way home from Crawfordsville and Chicago.
3. Apparently Howells did not go to Washington.
4. Hamilton, Ontario, is about forty miles southwest of Toronto. Howells could have seen the countryside from the train on his way to Toronto.

22 JUNE 1881, BELMONT, TO CHARLES D. WARNER

My dear Warner:

I'm awfully sorry, but I don't know the name of the Secretary of the Soc. for the Prevention of Home Studies for Young Men, and I have n't a circular. The more shame to me, for I am a Patron, I believe.[1] You shall have the umbrella again as soon as we can overcome our attachment to it. We care nothing for the silk, but we prize it for the associations. It reminds us of a visit, all too short, which you may consider stupid, but which was to us a season of pleasure alloyed only by the low spirits of our guest. I hope you are feeling constantly better and better, and I'm glad you're keeping out of Hartford for the present.— Sanborn for Thoreau is capital, and I'm glad you're not going to be weighted down with T. Parker.[2] I will try to see Norton before he goes back to Ashfield, and talk your enterprise up with him. Mrs. Howells joins me in love.

> Yours ever
> W. D. Howells.

June 22, 1881.

1. In a letter of 22 June 1881 (MH) Warner asked Howells or the secretary of the organization to send a circular on this society to Mrs. Chas. A. Jewell at Hartford, using the name "Promotion," however, instead of "Prevention." The background for the joking seems to be in Warner's visit at Belmont, beginning either 13 or 14 June. See Warner to Howells, 12 June 1881 (MH).
2. During the visit Warner saw Houghton about the "American Men of Letters" series. He also secured F. B. Sanborn's promise for writing *Henry D. Thoreau* (1882) in the series. The comment about Theodore Parker suggests that Warner had originally been asked to include a volume on the Unitarian clergyman and Transcendentalist.

2 JULY 1881, BELMONT, TO EDMUND C. STEDMAN

Belmont, July 2, 1881.

My dear Stedman:

With this terrible news about Garfield superseding and blotting out everything else,[1] I hardly know how to reply fitly to your two kind letters, and tell you what a glorious time I had at Yale.[2] I found myself in the midst of friends at once; but that did not prevent my missing you, and I enquired for you at once. I called on Mrs. Stedman, but she was not in, and I had not the pleasure of seeing her till we met at the President's reception. I was at the Commencement exercises as well as the dinner, and Lounsbury walked me all about and showed me the whole university.[3] I topped off the next day by going to the race at New London.—I learnt from Holt the fraternal interest you had taken in the high honor done me, and I wish to thank you with all my heart, and to beg you to thank my proposer for me.[4] Do you know his address? I should like to send him my next book.—The President introduced me at dinner in terms that made me blush for pride and pleasure; and I never longed so before to be able to make a speech in return. I noticed an atmosphere of enthusiasm and cordiality at Yale which seemed characteristic and peculiar, and which made me feel at once at home there.—I must now write on my title-pages *W. D. H. A. M. Harv. and Yale.* At the boat-race, "I perceived a divided duty," and hardly knew whether to weep or rejoice at the defeat of my first adoptive alma mater. I happened to wear a blue neck-tie; Miss Porter noticed it, and sent to know if I wore it purposely. Good bye. Thanks and thanks.—The cloud that is over us all, settles down on me again. It's terrible![5]

Yours ever
W. D. Howells.

1. Earlier in the day James A. Garfield was shot by Charles J. Guiteau at the Washington railway station; he did not die until 19 September.

2. Howells was given an honorary M. A. degree from Yale, having received one from Harvard in 1867.

3. Mrs. Laura Stedman, wife of E. C. Stedman. Noah Porter (1811–1892), Congregational clergyman and educator, was president of Yale (1871–1886). Thomas Lounsbury (1838–1915), professor of English at Yale, contributed essays on Chaucer and Shakespeare to the *Atlantic* in 1877 and 1878.

4. Henry Holt (1840–1926), the publisher, was a graduate of Yale in the Class of 1866. The proposer was Mason Young, as Stedman wrote Howells on 1 July 1881 (MH).

5. The Garfield assassination.

3 JULY 1881, BELMONT, TO WILLIAM C. HOWELLS

Belmont, July 3, 1881.

Dear father:

I have been thinking, ever since the terrible occurrence of yesterday, of the anxiety you must have suffered.[1] I did not hear of the assassination till the afternoon, and then I went into Boston at once. It was a very solemn city, with large crowds before all the newspaper offices, where bulletins were posted every half hour. When I came home the news was that Garfield could not live two hours; but this morning the papers brought the good news of his improvement, and I have just seen a private dispatch still more favorable in substance.—There was but one feeling, after the sorrow for Garfield, and that was shame at the thought of having Arthur for President. Of course, I feared for you, and I knew how anxious you would all be. I scarcely dare hope, even now; but the chances are certainly better.—In the relief we are feeling, I have let John go on with his preparations for keeping the Fourth, which the good fellow had himself proposed to suspend, when we heard that Garfield was dead. He has now pitched his tent, up in the woods, with four other boys, and I hope he will have a glorious time.—I was given the degree of Master of Arts by Yale, this week, and went to New Haven to the commencement, where I was received with all sorts of honors, and greatly enjoyed himself.—I have not answered anything in your letter; but I wish to suggest the consideration that you are probably not giving Sam any more money now than when you were letting him have all you got out of the Sentinel.[2] It seems to come to the same thing. And it is certainly better for you to have sold your half to Joe than given it to Sam.

All send love.

Your aff'te son
Will.

1. After the attempted assassination of President Garfield, at least part of the anxiety was over the retention of the consulship under a new president.

2. On Sam and the sale of the *Sentinel*, see Howells to V. M. Howells, 22 May 1881.

8 July 1881, Belmont, to Edwin D. Mead

Belmont, July 8, 1881.

My dear Eddy:

I thank you for your book,[1] which the publishers have made so handsome, and I have with the usual shame to ask your patience for my fault in not doing it sooner, and for not answering your first letter. You may be sure that I should not misunderstand anything in you or your essay, which I have not yet read with the fulness it merits, but in which I am quite ready to swear there is no fault but its subject. At your instigation, I bought "Sartor" and "Heroes," and I think your philosopher is a wonderful blatherskite,—a prophet of Commonplace with the Colic. But he is very well for a Scotchman.—I know you will let me speak freely. I do think the man was a humbug, and no better than a Joe Smith among the prophets[2]—gross and palpable in his literary imposture. I don't believe he wished the world well, or tried to make it better, and such continuous lines of thought as I find in him are harsh and inhuman. But very likely I'm wrong, and you are surely none the worse off thinking more of him than I do. Besides you have the great advantage of having read him thoroughly.—Winny and Elinor are at Dio Lewes's, Arlington Heights, for their Nerves;[3] but I shall be very glad to see you here at any time.

Yours affectionately
W. D. Howells.

1. E. D. Mead, *The Philosophy of Carlyle* (1881), published by Houghton, Mifflin & Co. Since it has only 140 pages, it is probably the "essay" Howells mentions in the next sentence.

2. Joseph Smith, the Mormon leader. In view of Norton's interest in Carlyle, it is surprising that Howells had not bought and read the two books earlier than this. On 22 April 1881 (NNC) he had written Conway: "We have been reading your Harper Carlyle paper with great pleasure in *you*. But I think it must require personal knowledge of that sick and ugly soul to make one even pity him." "Some Personal Recollections of Carlyle," by Henry James, Sr., appeared in the *Atlantic*, May 1881, under Aldrich's editorship though so soon after Howells' resignation that the acceptance by Howells was likely. See Howells to W. C. Howells, 31 January 1875, n. 1.

3. Dr. Dio Lewis (1823–1886) practiced in Buffalo (1847–1852), published papers on the treatment of cholera, and lectured widely on his new system of gymnastics. In 1860 he settled in Boston; he founded the Normal School for Physical Training in Lexington; he established a seminary for girls, in which physical development was a matter of major concern; and he edited *Dio Lewis's Monthly*.

10 JULY 1881, BELMONT, TO CHARLES E. NORTON

Belmont, July 10, 1881.

Dear friend:

As soon as our ill-advised mare, who seizes all emergent occasions, to kick in her stall and cap her hock, gets well enough to drive to Cambridge, I will go to see those pictures which you kindly tell me of.[1] But I am going first to try to "run my face" with your house keeper, without troubling Miss Theodora,[2] for I flatter myself that I look suspicious enough to be admitted instantly. Mrs. Howells and I always feel when we drive out, that it is in the characters of the village bar keeper and school ma'am; and I have a velvet coat and red neck-tie that clinch conjecture.—Just now Winny and her mother are away at Dio Lewis's, having another physician's prescription for Winny applied.[3] —I am getting on famously with my story, and when I go to Shady Hill I shall wish to borrow your Giusti's Proverbij Toscani. There is a proverb—Iddio non paga il Sabbato—which I think of using for a title, if I can't find a better.[4]—Yesterday my last and newest novel was published,[5] and I hope to send it to you to-morrow.

—We breathe freer at last about Garfield. But what a nightmare it has been! Now let us hope that he may rise from his bed with all the trammels which bound him to "politics" broken forever.[6] But there is some danger in the very universality of the sympathy shown—with a sweet & kindhearted man like him. How can he be made to feel that the best of it was evoked by the thought of whatever he had done for reform?

Yours ever
W. D. Howells.

1. On 3 July 1881 (MH) Norton, writing from Ashfield, asked Howells to look at two watercolor copies of Longhi paintings at $50 each.

2. In the same letter Norton suggested that Theodora Sedgwick, the late Mrs. Norton's youngest sister, would go to Shady Hill with Howells for him to see the pictures.

3. On 17 July 1881 (MH) Howells wrote to his father about Winny: "I see these days of her beautiful youth slipping away, in this sort of dull painful dream, and I grieve over her. 'Oh, papa, what a strange youth I'm having!' she said once with a burst of tears that wrung my soul. Well, to every one his own care." See also Howells to Mead, 8 July 1881, n. 3.

4. "God does not pay Saturdays"—a title Howells was considering probably for *A Modern Instance.* Many years later, on 6 April 1903 (MH; *Life in Letters*, II, 171), he wrote to Norton that he was thinking of using this title for a novel he was then finishing. See *The Son of Royal Langbrith*, HE, pp. xiii–xiv. *Proverbi Toscani* by Giuseppe Giusti, the poet, appeared in a new and enlarged edition in 1873.

5. *A Fearful Responsibility and Other Stories*, with copyright deposit date of 13 July.

6. By 10 July bulletins about Garfield were optimistic. On 13 July, for example, his doctors announced, "His gradual progress toward complete recovery is manifest and thus far without serious complications."

11 JULY 1881, BELMONT, TO ELIZABETH S. PHELPS (WARD)

Belmont, July 11, 1881.

Dear Miss Phelps:

I need not tell you how much I like Friends,[1] for you know that already, but I wish to thank you for remembering a poor old ex-editor with the book.

The close of the story, the working-out, is better even than I expected: the texture is wonderfully delicate and wonderfully fine; but then if you *have* gold in your hand you can beat it out to any subtilty you like, and steel you can draw to the tenuity of a hair. You were lucky in the preciousness of your theme—a great and simple one, the sort so hard to find that you wonder nobody found it before.[2]

I felt sorry for your poor man. Women, I always think can take care of themselves in matters of the affections, and can be what they like; but men are helpless and must be Caesar or nothing.

I was very greatly stirred up by your book, and thought a thousand things.

> Yours sincerely
> W. D. Howells.

1. *Friends: A Duet* was serialized in the *Atlantic*, January–July 1881.
2. In a letter to Howells, 10 March 1880 (MH), Miss Phelps describes the story of a young widow and her growing love for her former husband's friend as "just a study of one of those indefined relations with which society is full, and over which it is always perplexed." Of the end she says: "The light-natured reader will be glad she married him. The other kind will almost wish she had not."

14 JULY 1881, BELMONT, TO JAMES R. OSGOOD

Belmont, July 14, 1881.

My dear Osgood:

I am very glad to get your note of the 30th, and to learn of the good time you are having.[1] Everything goes prosperously here, and I am advancing the story rapidly,[2] in spite of having to turn back a good many times and rewrite and recast. So far, it does not lack incident of the mild sort in which I deal, and I think there will be a great deal of action throughout.

Before this comes, you will have received the advance sheets of Doctor Breen's Practice. At first I was disgusted with it, and then I concluded to go ahead and get the English copyright if I could.[3]

That announcement of a serial in the Y's. Companion is what I once talked to you of. It is the result of Mr. Butterworth's persistence, and I do not yet see the hour when I can write the thing.[4]

I had a good time last month at the Yale Commencement where they gave Aldrich and me degrees. Afterwards I went to the boat-race at New London. I saw Clemens at Montewese, and we arranged to push through the Library of Humor, if I finish the novel before the end of the year.[5]—The rest of my time has been spent at Redtop, though I shall probably go for a week's bathing to Duxbury soon, taking my shop with me, of course.

Your brother told me the other day that A Fearf. Resp. was starting off finely. They have made a very pretty book of it, and I am well content to appear under the old imprint again.[6]

With kindest regards to the Anthonys,[7]

Yours ever
W. D. Howells.

1. Osgood wrote Howells from London, 30 June 1881 (MH), about his "capital time" in Scotland and his plan to sail for Boston on 11 August.

2. *A Modern Instance.*

3. *Doctor Breen's Practice* began serialization in the August *Atlantic.* In his letter Osgood had reminded Howells to send sheets of the novel in advance in order to secure British copyright.

4. Hezekiah Butterworth (1839–1905), journalist and author, was an editorial associate of *Youth's Companion* from 1870 until his death. Howells did not contribute to the magazine until 1887, when it published his "Year in a Log-Cabin."

5. No letters between Howells and Clemens are extant between 19 April and 12 August 1881. The editors of *Twain-Howells,* p. 364, note that Howells spent a day with Clemens during the week prior to 17 July. Montewese is located in New Haven county, Connecticut.

6. Edward L. Osgood, for several years a banker with the Paris firm Drexel, Harjes, returned to America in 1878 to work for Houghton, Osgood & Co.; after its dissolution in 1880 he became a partner in his brother's firm. The "old imprint" was that of James R. Osgood & Co.

7. Andrew Varick Stout Anthony (1835–1906), a wood engraver, was a superintendent of fine editions with Osgood and other firms in Boston and a member of the literary department of Harper & Brothers (1894–1896).

6 AUGUST 1881, BELMONT, TO THOMAS B. ALDRICH

Belmont, Aug. 6, 1881.

My dear Aldrich:

It is most kind of you to ask this hospital to visit you, but for the hospital it is impossible. Winny is doomed to an indefinite season in bed, that being the uncertain cure of the nervous prostration from which she is suffering. We have not yet organized a nurse, and Mrs. Howells has worn herself out waiting on W., so that *she* is in bed, too. John and Pil and I are "just so's to be about," but we can't leave home. Thank you cordially, and tell Mrs. Aldrich, please, how grateful and sorry we all are.

If you are able to refrain from giving me those little digs in your notice which I used to deal you in mine, I shall believe you more of a saint and hero than I ever thought you. I'm getting ready to squirm, anyway; it's safest.[1]

By the way I've just finished my Police Report.[2] I've offered it nowhere. It would make 20 pp. for the January Atlantic, and if you want it for $300 'tis yours, as I am, ever,

W. D. H.

1. In his review of *A Fearful Responsibility*, *Atlantic*, September 1881, Aldrich included a few "digs" though they might have escaped the casual reader. Perhaps most obvious in its banter is the second paragraph, in which Aldrich suggests that Howells' new novella recalls too strongly *A Foregone Conclusion*: "We are more than half disappointed not to meet Don Ippolito coming down the narrow *calle* with his two handkerchiefs, like a Japanese *samurai* with his pair of swords."
2. "Police Report," *Atlantic*, January 1882.

14 AUGUST 1881, BELMONT, TO THOMAS W. HIGGINSON

Belmont, Aug. 14, 1881.

Dear Colonel Higginson:

I must tell you how glad I am of what you said in the Woman's Journal about the Queen's excluding the doctresses.[1] It was truly not so much the fault of an arrogant, narrow-minded old woman as of those inexpressible sneaks who submitted to it. What a shame! *Could* it have happened in any other country than England? Every word of your article was at once balm and fire to me. What a great thing it is *not* to be an Englishman! It's a sort of patent of nobility.

Yours sincerely
W. D. Howells.[2]

1. In an article, "A Royal Example; or, Woman vs. Women," *Woman's Journal*, 13 August 1881, Higginson wrote: "The newspapers inform us that in the International Medical Convention at London the majority of the committee of arrangements were in favor of admitting women physicians as members; but that they were finally excluded by the expressed wish of Queen Victoria." The article, after voicing strong criticism of the queen, concludes with the assertion that this proves the old adage that women are their own worst enemies. In his reply to this letter, Higginson wrote on 17 August 1881 (MH): "Glad you liked it.... Your closing climax is delicious & shall be expressed on yr. tombstone if you are cut off prematurely." The subject of women doctors was, of course, of great interest to Howells at this time because *Doctor Breen's Practice* had just begun to appear in the *Atlantic*.

2. George S. Hellman omitted this letter from "The Letters of Howells to Higginson," *Twenty-Seventh Annual Report of the Bibliophile Society, 1901–1929* (Cedar Rapids, Iowa: Torch Press [1929]), pp. 17–56. His note, dated July 1941, on the typed copy of the letter (NN) reads in part: "... I was unwilling to have it printed in the Bibliophile Society Year Book, and trust that it will never find its way into print.... Certainly in these days of the war, it is a great thing *to be* an Englishman."

14 AUGUST 1881, BELMONT, TO ANNE H. FRÉCHETTE

Belmont, Aug. 14, 1881.

Dear Annie:

Your lovely letter deserves a far better answer than I know how to write. I read it aloud at the table, and we all agreed, "Well, nobody begins to write such letters as Annie!"

As to your invitation to poor Winny, you don't know how gladly we would accept it if we could. I think we would all come to Ottawa and take a house there, and if that were impracticable, we would most gratefully accept your hospitality for her. But at present she has been put to bed for some weeks in order to try a sort of rest-cure. She is bathed, rubbed, and *lunched* continually. It is too soon yet to hope for any effect, but there seems sense in the theory. At any rate we have tried everything else in vain.

What a perfectly ravishing picture that is Vevie![1] We are very proud to show it:—she is so pretty and solemn and sweet, it makes me want to hug her. The quaint dress is very becoming to her. She is a curious mixture in looks of you and Fréchette both.—I am glad that you like A Fearf. Resp. You are right: it was the first fruits of my emancipation.[2] I am now six hundred pages (this size) deep in my story for next year's Scribner. It will begin in January.[3] I suppose I am about half through. This last week I wrote a hundred pages.—If Miss King is still in Ottawa, remember me to her; she wrote me a very touching little note about her sister, just after her death.[4]—We are all very much interested in your removal to New Edinburgh,[5] and want very much to see your pretty home, there. I hope we shall some time be able to do so. And I should like to see *Mole*.[6] That's a good name for a boy. We used to call

John, *Rat*.—By the way this is John's 13th birthday, and he is very happy in a number of presents. The Fairchild children have given him a silver-handled riding whip, and he is now fully equipped for the grey mustang I bought him.—Elinor wants me to say that she is going to write you as soon as she can. Then you will have some sort of adequate reply: I despise my letters.—Alden's note, you may be sure, is as gratifying to us as it was to you.[7] What a capital letter from your friend!—Love from all to all—including Aurelia and Henry.

> Your aff'te brother
> Will.

1. Marie Marguerite Fréchette, born 16 April 1878.
2. *A Fearful Responsibility* was the first fiction Howells published after resigning as editor of the *Atlantic*.
3. *A Modern Instance* began in the *Century*, December 1881.
4. Miss King has not been identified; her note is not extant.
5. New Edinburgh was a suburb of Ottawa.
6. Howells Fréchette.
7. Henry Mills Alden had evidently written to Annie about her *Harper's Monthly* article (see Howells to V. M. Howells, 10 April 1881, n. 5) and perhaps also about her short story (see Howells to A. H. Fréchette, 18 February 1877, n. 5). Alden (1836–1919), was the editor of *Harper's Monthly* (1869–1919), and Howells devoted an "Editor's Easy Chair" to him (December 1919) in which he called Alden "a man of rare gifts, a poet, a philosopher, a scholar, an acute critic, . . . an editor perfect in his time and place."

2 SEPTEMBER 1881, BELMONT, TO THOMAS B. ALDRICH

> Belmont, Sept. 2, 1881.

My dear Aldrich:

I have become so abjectly a contributor that I am getting doubtful about points in my work, and feel like asking you to bolster me up. If you think the account of the lost soul and the hostess in the latter part of the Police Report is too frank, please say so: one would not be a great French Realist if one could.[1]

—I see that I shall yet write in back-slope, and be very neat about my MS.

> Yours ever
> W. D. Howells.

1. The passage referred to appears in "Police Report," *Atlantic*, January 1882, where Howells introduces the trial of a prostitute and madam for robbing a customer by remarking: "One case came up on the occasion of my last visit which I should like to report verbatim in illustration, but it was of too lurid a sort to be

treated by native realism...." Howells had recurrent doubts about this piece. In sending Aldrich the manuscript on 27 August 1881 (MH), he remarked: "I guess this is pretty poor." None of Aldrich's replies have been located.

3 SEPTEMBER 1881, BELMONT, TO CHARLES D. WARNER

Belmont, Sept. 3, 1881.

My dear Warner:

Thanks for your kind letter of the 27th. There is no cause for anxiety in Winny's case:[1] the doctors agree, if in nothing else, that it is only a question of time as to her recovery; but in the meanwhile she has been ordered to bed, where she has spent the last month, and where she requires continual care and nursing. I was extremely sorry not to be with you at Ashfield,[2] but I could not get away.—Your uncertainty about the time of your going to Europe is matched by ours. I shall have my story done in time to start Jan. 1,[3] but we dread the winter voyage for Winny, and we shall not go before May.—Your accounts of Mrs. Warner's improvement delight us: how glorious to bring her home so much better.—But you say nothing of yourself. How is your poor malaria? We often think of you, and wish we had treated you better—not joked, or anything.—Osgood has come home in fine feather, and has begun his old tricks of lunching people. We had a perfectly lurid time when Clemens was here: Garfield was at his lowest, and we did everything but shed tears; it was the saddest lunch I ever saw. But nothing discourages Osgood, and he proposes something else this week.—I'm glad, of course, that you fancy Dr. Breen;[4] you remember my telling you the idea long ago when you and your wife first visited us here.—I suppose you mean Miss Gleason by the "female fool":[5] she is not rare in any highly unitarianized community. I confess that she amuses me.—I'm making the hero of my divorce story a newspaper man. Why has no one struck journalism before?—I am curious to see your Irving.[6] Did you get any sort of promise out of Norton or Curtis?[7]

All join me in love.

Yours ever
W. D. Howells.

1. On 27 August 1881 (MH) Warner had written that Winny's continued sickness "filled me with alarm."

2. C. E. Norton's summer residence. See Howells to W. C. Howells, 22 August 1880, n. 1.

3. *A Modern Instance.*

4. *Doctor Breen's Practice.*

5. Miss Gleason is a very minor character in the novel. In his letter Warner

praised the novel and asked, "But where did you pick up your female fool?" It is likely that the "female fool" of Warner's question referred to Mrs. Maynard.

6. *Washington Irving* (1881), in the "American Men of Letters" series.

7. Presumably Warner, as editor of the series, was trying to secure C. E. Norton and G. W. Curtis as authors.

11 SEPTEMBER 1881, BELMONT, TO WILLIAM C. HOWELLS

Belmont, Sept. 11, 1881.

Dear father:

I suppose you are breathing freer again in regard to poor Garfield, and feeling a little indignant with all of us that he was not moved long ago.[1] Talking of him makes me think at once of Winny, who is still in bed. Her doctor has been in the Adirondacks for the last fortnight, but will return this week, and then I think I shall insist upon his getting her up. In fact, I feel now as if I should like to put the case in the hands of Dr. Wesselhoeft again as soon as he gets home from Europe.[2] After being used to homeopathy, it is hard to have patience with allopathotic methods. Perhaps when Winny is once on foot again she may show a gain which we don't see as yet.—You ask me who the N. Y. Mail critic is. It is R. H. Stoddard, who is a persistent and rather silly detractor of mine.[3] Besides, I think that I know rather more about the business of writing novels than any critic living, and where I don't feel obliged by my consciousness to side with a man against my work, his censure doesn't worry me.—I suppose I shall be in Toronto about the end of November, and I shall certainly bring some of the children with me. I long to see you all again, and I shall stay as long as possible.—I don't know whether I've told you before that I'm making the hero of my new story a city newspaper man.[4] Incidentally there is some good-natured satire of modern "journalism." I have now written nine hundred pages of the story since May 15. It will be the longest novel I've yet written.—All join me in love to both of you at Toronto. I shall write next to Vic.

Your aff'te son
Will.

1. On 6 September Garfield had been taken to Elberon, New Jersey, a seaside resort between Long Branch and Asbury Park. There he again seemed to improve for a short time, but died on the nineteenth.

2. See Howells to W. C. Howells, 31 January 1875, n. 4.

3. Howells had probably known R. H. Stoddard since he sailed from New York

in 1861; see *Literary Friends and Acquaintance*, HE, pp. 77–78. The letters from Stoddard at Harvard appear cordial, though there is a gap between 1880 (the year Stoddard became literary reviewer of the New York *Mail*) and 1894. The letter of 12 May 1880 (MH), hints that he would like to have his collected *Poems* reviewed in the *Atlantic*, as they were by G. P. Lathrop, November 1880, in a most favorable way. The 1894 letter, 24 November (MH), thanks Howells for sending proof of his "frank and kind" remarks in "First Impressions of Literary New York," *Harper's Monthly*, June 1895.

    4. Bartley Hubbard in *A Modern Instance*.

2 OCTOBER 1881, BELMONT, TO GEORGE W. CABLE

Belmont, Oct. 2, 1881.

My dear Mr. Cable:[1]

    I have just finished The Grandissimes, and I must at least try to tell you how much I like it. I had heard it called faulty and confused in construction; that was the only blame I had heard of it, and that is mistaken. I found it thoroughly knit and perfectly clear, portraying a multitude of figures with a delicacy and unerring certainty of differentiation that perpetually astonished me. It is a noble and beautiful book, including all the range of tragedy and comedy; and it made my heart warm towards you, while I had the blackest envy in it. Deuce take you, how could you do it so well?—Aurora is one of the most delicious creatures I ever knew. My wife kept reading me that first call of Frowenfeld's on the Nancanou ladies, till I was intoxicated with their delightfulness. Oh the charm of their English! We speak nothing else now but that dialect. Raoul, Honoré, and the poor f.m.c.[2]—they have our hearts, Raoul especially. Of course you expected me to like Agricole too? He is admirable. Bras-Coupé episode most powerful;[3] the last chapter, exquisite—that woman left a sweet taste in my mouth; Honoré, with his gutteral *r*'s noble and charming; all the Grandissime tribe boldly sketched, or finely suggested. The book is full of atmosphere. You are a great fellow, and we all send your homage—our love.

Yours sincerely
W. D. Howells

    1. George Washington Cable (1844–1925) had published *Old Creole Days* (1879), a collection of New Orleans local color stories that had been appearing in magazines since 1873. Author of many novels, he left the South in 1885 because of his speeches and articles in behalf of the blacks. At the time of this letter, *The Grandissimes* had been in print for about a year and reviewed in the *Atlantic*, December 1880, by H. E. Scudder; but Cable had first met Howells in June 1881. On 18 October (MH; Lucy L. C. Biklé, *George W. Cable* [New York: C. Scribner's Sons, 1928], pp. 72–73, in part; Ekström, *Studia Neophilologica* 22 [1950], 51–52) Cable thanked Howells for his letter: "I have quaffed your sweet praise until I am simply in no condition to attend to business."

2. Honoré Grandissime, f.m.c. (free man of color), is the half-brother of the hero of the same name in the novel.

3. The story of Bras Coupé, slave and former African king, appears midway in the novel. See Arlin Turner, *George W. Cable* (Durham, N. C.: Duke University Press, 1956), pp. 94–95, for a discussion of its effect and sources. In treating the novel in *Heroines of Fiction* (1901), II, 234–44, Howells does not mention the Bras Coupé episode, but quotes extensively from the last chapter. Though last chapters are "apt to be an anti-climax," he remarks, this one is "subtly interpretative of Aurora's personality," with a love scene that "has to my knowledge scarcely been surpassed in its delicious naturalness."

5 OCTOBER 1881, BELMONT, TO THOMAS W. HIGGINSON

Would that your welcome letter had not come! I'm all agog, now. How would "A Modern Catastrophe" do? Or, "A Contemporary Trouble"?[1]

W. D. H.[2]

1. These titles are suggestions for *A Modern Instance*. In a letter of 3 October 1881 (MH) Higginson had suggested some other titles: "A Marriage begun & ended"; "The Custom of the Country"; "Except these Bonds." On 6 October (MH) he replied to Howells: "We don't think the 'Mod. Catastr' or 'Contemp. Trouble' half so good as yr. Mod. Instance or Complication, let alone the 'Except these Bonds' [¶] My wife suggests if you wish another Shakesperian 'Double Double Toil & Trouble'!"

2. Date and place of origin of this note, as well as the addressee, have been established by the postmark and address on the verso.

6 OCTOBER 1881, BELMONT, TO CHARLES FAIRCHILD

Belmont, Oct. 6, 1881.[1]

My dear Fairchild:

We shall probably go to Europe the 1st of January, for an absence of 18 months or 2 years; and I wish if possible to arrange our affairs in regard to Redtop. I write now rather than wait for your return, because I suppose you may have more leisure for this small business on your way home than you will have afterwards. I had hoped to tell you that Winsor had bought my Cambridge house; but after giving me some recent hopes he has finally disappointed me.[2]—I have now to propose that you take the Belmont house off my hands during my absence and let it to some friend of yours.[3] I will leave all my furniture in it, and your tenant can have the use of our things for nothing, on condition that I have the option of buying the place at $10,000 when I come back. I might then have sold the Cambridge house; at any rate I should do my best to sell it.

If this plan does not seem feasible, I do not now see any way but for me to give up Redtop to you finally, and store my furniture. I need not tell you how sorry I should be to do this; but I must—with Winny's expensive invalidism ahead of me—economize in every way; and I cannot carry the rent of Redtop while I am away.

We could leave the house perfectly furnished, down to the last detail for housekeeping, with nine first-rate beds. Perhaps Mr. Ned Atkins might hire it; or your brother might like to occupy it awhile.[4]

> Yours ever
> W. D. Howells.

Of course I could not expect you to forego any good chance of selling the house during my absence.

1. This letter exists in draft form only, as is indicated by the frequent cancellations and revisions and by the uncancelled postage stamp on the accompanying envelope. Whether Howells ever sent Fairchild a clear copy is uncertain.

2. Justin Winsor, who had been renting the house at 37 Concord Avenue.

3. Though Howells had built the Belmont house, in effect he rented it from Fairchild; he had the option to buy it since the time it was built. See Fairchild to Howells, 6 November 1877 (MH).

4. Edwin Farnsworth Atkins (1850–1926) received an honorary M. A. degree from Harvard in 1903. In the presidential address during the commencement exercises he was referred to as an "adventurous and successful planter in Cuba, judicious and liberal promoter of applied botany." The only brother of Charles Fairchild who has been identified is Lucius Fairchild (1831–1896), who was governor of Wisconsin (1866–1872) and U. S. minister to Spain (1880–1882). At the time of this letter he was evidently considering his resignation. Howells' house remained empty until 1883; see Howells to Fairchild, 15 March 1883 (MH).

23 OCTOBER 1881, BELMONT, TO WILLIAM C. HOWELLS

Belmont, Oct. 23, 1881.

Dear father:

It seems a long time since we heard from you; but I suppose you are all well. We are rejoicing over the rapid restoration of Winny to health. She is not strong yet; but she is down stairs, she walks out, is cheerful, and seems to be getting rid of her vertigo. Of course she has her ups and downs, and at times is very morbid; but still she is gaining, and gaining fast.

Last Sunday, after Elinor wrote, your friend Mr. Moore came out and took tea with us.[1] We all liked him very much—he is a modest, nice young fellow in every way; and I believe he has some good business prospects. I tried to do something for him with Osgood; but he had nothing that Mr. Moore could take hold of.

I expect now to be with you sometime about Thanksgiving—rather before than after—and to bring John and Pilla. The prospect now is that I shall get my story nearly done by that time;[2] but I may take my MS. with me, and work on it in the mornings. It is already as long as The Undiscovered Country, and it will be a fourth longer, when it is finished. The subject has great capabilities, and it interests me very much. It appears to me now that I shall make something good out of it. I write continuously at it, and I have begrudged the time I have had to give to the sittings for my portrait.[3] The painter has succeeded in getting a very good likeness in charcoal, and he promises to do it in oil and give it to me. As his price is $500 for a head, this is rather fine. With love to all from all,

Your aff'te son
Will.

1. Moore has not been identified.

2. Because of Howells' illness, with confinement in bed from about mid-November, he did not make the Toronto visit. Nor was *A Modern Instance* completely finished until June 1882.

3. Howells was sitting for the prominent American painter, Frederick P. Vinton (1846–1911), who became famous for his portraits of noted statesmen, authors, jurists, and professional men.

30 OCTOBER 1881, BELMONT, TO JAMES R. OSGOOD

Belmont, Oct. 30, 1881.

Dear Osgood:

I will speak with you about this note on Tuesday afternoon, when I expect to come in. It is the answer I supposed you would get.[1]

I have gone through Mr. John Esten Cooke's MS., and I can't advise you to take it.[2] There is not a human being in the book; the plot is improbable and not very novel. On its level the literature is good enough. But the level is not the highest.

Yours ever
W. D. H.

1. Howells' reference is unclear.

2. Perhaps *Fanchette by One of Her Admirers* (1883), the first novel by Cooke to be published after this date. Harper & Brothers had published Cooke's four previous books; and in spite of Howells' advice, Osgood published this one.

6 NOVEMBER 1881, BELMONT, TO JAMES R. OSGOOD

Belmont, Nov. 6, 1881.

My dear Osgood:

The cities I should expect to visit in Italy are Bologna, Parma, Modena, Verona, Brescia, Vicenza, Ferrara, Bergamo, Lucca, Padua, Trent, Pisa and Siena.[1] My notion is to treat them as I did "Ducal Mantua" in *Italian Journeys*, sketching the history of each, with contemporary light and incident, and making each study as attractive as possible with anecdote and adventure. I should seek rather interest than thoroughness, and I believe I should succeed, and make some sketches which people would like. It is the ground I know, and I should work con amore.

The papers would be about 14 "Atlantic" pages, each.

Yours ever
W. D. Howells.

1. Of these cities Howells wrote only about Lucca, Pisa, and Siena in *Tuscan Cities* (1886). But half the book is devoted to Florence, and there is an essay on "Pistoja, Prato, and Fiesole."

10 DECEMBER 1881, BELMONT, TO ANNIE A. FIELDS

Belmont, Dec. 10, 1881

Dear Mrs. Fields:

I have now been nearly four weeks in bed, with fever, and a thousand other things; but I am slowly getting better.—The first week of my sickness was the time I had meant to give to a review of your beautiful and interesting book;[1] and I know that you will believe that I deeply grieved at being prevented from writing of it. Of course Aldrich has had it well done;[2] but I cannot cease to regret that I should not have been able to do it.

The reading gave me a sad but constant pleasure: it kept dear Mr. Fields continually before me; I saw him, I heard him speak and laugh. Could I say more in praise?

Write me a line to say you forgive my delinquency, and excusing this shapeless note—the best I can do—believe me

Ever sincerely Yours
W. D. Howells.[3]

1. *James T. Fields: Biographical Notes and Personal Sketches* (1881). Fields had died on 24 April 1881.

2. The promised review did not appear in the *Atlantic*.

3. For Elinor Howells' addition to this letter, see Textual Apparatus.

15 DECEMBER 1881, CAMBRIDGE, TO WILLIAM C. HOWELLS

7 Garden st.
Cambridge, Dec. 15, 1881.

Dear father:

We have come down to this boarding-house, so that I can be handy to the doctor at all hours.[1] There has been a very persistent and tedious recurrence of the stricture, and Belmont was so far off that I suffered a great deal before I could get at the doctor; now I reach him in a few minutes. It is very trying, to have this thing recur; but he says it is only a matter of a few days, and that I need have but courage and patience.[2]

Elinor is kept a good deal at Belmont, putting the house in order to shut up for the winter. Then she will join me here with the children; and if I get well soon, we shall take a furnished house in Boston till spring.[3] I have an excellent nurse; and perfect care; so there is nothing to worry about.

With love to all

Your aff'te son
Will.

1. See Howells to W. C. Howells, 31 January 1875, n. 4.

2. Though Howells' illness has been generally accepted as a nervous breakdown (see Cady, *Howells*, I, 208–10; Lynn, *Howells*, pp. 253–54), this sentence suggests that the immediate physical symptom was a recurrent cystitis, so painful that apparently a doctor was needed to insert a catheter for urinating.

3. On 12 January 1882, they moved to 16 Louisburg Square.

TEXTUAL APPARATUS

Introduction

THE letters selected for inclusion in these volumes of Howells correspondence are printed in clear text in the form reproducing as nearly as possible their finished state. The record of the alterations which took place during composition and which are evidenced on the pages of the manuscripts is presented in the textual apparatus which follows, in combination with the record of editorial emendations. The letters have been editorially corrected only in specific details and only when the original texts would make no conceivable sense to the reader. Thus Howells' few eccentricities of spelling and punctuation and his occasional mistakes and oversights have generally been retained. However, inadvertent repetitions of letters, syllables, or words—usually a result of moving the pen from the end of one line to the beginning of the next—have been emended and recorded in the apparatus. In cases where the actual manuscripts are not available and transcriptions or printed versions of letters have served as the basis for printing here, errors in those materials have also been retained, since the actual source of the error—Howells, the transcriber, or the printer—cannot be identified.

Except where extraordinary conditions have made it impossible, the following procedures have been followed step-by-step in the preparation for publication of the text of each letter, whether the extant form of it is the original document or an unpublished or published transcription. First a clean, typed transcription of the final form of the extant material is prepared from a facsimile of it. Then duplicate copies of this prepared transcription are read and corrected against the facsimile by the editor of the volume and by one of the editors of the letters series. At the same time drafts of the apparatus material are prepared, recording all cancellations, insertions, revisions, and illegible words or letters in the text, as well as possible compounds, end-line hyphenated, which must be resolved as hyphenated or unhyphenated forms. These drafts of the apparatus also include questions about proper interpretation of textual details. The corrected and edited transcriptions and accompanying apparatus are conflated at the Howells Center and any discrepancies identified and corrected. At this stage transcriptions and textual apparatus are completely reread against the facsimile of the original. The resultant material is next checked by a different editor against the original holograph, copy, or printing; he verifies all details, answers insofar as possible all remaining questions, and indicates matter in the original which has not been reproduced in the working facsimile. This completes the process of preparing printer's copy.

At this point the texts of the letters—though not the corresponding apparatus—are set in type. The typset texts are proofread once against the facsimiles of the original documents and once more against the prepared printer's copy; necessary corrections are made in both typeset text and apparatus, and the apparatus is keyed to the line numbering of the typeset texts. After correction by the printer of the typeset text and the setting in type of the textual apparatus, these materials are proofread in full once more against the printer's copy, and the apparatus is proofread again separately. At every point at which revises are returned by the printer they are verified against the marked proofs.

This procedure—involving as many different people as possible from among the editors of the volumes, the series, and the Howells Edition staff—has been adopted to guarantee that the printed texts are as accurate as the combined energy and attention of a group of trained and experienced editors can make them. It will, we hope, warrant our statement that the errors, oversights, and possibly unidiomatic readings of the texts are those of the original documents and not of the editors. Further, since even the detailed textual record presented in this apparatus cannot fully indicate the physical condition of the letters, the editorial materials prepared during the assembly of these volumes are all being preserved, and can be consulted by anyone who wishes to see them—at the Howells Center at Indiana University as long as it is in operation for preparation of texts for "A Selected Edition of W. D. Howells" and in a suitable public depository thereafter.

The editorial considerations and procedures outlined above underlie the actual presentation of the letters printed in these volumes. Each letter is introduced by an editorial heading identifying the date and place of composition and the name of the correspondent to whom it is directed. The date and location identified in this heading may be different from those provided by the letter itself, since the content of the letter or other pertinent evidence can indicate that those details are inaccurate. When such cases arise, they are discussed in appropriate footnotes.

The translation of the ranges of handwritten and typewritten material and printed stationery into the stricter confines of the printed page obviously demands the adoption of certain formal and stylistic conventions. Regardless of their arrangement or placement on the original page, inside addresses are presented in one or more lines above the single line containing the place of origin and date provided in the letter. This format is followed regardless of the placement of the dateline at the beginning or at the end of a letter. When handwritten or printed letterheads provide more elaborate information than basic identification of place of origin and date, the additional information is omitted and its absence signaled by the appropriate placement of ellipses. The use of capitals or a combination of capitals and small capitals in printed letterhead forms has been reduced here to capitals and lowercase letters. In the printing of letters and datelines in the present text, italic type is used to indicate matter which occurs in the original as part of printed stationery, and roman to indicate portions supplied by Howells himself. The distinction between print and handwritten or typed portions of heading information can be significant in that a printed letterhead in particular does not necessarily indicate that the letter itself was written in that place. If Howells supplied location information different from that of a printed letterhead, the printed letterhead is considered simply a mark on the paper and has been ignored in the presentation of the text.

The beginning of the body of the letter after the salutation has been consistently set off by a paragraph even if Howells continued on the same line or used any other unconventional spacing. Similarly, the positions of the complimentary close (e.g., "Yours ever") and the signature in relation to the body of the letter have been standardized without regard to Howells' widely varying usage. The relative spacing of the indentations of paragraphs has been normalized to conform to the typography of these volumes; this principle has been applied also to unindented paragraph breaks which occur in the originals. The interruptive or appositive dash within sentences and the transitional dash between sentences (the latter almost the equivalent in sense of the paragraph break) have been set in standard typographical form, and relative length not indicated. The long *s* of Howells' youthful hand has been set consistently in the ordinary typographical form. Underlined words have been set in italics without regard to the position or relative length of the underlining; when the form of the underlining indicates, however, that Howells clearly intended to emphasize only part of a word (e.g., *every*one), then only that part has been italicized.

When texts are derived from machine-printed rather than handwritten telegrams, the full capitalization used there has been reduced to capitals and lowercase letters, with an appropriate note in the textual apparatus. The same procedure has been followed for letters typed on typewriters using only capital letters. Where texts are derived from copies of now-missing letters rather than from manuscripts, any typographical peculiarities of those forms—indentation, employment of capitals and small capitals in proper names, and so on—have been altered to conform to the format of the present edition. But only this strictly typographical alteration has been enforced; the errors in spelling and punctuation and the revisions and cancellations within these materials have all been considered textually significant and a potentially accurate record of the originals upon which they are based.

Postscripts which follow upon the signatures in the original letters are placed in this same position in the printed text, but marginal notes and postscripts placed eccentrically are printed where they seem to belong within or after the body of the letter, and their original locations indicated by editorial notes in the apparatus to the letter. The presence or absence of page and leaf numbering or the location of such numbering on the original pages has not been recorded.

In the preparation of the texts and apparatus, those marks, and those marks alone, in the text of the letter which could be interpreted as slips of the pen have been ignored. All other marks, including wiped-out words or letters, erased material, incomplete words either canceled or uncanceled, and random letters have been recorded. Illegible words or letters are identified in the apparatus by the abbreviation "*illeg.*"

The presentation of this information in the apparatus demands the use of certain symbols and abbreviations to conserve space. The record for each letter is introduced by the same editorial heading that introduces the item in the text proper. Then follows a note on the number of pages (i.e., sides of individual sheets or of segments of sheets created by folding which have been written on). Next is provided an abbreviated indication of the kind of text and the presence or absence of authorial signature (A.l. = Autograph letter; A.l.s. = Autograph letter signed; T.l. = Typescript letter; T.l.s. = Typescript letter signed; A.n. = Autograph note; A.n.s. = Autograph note signed; T.n. = Typescript note; T.n.s. = Typescript note signed). If the authorial text is of a kind not represented by these eight abbreviations, it is described fully (e.g., "Mostly in autograph of Elinor M. Howells"; "Telegraph form written in Howells' hand"; "Typed telegram"). If the text is based on a transcribed copy, that fact is noted togther with information about the source of the transcription, if known; if the transcription is a published text, the author, title, and other bibliographical information are provided —in the cases of both published and unpublished transcriptions the number of pages of text is ignored as textually irrelevant. This information is followed in turn by the standard abbreviation for the library in which the original document or extant transcription is located,[1] or by the short-form designation for a private collection.

Following this heading appears the record of the internal revisions and cancellations in the letter document and any emendations made by the editors. All such revisions, even in typed letters, may be assumed to be

---

1. The system of abbreviations used in this edition is that described in *Symbols of American Libraries*, 10th ed. (Washington: Library of Congress, 1969).

by Howells, unless otherwise noted in the apparatus. Each entry in this record begins with the citation of the number or numbers of the lines in the text of the printed letter in which the cited material occurs. This numbering is based on the count of full or partial lines of type, and begins with the first line of the document, whether that be inside address, date, or salutation; it does not include the formal editorial heading which precedes each letter.

Sentences, phrases, words, or parts of words inserted into the running text of the document are indicated in the record by placement within vertical arrows, ellipses being used to abbreviate passages of four or more words. Thus:

$\uparrow$evade$\downarrow$ with$\uparrow$out$\downarrow$ $\uparrow$directly . . . exchange.$\downarrow$

No distinction is made between words inserted above the line and those inserted below it or manuscript revisions fitted into typescript lines, and the color of ink or the medium (pencil, pen, typewriter) used for corrections or additions is not described. The presence or absence of a caret or other conventional symbol for the insertion of the material is not recorded. When a word has been written over some other word or part of a word, that fact is indicated by the use of the abbreviation "*w.o.*" (for "written over") following the final reading and preceding the original. Thus:

parties *w.o.* party   people *w.o.* ple

Words canceled in the original are indicated by placement in pointed brackets in the context of citation of sufficient words from the text of the letter (either before or after the canceled words or phrase) as printed in this edition to identify its location. Thus:

went ⟨to⟩   ⟨we went⟩ I walked

An italic question mark within brackets following a word indicates a degree of uncertainty about the interpretation provided. The combinations of these various symbols and abbreviations should be self-explanatory: e.g., $\uparrow$⟨this⟩$\downarrow$ indicates that the interlined word "this" has been canceled.

All editorial revisions are signaled in the apparatus by a left-opening bracket (]); preceding it appears the reading of the text as printed in this edition, and following it the reading of the original. When the editorial revision involves only the emendation of punctuation, each curved dash ($\sim$) following the bracket stands for a word preceding the bracket. When it has been necessary to supply words, letters, or marks of punctuation missing in the original not because of oversight or error in composition but because of the present physical condition of the document—badly faded ink, deteriorated or torn paper, blots, or water-spots—the reconstructed portions are signaled by being placed between vertical lines: Thus:

af|te|r |the| commit|tee| met

Virgules (slashes) are used to indicate the end of a line of writing in the original document. All other editorial comments, including description of the placement of postscripts and marginal notes or the presence in a document of notes or comments in another hand believed to be contemporary with the composition or receipt of the letter, as well as information about specific textual details not covered by the basic system of symbols and abbreviations outlined here, are provided in italic type within brackets.

In addition to the textual record which follows, this edition of letters contains a section headed "Word-Division," consisting of two separate lists: one, List A, indicates the resolution of possible compounds occurring as end-line hyphenations in the original documents, and the other, List B, the form to be given to possible compounds which occur at the end of the line in the present text. A description of the keying system employed in these lists and the process by which editorial decisions about the resolution of such end-lines were reached are provided in the headnote to that section.

C. K. L.
D. J. N.

Textual Record

---

2 January 1873, Boston, to Paul H. Hayne. 3 pp. A.l.s. NcD.

   7 exaggerated *w.o.* exg

5 January 1873, Cambridge, to Charles D. Warner. 4 pp. A.l.s. NjP.

   8 at the *w.o.* at one   9 this *w.o.* the   18 looking *w.o.* as
19 week's *w.o. illeg.*

3 February 1873, Boston, to Anne T. Howells. 4 pp. A.l.s. MH.

   6 yours *w.o. illeg.*   12 giving ⟨him⟩   16 ↑honestly↓
30 met *w.o. illeg.*   35 ⟨*illeg.*⟩ Their

5 February 1873, Boston, to William C. Howells. 4 pp. A.l.s. MH.

   5 that ⟨the⟩   5 send *w.o.* sent   19 ↑officers↓   20 ↑to say,↓
28 as inferior ⟨as inferior⟩

16 February 1873, Boston, to William C. Howells. 4 pp. A.l.s. MH.

   11 Henry's *w.o. illeg.*   16 little ⟨other⟩   16 this. *w.o.* think

6 March 1873, Cambridge, to Anne T. Howells. 4 pp. A.l.s. MH.

   7 you⟨r⟩   13 so⟨w⟩   16 ↑have↓   24 of *w.o.* ab

10 March 1873, Cambridge, to Henry James. 4 pp. A.l.s. MH.

   9 ⟨th⟩ another   15 ⟨notl⟩ notion   16 always ⟨,nearly alwa⟩
18 ⟨hard⟩ ↑impossible↓   20 ⟨t⟩ I   20 man↑,↓⟨ner⟩   22 ⟨all⟩ any
24 she *w.o.* the   25 ⟨I⟩ makes ⟨him appear⟩   28 weighed *w.o. illeg.*
37 voice *w.o. illeg.*   38 Delphic *w.o.* Depphic   45 *artista w.o. artiste*
48 soon *w.o.* sorr⟨y⟩   49 ⟨ag⟩ about   60 jolliest and *w.o.* jolliest,
69 is the *w.o.* is one   70 ↑there↓
78–82 five . . . . you.] [*in margin and across salutation and text, first page*]
83–85 Imagine . . . . sleighing.] [*in margin, second page*]
85 snow *w.o. illeg.*

16 March 1873, Boston, to William C. Howells. 4 pp. A.l.s. MH.

   9 thick *w.o.* thin   16 woe *w.o. illeg.*   19 up *w.o. illeg.*
24 carriage. She *w.o.* carriage. The

311

20 March 1873, Boston, to Charles W. Stoddard. 3 pp. A.l.s CSmH.

10 suggest *w.o.* advise   13 just *w.o. illeg.*

27 March 1873, Boston, to Hjalmar H. Boyesen. 4 pp. A.l.s. ViU.

28 ↑else↓

6 April 1873, Boston, to William C. Howells. 4 pp. A.l.s. MH.

20 sufficient⟨l⟩   25 not at ⟨at⟩
32–35 Elinor . . . . Will.] [*across letterhead and salutation, first page*]

20 April 1873, Boston, to William C. Howells. 4 pp. A.l.s. MH.

19 Urbana *w.o. illeg.*   23 glad ⟨of⟩   25 that *w.o.* than
26 ⟨Sup⟩ Sometimes   27 By *w.o.* But
29–34 for . . . . Will.] [*across letterhead, salutation, dateline, and text, first page*]

12 May 1873, Boston, to Henry James. 4 pp. A.l.s. MH.

4 ⟨Your⟩ Roman   5 number⟨ed⟩   15 social *w.o. illeg.*
19 ⟨4d *w.o.* 2d⟩↑IV↓   20 ⟨to⟩ that   27 Epicurean *w.o.* epicurean
33 Aldriches *w.o.* Aldrich's   39 across *w.o.* ag   40 budded⟨⟩⟩
49–53 Yours . . . . pains.] [*across letterhead, salutation, and dateline, first page*]

6 June 1873, Boston, to Francis Parkman. 3 pp. A.l.s. CLSU.

5 ↑you↓ with   19 ⟨which⟩ for   20 you↑r↓   20 rose-trees *w.o.* rose⟨es⟩
22–23 Yours . . . Howells.] [*across text, second page*]

8 June 1873, Boston, to Anne T. Howells. 4 pp. A.l.s. MH.

10 suppose the *w.o.* suppose he's   11 ↑editor has↓
19 Boyesen's *w.o. illeg.*   28 old *w.o.* or   43 five *w.o.* four
45–46 Your . . . Will.] [*across salutation, first page*]
47–49 Elinor . . . . cap.] [*across text, first page*]

11 June 1873, Boston, to Charles D. Warner. 4 pp. A.l.s. CSmH.

20 ⟨week.⟩ year.

20 July 1873, Cambridge, to William C. Howells. 8 pp. A.l.s. MH.

17 the *w.o.* one   23 Joe *w.o.* Jose   31 has *w.o.* was
38 *Arcadia*] [*the* r *is twice underlined beneath the single underlining of the entire word*]   40 back *w.o. illeg.*

20 July 1873, Cambridge, to James M. Comly. 8 pp. A.l.s. OHi.

18 August 1873, Boston, to William C. Bryant. 3 pp. A.l.s. George Arms, Albuquerque, N. M.

[*Written above letterhead, in Bryant's hand*: Answ'd; *and on fourth page, also in Bryant's hand*: W. D. Howells / Aug. 8. 1873.]

26 August 1873, Boston, to Henry James. 4 pp. A.l.s. MH.

8 the *w.o.* in   8 has *w.o.* had   15 whooping-cough⟨.⟩   18 ⟨t⟩his
21 ceiling *w.o.* celling   23 amused *w.o. illeg.*   23 letters ⟨ag⟩
28 Venetian⟨s⟩   36 left *w.o. illeg.*
40–43 Mrs. Howells . . . . Howells.] [*across letterhead, salutation, and text, first page*]

18 October 1873, Boston, to Thomas W. Higginson. 4 pp. A.l.s. NN.

5 ⟨*illeg.*⟩ author   18 ↑among↓   22 *ci*⟨a⟩
[*at top of fourth page, in Higginson's hand*: W D Howells / His poems &c]

21 October 1873, Boston, to Anne T. Howells. Location of MS. unknown. Typed copy at MH.

5 December 1873, Boston, to Henry James. 4 pp. A.l.s. MH.

6 these *w.o.* this   12 cypress *w.o.* sypress   28 at it *w.o.* it it
29 at it *w.o.* it it   30 of the *w.o.* of T   30 ⟨February no.⟩ January
42 ⟨in⟩ were   57 ⟨once.⟩ twice   63 amongst ⟨t⟩
66–71 sister . . . brother.] [*across letterhead, salutation, and dateline, first page*]

11 December 1873, Boston, to Thomas B. Aldrich. 1 p. A.l.s. MH.

1 *Monthly*,] [*Howells cancelled the next line of the printed letterhead*: No. 124, Tremont Street,—*the editorial offices had just been moved to Cambridge*]   2 Dec. *w.o.* Nov.   6 pierced⟨,⟩

12 December 1873, Cambridge, to James M. Comly. 3 pp. A.l.s. OHi.

15 ⟨of⟩ chapters   33 Please . . . Jefferson.] [*across letterhead, first page*]

17 December 1873, Cambridge, to Whitelaw Reid. 1 p. A.l.s. DLC.

11 naming *w.o.* namig
18–21 Dear . . . . WR] [*in Reid's hand, opposite first page*]
22–23 Did . . . . H.] [*in Hay's hand, immediately below Reid's note*]

27 December 1873, Cambridge, to Edmund C. Stedman. 3 pp. A.l.s. NNC.
12 ↑not↓
[*holograph shows other words and phrases in various hands; above letterhead, first page*: W. D. Howells *below dateline, first page*: Book *on verso of second page*: ⟨My dear / My dear Mother: / Pray let me know / whether you⟩]

28 December 1873, Cambridge, to Charles D. Warner. 1 p. A.l.s. CtHT.

11 on *w.o.* in

28 December 1873, Cambridge, to Bayard Taylor. 4 pp. A.l.s. NIC.

11 ↑rejected↓   16 I. ⟨do.⟩   19 mere ⟨natest⟩   30 ⟨*illeg.*⟩ in

9 January 1874, Cambridge, to Melanchthon M. Hurd. Location of MS. unknown. *Life in Letters*, I, 183–84.

18 January 1874, Cambridge, to Victoria M. Howells. 4 pp. A.l.s. MH.

18 ⟨up⟩ about   25 ↑say↓   29 I think *w.o.* I *illeg.*

22 January 1874, Cambridge, to Ralph Waldo Emerson. 3 pp. A.l.s. MH.

5 poem *w.o.* some   17 ⟨pub⟩ poem
[*on verso of second page, in another hand*: W D Howells / Jan '74]

24 January 1874, Cambridge, to Hjalmar H. Boyesen. 4 pp. A.l.s. ViU.

10 Hulder, according *w.o.* Hulder, an   12 care⟨f⟩
19–21 Mrs. . . . Howells.] [*across dateline, salutation, and text, first page*]

6 February 1874, Cambridge, to Benjamin W. Lacy. 3 pp. A.l.s. MH.

19 conclusive *w.o* conclusion

17 February 1874, Cambridge, to Charles D. Warner. 2 pp. A.l.s. CtHT.

   7 5th *w.o.* 4th   8 in *w.o.* on   14 ↑will↓

17 March 1874, Cambridge, to Charles D. Warner. 4 pp. A.l.s. CtHT.

   11 ⟨could⟩ ↑can↓   13 Republic *w.o.* republic
20 *Prosperous w.o. Prosperet*   22 Commerce *w.o.* commerce
24 Decline *w.o.* decline   24 Up *w.o.* up   28 substance *w.o.* subj

21 March 1874, Cambridge, to James M. Comly. 4 pp. A.l.s. OHi.

   13 more than the] more the   13 they *w.o.* They   16 of *w.o.* a
18–22 desire . . . . W. D. H.] [*across dateline, salutation, and text, first page*]

24 March 1874, Cambridge, to Hjalmar H. Boyesen. 3 pp. A.l.s. ViU.

   13 ⟨stot⟩ ↑sort↓   21 at me every day] at me every me ⟨at⟩ every day

27 March 1874, Cambridge, to James Maurice Thompson. 4 pp. A.l.s. OFH.

   6 splendid *w.o.* splendor   10 four *w.o.* five   11 ↑to contributors↓
12 work *w.o.* word   18 cover *w.o.* covered   27 ⟨—⟩ He
28 ↑hit *w.o.* hid↓

22 April 1874, Cambridge, to Edwin D. Mead. 2 pp. A.l.s. CLSU.

   [*Above dateline, in another hand*: Howells.]

25 May 1874, Cambridge, to James R. Lowell. 4 pp. A.l.s. MH.

   6 ↑which we have↓   13 you've *w.o.* your   15 your⟨'e⟩
18 ⟨*illeg.*⟩ wish   31 love⟨s you⟩   36 where *w.o.* way
[*in margin, fourth page, in another hand*: 25 May, 1874]

10 June 1874, Jaffrey, New Hampshire, to Hjalmar H. Boyesen. 3 pp. A.l.s. ViU.

   21 ↑their↓ harps

9 July 1874, Jaffrey, New Hampshire, to William C. Howells, 4 pp. A.l.s. MH.

   7 good.] [*Howells wrote* good! *and then cancelled the upper part of exclamation point*]   13 reside with you] reside you   17 ↑period of↓
19 one of] of ↑one↓   20 him *w.o. illeg.*   22 Aurelia *w.o.* Aurelie

11 July 1874, Cambridge, to Samuel L. Clemens. 3 pp. A.l.s. CU.

7 ↑thus↓   8 ⟨to⟩ ↑with↓   13 ⟨him⟩ me

14 August 1874, Cambridge, to Henry W. Longfellow. 3 pp. A.l.s. MH.

15 ↑been↓   21 again *w.o.* at

16 August 1874, Jaffrey, New Hampshire, to Aurelia H. Howells. 4 pp. A.l.s. MH.

3 ↑fort↓night   5 to *w.o. illeg.*   7 ⟨fr⟩ French   15 ↑of French↓
26 ⟨month⟩ week   30 Cambridg|e| 35 ⟨*illeg.*⟩ will

25 August 1874, Jaffrey, New Hampshire, to Francis J. Garrison. 3 pp. A.l.s. NjP.

1 September 1874, Cambridge, to Bret Harte. 2 pp. A.l.s. TxU.

4 ↑of↓   6–7 ↑for examination↓   11 ⟨I⟩ if   12 matter *w.o.* ,

8 September 1874, Cambridge, to Samuel L. Clemens. 4 pp. A.l.s. CU.

[In upper right corner, first page: 74]
6 ↑think↓   14 ↑and touching↓   24–25 ↑even for you↓   29 ⟨for⟩ to

24 September 1874, Cambridge, to John B. O'Reilly. 4 pp. A.l.s. ViU.

5 reply *w.o.* to   10 expl⟨ic⟩icitly
18 (*I Promessi Sposi.*)] [*Howells first wrote*: ("Promessi Sposi."), *then
wrote "I over the opening quotation marks, cancelled the closing quotation marks, and underlined* Promessi Sposi]   24 ↑making↓

3 October 1874, Cambridge, to Melanchthon M. Hurd. 2 pp. A.l.s. MdBJ.

6 ↑to↓ connect   7 apostrophe⟨s⟩

18 October 1874, Cambridge, to William C. Howells. 4 pp. A.l.s. MH.

7 was *w.o.* is   8 week *w.o.* weak

24 October 1874, Newport, Rhode Island, to Anne T. Howells. 12 pp. A.l.s. MH.

6 ↑was↓   13 feeble *w.o. illeg.*   16 it⟨s⟩
27 opportunity *w.o.* opportunly   31 could *w.o.* would   34 ↑here,↓
41 ⟨cast⟩ catastrophe   42 if ⟨If⟩   43 with ⟨the⟩
46 married; *w.o.* married.   47 she] She   51 Ms. *w.o.* Mss.   52 ↑my↓

14 November 1874, Cambridge, to John Augustin Daly. 3 pp. A.l.s. DFo.

  8 ↑certainly,↓   15 these *w.o.* this
[*on verso of second page, in another hand*: W. D. Howells / Nov 1874]

23 November 1874, Cambridge, to Samuel L. Clemens. 3 pp. A.l.s. CU.

  [*Above letterhead, first page, probably in Howells' hand*: 1st Miss]
  12 A *w.o.* a   14 read⟨s⟩ it,⟨–⟩   15 think *w.o.* thing
26 world. *w.o.* world,

29 November 1874, Cambridge, to William C. Howells. 4 pp. A.l.s. MH.

  7 ⟨types⟩ takes   10 build *w.o.* built

30 November 1874, Cambridge, to Hjalmar H. Boyesen. 2 pp. A.l.s. ViU.

  2 30 *w.o.* 20   10 a *w.o.* *illeg.*
23 The . . . Annie's.] [*in margin, second page*]

5 December 1874, Cambridge, to James M. Comly. 3 pp. A.l.s. OHi.

  20–21 undischarged *w.o.* undiccharged   21 in *w.o.* im

8 December 1874, Cambridge, to Edmund C. Stedman. 4 pp. A.l.s. NNC.

  13 ↑or . . . me↓   16 ⟨publishers *w.o.* publication⟩ publishers
19 care *w.o.* g   23 all *w.o.* of   31 past,] ~„   36 Yurs *w.o.* Yours

15 December 1874, Cambridge, to Wendell P. Garrison. 3 pp. A.l.s. NjP.

  14 victimization *w.o.* victimigation   21 the way *w.o.* thus way
26 ↑my↓   27 motives *w.o.* motion

18 December 1874, Cambridge, to the Editor of the *Evening Transcript*.
1 p. Author's draft signed. CSmH.

  1 The *w.o.* the   3 ⟨that⟩ you   5 color *w.o.* l
6 and ⟨in mentioning Mr. Fields,⟩   7 ↑some of↓
8 Fields. ⟨If that gentleman needed any defence, I should be quite
ready to offer it, for I⟩   8 added ⟨, perhaps,⟩ that ⟨he⟩   9 ⟨I thought⟩ he

19 December 1874, Cambridge, to Belton O. Townsend. 3 pp. A.l.s.
E. N. Zeigler, Florence, S. C.

20 December 1874, Cambridge, to William C. Howells. 4 pp. A.l.s. MH.

  14 you've been having] you've having

28 December 1874, Cambridge, to Charles E. Norton. 3 pp. A.l.s. CSmH.

　11 lifelike *w.o.* lifelife　　22 ⟨I⟩ a wife

8 January 1875, Cambridge, to Thomas B. Aldrich. 2 pp. A.l.s. MH.

　12 give *w.o.* gave

9 January 1875, Cambridge, to William C. Howells. 3 pp. A.l.s. MH.

　12 the austerity of several] ↑the austerity↓ several　　16 talking] talk
24 play *w.o.* Q　　25 ⟨—I⟩ in　　26 cast⟨e⟩　　34 write *w.o. illeg.*

31 January 1875, Cambridge, to William C. Howells. 4 pp. A.l.s. MH.

　10 provided *w.o.* proba　　21 keep *w.o. illeg.*
28 ⟨*illeg.*⟩ creature's head ↑on↓)　　29 every ⟨morning,⟩　　36 ⟨weeks⟩ days

10 February 1875, Cambridge, to Thomas B. Aldrich. 2 pp. A.l.s. MH.

　4 from *w.o.* for　　5 Pine *w.o.* pine　　9 thing *w.o.* think
13 the "Rococo" *w.o.* their "Rococo"　　14 heart⟨?⟩
14 ↑and . . . stuck-up.↓　　17 that ⟨da⟩
19 I've not] I've have↑n't↓ [*the inserted* n't *is in another hand*]

28 February 1875, Cambridge, to Samuel L. Clemens. 2 pp. A.l.s. CU.

　8 give *w.o.* ca　　14 ⟨*illeg.*⟩ missed

7 March 1875, Cambridge, to William C. Howells. 4 pp. A.l.s. MH.

　19 by *w.o.* in

6 April 1875, Bethlehem, Pennsylvania, to Henry W. Longfellow. 2 pp.
A.l.s. MH.

　11 ↑in↓

25 April 1875, Cambridge, to Aurelia H. Howells. 4 pp. A.l.s. MH.

　7 disrepair *w.o.* dicrepair　　19 ⟨with⟩ ↑were↓
21 it to Arlington] it Arlington　　25 suppose *w.o.* supper

2 May 1875, Cambridge, to William C. Howells. 4 pp. A.l.s. MH.

　2 May *w.o.* A　　7 children *w.o.* chill　　11 had *w.o.* have
17 was *w.o.* is　　23 than *w.o.* that　　25 Howells *w.o.* of

28 May 1875, Cambridge, to George H. Warner. 3 pp. A.l.s. Mark Twain Memorial, Hartford, Conn.

7 see⟨m⟩   8 any *w.o.* and   11 ↑others↓   15 regards *w.o.* regre

4 June 1875, Cambridge, to Charles D. Warner. 4 pp. A.l.s. CtHT.

24 Centennial *w.o.* O   33 scared *w.o. illeg.*
36–39 Just . . . . Howells.] [*across letterhead, dateline, and text, first page*]

27 June 1875, Cambridge, to William C. Howells. 4 pp. A.l.s. MH.

6 ⟨last⟩ Friday   11–12 ↑(it's . . . frightful)↓   14 bell⟨-⟩ring
14 two *w.o.* too   22 possibility *w.o.* prospect   22 worse ⟨the⟩
25 You⟨r⟩   26 ↑named↓   31 ↑but↓   36 I *w.o.* we

18 July 1875, Cambridge, to Annie A. Fields. 3 pp. A.l.s. George Arms, Albuquerque, N. M.

11 tenant of] tentant⟩ of   13 down *w.o.* t

29 July 1875, Cambridge, to Whitelaw Reid. 4 pp. A.l.s. DLC.

6 assure⟨s⟩   6 knowledge *w.o.* n   6 ↑that↓   9 ↑absurd↓
14 ⟨wish⟩ ↑desire↓   16 ↑not↓   16 ⟨f⟩ neglected   16 The *w.o.* the
17 its] its'   28 ↑again or not↓   31–32 ↑me as↓

2 August 1875, Shirley Village, Massachusetts, to Francis J. Garrison. 3 pp. A.l.s. NjP.

4 ↑you↓   12 ⟨I⟩ here   18 an⟨o⟩   23 C.↑hristopher↓

4 September 1875, Shirley Village, Massachusetts, to Charles D. Warner. 4 pp. A.l.s. CtHT.

1 Sept. *w.o.* O   5 I ⟨I⟩ suppose   11 paper for] ∼.∼   18 ↑real↓
23 got *w.o.* good   23 ⟨paper⟩ ↑chapter↓   26 you've *w.o.* your
32 little *w.o. illeg.*
36 *Orienting* is delightful!] [*across salutation and letterhead, first page*]

17 September 1875, Chesterfield, New Hampshire, to David A. Wells. 2 pp. A.l.s. DLC.

2 Chesterfield *w.o.* c
13 him.] [*Howells cancelled the upper part of a question mark, leaving the period*]

6 October 1875, Quebec, to James A. Garfield. 2 pp. A.l.s. DLC.

1 Qu|ebec, Oc|t.   2 |Dea|r   10 |You could intro| 11 |because|
14 ⟨My⟩ The   16 of *w.o.* at
[*on verso of second page, in another hand*: W. D. Howells]

24 October 1875, Cambridge, to Charles D. Warner. 4 pp. A.l. CtHT.

1 |*Atlantic*| 2 |*Cambridge,*| 3 |My|
13 always went *w.o. illeg.* went   13–14 -class *w.o. illeg.*   18 your *w.o.* h
21 Tri|bune. He| 22 . . .] [*one or more words excised*]
26 Bret *w.o.* Brat   31 ⟨cold⟩ ↑still↓
33 [*complimentary close and signature excised*]
34 Write!] [*above dateline, first page*]

8 November 1875, Cambridge, to William Wetmore Story. 1 p. A.l.s. IEN.

11 think⟨s⟩

14 November 1875, Cambridge, to Hjalmar H. Boyesen. 2 pp. A.l.s. ViU.

2 Nov. *w.o.* F   10 strive *w.o. illeg.*   11 ⟨think⟩ ↑believe↓

21 November 1875, Cambridge, to Samuel L. Clemens. 2 pp. A.l.s. CU.

22 November 1875, Cambridge, to James T. Fields. 2 pp. A.l.s. CSmH.

6 consider it *w.o.* consider a
6 consider it successful] consider it a successful
10 blame *w.o. illeg.* ↑you↓   11 ⟨to the paper⟩ to have
12 will send *w.o.* wish send

27 November 1875, Cambridge, to William C. Howells. Location of MS.
unknown. *Life in Letters*, I, 213–14.

11 perhaps] perhraps

18 December 1875, Cambridge, to John Hay. Location of MS. unknown.
Life in Letters, I, 214–15.

19 December 1875, Cambridge, to James R. Lowell. 2 pp. A.l.s. MH.

6 done, and *w.o.* none, and   8 ↑committed↓   10 ↑did↓
13 word *w.o.* world   14 this *w.o.* these   18 before *w.o.* first

21 December 1875, Cambridge, to James R. Lowell. 1 p. A.l.s. MH.

6 I *w.o.* j

26 December 1875, Cambridge, to William C. Howells. 4 pp. T.l.s./A.l.s. MH.

1–9 Cambridge. . . . blunder.] [*Howells' typescript; all in capital letters*] 7 almost any] almostany 9 correct ⟨h⟩
9 —It] [*begin Howells' autograph*] 13 Christmas *w.o.* christmas
16 grand *w.o. illeg.* 16 tableau⟨x⟩ ↑in . . . parlor.↓ 16 all ⟨all⟩

5 January 1876, Cambridge, to Charles D. Warner. 4 pp. A.l.s. CtHT.

12 no⟨w⟩ 14 steadily *w.o. illeg.* 15 seem ⟨best⟩
18 ⟨fellow⟩ ↑feeling↓ 25 you've *w.o.* your 34 read] ready
35 ⟨wanted⟩ was 46 Republican.] ~ 47 both *w.o.* her 47 ↑of you↓

23 January 1876, Cambridge, to William C. Howells. 7 pp. T.l. MH.

[*Typed entirely in capital letters, many of which Howells had to retrace by hand because of the inadequate performance of his typewriter. These retracings as well as inserted spaces (#) and punctuation marks in ink are not listed below. Undeleted typed word fragments at the ends of lines are also not recorded*]

4 ↑as↓ 5 consider] consid-/ 6 read it ⟨read⟩ ↑yet↓
7 ⟨*illeg.*⟩ before 7 & ↑I↓ 8 ↑you↓ 9 sor↑r↓y 10 ⟨*illeg.*⟩ your
12 intelligence *w.o.* intellihence 12 as↑h↓amed 16 fellow⟨'⟩s
19 t↑a↓kes 24 pat↑i↓ent 25 disad-/ *w.o.* disada 30 ⟨ar'd⟩ abroad
32 w'd⟨w⟩ 32 chil-/ *w.o.* child 33 va↑s↓t 38 ⟨t⟩the end
40 mercury *w.o.* mercuria 40 s↑t↓ood 40 an⟨a⟩ 43 leaves] lwaves
43 ⟨su⟩ suppose 46 for⟨t⟩ 46 ⟨a *w.o.* d⟩ advise 47 her] hr
47 without ⟨r⟩ 48 a *w.o. illeg.* 48 maga-/ *w.o.* magazi
52 of you] of of you

13 February 1876, Cambridge, to William C. Howells. 4 pp. A.l.s. MH.

10 up ⟨, and⟩ 21 for *w.o.* but

22 February 1876, Cambridge, to Charles D. Warner. 4 pp. Al.s. CtHT.

13 ↑can↓

3 March 1876, Cambridge, to Thomas B. Aldrich. 2 pp. A.l.s. MH.

19 March 1876, Cambridge, to William C. Howells. 4 pp. A.l.s. MH.

11 ⟨and⟩ he came 15 ⟨th⟩ we 18 ⟨betray⟩ between
20 ↑this morning↓ 22 sister *w.o. illeg.*

2 April 1876, Cambridge, to Thomas B. Aldrich. 2 pp. A.l.s. MH.

5 first *w.o.* one　　10 so.] [*upper part of question mark cancelled to produce a period*]

9 April 1876, Cambridge, to William C. Howells. 4 pp. A.l.s. MH.

2 April *w.o.* March　　30 ago *w.o. illeg.*　　34 Auerbach *w.o.* auerbach
36–39 Your . . . . family.] [*across letterhead, first page*]

24 April 1876, Cambridge, to John Augustin Daly. 3 pp. A.l.s. DFo.

9 so ⟨there⟩　　9 the *w.o.* s　　9–10 ⟨⟨⟩for the reader's intelligence,⟨⟩⟩
12 ↑car↓　　20 help] [*a cancelled caret follows this word*]
20 ↑for your purpose↓
[*on verso of second page, in another hand*: W. D. Howells / Apl. 1876]

13 May 1876, Cambridge, to Oliver W. Holmes. 2 pp. A.l.s. DLC.

5 ↑you↓ give

15 May 1876, Cambridge, to William C. Howells. 4 pp. A.l.s. MH.

8 June 1876, Cambridge, to John Augustin Daly. 2 pp. A.l.s. DFo.
9 ↑that↓
[*on verso of second page, in another hand*: M. Howells / June 1876]

10 June 1876, Cambridge, to Sarah Orne Jewett. 4 pp. A.l.s. NNC.

7 ↑then↓　　8 ↑in↓ it　　12 ↑being↓
12–13 is drawn distinctly] is drawn is distinctly　　20 all *w.o.* our

18 June 1876, Shirley Village, Massachusetts, to William C. Howells.
4 pp. A.l.s. MH.

7 ⟨"⟩woman"　　8 ⟨of⟩ our　　9 atmosphere *w.o. illeg.*

20 July 1876, Cambridge, to Rutherford B. Hayes. 4 pp. A.l.s. OFH.

8 ⟨"⟩biography　　10 ↑some↓　　11 ↑you↓ kindly　　15 ↑use↓
21 bespatter ⟨from⟩　　22 will *w.o.* is　　23 ↑in the magazine↓
24 he's *w.o.* he'll

30 July 1876, Townsend Harbor, Massachusetts, to William C. Howells.
4 pp. A.l.s. MH.

1 30 *w.o.* 20　　23 ↑want to↓　　24 material *w.o. illeg.*
29 Will.] [*across printed letterhead, first page*]

8 August 1876, Townsend Harbor, Massachusetts, to James R. Lowell. 4 pp. A.l.s. MH.

8 ↑be↓   12 ↑them to↓   22 pleasure *w.o. illeg.*
27 Howells.] [*across printed letterhead, first page*]

20 August 1876, Townsend Harbor, Massachusetts, to Edmund C. Stedman. 3 pp. A.l.s. George Arms, Albuquerque, N. M.

4 heart⟨y⟩   7 ⟨k⟩now   11 I'm *w.o.* I've
[*above dateline, first page, in another hand*: "Sister Beatrice"; *on verso of second page, in Stedman's hand*: W. D. Howells / Aug. '76]

23 August 1876, Townsend Harbor, Massachusetts, to Webb C. Hayes. 3 pp. A.l.s. OFH.

3 pack|age| 3 ↑of | letters|↓   4 purpos|e| 5 than⟨t⟩
5 tell what⟨e⟩   6 thei|r| absurd |in| 9 |be| 9 ↑him↓
10 follies *w.o.* followed   11 ↑his↓   11 afte|r| 12 ⟨would⟩ wounded
[*on verso of second page, in another hand*: Howells. W D. /Townsend Harbor. / Aug 23. 76.]

Late August or early September 1876, Cambridge[?], to Francis J. Garrison. 2 pp. A.l.s. NjP.

6 ↑Mass.,↓

7 September 1876, Cambridge, to Rutherford B. Hayes. 4 pp. A.l.s. OFH.

[*At top of first page, in another hand*: W. D. Howells]

17 September 1876, Townsend Harbor, Massachusetts, to Bayard Taylor. 3 pp. A.l.s. NIC.

6 ⟨As⟩ Its   8 miles *w.o.* minute

19 September 1876, Cambridge, to Hjalmar H. Boyesen. 4 pp. A.l.s. ViU.

9 ↑not↓   10 supported *w.o. illeg.*   20 me was *w.o.* me wh
22 ↑as it is,↓   24 gone *w.o. illeg.*   25 ↑spun-out↓
28–31 busy .... Howells.] [*across letterhead, salutation, and dateline, first page*]

24 September 1876, Townsend Harbor, Massachusetts, to Charles E. Norton. 4 pp. A.l.s. MH.

11 ⟨too⟩ ↑so↓   19 ⟨the⟩ ↑such a↓   22 ↑we↓ all   22 ⟨o⟩for
22 Cambridge *w.o.* cambridge   25 ⟨both⟩ ↑book↓

27–30 told . . . . Howells.] [*across printed letterhead and dateline, first page*]

11 October 1876, Cambridge, to Thomas B. Aldrich. 2 pp. A.l.s. MH.

12 November 1876, Cambridge, to William C. Howells. 4 pp. A.l.s. MH.
    2 ⟨Oct.⟩ Nov.   15 effect *w.o.* affect   20 ↑to↓   22 ↑would↓
25–26 son Will.] [*across letterhead, first page*]

30 November 1876, Cambridge, to Samuel L. Clemens. 4 pp. A.l.s. CU.
    8–9 you of them.] ∼.∼∼.   11 ↑our↓   15 doubt *w.o. illeg.*
19–20 when you are gone] when are gone

4 December 1876, Cambridge, to James R. Lowell. 2 pp. A.l.s. MH.
    10 thing⟨s⟩

18 December 1876, Cambridge, to Charles D. Warner. 3 pp. A.l.s. CtHT.
    13 kind ⟨not⟩

31 December 1876, Cambridge, to William C. Howells. 4 pp. A.l.s. MH.
    9 it *might w.o. illeg.*   18 of Winny's *w.o. illeg.*   20 ↑since . . . you↓
31 ↑the↓ Williston   32 really *w.o.* rially   33 ↑first↓
35–36 affectionate son Will.] [*across letterhead, first page*]

9 January 1877, Cambridge, to Oliver W. Holmes. 3 pp. A.l.s. DLC.
    10 ↑you↓

18 February 1877, Cambridge, to Anne T. Howells. 4 pp. A.l.s. MH.
    19 You⟨r⟩   20 A Foregone *w.o.* a Foregone
27–29 All . . . . Will.] [*across letterhead, salutation, and dateline, first page*]

22 February 1877, Cambridge, to John Hay. Location of MS. unknown.
Life in Letters, I, 230–31.

18 March 1877, Cambridge, to James R. Osgood. 3 pp. A.l.s. MH.
    13 ⟨the⟩ connection   15 ⟨ur⟩beg   17 ↑my↓ name

25 March 1877, Cambridge, to Marianne W. Batchelder. 4 pp. A.l.s.
George Arms, Albuquerque, N. M.

   5 ⟨ough⟩ out   6 Sacramento *w.o.* sacramento   18 loss *w.o. illeg.*
18 ⟨yet⟩ we   22 ↑been↓
[*next to signature, in another hand*: W. D. Howells / M'ch 1877.]

1 April 1877, Cambridge, to Charles D. Warner. 8 pp. A.l.s. CtHT.

   21 want] wont   22 ⟨⟨⟩Not   22 compel *w.o.* compl   27 ↑to read↓
28 ⟨fortune⟩ fate   39 was *w.o. illeg.*
[*several notations, in another hand, appear in margins; fourth page*:
Apr 77 *eighth page*: '77 *and* W. D. Howells / Apr 77]

7 April 1877, Cambridge, to William K. Rogers. 3 pp. A.l.s. OFH.

[*On verso of second page, in another hand, the following endorsement*:
Howell, W. D. / Cambridge, Mass. / Apl. 7/77. / Rel. to promotion /
of his father in the / Diplomatic Service. / Ansd. / Apl 10/77.]

   4 ⟨rela⟩ regard   8 Queb|ec,| 9 ↑when . . . vacancy↓   13 ↑ask you to↓

8 April 1877, Cambridge, to William C. Howells. 6 pp. A.l.s. MH.

   4 arrival *w.o.* arrived   8 ⟨b⟩ missed   11 her *w.o.* him
12 ↑and silk↓ [*in Elinor Howells' hand*]   23 ⟨sell⟩ silver
23 ↑and silk↓ [*in Elinor Howells' hand*]   28 for *w.o. illeg.*
28 ⟨but⟩ and   29 ⟨at⟩ ↑to↓

9 April 1877, Cambridge, to Rutherford B. Hayes. 4 pp. A.l.s. OFH.

[*Above dateline, first page, in another hand*: President]
   19 cordially *w.o.* cordialy
20–22 united . . . Howells.] [*across dateline and salutation, first page*]

22 April 1877, Cambridge, to William C. Howells. 4 pp. A.l.s. MH.

   2 ⟨Cambr⟩ April   11 ⟨th⟩ a   18 Did *w.o.* Do   19 ⟨drg⟩ dragged

25 April 1877, Cambridge, to Francis J. Garrison. 1 p. A.n.s. NjP.

28 May 1877, Cambridge, to Rutherford B. Hayes. 3 pp. A.l.s. OFH.

   7 you, ⟨to say⟩ that   7 assure ↑you↓   7 ↑have↓ written
10 only *w.o.* no   12 happy *w.o.* happiness
[*on verso of second page, in another hand, the following endorsement*:
Cambridge Mass. / May 28. 1877. / Howells W. D. / Never should

have written / could he have anticipated / that Mr Lowell would / have declined Austrian / Mission—He had / every reason to believe / that Mr L would / accept. / If the President & Mrs / Hayes go to Boston / on 17 June—tenders / the hospitalities of his house]

5 June 1877, Cambridge, to Moncure D. Conway. 4 pp. A.l.s. NNC.

  6 ⟨k⟩now   10 ⟨that⟩ you   25 ⟨ab⟩ be

19 June 1877, Montreal, to Elinor M. Howells. 4 pp. A.l.s. MH.

  13 Is↑n't↓   15 they've *w.o.* there   17 summer⟨'s⟩   17 days *w.o. illeg.*
19 Dear *w.o. illeg.*   21 the *w.o. illeg.*
25 I'll . . . Herald.] [*across dateline and salutation, first page*]

2 July 1877, Cambridge, to William C. Howells. 4 pp. A.l.s. MH.

  2 2 *w.o.* 1   10 party *w.o. illeg.*   12 were] were / were   22 hear⟨t⟩

2 July 1877, Cambridge, to Thomas W. Higginson. 3 pp. A.l.s. NN.

  10 the *w.o.* it ↑book↓   10 Roland⟨e⟩   10 Burroughs⟨*illeg.*⟩
13 field ⟨alone⟩   15 auto.)⟨,⟩   16 the *w.o.* it ↑essay↓
17 ⟨all⟩ collateral   17 time and] ∼. ∼   21 ↑shall↓

4 August 1877, Cambridge, to William C. Howells. 4 pp. A.l.s. MH.

  9 ↑come↓   18 ⟨reb⟩ rigged

28 August 1877, Cambridge, to Belton O. Townsend. 3 pp. A.l.s. E. N. Zeigler, Florence, S. C.

  4 m|e| 9 d|estiny| 9 |it is| 10 sur|e; in| 10 that *w.o. illeg.*
14 |press?| 15 way |o|f   15 ↑short↓   17 forsaking *w.o. illeg.*

2 September 1877, Cambridge, to John Hay. Location of MS. unknown. *Life in Letters*, I, 239–40.

2 September 1877, Cambridge, to William C. Howells. 4 pp. A.l.s. MH.

  4 ⟨t⟩ now   8 ⟨*illeg.*⟩ season   21 ⟨*him*⟩ his   25 and *w.o. illeg.*

11 September 1877, Cambridge, to William H. Bishop. Location of MS. unknown. *Life in Letters*, I, 240–41.

14 October 1877, Cambridge, to A. W. Whelpley. 2 pp. A.l.s. OCHP.

10 happened ⟨to me⟩   11 State⟨'⟩   11 Ohioan⟨'⟩

21 October 1877, Cambridge, to Charles D. Warner. 3 pp. A.l.s. CtHT.

2 21 *w.o.* 20   8 ↑more↓   14 ⟨week⟩ day

28 October 1877, Cambridge, to James R. Osgood. 2 pp. A.l.s. NjR.

4 ↑⟨what hour⟩↓   14 Alfieris *w.o.* Affieris

14 November 1877, Cambridge, to Lawrence Barrett. 8 pp. A.l.s. NjP.

5 is *w.o.* it   9 situ|a|tions   19 while *w.o.* which
20 ↑drawn . . . comedy↓   21 element.] ~   23 Hay *w.o.* she
32 ↑way↓   34 ↑of↓   36 The⟨y⟩   39 infer⟨r⟩   42 should↑n't↓
42 with⟨out⟩   53 This . . . scene.] [*in margin, seventh page*]
55 ↑sufficiently↓
[*on verso of eighth page, in another hand*: Howells. / 77.]

24 November 1877, Cambridge, to William C. Howells. 4 pp. A.l.s. MH.

9 when she] when she / she   13 feel *w.o. illeg.*   23 year⟨s⟩
29 ⟨Do⟩ I suppose   30 ⟨written to⟩ asked   38 feel *w.o.* felt

27 November 1877, Boston, to James R. Osgood. 2 pp. A.l.s. MH.

14 ↑you↓   14 ⟨exp⟩ exasperating

2 December 1877, Cambridge, to Edmund C. Stedman. 1 p. A.l.s. NNC.

5 gracefullest *w.o.* gracefully   8 attaint ⟨ready to attain,⟩ ↑us↓

19 December 1877, Cambridge, to Charles E. Norton. 2 pp. A.l.s. MH.

9 before *w.o.* long

22 December 1877, Cambridge, to William C. Howells. 4 pp. A.l.s. MH.

4 ↑the way of↓   5 Burchard Hayes's] Burchard'⟨s⟩ Hayes⟨e⟩'s
5 held *w.o. illeg.*   8 write.] ~   9 World ⟨may⟩
17 giving] giving / giving   28 ↑first↓

25 December 1877, Cambridge, to Samuel L. Clemens. 3 pp. A.l.s. CU.

8 year⟨,⟩   9 fatality *w.o.* fr   14 my *w.o. illeg.*   17 ↑to↓ exaggerate
23 at *w.o.* on

6 January 1878, Cambridge, to Samuel L. Clemens. 2 pp. A.l.s. CU.

  2 1877] [1878 *is written over in another hand*]   16 ⟨hefp⟩ help

6 January 1878, Cambridge, to William C. Howells. 4 pp. A.l.s. MH.

  5 if I can] if can   9 to *w.o. illeg.*   28 L↑-↓i↑-↓g
32 before *w.o.* began   33 persons⟨,⟩

12 January 1878, Cambridge, to Charles D. Warner. 2 pp. A.l.s. CtHT.

19 January 1878, Cambridge, to William C. Howells. 4 pp. A.l.s. MH.

  2 19 *w.o.* 20   8 success⟨ful⟩↑ive↓   10 approach *w.o. illeg.*
19 Dr *w.o.* W   27 spend *w.o.* spent   27 ↑quarterly↓
35 up,] [*word written over comma after* him]   35 their *w.o.* they
37 agreeable *w.o.* agreed   41 Your] You'r⟨e⟩

30 January 1878, Cambridge, to James A. Garfield. 3 pp. A.l.s. DLC.

  4 ⟨p⟩ back   15 ↑you↓   16 ⟨*illeg.*⟩ administrational

25 February 1878, Cambridge, to William Bigelow. 2 pp. A.l.s. MA.

  10 be-/↑-wail↓   18 Hayese⟨'⟩s

14 March 1878, Cambridge, to Hjalmar H. Boyesen. 4 pp. A.l.s. ViU.

  8 ⟨I⟩ present   10 inspiration ⟨of⟩   15 ↑all↓ the   15 ↑once↓
24 mean⟨t⟩   24 treat *w.o.* try   33 ⟨onc⟩ wont   33 my-⟨out⟩/self

19 March 1878, Cambridge, to Lawrence Barrett. 3 pp. A.l.s. NjP.

  2 19 *w.o.* 29   13 she *w.o.* sho⟨uld,⟩   13 ⟨make it⟩ ↑find it taken in a↓
13 ⟨own⟩ owe   18 ⟨fir⟩ opening

31 March 1878, Cambridge, to William C. Howells. 3 pp. A.l.s. MH.

  6 ↑sorry to↓   7 find *w.o.* T   11 ↑be↓   15 only *w.o.* merely
20 ↑most↓

9 April 1878, New York, to Rutherford B. Hayes. 3 pp. A.l.s. MH.

  3 your *w.o. illeg.*   9 began *w.o. illeg.*   10 ↑(I saw this.)↓
12 ↑(in my presence)↓   13 from *w.o.* of   14 ⟨all⟩ ↑what↓
18 falling from the] falling / the   19 judge *w.o. illeg.*

14 April 1878, Boston, to William C. Howells. 4 pp. A.l.s. MH.

9–10 out to] out / out to   26 ↑like↓   28 burn *w.o. illeg.*

16 April 1878, Boston, to Charles E. Norton. 3 pp. A.l.s. MH.

7 ↑be↓   12 Quinze *w.o.* Seize   12 abide *w.o. illeg.*   18 a⟨s⟩
20 nearer *w.o. illeg.*

4 May 1878, Boston, to Thomas S. Collier. 3 pp. A.l.s. NjR.

7 ⟨*illeg.*⟩ now   19 Or⟨e⟩   26 ⟨tw⟩ a

2 June 1878, Boston, to Samuel L. Clemens. 4 pp. A.l.s. CU.

6 you⟨r⟩   7 welcome *w.o.* wellcome   8 ⟨truly⟩ still
17 to keep to] to keep to keep to   42 Clemens⟨'s⟩
48 another *w.o. illeg.*   48 ⟨with⟩ at   49 dullest ⟨I⟩
51–54 Affectionately . . . . enterprises.] [*across letterhead, salutation, and dateline, first page*]

2 June 1878, Boston, to William C. Howells. 4 pp. A.l.s. MH.

8 ↑of introduction↓   8 a *w.o.* an   19 you *w.o. illeg.*

16 June 1878, Boston, to William C. Howells. 4 pp. A.l.s. MH.

17 must *w.o. illeg.*   30 politicians *w.o.* pop   30 die *w.o.* dy

21 July 1878, Belmont, to William C. Howells. 4 pp. A.l.s. MH.

5 mo|ve| 11 wrote⟨*illeg.*⟩   14 |sy|stem   15 enti|re| 26 ↑the pony↓
[*in margin, first page, in Victoria Howells' hand*: Please return this to us, as father has / not answered it, V. M. H.]

23 August 1878, Boston, to William Wetmore Story. 3 pp. A.l.s. TxU.

6 Rabbi's *w.o. illeg.*   7–8 ↑its philosophic . . . well as↓
16 ↑(the latter)↓   19 ⟨*illeg.*⟩ never

4 September 1878, Boston, to Charles E. Norton. 2 pp. A.l.s. MH.

4 ⟨say⟩ ↑send↓   4 ↑the↓ proofs   8 ⟨Nationals,⟩ Nationals
19 Aff'te⟨'⟩ly

8 September 1878, Belmont, to William C. Howells. 4 pp. A.l.s. MH.

10 ↑his↓   11 soon *w.o.* now   17 pages *w.o. illeg.*

18 September 1878, Boston, to Horatio S. Noyes. Location of MS. unknown. Handwritten transcription by Mrs. Gertrude Noyes at InU.

23 September 1878, Boston, to William C. Howells. 4 pp. A.l.s. MH.

   18 ↑here↓   21 fever *w.o.* fie   23 the *w.o.* that   25 dollar.⟨s⟩
28 ⟨flattering⟩ highly

6 October 1878, Boston, to William C. Howells. 4 pp. A.l.s. MH.

   5 ↑—whom . . . much—↓   14–15 (I . . . company.)↓   29 ⟨o⟩for

29 October 1878, Boston, to John Hay. Location of MS. unknown. *Life in Letters*, I, 259–60.

30 October 1878, Boston, to Horace E. Scudder. 1 p. A.l.s. MH.
[*In upper left corner, in another hand*: Bryant vol II]
   4 will *w.o.* is   8 surface *w.o.* surfice   8 ↑the↓ new

11 November 1878, Boston, to Henry W. Longfellow. 2 pp. A.l.s. MH.

21 November 1878, Belmont, to Hjalmar H. Boyesen. 4 pp. A.l.s. ViU.

   11 ↑in English↓   11 I *w.o. illeg.*   17 Literatur⟨e⟩   41 ⟨and⟩ has

24 November 1878, Boston, to Edmund C. Stedman. 2 pp. A.l.s. NNC.

   5 know what to] know/ to   5 of *w.o. illeg.*   5 so *w.o.* it
5 ↑sad a thing.↓   10 ↑as . . . say,↓
[*on verso of second page, in another hand*: W. D. Howells. / Nov. 24/78]

4 December 1878, Boston, to Thomas B. Aldrich. 3 pp. A.l.s. MH.

   5 written *w.o.* in   6 ⟨note⟩ letter   9 ↑as↓   10 ↑with you↓
14 it's *w.o.* st   14 stories *w.o. illeg.*   15 Why ˙*w.o.* what
21 Yours *w.o.* yours

1 January 1879, Boston, to Arthur G. Sedgwick. 3 pp. A.l.s. ViU.

4 January 1879, Boston, to Rutherford B. Hayes. 3 pp. A.l.s. OFH.

   2 1879 *w.o.* 1878   7 dialect *w.o. illeg.*

19 February 1879, Boston, to Ellen Hutchinson. 2 pp. A.l.s. CtY.

   3 Miss *w.o.* Mrs.

19 February 1879, Boston, to Charles D. Warner. 3 pp. A.l.s. CtHT.

5 for that *w.o.* for it   17–18 "I . . . . it."] [*on verso of first page*]

7 March 1879, Boston, to Richard G. White. 2 pp. A.l.s. NHi.

11 there is] there there is   12 ↑that↓   16 ⟨of⟩ on

10 March 1879, Boston, to Horace E. Scudder. 2 pp. A.l.s. MH.

10 Scudder *w.o.* St   12 my *w.o.* me   15 As *w.o.* An
16 Reservoir *w.o.* reservoir   19–20 What . . . fallen.] [*in margin, first page*]

16 March 1879, Boston, to Rutherford B. Hayes. 2 pp. A.l.s. OFH.

7 had *w.o.* have
[*on verso of second page, in another hand*: Howells / 1879]

17 March 1879, Boston, to James P. Stabler. Location of MS. unknown. Clara M. and Rudolf Kirk, eds., *William Dean Howells*: *Representative Selections* (New York: Hill and Wang, 1950; reprinted 1961), p. cxxxv.

1–2 The . . . 1879.] [*the Kirks omit these lines, but introduce the text of the letter with this statement*: Howells replied on March 17, 1879, from the office of *The Atlantic Monthly*]
[*For Stabler's note on the verso of the letter, see p. 221, n. 2*]

31 March 1879, Boston, to Samuel A. Green. 2 pp. A.l.s. MHi.

4 ↑for↓   8 fact⟨s⟩

31 March 1879, Boston, to Annie A. Fields. 3 pp. A.l.s. CSmH.

7 Gloucester⟨s⟩   7 ↑sufferers,↓   11 And *w.o.* *illeg.*

12 April 1879, Boston, to William H. Bishop. Location of MS. unknown. *Life in Letters*, I, 267–68.

22 April 1879, Boston, to Lawrence Barrett. 3 pp. A.l.s. NjP.

5 into dialogue] into / into dialogue   9 ↑that↓   10 ↑in soliloquy↓
13 it⟨'⟩s   13 roughness *w.o.* *illeg.*   17 ⟨But⟩ If   18 royalties⟨⟩⟩
20 royalties] [*added in margin*]

23 April 1879, Boston, to George W. Curtis. 2 pp. A.l.s. MB.

7 Fortnightly *w.o.* Forth

2 May 1879, Boston, to John Hay. Location of MS. unknown. *Life in Letters*, I, 268–70.

4 May 1879, Boston, to William C. Howells. 3 pp. A.l.s. MH.

16 ⟨of⟩ absolutely   19 and *w.o. illeg.*   19 ⟨which⟩ on
23 ⟨Belmont⟩ leave

18 May 1879, Boston, to Samuel P. Langley. 4 pp. A.l.s. MH.

7 ⟨some bewilderment on⟩ your ⟨part⟩ ↑uncertainty↓   8 ⟨affair⟩ ↑care↓
8–9 story—as you . . . end.] story—a [*Howells inadvertently did not in-clude the word* a *in the long cancellation that follows*] ⟨bewilderment like that of an author who reads himself in a free translation.⟩ ↑as you will have seen if you have since had patience to hold↓. ⟨If you ↑have since↓ held⟩ out to the end↑.↓, ⟨your mystification *w.o.* mystified must have increased.⟩.   10–11 ↑—and . . . kind—↓
22 never knew anyone] never / anyone   27 month⟨'⟩s

18 May 1879, Boston, to Edmund C. Stedman. 2 pp. A.l.s. NNC.

4 ⟨very⟩ vacation   5 ↑in . . . introduction↓
[*on verso of second page, in another hand*: W. D. Howells / May 18/79]

20 June 1879, Boston, to Charles D. Warner. 2 pp. A.l.s. CtHT.

7 ⟨the⟩ it   14 ↑in mind↓   15 Adirondacks *w.o.* Aro
18 course] [*added in margin*]

22 June 1879, Boston, to James R. Lowell. 4 pp. A.l.s. MH.

4 ↑me↓   7 ⟨public⟩ ↑part↓   18 day⟨s⟩   26 ↑in Froude's Caesar,↓
31 distance *w.o. illeg.*   54 played *w.o. illeg.*   54 now *w.o.* not
55 a *w.o.* an   57 play⟨ed⟩   58 egotism.] [*upper part of exclamation point cancelled to make period*]   67 him *w.o. illeg.*   70 ⟨wide⟩ noisy
73–74 Yours . . . Howells.] [*across letterhead, salutation, and text, first page*]

29 June 1879, Belmont, to Annie A. Fields. 4 pp. A.l.s. CSmH.

9 on *w.o.* at   10 ⟨t⟩we belonged

20 July 1879, Boston, to William C. Howells. 4 pp. A.l.s. MH.

16 ↑later↓   20 mad⟨e⟩   24 foot *w.o.* firs

24 July 1879, Boston, to William Wetmore Story. 4 pp. A.l.s. TxU.

4 that ⟨that⟩   8 ↑too purely↓   9 ⟨of⟩ in   12 ↑the↓ paper
14 ⟨f⟩ most   18 have *w.o. illeg.*   20 exhibition *w.o.* E
29 from you only] from only

7 August 1879, Belmont, to Rutherford B. Hayes. 2 pp. A.l.s. OFH.

20 August 1879, Boston, to Achille Fréchette. 1 p. A.l.s. CSmH.

9 September 1879, Boston, to Samuel L. Clemens. 3 pp. A.l.s. CU.

2 September *w.o.* Aug.   2 9 *w.o.* 10   4 Sleepeth] [*word enclosed in
quotation marks, pencilled in by another hand*]   7–8 Have . . . papers?]
[*sentence enclosed in parentheses, pencilled in by another hand*]
12 ↑me↓

17 September 1879, Boston, to Thomas W. Higginson. 2 pp. A.l.s. NN.

6 of *w.o. illeg.*   17 It *w.o.* B
[*at top of second page, in Higginson's hand*: Howells—my crit.]

17 September 1879, Boston, to Samuel L. Clemens. 3 pp. A.l.s. CU.

3 (Belmont . . . P. O.)] [*in upper right corner, first page*]
5 a journey] a/ a journey   16 you⟨r⟩   17 ⟨you⟩ usual

16 November 1879, Boston, to William C. Howells. 3 pp. A.l.s. MH.

7 to↑-↓day   27–28 want ↑you↓   41 ⟨all⟩ always

26 December 1879, Boston, to Rutherford B. Hayes. 1 p. A.l.s. OFH.

31 December 1879, Boston, to Charles D. Warner. 2 pp. A.l.s. CtHT.

2 *1879 w.o. 1887*   7 of *w.o.* as   7 ⟨ask⟩ essay

8 January 1880, Boston, to Erastus Brainerd. 3 pp. A.l.s. NjP.

9 adaptation⟨s⟩   10 |and| I   10 upon *w.o.* on   10 concep|tion|
11 are *w.o.* is   11 ⟨largely⟩ essentially   13 ↑liked↓
18 ⟨lof⟩ profoundly   19 ⟨imbued⟩ ↑touched↓   20 and *w.o.* or
20 in the] in / in the   25 the drama *w.o.* it   26 very *w.o.* sin

29 January 1880, Boston, to William H. Bishop. 2 pp. A.l.s. CSmH.

29 February 1880, Boston, to William C. Howells. 3 pp. A.l.s. MH.

   9 ever *w.o.* even   12 amusing *w.o. illeg.*   24 again *w.o. illeg.*
26 at *w.o.* as   26 school *w.o. illeg.*

12 March 1880, Boston, to Charles D. Warner. 2 pp. A.l.s. CtHT.

[*In margin of second page, in another hand*: W. D. Howells / March/80]

21 March 1880, Boston, to William H. Bishop. Location of MS. unknown. *Life in Letters*, I, 281–82.

22 March 1880, Boston, to Samuel L. Clemens. 2 pp. A.l.s. CU.

[*At top of first page, in Clemens' hand*: Remail this / to me, Joe. / Mark.]

   10 ↑the idea↓   10 which *w.o.* while   11 ⟨l⟩ Well   14 ↑of↓
16 ↑here↓   16 mid *w.o.* in

17 April 1880, Boston, to William C. Howells. 3 pp. A.l.s. MH.

   20 full *w.o. illeg.*   29 publish *w.o. illeg.*   29 ↑rate↓

22 April 1880, Boston, to Henry W. Longfellow. 1 p. A.l.s. MH.

25 April 1880, Boston, to Samuel L. Clemens. 3 pp. A.l.s. CU.

   5 one *w.o.* once   11 the *w.o.* her

29 April 1880, Boston, to Edmund C. Stedman. 1 p. A.l.s. NNC.

   4 my *w.o.* an   5 ⟨kind⟩ his   12 P. S. . . . Atlantic?] [*in margin*]

2 May 1880, Boston, to William C. Howells. 3 pp. A.l.s. MH.

   5 gave *w.o.* is   12 think⟨ing⟩   13 ↑in . . . posture,↓   14 effect⟨s⟩
15 ↑him↓   16 amuse *w.o. illeg.*   28 imagined *w.o.* imaged
42 return ⟨one of⟩   44 dim, ⟨*illeg.*⟩   44–50 life . . . . Will.] [*across top of first page*]   49 aff'te] afftee'

3 May 1880, Boston, to Thomas W. Higginson. 2 pp. A.l.s. NN.

   7 ↑allusion to↓   9 be *w.o.* ne   13 It⟨'⟩s

17 May 1880, Boston, to William C. Howells. 3 pp. A.l.s. MH.

   4 ↑I↓   8 round *w.o. illeg.*   9 with *w.o.* —

17 May 1880, Boston, to Rutherford B. Hayes. 2 pp. A.l.s. OFH.

[*At top of first page, in another hand*: Howells]
   7 greater *w.o. illeg.*   10 an⟨d⟩   11 visit⟨s⟩   15 he *w.o. illeg.*

10 June 1880, Boston, to Sylvester Baxter. 1 p. A.l.s. ViU.

14 June 1880, Boston, to Samuel L. Clemens. 2 pp. A.l.s. CU.

   8 ⟨you⟩ the

14 June 1880, Boston, to Hjalmar H. Boyesen. 2 pp. A.l.s. ViU.

   5 doesn't *w.o.* doen   11 thirty-three *w.o.* 33
12 any the] any-/ the *w.o.* any-/thing

20 June 1880, Belmont, to William C. Howells. 3 pp. A.l.s. MH.

   16 ↑you,↓

4 July 1880, Belmont, to Charles E. Norton. 3 pp. A.l.s. MH.

   6 ↑readers↓

8 July 1880, Boston, to James Maurice Thompson. 2 pp. A.l.s. OFH.

   9 Europe *w.o.* europe   10 before *w.o.* a   14–15 ↑poems . . . on↓
15 those *w.o. illeg.*   20 live *w.o.* have

21 July 1880, Boston, to Thomas W. Higginson. 3 pp. A.l.s. NN.

   6 notice⟨s⟩   7 they *w.o.* it   15 I *w.o.* ,   15 ↑suppose,↓   15 ↑early↓

25 July 1880, Boston, to William C. Howells. 3 pp. A.l.s. MH.

   4 have *w.o.* had   9 Old *w.o.* old   15 ↑that↓   23 days⟨'⟩
31 ⟨*illeg.*⟩ only   32 this *w.o.* these   42 ⟨Gol⟩ Leslie

28 July 1880, Boston, to Thomas B. Aldrich. 3 pp. A.l.s. MH.

   18 ⟨month⟩ ↑while↓   20 have had] have / have had

22 August 1880, Boston, to William C. Howells. 2 pp. A.l.s. MH.

   9 and ↑in↓   18 Sherman *w.o.* sherman   22 do *w.o.* day
26 it *w.o.* at

24 August 1880, Boston, to Thomas W. Higginson. 2 pp. A.l.s. NN.

8 ask⟨ed⟩   14 begun, *w.o.* because   21 of *w.o. illeg.*
22 ⟨*illeg.*⟩ enjoyment   19–22 This . . . . feels.] [*at bottom and around
margins of second page*]

29 August 1880, Boston, to Charles E. Norton. 2 pp. A.l.s. MH.

6 ↑a↓   12 I↑'ve↓   15 it *w.o.* is   20 like *w.o.* live   23 ↑of↓ us
22–25 the mobiglie . . . . Howells.] [*in margin and across letterhead,
first page*]

14 September 1880, Boston, to Moncure D. Conway. 2 pp. A.l.s. NNC.

16 ↑was↓   22 I . . . Hoadley.] [*across letterhead, first page*]

17 October 1880, Belmont, to William C. Howells. 3 pp. A.l.s. MH.

17 both⟨s⟩   17 rejoicing *w.o. illeg.*   24 ⟨to⟩ ↑in↓

22 October 1880, Boston, to Whitelaw Reid. 2 pp. A.l.s. DLC.

2 22 *w.o.* 21   10 grieve *w.o.* greve   19 Eastern *w.o.* eastern
22 makes *w.o. illeg.*

5 December 1880, Boston, to William C. Howells. 2 pp. A.l.s. MH.

14 but he *w.o.* but his   18 donkey *w.o. illeg.*

6 December 1880, Boston, to Henry Demarest Lloyd. 1 p. A.l.s. WHi.

13 December 1880, Belmont, to Samuel L. Clemens. 3 pp. A.l.s. CU.

6 too *w.o.* two   31 real *w.o.* ni   31 ↑to the prince↓

10 January 1881, Belmont, to Henry O. Houghton. 1 p. Author's copy
signed. MH.

[*At bottom of page, in Howells' hand*: copy *to the left of text, also in
Howells' hand*: Copy of letter to Mr. Houghton (*w.o.* Osgood)]

14 January 1881, Belmont, to Henry O. Houghton. 3 pp. Copy, probably
in Elinor Howells' hand. MH.

24 ↑for me↓

4 February 1881, Belmont, to James R. Osgood. 1 p. A.l.s. MB.

3 ↑leave↓

8 February 1881, Boston, to Horace E. Scudder. 2 pp. A.l.s. MH.

 8 personal *w.o.* pes   13 few *w.o.* four

13 February 1881, Belmont, to William C. Howells. 3 pp. A.l.s. MH.

 6 ↑(for three years)↓   8 republication *w.o. illeg.*   9 ⟨my⟩ ↑a↓

17 February 1881, Boston, to James R. Osgood. 2 pp. A.l.s. MH.

[*Written in Osgood's hand on the second page are two notes, the first of which has been cancelled*: ⟨Letter received. Do whatever seems / ⟨wise⟩ ↑best↓. I leave for home to-day. / Should like to see you on Sunday. / ⟨Could⟩ ↑Perhaps↓ you ↑can↓ delay till then.⟩ *The second note reads*: Letter received. Do whatever / seems best. Shall be home / Sunday. Perhaps you / can delay till then, & talk it over.]

18 February 1881, Belmont, to James R. Osgood. 4 pp. A.l.s. ViU.

27 February 1881, Boston, to Rose Terry Cooke. 2 pp. A.l.s. CtHi.

 5 invisible *w.o.* ins

10 April 1881, Boston, to Victoria M. Howells. 3 pp. A.l.s. MH.

 9 ↑been↓   18 ↑all↓   18 ⟨got⟩ a   28 ⟨wh⟩ was

17 April 1881, Boston, to James R. Osgood. 3 pp. A.l.s. MH.

 3 closing *w.o.* clearing   10 Humor *w.o.* humor

17 April 1881, Boston, to Samuel L. Clemens. 5 pp. A.l.s. CU.

 4 to you *w.o. illeg.* you   5 decency *w.o. illeg.*   7 ⟨aba⟩ a
12 that ⟨if⟩   15 how *w.o. illeg.*   36 finishing ⟨up⟩

28 April 1881, Xenia, Ohio, to Elinor M. Howells. 2 pp. A.l.s. MH.

 5 a *w.o.* an   6 Between *w.o. illeg.*   16–17 This . . . Eureka.] [*in margin and across dateline and salutation, first page*]

1 May 1881, Crawfordsville, Indiana, to Winifred Howells. 2 pp. A.l.s. MH.

 5 ↑my↓   6 Friday *w.o.* last   9 broke *w.o. illeg.*
17 all go] all / all go   17–21 all . . . . nice.] [*across saluation and text, first page*]

22 May 1881, Belmont, to Victoria M. Howells. 3 pp. A.l.s. MH.

6 ⟨left⟩ got 7 Cambridg|e| 8 put *w.o.* you
10 a mortgage *w.o.* a most 14 ⟨y⟩ he 23 ⟨be⟩ more
35 China *w.o.* china 35–36 to⟨day,⟩ ↑you to↓-morrow

22 June 1881, Belmont, to Charles D. Warner. 2 pp. A.l.s. CtHT.

4 ↑a↓ Patron 9 guest⟨s⟩

2 July 1881, Belmont, to Edmund C. Stedman. 3 pp. A.l.s. NNC.

[*Above and below dateline, first page, in another hand*: W. D. Howells /
1881] 5 ⟨I⟩ glorious 14 ↑to↓ thank

3 July 1881, Belmont, to William C. Howells. 3 pp. A.l.s. MH.

7 came *w.o. illeg.* 11 ↑that↓ was ⟨then⟩ 11 ↑at the thought↓
14 In *w.o.* On 20 where *w.o.* which 21 ⟨y⟩ anything
24 you⟨r⟩ got 24–29 Sentinel . . . . Will.] [*in margins of first two pages
and across salutation*]

8 July 1881, Belmont, to Edwin D. Mead. 4 pp. A.l.s. NjR.

5 in ↑not↓ 11 ⟨a⟩ very 13 imposture *w.o.* imposition 17 off] of

10 July 1881, Belmont, to Charles E. Norton. 4 pp. A.l.s. CSmH.

6 face] [*doubtful reading; could be* fate]
12 having another] having / having another 15 ↑il↓ 18 breathe⟨r⟩

11 July 1881, Belmont, to Elizabeth S. Phelps (Ward). 3 pp. A.l.s. NjP.

[*In another hand across top of first page*: This is so delicate and lovely,
it will give you / pleasure. Please return it.]

14 July 1881, Belmont, to James R. Osgood. 3 pp. A.l.s. MB.

7 of the] of / of the 9 ↑comes,↓ 10 At *w.o.* It
12 announcement *w.o.* acc 12 once *w.o.* w 15 good *w.o.* got

6 August 1881, Belmont, to Thomas B. Aldrich. 4 pp. A.l.s. MH.

14 August 1881, Belmont, to Thomas W. Higginson. 2 pp. A.l.s. NN.

9–11 nobility. . . . Howells.] [*in margin and across salutation, first
page*]

14 August 1881, Belmont, to Anne H. Fréchette. 3 pp. A.l.s. MH.

  8 there, ⟨but⟩   17 ↑you↓ like   19 six⟨t⟩   21 ↑last↓   27 he *w.o.* is

2 September 1881, Belmont, to Thomas B. Aldrich. 2 pp. A.l.s. MH.

  6 the Police *w.o. illeg.* Police

3 September 1881, Belmont, to Charles D. Warner. 6 pp. A.l.s. CtHT.

  17 ↑we↓

11 September 1881, Belmont, to William C. Howells. 3 pp. A.l.s. MH.

  7 ↑but↓   20 ↑know↓   23 ⟨J⟩ May   24 you⟨r⟩

2 October 1881, Belmont, to George W. Cable. 3 pp. A.l.s. LNHT.

  10 blackest *w.o.* blacket   11 it ⟨it⟩ so   11 ↑one↓

5 October 1881, Belmont, to Thomas W. Higginson. 1 p. A.n.s. NN.

[*Below signature, in Higginson's hand*: Wm Dean Howells]

6 October 1881, Belmont, to Charles Fairchild. 3 pp. Author's draft signed. MH.

    7 ↑to tell↓   11 all *w.o. it*
15 sell it. ⟨Or, if you could take the Cambridge house at $13,000 *w.o. illeg.* ↑13,000↓ I would buy Redtop at once, and take the risk of finding a tenant.⟩   16 ⟨neither of⟩ thes⟨e⟩   16 this] thes
16 plan⟨s⟩ does ↑not↓ seem⟨s⟩   17 to you *w.o.* at once   22 Mr. *w.o.* Mrs.

23 October 1881, Belmont, to William C. Howells. 3 pp. A.l.s. MH.

  20 some↑thing↓   21 continuously *w.o. illeg.*   23 likeness ⟨; the⟩

30 October 1881, Belmont, to James R. Osgood. 2 pp. A.l.s. MH.

  4 ⟨what⟩ the   5 can't *w.o. illeg.*

6 November 1881, Belmont, to James R. Osgood. 2 pp. A.l.s. MB.

  3 cities *w.o.* city   5 "Ducal⟨-⟩Mantua"   7 making *w.o. illeg.*

10 December 1881, Belmont, to Annie A. Fields. 5 pp. A.l.s. CSmH.

  7 grieved] grived   7 Of *w.o.* It
[*on verso of fifth page, in Elinor Howells' hand*: Dear Mrs Fields: /

Mr Howells is still in bed except for two hours sitting up during the day—& very, very nervous / Affectionately / Elinor M Howells]

15 December 1881, Cambridge, to William C. Howells. 2 pp. A.l.s. MH.

 5 doctor *w.o. illeg.*   9 a matter] a / a matter   9 ⟨have⟩ courage 13 ↑we↓

Word-Division

In the two lists below, entries are keyed to the line numbers of the letter texts; the line-count includes all lines of type of a letter proper, beginning at the internal address or dateline. List A records compounds and possible compounds hyphenated at the end of the line in the authorial document or extant transcription used as copy-text for the present edition, and indicates how these end-line hyphenated forms have been resolved. If the compounds occur in consistent form elsewhere in the authorial document or in other such materials of the same general period in time, including literary manuscripts, then resolution was made on that basis; if these other occurrences are inconsistent, resolution was based on the form in closest proximity in time to the possible compound in question. If neither of these resources was sufficient, then resolution was based on the evidence of published texts of Howells' works or on the prevalent usage of the period. List B is a guide to transcription of compounds or possible compounds hyphenated at the end of the line in the present text: compounds recorded in this list should be transcribed as given; words divided at the end of the line and not listed should be transcribed as one word.

LIST A

10 March 1873, to H. James		84	heart-breaking
20 April 1873, to W. C. Howells		5	book-noticing
12 May 1873, to H. James		37	to-day
8 June 1873, to A. T. Howells		27	wall-paper
8 June 1873, to A. T. Howells		48	lady-like
11 June 1873, to C. D. Warner		12	fellow-men
20 July 1873, to W. C. Howells		11	picture-tiles
26 August 1873, to H. James		19	mantel-piece
18 October 1873, to T. W. Higginson	23,	24	anti-climax
9 January 1874, to M. M. Hurd		24	nonpartizan
22 April 1874, to E. D. Mead		8	greenbacks
14 August 1874, to H. W. Longfellow		11	to-morrow
24 September 1874, to J. B. O'Reilly		16	standpoint
24 October 1874, to A. T. Howells		36	human-nature
9 January 1875, to W. C. Howells		22	-a-brac

25 April 1875, to A. H. Howells	7	over-joyed
27 November 1875, to W. C. Howells	11	strength-gaining
5 January 1876, to C. D. Warner	6	handwriting
5 January 1876, to C. D. Warner	20	book-public
13 February 1876, to W. C. Howells	32	twenty-times
9 April 1876, to W. C. Howells	8	snow-drifts
9 April 1876, to W. C. Howells	24	dressing-room
August/September 1876, to F. J. Garrison	9	to-morrow
24 September 1876, to C. E. Norton	8	firm-willed
18 February 1877, to A. T. Howells	9	water-bouquet
22 February 1877, to J. Hay	9	fellow-countryman
1 April 1877, to C. D. Warner	11	side-light
4 August 1877, to W. C. Howells	7	to-day
11 September 1877, to W. H. Bishop	22	good-natured
14 November 1877, to L. Barrett	11	love-making
24 November 1877, to W. C. Howells	15	Thanksgiving
14 March 1878, to H. H. Boyesen	16	forty-one
21 November 1878, to H. H. Boyesen	22	oversetter
31 March 1879, to A. A. Fields	9	slide-up-
29 June 1879, to A. A. Fields	5	nose-bleeding
17 September 1879, to T. W. Higginson	17	stopping-short
17 May 1880, to R. B. Hayes	14	apple-blossoms
28 July 1880, to T. B. Aldrich	8	fly-leaves
17 October 1880, to W. C. Howells	7	*nonpartizan*
1 May 1881, to W. Howells	8	sons-in-law
22 June 1881, to C. D. Warner	5	overcome
8 July 1881, to E. D. Mead	10	blatherskite
8 July 1881, to E. D. Mead	11	Scotchman
14 July 1881, to J. R. Osgood	6	rewrite

LIST B

21 October 1873, to A. T. Howells	5–6	Inter-Ocean
17 February 1874, to C. D. Warner	12–13	hard-hearted
16 August 1874, to A. H. Howells	19–20	corkscrew-attachment
8 September 1874, to S. L. Clemens	18–19	over-running
8 September 1874, to S. L. Clemens	25–26	tumble-bug
9 January 1875, to W. C. Howells	4–5	to-morrow
27 June 1875, to W. C. Howells	11–12	boarding-house
4 September 1875, to C. D. Warner	14–15	six-monthser
24 October 1875, to C. D. Warner	13–14	first-class
21 November 1875, to S. L. Clemens	15–16	treasure-hunting
26 December 1875, to W. C. Howells	9–10	type-writer

19 March 1876, to W. C. Howells	8–9	bath-room
15 May 1876, to W. C. Howells	7–8	to-morrow
8 August 1876, to J. R. Lowell	24–25	tumble-down
21 November 1878, to H. H. Boyesen	33–34	hill-top
10 March 1879, to H. E. Scudder	11–12	forty-two
18 May 1879, to S. P. Langley	22–23	one-sided
7 August 1879, to R. B. Hayes	4–5	king-catcher
21 March 1880, to W. H. Bishop	16–17	inter-continental
29 August 1880, to C. E. Norton	13–14	to-morrow

List of Howells' Correspondents

The following alphabetical list of Howells' correspondents provides page references for (1) letters written by Howells TO others and (2) letters FROM others addressed to Howells. Page numbers in italic type indicate letters appearing in full or as fully as the source permits; page numbers in roman type indicate letters cited in footnotes, with "cited" used broadly to mean quotation from a letter, description of part of its contents, or mention of it whether printed in this edition or not. The few cited letters *about* Howells, e.g., to Boyesen from Turgenev, appear not in this list but in the main index.

Adams, Charles F., FROM 271

Adams, Henry, FROM 112

Aldrich, Thomas B., TO *42*, 49, *86-87*, *90*, *122*, *124*, 124-25, 127, *140-41*, *215*, 215, 259, *262-63*, 263, 275, 292, 294, 295; FROM 87, 123, 194

Appleton, Thomas G., FROM 245

Barrett, Lawrence, TO 150, *177-79*, *192-93*, 193, 224, 224, 243; FROM 177, 193, 206-07, 211, 224, 226, 266

Batchelder, Marianne W. (Mrs. S.), TO *159-60*

Baxter, Sylvester, TO *255*

Bigelow, William, TO *190*, 209

Bishop, William H., TO 153, 154, *174*, 223, *243-44*, 246

Boston *Evening Transcript*, Editors of, TO *82-83*, 85

Boyesen, Hjalmar H., TO *5*, *21-22*, 38, *52-53*, 53, *57*, 57, *61*, 62, *78*, 79, *108*, 108, *138-39*, 141, 151, *191-92*, 198, *212-13*, 213, 214, *256*; FROM 62, 256

Brainerd, Erastus, TO *242-43*

Bryant, William C., TO *33-34*; FROM 34

Cable, George W., TO *297*; FROM 297

Church, Francis P. (or William C.), TO 74, 158

Clemens, Samuel L., TO 7, 49, 63, *63-64*, 67, *68-69*, 69, 74, 75, *75-76*, *91-92*, 91, 109-10, 116, 124, 141, *142-43*, 155, 182, *184*, *185*, 188, *199-200*, 201, 224, 237, 239, 247, 249, 250, 255, *255*, 262, 271, 272, 280, *280-81*, 282; FROM 64, 67, 75, 76, 91, 109, 110, 112, 150, 184, 185, 186, 200, 237, 239, 248, 255, 268, 272, 282

Collier, Thomas S., TO 192, *198*

Comly, James M., TO *32-33*, 33, 38, 40, *43*, 48, *56*, 57, 79, 133

Conway, Moncure D., TO *166-67*, 210, *266-67*, 288

Cooke, Rose T., TO *278*; FROM 278

Curtis, George W., TO *224-25*

Daly, John A., TO *74-75*, *126*, 128, *129*, 129; FROM 75, 125-26, 129

De Forest, John W., FROM 8, 67

Dwight, John S., TO 38

Eggleston, George C., FROM 29

Emerson, Ralph W., TO 49, *51-52*, 52; FROM 52

Fairchild, Charles, TO 187, *298-99*, 299; FROM 299

Field, Roswell M., FROM 206

Fields, Annie A. (Mrs. J. T.), TO 40, *99-100*, 116, 120, 222, 223, *232-33*, 301

Fields, James T., TO *110*, 118, 120; FROM 110, 111

Fréchette, Achille, TO *236*, 237

Fréchette, Anne H. (Mrs. A.), TO *293-94*, 294. See also Howells, Anne T.

Garfield, James A., TO *105*, 105, 106, *189*, 257, 279

Garrison, Francis J., TO 49, *66-67*, 67, 100, *101-02*, 102, 104, 131, *136*, *165*, 171; FROM 194

Garrison, Wendell P., TO *81-82*, 82

Gilder, Richard W., TO 98

Green, Samuel A., TO 153, *221-22*

Hale, Edward E., FROM 245

Harte, Bret, TO *68*; FROM 68

Hay, John, TO *112-13*, 151, *157-58*, *172*, 173, 207, 210, 224, *225-26*, 262; FROM 113, 158, 177, 211, 226

Hayes, Rutherford B., TO *131-32*, 131,

137, 142, 149-50, *163-64*, 164, *165-66*, 166, *194-95*, 200, 202, 211, *216-17*, 220, *235-36*, 236, *241*, *254*, 270; FROM 131, 133, 136, 164, 195, 220, 236, 241
Hayes, Webb C., TO *135-36*
Hayne, Paul H., TO *10*; FROM 10
Higginson, Thomas W., TO 5, *36-37*, 37, 154, 165, *169*, 177, 180, 207, *238*, 252, 252, *259-60*, 260, *264-65*, 265, *292*, *298*; FROM 238, 252, 260, 293, 298
Holland, Josiah G., FROM 246
Holmes, Oliver W., TO *127*, 149, *156*, 156; FROM 51, 127
Houghton, Henry O., TO 152, 272, *272-73*; FROM 132
Houghton, Mr. and Mrs. Henry O., TO 276
Howells, Anne T., TO 5, *12*, 14, 15, *16*, 23, 24, *28-29*, 35, *37-38*, 41, 42, 43, 51, 59, 72, *72-74*, 79, 80, 88, 132, *156-57*. *See also* Fréchette, Anne H. (Mrs. A.).
Howells, Aurelia H., TO 38, *65-66*, *94*, 234
Howells, Elinor M., TO *167*, 282, 283
Howells, Joseph A., TO 63
Howells, Victoria M., TO 4, *50*, 72, 74, 116, 212, 241, 267, *278-79*, 279, *284-85*, 287, 294
Howells, William C., TO 3, 4, 7, 13, *13-14*, 14, *14-15*, 16, *19-20*, 22, *22-23*, *24*, 24, 26, 27, 29, *31-32*, 32, 35, 36, 38, 56, 61, 62, *62-63*, 64, 65, *71-72*, 72, 75, 76, *76-77*, 77, *84-85*, 85, *87-88*, 88, *89-90*, 92, 92, 93, *95*, 98, *98-99*, 99, 102, *111-12*, 112, *115-16*, *118-19*, 120, *120*, 121, *123*, 124, *125-26*, 126, 127, *128*, 128, 130, *130-31*, 131, *132-33*, 133, 138, 140, *141-42*, *143-44*, *144-45*, 145, 149, 151, 152, 154, 155, 157, 162, *162-63*, *164*, *168*, *170*, *173*, *179-80*, 180, *182-83*, *186-87*, 187, *188-89*, *193-94*, 194, 195, *195-96*, *200-01*, *201-02*, 203, 206, *207-08*, 208, 209, 211, 220, 226, *226-27*, 227, 232, *233-34*, 234, 236, 237, *240-41*, 241, 243, *244-45*, 245, *247-48*, 248, 250, *250-51*, 252, 253, 257, 258, *261-62*, 262, *263-64*, 264, 266, *267-68*, 270, 270, 272, 274, *275-76*, 277, 285, 287, 288, 289, *296*, 296, *299-300*, *302*, 302
Howells, Winifred, TO 283, *283*
Hurd, Melanchthon M., TO *48-49*, 67, 71
Hutchinson, Ellen, TO 151, 217, 218
James, Henry, Jr., TO 6, *17-19*, 19, 20, 22, 24, *25-26*, *34-35*, 35, *39-40*, 45, 77, 138; FROM 26, 35, 41, *41-42*, 91, 122, 151, 153, 154, 232, 258

James, Henry, Sr., FROM 78
Jewett, Sarah O., TO 5, *129-30*
Kemble, Fanny, FROM 98, 110
Krebiehl, H. E., TO 243
Lacy, Ben W., TO *53*; FROM 54
Langley, Samuel P., TO 153, *227-28*; FROM 228
Lathrop, George P., FROM 214
Lavelle y Romero, José A. de, FROM 171
Linton, William J., TO 230
Lloyd, Henry D., TO *270*
Longfellow, Henry W., TO 63, *64-65*, 65, *93*, 212, *249*; FROM 65, 279
Lowell, James R., TO *60*, 61, *114*, *115*, *134*, 138, *143*, *230-31*; FROM 60, 61, 114, 115, 134, *231-32*
Mason, Frank, FROM 177
Matthews, Brander, TO 197
Mead, Edwin D., TO *59*, 270, *288*, 289
Mead, William R., TO 190-91
Mitchell, S. Weir, TO 217
Morley, John, FROM 245
Niles, Thomas, TO 130
Norton, Charles E., TO 8, 36, 56, 66, 78, *85-86*, 138, *139-40*, 152, 154, 155, *182*, 184, *197*, *205*, 205, 210, 242, *258*, *258*, 263, 265, *265-66*, *289*, 289; FROM 140, 164, 258, 289
Noyes, Horatio S., TO 207
O'Reilly, John B., TO *70*, 124; FROM 70
Osgood, James R., TO 152, *158-59*, 159, 172, 176, *177*, 179, *180-81*, 181, 272, 273, 274, 274, 276, 277, 280, *290-91*, 300, *301*; FROM 111, 159, 237, 273, 276, 280, 291
Parkman, Francis, TO 27, 72; FROM *27-28*
Parton, James, TO *51*; FROM 67
Perry, Thomas S., TO 213-14
Phelps, Elizabeth S., TO *290*; FROM 290
Piatt, John J., FROM 175
Pope, Charles R., TO *64*; FROM *64*; AGREEMENT 63
Preston, Harriet W., FROM 67, 79
Reed, Samuel R., FROM 175
Reid, Whitelaw, TO *44*, 87, *100-01*, *269*, 269; FROM 44, 269
Rogers, William K., TO 149, *161-62*, 163, 165, 168, 170; FROM 162
Rose, George M., FROM 264
Sangster, Margaret, FROM 29
Scudder, Horace E., TO *211*, 219, *274-75*; FROM 275
Sedgwick, Arthur G., TO *216*, 243
Smith, Goldwin, FROM 248

Smith, Susan E. (Mrs. S. M.), FROM 80
Smith, William H., FROM 143
Stabler, James P., TO *221*; FROM 221
Stedman, Edmund C., TO 41, *45*, 49, 79, *80-81*, 81, *135*, 141, *181*, *214*, 214, 215, *228-29*, *250*, *286*; FROM 45, 81, 214, 250, 286
Stephen, Leslie, FROM 239
Stoddard, Charles W., TO 11, *20-21*, 21
Stoddard, Richard H., FROM 297
Story, William W., TO *107*, *204*, *234-35*; FROM 108, 235
Tauchnitz, Christian B., FROM 237
Taylor, Bayard, TO 45, *46-47*, 47, 48, *138*; FROM 47, *47-48*, 48
Thompson, [James] Maurice, TO *58*, 58, *259*; FROM 282-83
Ticknor, Benjamin H., FROM 162
Townsend, Belton O., TO *83-84*, 84, 165, *171*, 171
Turgenev, Ivan, FROM 79

Twain, Mark (pseud.). *See* Clemens, Samuel L.
Ward, Elizabeth S. P. *See* Phelps, Elizabeth S.
Warner, Charles D., TO 5, 8, *10-11*, 11, *30*, *46*, 49, *54*, 54, *55*, 56, 57, 59, 72, 86, 96, *97*, 98, 102, *102-03*, 103, 104, *106*, *116-17*, *121-22*, 133, *144*, 154, 157, *160-61*, 165, *175-76*, 176, 183, 184, 187, *187-88*, *218*, 229, 229, *242*, 244, *245*, 245, 255, *285*, *295*; FROM 30, 46, 54, 55-56, 103-04, 107, 110-11, 118, 122, 144, 161, 242, 245, 285, 295-96
Warner, George H., TO *96*, 107; FROM 96
Wells, David A., TO *104*, 104-05
Whelpley, A. W., TO *174-75*, 175, 179; FROM 175
White, Richard G., TO *218-19*
Whittier, John G., FROM 110
Woolson, Constance F., FROM 110, 179

Index

This index records all names of persons, organizations, monuments, ships, hotels, public buildings, and titles of magazines and books (the last recorded under the names of authors, if known). It excludes the names of relatives of Howells' correspondents when they are mentioned for the primary purpose of sending love or minor information; the titles, journals, or publishers of post-1920 criticism and scholarship; and geographical names and government divisions. Some topics are listed as independent entries, but most can be found under Howells' name, where information is divided into two major lists: WORKS and TOPICS. The TOPICS section is further subdivided.

Within entries, the general order of information is: brief and/or general references; citation of correspondence other than that with Howells (e.g., Turgenev to Boyesen); works by that person, including reviews and presumably unpublished work; and descriptive modifications, arranged in ascending page order. Finally, the frequent occurrence of some dozen entries has required the use of "passim" (e.g., "*Atlantic*, WDH as editor and contributor, 3–295 passim").

Italic numbers designate pages on which significant biographical information is given. An asterisk preceding an entry indicates that a full record of correspondence between Howells and the person or institution so marked is provided in the separate "List of Howells' Correspondents," pages 345–347, the headnote of which explains its arrangement.

*Adams, Charles F., 137, *138*, 142; "A Disputed Election...," 143-44; approves Lloyd essay, 271

*Adams, Henry, *North American Review* (ed.), 27, 35, 36; entertains WDH, 4, 111, 112

Agassiz, Jean L. R., 40, 42; Lowell's poem on, 60, 61

Aiken, George L., *Uncle Tom's Cabin* (play), 126

Ainsworth, 37, 38

Aitiaiche (pseud.). *See* Fréchette, Anne H. (Mrs. A.).

Alabama Claims, 25, 26-27

Alden, Henry M., *294*

*Aldrich, Thomas B., 48, 75, 259, 275; letter from H. O. Houghton cited, 273; *Cloth of Gold*... (reviewed by E. Fawcett), 263; "The Legend of Ara-Coeli," 122, 123; "Mademoiselle Olympe Zabriskie," 58, 59; *Marjorie Daw*, 59; *A Midnight Fantasy*... (WDH on), 86-87, 181; "Our New Neighbors at Ponkapog," 215; "The Pine and the Walnut," 90; *Prudence Palfrey* (WDH on), 42, 58, 59; *The Queen of Sheba*, 122, 123, (reviewed by WDH) 176; review of *A Fearful Responsibility*, 292; R. Keeler essay (returned by WDH), 49; "Rococo" (WDH on), 90; "Spring in New England," 90, 91; *The Stillwater Tragedy*, 215, (reviewed by W. C. Brownell and WDH) 262, 263; "Unsung" (John Howells on), 124; "A Visit to a Certain Old Gentleman," 122, 123; *XXXVI Lyrics and XII Sonnets...*, 262, 263; sale of *Every Saturday*, 40, 42; criticized by C. H. Webb, 44; and WDH, 58, 80; and Lowell, 60, 61; and *Atlantic*, 84, 140-41, 250, 276, 278, 288; visited by WDH or WDHs, 86, 87, 106, 124; entertained by Osgood, 91, 92; European trip, 92, 106; residences, 119, 199; quarrel with WDH, 215; and Harvard and Yale, 232, 291; and J. T. Fields, 233, 301

Aldrich, Mr. and Mrs. Thomas B., dinner at Jameses, Sr., 25, 26; entertained

by WDHs, 113, 209; European trip, 232, 233
Alfieri, Vittorio, WDH on, 177
Allen, William, *106*
Allibone, S. A., *Critical Dictionary . . .* , 85, 86
American Land Emigrant Co., 96
American Publishing Co., 54, 107; and WDH's Venetian history, 55
American Woman Suffrage Association, 54
Amory, Thomas C., 50, *51*
Anderson, Charles R., 71
Annon, Annie R., "An After-Thought," 45; "Little Muriel," 45
Anspach-Baireuth, Margravine of. *See* Craven, Elizabeth.
Anthony, Mr. and Mrs. Andrew V. S., *291*
*Appleton, Thomas G., 142, 143; entertains WDH, 4, 88
Arabian Nights' Entertainments, 232
Archaeological Institute of America, 266
Arms, George, 192, 198. *See also* Gibson-Arms.
Arthur, Chester A., 220, 287
Ashfield Academy Fair, 263, 264, 265, 266, 295
Ashtabula *Sentinel*, 184; editorials and news items, 23, 79, 80, 167, 168, 201, 202, 208; publishes W. C. Howells' "Familiar Letters from the Editor," 32, 63, 72, 95, 202, 203, 204, 240; business arrangements, 142, 240, 241, 284, 287
Astor, John J., 113, 196
Astor, Mrs. John J., 112
Astor, William W., 112, *113*, 172
Atkins, Edwin F., *299*
Atlantic, WDH as editor and contributor, 3-295 passim; "Contributors' Club," 144, 152-53; (and Aldrich) 140-41, 215; (and Boyesen) 141; (and Clemens) 141, 249; (and Stedman) 141; (and Hay) 157, 158; (and W. C. Howells) 180; (and Hay, Woolson on *Daisy Miller*) 232; WDH resigns, 152, 273, 275; Aldrich offered editorship, 273; publishes James, Sr., essay, 288; publishes E. S. Phelps novel, 290; publishes Aldrich review of *A Fearful Responsibility*, 292; publishes Lathrop review of R. H. Stoddard poetry, 297; publishes Scudder review of Cable novel, 297

Atlantic dinner (1874), 82-83, 84, 85
Atlas, 69
Aucassin and Nicolette, 181
Auerbach, A. B., publishes *Voreilige Schlüsse*, 125, 126
Auerbach, Berthold, 125
Augusta, 204
Austen, Jane, WDH on, 157

Baird, Henry C., "Money and Its Substitutes," 105-6
Ballou, Ellen B., 43, 104, 242, 252, 272, 273
Bancroft, George, 253; *History of the United States*, 253
Banks, Nathaniel P., 209, 210
Banner of Light, reviews *The Undiscovered Country*, 261, 262
Baptists, 69
Barberini, Palazzo, Rome, 234
*Barrett, Lawrence, *173*, 180, 181; and *A Counterfeit Presentment*, 150-51; (Cincinnati) 174-75; (Cleveland) 177, 178, 179; (possible withdrawal) 185, 188; (Boston) 191, 192-93; (1877-1878) 216; and *Yorick's Love*, 150-51; (dissatisfaction) 206-7, 208; (revision) 210, 211; (Philadelphia and Boston) 243; payment to B. Taylor estate, 226; and "Civil Death," 266
Barrière, Théodore, *Les Filles de Marbre*, 193
Barry, John S., "Old Trees," 81-82
*Batchelder, Marianne W. (Mrs. S.), 159-60
Batchelder, Samuel, *160*
*Baxter, Sylvester, interview with Warner and Clemens, 255
Bayliss, Garland, 138
Beecher, Henry W., 95-96, 97
Belford Brothers, pirate *Their Wedding Journey* and *A Chance Acquaintance*, 167, 227; pirate Clemens book, 239
Belfords, Clarke & Co., pirate *The Lady of the Aroostook*, 227, 264
Belknap, William W., 122, *123*
Benson, Eugene, 142, *143*
Bergsöe, Wilhelm, *I Sabinerbjergene* (reviewed by Boyesen), 21, 22
Berman, Milton, 27
Bennett, George N., 140
Bettina, 204
Bible, 196, 209
Biklé, Lucy L. C., 297
*Bigelow, William, *190*, 209

*Bishop, William H., "Deodand," 243, 244; *Detmold*, 174, (reviewed by WDH) 223, 246; *The House of the Merchant Prince* (WDH on), 246; "McIntyre's False Face," 243, 244; reviews on art and architecture, 244; "Open Letters from New York," 153, 174; "Two New York Exhibitions," 223

Bjornson, Bjornstjerne, *The Happy Boy* and *The Fisher Maiden* (reviewed by WDH), *108*; compared with Boyesen, 5, 108, 139; met and described by WDH, 270

Black, William, 160, *161*; *MacLeod of Dare* (WDH on), 161

Blackwood's Edinburgh Magazine, 23, 107, 108, 204, 205

Blaine, James G., *131*

Blanchette, Joseph G., *183*

Bland-Allison Act, 202, 220

Bliss, Elisha P., 111, 112; and WDH's Venetian history, 54, 55; and Warner's books, 106, 107, 121, 122

Blobby (WDH's horse), 241, 270

Bloodgood, D. W., "Meteorology," 82

Booth, Bradford A., 68

Booth, Edwin, *173*

Boott, Francis, *138*

Boston *Courier*, 213

Boston *Daily News*, 162

*Boston *Evening Transcript*, 82-83, 85, 268

Boston *Herald*, 167, 168, 255

Boston Journal of Chemistry, 90

Boston Museum, 193, 206, 231, 232

Boston Museum of Fine Arts, 197

Boston Music Hall, 11

Boston *Pilot*, 70

Boston Symphony, 38

Boston University School of Medicine, 90

*Boyesen, Hjalmar H., 5, 24, 25, 66, 116, 198; letter from Turgenev cited, 61, 62; "Annunciata" (WDH on), 213, 214; "Aslang" (unidentified), 52, 53; *Falconberg* (WDH on), 108, 138-39; *Gunnar*, 28, 29, 139; "Henrik Ibsen," 57; *Idyls of Norway* . . . , 256; "Ilka on the Hill-Top," 212, 213; "Legend of the M. S." (unpublished), 21, 22; "Literary Aspects of the Romantic School," 78, 108; "The Lost Hellas" (WDH on), 256; "Necken," 21, 22, 52, 53; *A Norseman's Pilgrimage*, 57, 139; "Novalis and the Blue Flower," 78,

108; "The Ravens of Odin," 52, 53, 57; review of W. Bergsöe book, 21, 22; review of P. Heyse book, 212, 213; review of J. H. Schmidt book, 212, 213; "St. Olaf's Fountain" (WDH and Longfellow on), 21, 22; "Social Aspects of the German Romantic School," 78; "The Story of an Outcast," 57; other rejections and advice by WDH, 21, 22; described by WDH and Elinor, 22, 89; visits W. C. Howells and WDHs, 28, 99; asked for "Contributors' Club" paragraphs, 141; marriage, 191, 192

*Brainerd, Erastus, reviews of *Yorick's Love*, 242, 243

Brandes, Georg, *Die Hauptströmungen der Literatur* . . . (reviewed by Perry), 78, 79

Brewer, Tom, 39, 40

Bristow, Benjamin H., *189*

Brontë, Charlotte, *Jane Eyre* (WDH on), 157

Brontë, Emily, *Wuthering Heights* (WDH on), 157

Brooks-Baxter war, 138

Bross, Miss, 12, *13*, 23

Bross, family, 12, 13

Brown & Wells, 225

Brown, George W., "English Civil Service Reform," 224, 225; "Socialism and Germany," 224, 225

Brown, Mrs., 37

Brown, Owen, 49

Browne, Charles F., 39, 41

Brownell, W. C., "Notes" (review of Aldrich novel), 262, 263; "The Novels of Mr. Howells" (review of *The Undiscovered Country*), 258-59, 262, 263

Brunswick Hotel, Boston, 268

*Bryant, William C., 196, 230; *Orations and Addresses*, 33, 34; *A Popular History* . . . (with S. H. Gay; reviewed by Scudder), 211; *Thanatopsis* (reviewed by WDH), 230

Buck, Dudley, Centennial cantata, *138*

Buffalo *Courier*, 37, 38, 113

Bugbee, James M., "Boston Under the Mayors, 1822-1880," 222; "Mysterious Disappearances," 153, 221, 222

Bull, Ole, 247-*48*, 249

Bull, Mrs., 248, 270

Bullard, Francis, 197

Bunker Hill Centennial, 97, 98

Burlingame Treaty, 220

Burroughs, Stephen, *Memoir*, 169, *170*
Butler, Benjamin F., *209-10*
Butterworth, Hezekiah, *291*
Byron, Henry J., *Not Such a Fool as He Looks*, 95, *96*

*Cable, George W., *297*; *The Grandissimes* (WDH on; reviewed by Scudder), 297-98; *Old Creole Days*, 297
Cabot, Hannah J. (Mrs. S.), 36
Cabot, Lilla, 35, 36. *See also* Perry, Lilla C. (Mrs. T. S.).
Cabot, Samuel, 36
Cady, Edwin H., 7, 10, 15, 41, 93, 302
Caesar, Julius, 290
Calderón, Pedro, 166
The Californian, 44
Cambridge Hospital, 15
Cambridge University, 86
Capitol, U.S., 253
Carducci, Giosué, *Levia Gravia*, 102, *103*
Carlos, Don, of Asturias, 226
Carlyle, Thomas, 89, 90; *Heroes and Hero-Worship*, 288; *History of Friedrich II. of Prussia*, 169; *Sartor Resartus*, 288; WDH and others on, 288
Cary, Caroline E. *See* James, Caroline E. (Mrs. G. W.).
Cary, Richard, 130
Casanova, Giovanni J., 197
Casey, 62, 63
Cellini, Benvenuto, 85; *Autobiography*, *169*
Centennial Exhibition, 128, 130, 138
Century, 107, 282; publishes Boyesen article, 57; publishes *A Modern Instance*, 152, 277, 294; publishes *Tuscan Cities*, 280
Century Club, 213, 215
Cervantes, *Don Quixote* (WDH on), 183, 184
Channing, William E., *Thoreau*, 36, 37
Charles VIII, of France, 86
Charley (W. C. Howells' horse), 233
Chaucer, Geoffrey, essay by Lounsbury, 286
Chester, Joseph L.. *Some Account of the Taylor Family*, 167
Chicago *Inter-Ocean*, 4, 13, 24, 37, 38
Chicago *Tribune*, 270
Child, Francis J., 184, 185, 256
Child, Lydia M., 66, *67*
Chinese Exclusion Act, 220
Christ Church, Oxford University, 172
Church, Francis P., 116

*Church, Francis P. (or William C.), 74, 88, 195, 196
Church, William C. *See* Church, Francis P.
Cincinnati *Commercial*, publishes Annie Howells' Boston letters, 37, 38; publishes Piatt review of *A Counterfeit Presentment*, 175
Cincinnati *Gazette*, publishes S. R. Reed review of *A Counterfeit Presentment*, *175*
Cincinnati Law School, 267
Cincinnati Public Library, 175
Cincinnati *Times*, reviews *A Counterfeit Presentment*, 175
Clapp, Henry, Jr., *The Pioneer* (ed.), 102
Clark, John S., 27, 167
Clarke, Edward H., 50; *Sex in Education*, *51*
Clarke, John T., *266*
Clarke, Miss, 283
Clarke, Mr., 282, 283
Clemens, Jean, 263
Clemens, John M., 255, 256
Clemens, Olivia L. (Mrs. S. L.), 56; Limerick letter from Clemens cited, 75, 76
Clemens, Orion, 239, 255
*Clemens, Samuel L., 49, 116, 177, 188, 201, 233, 258; Limerick letter to Olivia cited, 75, 76; letters to Emerson, Longfellow, and Holmes cited, 185-86; letter from Longfellow cited, 186; *The Adventures of Tom Sawyer* (edited by WDH), 7, 109-10; *Ah Sin* (with Harte), 143; autobiographical piece (not extant; WDH on), 255-56; "Cap'n Simon Wheeler, the Amateur Detective," 199, 200; "Colonel Sellers" (reviewed by WDH), 95; "Colonel Sellers as a Scientist" (with WDH), 199, 200; Etiquette burlesque (unfinished), 281, 282; "Extract from Captain Stormfield's Visit to Heaven," 200; "Facts Concerning the Recent Carnival of Crime in Connecticut" (WDH on), 127; *The Gilded Age* (with Warner; WDH on), 46, 54; "A Literary Nightmare," 109; "The Loves of Alonzo Fitz Clarence and Rosannah Ethelton," 184; *Mark Twain's Sketches, New and Old*, 69, (reviewed by WDH), 109, 110; "A Murder, a Mystery, and a Marriage" (unpub-

lished), 124; obituary eloquence (sketch), 249-50; "Old Times on the Mississippi" (WDH on), 7, 76, 91, 92, 97, (pirated) 239; play about Orion (projected with WDH), 239; *The Prince and the Pauper* (reviewed by WDH), 271-72; review of J. Habberton's *Helen's Babies* (unpublished), 142, 143; *Roughing It* (WDH on), 109; "Some Learned Fables" (WDH on), 68-69; "Some Rambling Notes of an Idle Excurison," 153; speech at the Whittier birthday dinner, 153, (WDH and others on), 182, 184-86; *The Stolen White Elephant Etc.*, 237; "A Telephone Conversation" (WDH on), 249, 250; *A Tramp Abroad*, 237, (reviewed by WDH), 247, 255; "A True Story" (WDH on), 68-69; "Unconscious Plagiarism" (Holmes breakfast speech), 153; friendship with WDH, 6-7, 91, 96, 113; collaboration with WDH, 7; visits WDH or WDHs, 7, 75, 76, 94, 142-43, 268, 295; visited by WDH or WDHs, 11, 54, 56, 57, 123, 124, 291; drama and WDH, 63, 64, 74, 75; and *Atlantic*, 84, 85, 141, 153, 199, 237; sends Aldrich photographs, 87; sells WDH typewriter, 111, 112; portrait by F. D. Millet, 143; on Harte's consulship, 150, 195; on *A Counterfeit Presentment*, 185; interviewed by S. Baxter, 255; copyright, 262; at H. O. Houghton dinner, 276; negotiation on *Mark Twain's Library of Humor*, 280-82, 291

Clemens, Mr. and Mrs. Samuel L., entertain WDHs, 7, 91, 92, 93, 280, 281; visit WDHs, 247, 248, 249; Jean born, 263

Clemens, Susy, *200*

Cleveland *Herald*, 37, 38, 50

Cleveland *Leader*, publishes F. Mason review of *A Counterfeit Presentment*, 177; publishes Hay speech, 226

Coggeshall, William T., *Poets and Poetry of the West* (ed.), 212

Cole, Thomas, 33

*Collier, Thomas S., *Song Spray*, 198

Collins, Wilkie, 246

Columbia College (or University), 113

Comalada, Miguel, *Desiderius*, 85, 86

Comly, Elizabeth S. (Mrs. J. M.), 33

*Comly, James M., article (promised), 43, 44; item on WDH and Columbus, 32;

lecture, 32; and Annie Howells, 4; and Hayes, 132, 133

Concord and Lexington Centennial, 94

Congregational Church, Independent, 11

Congregationalism, 57

Congressional Globe, 23

Conkling, Roscoe, 220

Conway, Eustace, 267

*Conway, Moncure D., 210, 228; "The Romance of a Family," 166, 167; "Thomas Carlyle," 288

Conway, Mr. and Mrs. Moncure D., 267

Conwell, Russell H., *Life . . . of . . . Hayes*, 137

Cook, Lucy, *254*

Cooke, John E., *Fanchette . . .* (WDH on), 300

Cooke, Josiah P., *258*

*Cooke, Rose T., *Huckleberries Gathered . . .*, *278*; *Somebody's Neighbors*, 278; on WDH's resignation, 278

Coolbrith, Ina, *Poems of C. W. Stoddard* (ed.), 21

Coolidge, Eleanora W. R. (Mrs. J. R.), 50, *51*

Coolidge, Joseph R., *50-51*

Cooper, James F., 33

Cornell University, 24, 25

Cornhill, 239

Cornwall, Barry (pseud.). See Procter, Bryan W.

Cortissoz, Royal, 217

Cowper, William, G. Smith's book and WDH on, 257, 261-62

Cozzens, Frederick S., *The Sparrowgrass Papers* (WDH on), 203, 204; *Works* (reviewed by WDH), 204

Cranch, Christopher P., *The Bird and the Bell* (WDH on), 115

Craven, Elizabeth, *Mémoires*, *169*

Crocker, Samuel R., 37, *38*, 41

Curtis, Benjamin R., 50, *51*

*Curtis, George W., and Hayes, 136; and G. W. Brown, 224; and Garfield, 263-64; and Warner, 295, 296

Curtis, Jessie, 181

Cushing, Caleb, *The Treaty of Washington* (reviewed by Annie Howells), 24

*Daly, John A., 128; offered and considers plays by WDH, 74-75, 125-26; production of Tamayo y Baus play, 210, 211

Daly's Theatre, New York, 75
Dart, William A., 170
Dartmouth College, 90
d'Aste, Ippolito, *Sansone* (trans. by WDH), 8, 62, 63, 64
David, 90
Davison, Kenneth E., 254, 264
Dean, Alec or Alexander, 116
Dean, Caroline, 179-*80*, 207-08
Dean, Lile (Mrs. W.), 278, 279
Dean, William, 278, 279
Dean, William B., 179, 180
*De Forest, John W., review of J. A. Froude book, 232; on *A Foregone Conclusion*, 8, 67
De Kalb, John, 101
Delmonico's, New York, 195
Democratic Party, 209, 210, 253, 254; and G. H. Pendleton, 105; and S. J. Tilden, 134; in 1876, 137, 138, 142; and F. O. Prince, 168; and A. G. Thurman, 190
Dennett, John R., 17, 19, 25, 26
Deutsche Rundschau, publishes H. Homberger article on WDH, 213
Deutschland (ship), 116, 118
Dickens, Charles, *David Copperfield*, 56; *Martin Chuzzlewit*, 69, 102
Dio Lewis's Monthly, 288
Disraeli, Benjamin, 111
Dodge, Theodore A., 40, *42*
Dred Scott Case, 51
Drexel, Harjes & Co., 291
Duffy, Charles, 45
*Dwight, John S., 38
Dyer, Louis, review of J. P. Mahaffy book, 269; visits WDH or WDHs, 213, 227, 261; on *Yorick's Love*, 243; recommended to Reid, 269

Eastlake, Charles, 34, *35*
Edel, Leon, 26, 35, 41, 91, 107, 122, 158, 232
Edmunds, George F., 189, *190*
Edwards, Mrs. M. A., 25, 27
Eggleston, Edward, 29, 59
*Eggleston, George C., 28, 29, 58, 59, 136
Eichberg, Julius, 134
Ekström, Kjell, 297
Eldridge, Mr., 234, 235
Electoral Count Act, 190
Eliot, Charles W.,...*Report of the Superintendent of Public Schools* (reviewed by Scudder), 219, 220
Eliot, George, 8, 67, 243; *Middlemarch* (WDH on), 23

Ellwood, Thomas, *The History of the Life of* . . . , 169
Emerson, Ellen T., 185
*Emerson, Ralph W., 5, 48; letter from Clemens cited, 185-86; "Boston," 49, 51-52; seconds WDH for Saturday Club, 77, 78; response to Whittier birthday dinner and Clemens, 182, 184, 185
England, Church of, 86
Epicurus, 25
Episcopalianism, 69. *See also* WDH: Religion.
Episcopal Theological School, 252
Estébanez (pseud.). *See* Tamayo y Baus, Manuel.
Euripides, 267; *Medea*, 140
Evarts, William M., 150, 164, *168*, 253, 254
Every Saturday, 40, 42

*Fairchild, Charles, letters to and from J. W. Harper, Jr., cited, *268*; and Redtop, 187, 298-99
Fairchild, Charles, family, 294
Fairchild, Elisabeth N. (Mrs. C.), 282
Fairchild, Lucius, 299
Faneuil Hall, 52
Farmers' Clubs or Granges, 25
Fawcett, Edgar, review of Aldrich book, *263*
Fenian raids (1866), 137
Ferguson, J. DeLancey, 10
Ferguson, Thomas, 43
Fertig, Walter L., 282
Feuillet, Octave, *The Story of Sibylle* (reviewed by Annie Howells), 12, 13
*Field, Roswell M., *193*; rejects *Out of the Question*, 206
Fieldat (pseud.). *See* Lavelle y Romero, José A. de.
*Fields, Annie A. (Mrs. J. T.), 120, 130; *James . T. Fields* (WDH on), 301; on *The Lady of the Aroostook*, 222, 223
*Fields, James T., 118, 121; *Ballads and Other Poems*, 233; " 'Barry Cornwall' and Some of His Friends," 110, 111; "The Owl-Critic" (WDH and others on), 233; succeeded by WDH, 4; early rejection of WDH's contributions, 82-83; on "Private Theatricals," 110; illness and death, 232, 233; at H. O. Houghton dinner, 276; recalled by WDH, 301
Fields, Mr. and Mrs. James T., invite WDHs to Manchester, 99-100; annual

Christmas party, 116; visit WDHs, 213; entertain WDHs, 247-48, 261, 263

Fields, Osgood & Co., 59

Fifth Avenue Theatre, New York, 75, 211

Filiasi, Giacomo, *Memorie storiche de'Venuti . . .* , 85, 86

Fiske, John, "The Unseen World," 101; European trip, 25, 27; building house, 166, 167

Fitchburg Railroad, 187, 192, 259

Flaubert, Gustave, 213

Flynn, Gerard, 243

Force Acts, 232

Fortnightly Review, 224, 225

*Fréchette, Antoine Léonard Achille, 157, *161*, 236-37

*Fréchette, Anne H., "The Chances of War . . . ," 294; "Life at Rideau Hall," 279, 294; *Popular Sayings from Old Iberia* (with J. A. de Lavelle y Romero; reviewed by WDH), 170; vivid experience, 240; visits W. C. Howells family, 279; invites Winifred to Ottawa, 293. *See also* Howells, Anne T.

Fréchette, Mr. and Mrs. Achille, 180

Fréchette, Howells, 279, 293, 294

Fréchette, Louis, *157*

Fréchette, Louis H., 157; *Pêle-Mêle* (reviewed by WDH), *208*

Fréchette, Marie M., 233, 293, 294

Friedrich I, of Prussia, 169

Friedrich II, of Prussia, 169

Froude, James A., *Caesar* (read by WDH; reviewed by De Forest), 230, 232

Fuller, George, "The Romany Girl," *223*; "She Was a Witch," 223; Bishop and WDH on, 223

Gage, William L., *176*

Galaxy, 54, 195; publishes Boyesen poem and story, 21, 22, 53, 57; publishes Annie Howells' novel, 74, 78, 99, 115, 116, 119, 124; absorbed by *Atlantic*, 152, 186, 187; WDH secures *The American* from, 158

*Garfield, James A., 23, 150; "The Currency Conflict," 105-6; letter of acceptance, 261, 262; "Presidential Elections," 189, 190; and W. C. Howells consulship, 194; 278-79; campaign, 257, 264, 267, 268; assassination, 286, 287; last days and death, 295, 296; WDH on, 289, 290

Garfield, Mr. and Mrs. James A., 253, 254, 257

*Garrison, Francis J., 49, 67, 82, 100, 104, 127, 131, 171; note from Elinor cited, 137; *The Life of William Lloyd Garrison* (with W. P. Garrison), 67; on Christopher Robinson family, 101-2

*Garrison, Wendell P., *The Life of William Lloyd Garrison* (with F. J. Garrison), 67; "The Magazines for December" (on WDH), 81-82

Garrison, William L., 102; *The Liberator* (ed.), 67

Gautier, Théophile, *Théâtre de . . .* (reviewed by James), 25, 26

Gay, Sydney H., *A Popular History . . .* (with Bryant; reviewed by Scudder), 211

German revolution of 1848, 132

Gibbon, Edward, WDH on, 176, 177, 183, 186, 187

Gibson-Arms, 170

Gibson, William M. *See* Gibson-Arms and Smith-Gibson.

Gilbert, William S., *H. M. S. Pinafore*, 234

*Gilder, Richard W., 282; *The New Day* (WDH on), 106, *107*; recommends Lathrop, 98; relation with Warner and WDH, 121

Giovanna, 204

Giusti, Giuseppe, *Proverbi Toscani*, 289

Glasrud, Clarence A., 192

Godkin, Edwin L., 97, 98, 143, 205

Goldoni, Carlo, 177, 180, 185; *Memoirs*, 169, 170

Good Company, 130

Gould, G. M., 81, 214, 229, 250

Graham, Mr. and Mrs. James L., 47, 48

Grand Trunk Railroad, 209

Grant, Ulysses S., 123, 141, 202; and WDH, 145; dinner for, 150, 267-68

Graphic (New York *Daily*?), 32, 33

Gray, Asa, 97, *98*, 142, 143; "Longevity of Trees," 82

Gray, David, *113*

Gray, Horace, 50, *51*

Green, Harvey, 15

*Green, Samuel A., 221-22

Greene, George W., 88, 194; "General John De Kalb," 101

Greenough, James B., *The Queen of Hearts* (reviewed by WDH), *88*, 120, 121

Greenough, Robert B., 120

Greenslet, Ferris, 87, 123, 233

Greve, C. T., 175
Grillparzer, Franz, *Medea*, 140
Grosvenor, Charles H., 104, *105*
Guild, Lilly, 125
Guiteau, Charles J., 286
Gurney, Ephraim W., 40, 41

Habberton, John, *Helen's Babies* (reviewed by Clemens), 142, 143
*Hale, Edward E., 245; *His Level Best* ... (reviewed by Annie Howells), 12, 13
Halfmann, Ulrich, 214
Hall, Charles F., *49*
Hansen-Taylor, Marie, 196
Hardenberg, Friedrich von, 78, 108
Harper & Brothers, 136, 291; copyright, 239, 261, 262; negotiations with WDH, 266, 268; publishes J. E. Cooke novels, 300
Harper, J. W., Jr., letters to and from Fairchild cited, 268
Harper, Joseph H., 195, 196
Harper's Ferry, Raid on, 49
Harper's Monthly, religious reputation, 48, 69; publishes Aldrich poem, 90; publishes J. T. Fields article, 110, 111; publishes Annie Howells story and article, 157, 279, 294; publishes Clemens story, 200; and Whitman, 250; publishes Conway article, 288; publishes "First Impressions of Literary New York," 297
Harper's Weekly, 264
Harrison, Jonathan B., 266, 269; *Certain Dangerous Tendencies in American Life* (WDH on), 154, 205, 209; "The Nationals..." (WDH on), 205, 209
*Harte, Bret, 229; *Ah Sin* (with Clemens), 143; "For the King," 68; *Gabriel Conway* (WDH on), 106, 107, 117, 118; "Ramon," 68; story (unidentified), 68; entertained by WDHs, 5, 194, 195; compared with WDH, 45, 213; appointment as consul, 150, 194-95, 199, 200
Hartford *Courant*, 66; publishes notice of "Edward Gibbon," 183; publishes Warner review of *A Counterfeit Presentment*, 185
Harvard Advocate, 127
Harvard College (or University), (and Aldrich) 232; (and E. F. Atkins) 299; (and E. Brainerd) 243; (and G. W. Brown) 225; (and E. H. Clarke) 51;

(and J. P. Cooke) 258; (and Louis Dyer) 213, 269; (and Fairchild) 268; (and Asa Gray) 98; (and S. A. Green) 222; (and J. B. Greenough) 88; (and B. A. Hayes) 183; (and R. B. Hayes) 150, 166, 168; (and G. Hoadley) 267; (and John M. Howells) 166; (and WDH) 123, 232, 233, 286; (and C. F. McKim) 190; (and T. Parsons) 20; (and F. O. Prince) 168; (and S. D. Robbins) 228; (and N. S. Shaler) 257; (and J. Trowbridge) 258; (and E. Washburn) 160; (and J. Winsor) 203
Hawley, Joseph R., 267-*68*
Hawthorne, Nathaniel, 52, 235; *The Complete Works*, 98; effect compared with *Yorick's Love*, 210, 243; on America, 231
*Hay, John, 173, 207, 212, 224; letters from and to Reid, 44; "Col. John Hay on Negro Exodus" (WDH on), 225, 226; "Corrupting Influences of the 'Postal Card,' " 157, 158; defense of *Daisy Miller*, 232; resigns from New York *Tribune*, 112, 113; tribute by Stedman, 135; on *A Counterfeit Presentment*, 177; on *Yorick's Love*, 210-11; in Europe, 199; entertained by Reid, 213; Assistant Secretary of State, 240, 241; copyright, 262
Hay, Mr. and Mrs. John, visit WDHs and discuss *A Counterfeit Presentment*, 178
Hayes, Birchard A., 168, 182, *183*
Hayes, Fanny, *254*
Hayes, Lucy (Mrs. R. B.), 217
Hayes Memorial Library, 136
*Hayes, Rutherford B., 106, 200, 257; subject of *Sketch of ... Hayes*, 8, 129, 133, 136; nomination, *131*; campaign biographies of, 131; and WDH, 137, 138, 145, 149-50; Norton's opinion of, 139, 140; in 1876 election, 142, 143, 189, 190; Holmes on, 156; characterized by WDH, 158, 189, 202, 220; appointments of H. M. Ticknor, W. H. Smith, Harte, King, 162, 183, 194-95, 216-17; and Lowell, 163, 164, 231, 232, 235-36; invites WDHs to White House, 163-64, 168, 180, 251; invited by WDHs, 165-66; visit to New England, 168; relation with W. R. Mead, 190, 191; California trip, 220, 264; message on Turgenev, 241; gift to Elinor, 251; entertains WDHs, 251, 253-54; copyright, 262

Hayes, Mr. and Mrs. Rutherford B., 253-54

*Hayes, Webb C., 135, *136*, 254

*Hayne, Paul H., 5; "The Woodlake," *10*

Hazlitt, William C., *The History ... of Venice*, 85-86

Hearn, Mrs., 218

Hearth and Home, 28, 29, 37, 38

Heine, Heinrich, 111

Hellman, George S., 37, 293

Herbert, Edward, of Cherbury, *Autobiography*, 169

Herolt, Jean, *Sermones Discipuli*, 135

Heyse, Paul, *Das Ding an Sich* ... (reviewed by Boyesen), 212, 213

Higginson, Mary C. (Mrs. T. W.), 37

*Higginson, Thomas W., 165, 177, 180, 207; *Atlantic Papers*, 169; "Howells" (WDH on), 238; "Mademoiselle's Campaigns," 169; *Oldport Days* (reviewed in *Atlantic*), 36, 37; "The Reed Immortal," 252; review of *The Undiscovered Country*, 259-60, 265; "A Royal Example" (WDH on), 292-93; "A Search for the Pleiades" (WDH on), 264-65; *Short Studies of American Authors* (WDH on), 238, 252; *Woman's Journal* (ed.), 54; and WDH, 58, 59, 114; titles for *A Modern Instance*, 298

Hillard, George S., 234; *Six Months in Italy*, 235

Hinsdale, B. A., 262

Hinton, Richard J., "The Howells Family," 88

Hoadley, George, *267*

Hoar, Elizabeth, 123, 124

Hoar, George F., 189, *190*

Hoar, Samuel, *124*

*Holland, Josiah G., 250, 282; *Arthur Bonnicastle*, 80, 81; *Kathrina* (reviewed by WDH), 196; *The Mistress of the Manse* (WDH on), 80, 81; *Plain Talks on Familiar Subjects* (reviewed by WDH), 196; and WDH, 39, *41*, 80, 81, 104; reconciliation with WDH, 196, 246

*Holmes, Oliver W., 5, 88, 231, 236; letter from Clemens cited, 185-86; "A Ballad of the Boston Tea-Party," 52; "How Not to Settle It" (WDH on), 149, 156; "How the Old Horse Won the Bet," 127; "The New Portfolio," 232; dines with WDH, 50, 51; on the Saturday Club, 77-78; at *Atlantic* dinner, 85; Atlantic breakfast for, 153; response to Whittier birthday dinner and Clemens, 182, 184, 185, 186

Holt, Henry, *286*

Homberger, Heinrich, *213*-14; review of "Private Theatricals," 212-13; "William Dean Howells" (review of *A Foregone Conclusion*), 213

Homer, 154

Hooker, Isabella B. (Mrs. J.), 56, 57

Hooker, John, 56, 57

Horton, Edwin J., 32-33

*Houghton, Henry O., 60, 86, 134; letter to Aldrich cited, 273; as proprietor of *Atlantic*, 66, 67; proposes Hayes biography, 131, 132, 133; response to Clemens speech at Whittier birthday dinner, 184; offers new contract, 273; and WDH's salary, 275, 276; entertains WDH, 276; publishes "American Men of Letters," 285. *See also* Hurd & Houghton and several Houghton companies.

*Houghton, Mr. and Mrs. Henry O., 89

Houghton, H. O., & Co., 61, 67, 83; relation with New York *Tribune*, 100, 101; buys *Atlantic* and *Every Saturday*, 39-40, 42, 48, 50

Hougton, Lord. *See* Milnes, Richard M.

Houghton, Mifflin & Co., founded, 251, 252; publishes Aldrich books, 263; and WDH, 272; publishes E. D. Mead book, 288; publishes *The Undiscovered Country*, 261, 276

Houghton, Osgood & Co., 242, 251, 252, 291

House, Edward H., 268

Howard, Cordelia, 126

Howard, G. C., 125, *126*

Howard, Mrs. G. C., 125, 126

Howard, James Q., *The Life ... of ... Hayes*, 133, 136, 137

Howel, Laurence, *The Case of Schism in the Church of England ...*, 86; *Desiderius* (trans.), 85, 86

*Howells, Anne T. (WDH's sister), 35, 41, 42, 51, 59, 80, 132; Boston letters, 37, 38, 43, 50; "The Chances of War ...," 157, 294; "Life at Rideau Hall," 157, 279, 294; "Reuben Dale," 78, 79, 88, 99, 119, 120; (blunder in), 115, 116; (WDH on), 73-74, 123, 124; review of C. Cushing book, 24; review of O. Feuillet book, 12, 13; review of E. E. Hale book, 12, 13; story (pro-

jected), 38; "A Tour in a Basket"
(unpublished), 16; literary career, 4,
23, 24, 28; in *A Chance Acquaintance*,
13, 14, 16; in Chicago newspaper office, 15; appearance, 28; as Boston correspondent, 37-38, 40, 50, 72; marriage, 157, 161, 164, 165, 167. See
also Fréchette, Anne H. (Mrs. A.).
*Howells, Aurelia H. (WDH's sister),
diary (unpublished), 118; notice in
Literary World, 183; study of French,
65-66
Howells, Beatrice (WDH's niece), 98, 99
Howells, Clara (WDH's cousin), 283
*Howells, Elinor M. (WDH's wife), 156,
251, 292; letter to F. J. Garrison cited,
137; letters to W. R. Mead cited, 191;
letter to Lucy Hayes cited, 217;
"Venetian Diary" (unpublished), 283;
helps design 37 Concord Avenue, 3,
31; relatives, 8, 59, 124, 131, 132, 149;
on *A Chance Acquaintance*, 18; on
A Foregone Conclusion, 29, 75; on
WDH's fiction, 103; on "Private Theatricals," 110; on *Sketch of . . . Hayes*,
117; on WDH's poem about Gloucester disaster, 223; on *The Undiscovered Country*, 265; on *A Fearful
Responsibility*, 266; on WDH's letter
to Clemens, 280-81; health, 20, 99,
245, 281, 288, 289; on books by others,
(Turgenev) 61; (Clemens) 75, 143, 247;
(Boyesen) 89, 213; (Harte) 143; visits,
54, 57, 91, 92, 253-54; advises on
Redtop, 187, 190, 191; on WDH's
illness, 302
Howells, Eliza W. (Mrs. J. A., WDH's
sister-in-law), 66, 98, 99
Howells, Hannah (Mrs. H. C., WDH's
aunt), 12, 13
Howells, Henry I. (WDH's brother), 14,
15, 50, 240-41, 250-51
Howells, Henry C. (WDH's uncle), 13
Howells, Henry C., Jr. (WDH's cousin),
95, 96, 196
Howells, John M. (WDH's son), health,
12, *13*, 14; on his father, 22-23; trips,
31-32, 123, 124, 206; on literature,
124, 209; interests, 166, 201, 219, 230,
259; schooling, 206, 230; walks with
father, 241; on women in politics,
244; gift of playing pipe, 264, 294;
celebrates Fourth of July, 287; once
nicknamed "Rat," 294
Howells, Joseph (WDH's uncle), 283

*Howells, Joseph A. (WDH's brother),
66; visits WDHs and Deer Isle, 31,
32; illness, 94, 275; newspaper career,
142, 284, 285, 287; meets Barrett, 173;
visits WDHs, 240
Howells, Mr. and Mrs. Joseph A., 167
Howells, Mary D. (WDH's mother), 225
Howells, Mary E. (WDH's niece), 98,
99, 187
Howells, Mildred (WDH's daughter),
Life in Letters, 40, 110, 133, 162, 164,
166, 194, 211, 217, 227, 228, 241,
243, 262, 272, 274, 283, 289; birth,
3, 12, *13*; described, 18; note on Emerson poem, 52; toy animal, 89, 90, 92;
activities, 120, 186, 244; anecdotes
about, 196; playhouse, 234
Howells, Samuel D. (WDH's brother),
167, 247, 248; characterized by WDH,
173; support of, 284, 285, 287
Howells, Susan B. (Mrs. T., WDH's
great-grandmother), letter to daughter
cited, 252
Howells, Theodora (WDH's cousin), 77,
95, 96
Howells, Thomas (WDH's great-grand-
father), 252
*Howells, Victoria M. (WDH's sister),
212, 241, 287, 294; "The Sheriff's
Daughter" (unpublished), 87, 88, 115,
116, 118; scolds WDH, 173
*Howells, William C. (WDH's father),
16, 61, 64, 65, 120, 127, 138, 140, 157,
192, 195, 211, 220, 232, 237, 243, 246,
250, 258, 266, 272, 274, 277, 295; editorial on congressional salaries, 23;
"Familiar Letters from the Editor,"
63, 72, 95, 202, 203, 204, 240, 241;
Indian essay in *Atlantic*, 180; lecture
on printing (unidentified), 183, 184;
letters on Ohio trip, 31, 32; *The Science of Correspondences*, 227; as consul
in Quebec, 3-4, 61, 77, 200, 201; as
Swedenborgian, 6, 188; advised on consular duties by WDH, 62, 163; and
languages, 65; invited to visit WDHs,
133, 188-89, 203, 209, 240; business
affairs, 142, 240, 241, 284, 285; seeks
consular promotion, 145, 149, 150; as
consul in Toronto, 161, 162, 163, 193,
194, 196, 201, 202; changes houses in
Toronto, 244, 247, 250, 257, 261; and
Garfield, 264, 278-79, 287; visits Jefferson, 268

Howells, W. D.:
WORKS

Aldrich article (proposed), 80
"Alfieri," 177
"Avery," 212
Blindfold novelette (projected), 124
Bühnenspiele ohne Coulissen. See
"Private Theatricals."
"Buying a Horse," 199, 201, 203, 204
"Carlo Goldoni," 169, 170, 177
Cervantes life (projected), 183, 184
A Chance Acquaintance, 77, 164;
James on, 6, 17, 19, 25, 26, 39-41;
analyzed and interpreted by WDH,
7, 17, 53-54; Elinor Howells on, 18;
composition, serialization, and pub-
lication, 12, 13, 15, 16, 22, 24, 25,
26, 35; family prototypes, 13-14;
Parkman on, 27-28; reviewed by
Rochester *Democrat*, 28-29; reviewed
by Warner and *Nation*, 30; reception in Boston society, 50; Turgenev on, 62; Parton on, 67; pirated, 167, 227
"Choice Autobiographies" (ed.), 151;
preparation, 164, 165, 169, 170;
publication, 177, 186, 187; reception, 183, 206, 207
"Civil Death" (trans.; unlocated), 265,
266
"Colonel Sellers as a Scientist" (with
Clemens), 199, 200
"Concerning Timothy Titcomb" (review of J. G. Holland, *Plain Talks
on Familiar Subjects*), 196
A Counterfeit Presentment, revisions,
150, 151, 177-79; Cleveland, 172, 177;
Cincinnati premiere, 174-75; New
England reception, 185; reviewed
by Warner, 185; Worcester performance, 186, 187; self-analysis, 187-88;
Boston performance, 191, 192-93,
193-94, 206; Aldrich and F. J. Garrison on, 194; L. Wallack's interest,
216; in abeyance, 231, 232
"Diary . . . 1850-1859" (MS.), 183
Doctor Breen's Practice, James on,
154; composition, 152; beginnings,
239, 240; difficulties with, 258, 263;
recommences, 265, 269; British copyright, 291; and women doctors, 293;
Warner on, 295-96
"Doorstep Acquaintance," J. J. Astor
on, 196

"Drama" (review of S. L. Clemens,
"Colonel Sellers"), 96
"Ducal Mantua" (as model for *Tuscan Cities*), 301
"Editor's Easy Chair" (on H. M. Alden), 294
"Edward Gibbon," 176, 177; noticed
by Hartford *Courant*, 183
A Fearful Responsibility, 258; composition, 152, 293, 294; Elinor Howells on, 266; completion, 281, 282;
publication and sales, 289, 291; reviewed by Aldrich, 292
"First Impressions of Literary New
York," 297
A Foregone Conclusion, 7-8, 68, 72,
75; De Forest on, 8, 67; beginnings,
17, 19, 22, 26, 27, 29, 35, 36, 77;
completion, 39, 41, 43, 53, 58, 64,
65; reception generally and by Parton, Clemens, H. W. Preston, F. J.
Garrison, and Roman Catholics, 66-
67, 70, 123, 124; projected as play,
74-75; publication and sale, 77, 85;
responses to ending, 78, 79; Stedman on, 80, 81; Hay on, 113; German translation, 125, 126; James
on, 154; manuscript of, 157; reviewed by H. Homberger, 213;
Tauchnitz edition, 237; compared
with *A Fearful Responsibility*, 292
"Forlorn," 36-37
"Four New Books of Poetry," 115
"A French Poet of the Old Regime,"
177
"Frederika Sophia Wilhelmina," 169
Heroines of Fiction, 23, 157, 161, 298
"The Hero of the Summer." See "Private Theatricals."
Impressions and Experiences, 184
Italian Journeys, 47, 48, 103, 301
The Lady of the Aroostook, composition, 151, 206, 207, 217; James on,
151, 232; Hay on, 210, 211; Sted-
man on, 214, 215; Warner on, 217;
E. Hutchinson on, 217, 218; ana-
lyzed by WDH, 221, 226; Annie A.
Fields on, 222, 223; pirated, 226,
227, 237, 264; origin, 227-28; reviewed by G. E. Woodberry, 232;
reception, 235; Tauchnitz edition,
237; Higginson on, 238; compared
with *Daisy Miller*, 246
"The Late Horatio S. Noyes," 162
"Lord Herbert of Cherbury," 169
Literary Friends and Acquaintance

(as background information), 61, 76, 94, 166, 182, 185, 229, 232, 297

Mark Twain's Library of Humor, 280-82, 291

Memoirs of Carlo Goldoni (ed.), 180

Memoirs of Edward Gibbon (ed.), 183, 186, 187

A Modern Instance, early conception, 8, 140; Crawfordsville trip, 59, 282-83; delay in completion, 149, 300; prospectus, 152, 277; progress with, 280, 281, 282, 289, 290, 291; stages in writing, 293, 294, 295, 296; journalism in, 295, 296, 297; alternative titles, 298

"Mr. Aldrich's Fiction," 263

"Mr. Parkman's Histories," 72

Mrs. Farrell. See "Private Theatricals."

My Literary Passions, 15, 157

My Mark Twain (as background information), 76, 94, 182, 185, 247

My Year in a Log Cabin, 15

New Leaf Mills, 15

"New Medea." *See A Modern Instance.*

"A New Play." *See Yorick's Love.*

Out of the Question, 8; composition, 128, 129, 140; analyzed by WDH, 151; WDH and Hay on, 158; publication, 158-59; rejection by R. M. Field, 206

The Parlor Car, 8; idea of, 75; completion, 124-25; and Daly, 124-25, 126-27, 129

"The Pilot's Story," 45

"Pistoja, Prato, and Fiesole," 301

Play about Orion (projected with Clemens), 239

Poem on Gloucester disaster (unidentified), 222, 223

Poems (1873), 35, 36, 37, 212; reviewed by James and *Literary World*, 39, 40-41

Poems of Two Friends (with Piatt), 138

Poets and Poetry of the West (contr.), 212

"Police Report," overfrankness, 154, 294-95; offered to *Atlantic*, 292

"Private Theatricals," delay in book publication, 8, 111, 122, 123; composition, 92, 93, 95, 96, 97, 98; completion, 101, 102, 103; reception by J. T. Fields, Kemble, Woolson, Whittier, Warner, and Osgood, 110-11; analyzed by WDH, 113; Lowell on, 114; Warner, Mrs. Warner, Springfield *Republican* on, 117, 118; Warner on, 121, 122; reviewed by H. Homberger, 212-13

"Ralph Keeler," 48

"Recent Italian Comedy," 60

"Recollections of an Atlantic Editorship," 69

"Romance," 178, 179

REVIEWS and NOTICES

Aldrich, T. B., *The Queen of Sheba*, 176

Bishop, W. H., *Detmold*, 223

Bjornson, B., *The Happy Boy* and *The Fisher Maiden*, 108

Bryant, W. C., *Thanatopsis* (illus. by W. J. Linton), 230

Clemens, S. L., "Colonel Sellers" ("The Drama"), 96; *Mark Twain's Sketches, New and Old*, 109, 110; *The Prince and the Pauper*, 272; *A Tramp Abroad*, 247, 255

Cozzens, F. S., *Works*, 204

Fréchette, A. H., and J. A. de Lavelle y Romero, *Popular Sayings from Old Iberia*, 170

Fréchette, L. H., *Pêle-Mêle*, 208

Greenough, J. B., *The Queen of Hearts*, 88, 121

Holland, J. G., *Kathrina*, 196; *Plain Talks on Familiar Subjects* ("Concerning Timothy Titcomb"), 196

James, H., Jr., *Hawthorne*, 153, 245; *A Passionate Pilgrim*, 90-91

King, C., *Mountaineering in the Sierra Nevada*, 217

Lavelle y Romero, J. A. de, and A. H. Fréchette, *Popular Sayings from Old Iberia*, 170

Le Moine, J. M., *L'Album du Tourisme*, 27, 28

Monti, L., *Adventures of an American Consul*, 279

Morris, W., *Love Is Enough*, 35

Smith, G., *Cowper*, 257

Stedman, E. C., *The Poetical Works*, 45

Stoddard, C. W., *South-Sea Idyls*, 44

Thompson, J. M., *Witchery of Archery*, 259

Warner, C. W., *Backlog Studies*, 11; *Being a Boy*, 176; *In the Levant*, 144

Whittier, J. G., *The River Path*, 181
Samson (trans.), 8; arrangements, 62, 63, 64; acceptance, 69
"A Sennight of the Centennial," 128
"A Shaker Village," 101, 102, 103
"Signorial Cities." See *Tuscan Cities*.
"Sketch of George Fuller's Life," 223
Sketch of ... Hayes, 8, 129; preparation, 132, 133, 134; composition, 135-36, 136-37; analyzed by WDH, 137, 139-40; Norton on, 140
The Son of Royal Langbrith, 289
Their Wedding Journey, 212; compared with *A Chance Acquaintance*, 12, 13, 15, 24, 29; omitted episode, 16; and Turgenev, 57, 61, 62, 79; pirated, 167, 227
"Thomas Ellwood," 169
Tuscan Cities, 280, 301
The Undiscovered Country, 103, 249, 250, 251, 252, 276; and spiritualism, 151, 152; James on, 154; beginning, 187; finishing, 231, 232, 234, 235, 239, 240, 241; E. E. Hale and T. G. Appleton on, 244, 245; episodes and details in, 246, 260; possibly pirated, 248, 264; sales, 257; C. E. and Grace Norton on, 258; reviewed by W. C. Brownell, 258-59, 262, 263; reviewed by Higginson, 260, 265; reviewed in *Banner of Light*, 261, 262; Elinor Howells on, 265; reviewed by Reid, 269; compared with *A Modern Instance*, 277, 300
The Vacation of the Kelwyns, 103
Venetian histories (projected), 8, 18, 19, 55, 56, 72, 85, 97
Venetian Life, 33, 40, 42, 229, 269; published by Tauchnitz, 47, 48; and Turgenev, 57, 62
Voreilige Schlüsse. See A Foregone Conclusion.
A Woman's Reason, difficulties with, 151-52, 198; beginnings, 191, 192, 199; put aside as failure, 206, 207
"Year in a Log-Cabin," 291
Years of My Youth (as background information), 15, 236, 252, 283
Yorick's Love (trans.), 150-51, 251; beginnings, 171, 178; revisions, 206-7, 208, 224; Cleveland premiere, 210-11; Hay and WDH on, 210-11; Cincinnati and San Francisco, 226; reviewed by E. Brainerd, 242-43

TOPICS:
Culture, aspects of: *art*, 180-81, 197; on G. Fuller, 223; on D. G. Rossetti, 266-67; *divorce*, 152, 277; *domestic life*, 101-2, 128; *gilded age*, 23; *immigration*, 137, 138; *propriety*, sister as journalist, 4, 15; sister's novel, 73-74, 124; pectoral imagery, 90; and Norton, 154, 197; response to Whittier birthday dinner and Clemens, 182, 184-86; and Matthews, 197; and R. G. White, 218, 219; and "Police Report," 294-95; *women*, 191, 221; maltreatment, 221-22; as doctors, 292-93
Culture, national: *America vs. Europe*, 60, 119; *English*, 292-93; *Italian*, 18, 19, 20; *Jewish*, 111; *Southern American*, 10
Family: *children*, at Christmas, 115-16; companionship with, 119, 155, 209; neglects moral advice, 203; *parents*, father, 131, 163, 188-89, 257
Financial affairs: *contracts*, with C. R. Pope, 63; with Osgood, 152, 274; with Barrett, 224; with Houghton and Osgood, 272, 273; advice to Bishop, 223; *editorship*, 275, 276; *expenses*, 59, 176; *royalties*, 59, 63, 129, 224
Health: *medical treatment*, 296; *mental and physical* (1881-1882 illness), 149, 152, 155, 300, 301, 302; *physical* (variety of illnesses), 76-77, 133, 226, 284
Languages: *English* (Americanisms), 219; *French*, 65-66, 72
Literary movements: *local color*, 265; *realism*, technique of, 7, 246; propriety in, 154, 294-95; ideality in, 213, 217
Literature, forms of: *autobiography*, 169; *criticism*, 83-84, 154-55, 296; *drama*, middle form, 140, 151, 158; character, 177-78; production, 194; tragedy, 243; *fiction*, style, 5, 108, 139, 297-98; character, 8, 53-54, 103, 277, 297-98; narrator, 53-54, 130; melodramatic, 73-74, 117; juvenile, 109; theory of, 152, 154, 160-61, 238, 290; disparagement, 157; of New York, 246; *journalism*, 153, 174, 295, 296, 297; *poetry*, 22, 58; *travel writing*, 5, 117, 301

Literature, national: *American*, 230-31; *English*, 230-31, 244

Philosophy: *ethics*, 238

Politics: *appointments*, Swiss mission, 131, 142, 144-45, 159, 161-62, 163, 164, 278, 279; various, 149-50; Lowell, 163, 164, 165, 166, 235-36; King, 216-17; *consulships*, father, 142, 145, 161-62, 168, 193, 194, 278-79, 287; various, 149-50; H. M. Ticknor, 161-62; Harte, 194-95; *copyright*, 227, 236-37, 261, 262, 284, 285; *democracy*, 24; *parties*, free trade and currency, 104-6; Republicans in 1876, 131, 141, 142; Republicans in 1877-1881, 150; Republicans in 1878, 202; Garfield campaign, 261, 267-68; *presidency, see* Hayes, Rutherford B.

Reform: *antislavery*, 125; *business*, 154, 270; *education*, 105; *equalitarianism*, 225, 257; *labor*, 154, 205; *single tax*, 154; *socialism*, 225; *unions*, 24, 25

Religion: *Episcopalianism*, 252; *Moravians*, 93; *Puritanism*, 88; *Quakerism*, 88, 169; *Roman Catholicism*, 252; and *A Foregone Conclusion*, 70, 123, 124; and marriage, 157, 164, 165; *skepticism*, in the *Atlantic*, 48, 49, 66, 67, 69, 181; *Shakerism*, 3, 103, 131; *spiritualism*, in *The Undiscovered Country*, 151, 152, 187, 261, 262; *Swedenborgianism*, 6, 188, 203; *Unitarianism*, 252, 295

Residences: 37 Concord Avenue, moves into, 3; described, 9, 24, 28, 31, 32, 34, 93; building, 12, 18, 20, 23; preferred to Mark Twain's house, 93; compared with Redtop, 155; leaves, 203; renting and selling, 202, 298, 299; Belmont and Redtop, described, 155, 188-89, 192, 213; and Norton, 155, 197; visitors, 155, 206, 209; building, 186, 187, 190-91, 194, 199; planting, 201, 248; financing, 202, 268, 298-99; moves into, 203; neighbors, 228; and Lowell, 230; compared with White House, 254; leaves, 298-99; 28 Brimmer Street, 278, 279, 281; 7 Garden Street, 302; 16 Louisburg Square, 302

Self-conceptualization: *aging*, 256, 266; *appearance*, 116, 289, 300; *career*, 19-20, 57, 119, 135, 249, 274; *death*, 159-60; *friendships*, 30, 33, 79, 215; *influence*, 191, 256; *shortcomings*, 203; *youth*, recalled, 125, 145, 183, 264, 282

Society: *Boston*, 4, 50, 51, 77, 78; *Cambridge*, 4, 40; burden of, 87-88, 99, 119, 186, 197; *Newport*, 170

Travels: Deer Isle (1873), 31-32; Ohio (1873), 33, 35, 36; Quebec, 4, (1874), 62; Jaffrey (1874), 3, 60, 62, 64, 65; Newport (1874), 66, 71, 72; Bethlehem (1875), 92, 93, 99; Shirley Village (1875), 3, 100, 101, 103, 104, 119; Chesterfield (1875), 100, 103, 104, 105; Quebec (1875), 94, 99, 100, 103, 105, 106; Philadelphia (1876), 127, 128; Shirley Village (1876), 3, 120, 130-31, 131-32; Townsend Harbor (1876), 3, 8, 131, 132, 134, 137, 138, 140; Newport (1877), 157; Conanicut (1877), 161, 162, 166, 167, 168, 172, 173; Quebec (1877), 161, 167; New York (1878), 195-96; Toronto and Ohio (1879), 225, 233, 237, 239, 240, 241; Washington (1880), 149, 150, 251, 252, 253-54; Manchester (1880), 261, 263; Duxbury (1880), 261, 263; Ashfield (1880), 258, 263, 265, 266; New York (1881), 275; Crawfordsville (1881), 59, 282-83; Toronto (1881), 285; New Haven (1881), 286, 287; Duxbury (1881), 291; Toronto (planned in late 1881), 152, 296, 300; Europe (planned in 1882), 112, 280, 281, 295, 298, 301

Writing: *editing, Atlantic* policy, 5, 152-53, 211; and public opinion, 49; duties, 58, 64, 66; and religion, 66, 67, 69; and plagiarism, 81-82; and newspapers, 100-1; differences with H. O. Houghton, 152, 273; tired of, 274, 275; *letters*, 58, 152, 294; *reviewing*, in *Atlantic*, 5, 36, 144; theory of, 12; *style*, 114, 231; *typewriter*, 111, 112, 115, 116

Howells, W. D. II (WDH's nephew), 66

*Howells, Winifred (WDH's daughter), 12, *13*, 59; poem noticed in New York *Tribune*, 164, 165; poem in *Youth's Companion*, 268; described, 33, 125; activities, 115, 116, 186-87, 201; Quebec visit, 145, 162, 166; invalidism, 149, 275, 279, 299; WDH on invalidism, 155, 283, 289; schooling, 157, 206, 230, 245; social life, 247, 248; visits N. S. Shalers, 257; visits Ashfield, 258, 263; onset of invalidism, 270; at Dio

Lewis's, 288, 289; rest cure, 292, 293, 295; change of doctors, 296; much better, 299

Hurd & Houghton, publish *Venetian Life*, 40, 42, 47, 48; and *Atlantic*, 43; and Scudder, 87, 275; publish *Sketch of . . . Hayes*, 137

*Hurd, Melanchthon M., 66, 67

*Hutchinson, Ellen, 217, 218; *Library of American Literature* (ed. with Stedman), 217

Ibsen, Henrik, 57

Independent, publishes James review of *Poems* (1873), 40

International Medical Convention, 293

Irving, Washington, 33; *Conquest of Granada*, 236; WDH and Warner on, 229, 230, 242, 245

Italian Free Church Mission, 283

James, Caroline E. C. (Mrs. G. W.), 42

James, Garth W., 40, *42*

*James, Henry, Jr., 20, 22, 24, 29, 45, 77, 138, 179, 228; *The American*, 6; WDH and Hay on, 153, 158; "A Chain of Italian Cities" (WDH on), 34, 35, 39, 42; *Daisy Miller*, 153, 154; WDH, Woolson, and Hay on, 230; compared with *The Lady of the Aroostook*, 246; "Eugene Pickering," 41; *The Europeans*, 153; "Gabrielle de Bergerac," 158; *Hawthorne* (reviewed by WDH), 153, 245; "The Last of the Valerii" (WDH on), 18, 19, 39, 41; letters in *Nation*, 34; "The Madonna of the Future" (WDH on), 17-18, 19; Paris letters, 106, 107; *A Passionate Pilgrim*, 18, 19; (reviewed by WDH), 90-91; *The Portrait of a Lady*, 153; reviews of *Poems* (1873), 39, 40; review of *Théâtre de Théophile Gautier*, 25, 26; *Roderick Hudson*, 6, 18, 19; "A Roman Holiday" (WDH on), 25, 26; "Roman Neighborhoods" (WDH on), 34, 35; "Roman Rides" (WDH on), 25, 26; "Siena," 39, 41, 42; *Transatlantic Sketches*, 18, 19; *Washington Square*, 153, 154; association with WDH, 6; on *A Chance Acquaintance*, 6, 17, 19, 39, 41; breakfast with WDH, 106; Warner on, 106, 107; in Europe, 113, 121, 122; on *The Lady of the Aroostook*, 151, 232; on *A Foregone Conclusion*, 154; on *Doctor Breen's Practice*, 154; on *The Undiscovered Coun-*

try, 154; compared with G. W. Brown, 225; compared with WDH, 265

*James, Henry, Sr., *Society the Redeemed Form of Man*, 23, 188, 189; "Some Personal Recollections of Carlyle," 89, 90, 288; entertains WDH or WDHs, 6, 26; proposes WDH for Saturday Club, 77, 78; visited by WDH, 188

James, Mr. and Mrs. Henry, Sr., 40, 42, 88, 89

James, Mrs. Henry, Sr., 39

James, William, 34

Janson, Kristofer, 256

Jefferson, Thomas, 50, 51

Jesus College, Cambridge University, 86

Jewell, Mrs. Charles A., 285

*Jewett, Sarah O., *Deephaven* (WDH on), 5, 130; "Deephaven Excursions," 130; "Hallowell's Pretty Sister," 129, 130

Jews. See WDH, Culture, national.

Johnson, Andrew, 51

Johnson, Samuel, 258-59

Jones, Erasmus W., "The Welsh in America," 95, 96

Josephine, 240

Katy, 261

Kearney, Dennis, 220

Keeler, Ralph, "Owen Brown's Escape from Harper's Ferry," 49; returns from Europe, 25, 26; death, 47, 49; obituary by WDH, 48

Keen, Elizabeth M., 191, *192*

*Kemble, Fanny, "Old Woman's Gossip," 97, *98*, 120, 121; notice in New York *Tribune*, 101

King, Clarence, miscellaneous articles (1871-1875), 217; *Mountaineering in the Sierra Nevada* (reviewed by WDH), 217; appointment by Hayes, 150, 216-17

King, Miss, 293, 294

Kirk, Clara M. and Rudolf, 221

Kirk, Rudolf, 221

*Krehbiehl, H. E., 243

*Lacy, Ben W., 53-54

Lamb, Charles, 11, 75

Lane, Miss, 35

Lanes, 62, 63, 156-57

*Langley, Samuel P., 227-*28*; "Wintering on Aetna," 153, 228

Lanier, Sidney, letter to B. Taylor cited, 71; "Corn" (WDH on), 71

Larochejaquelein, Marquise de, *Mémoires*, *169*

*Lathrop, George P., *The Complete Works of Nathaniel Hawthorne* (ed.), *98*; "Left Out" (WDH and Warner on), 144; review of R. H. Stoddard poems, 297; review of B. Taylor poems, 215; as assistant editor of *Atlantic*, 97, 98, 103, 104, 106; resignation, 213, 214

Lathrop, Rose H. (Mrs. G. P.), 98

*Lavelle y Romero, José A. de 186, 187, 242, 279; *Popular Sayings from Old Iberia* (with A. H. Fréchette; reviewed by WDH), *170-71*

Leander, Brother, 120

Lee and Shepard, 103, 104

Lee, Higginson & Co., 268

Lefaivre, Albert A., 227; American poetry article (unidentified), 226

Lefaivre, Alfred, 227

Leipzig, University of, 225

Le Moine, J. M., *L'Album du Tourisme* (reviewed by WDH), 27, 28

Le Sage, Alain R., *Gil Blas*, 109, 127

Le Sueur, W. D., *248*

Lewis, Dio, 270, *288*, 289

Lind, Ilse D., 107

*Linton, William J., 244; "Art Engraving on Wood," 229, *230*; *Editorial Right*, 229, 230; illustrations for *Thanatopsis*, 230

Literary World, 38; notice of WDH's resignation, 54; reviews *Poems* (1873), 40-41; publishes Aurelia Howells' notices, 183; publishes Higginson article on WDH, 238

*Lloyd, Henry D., "Story of a Great Monopoly," 154, *270-71*; *Wealth Against Commonwealth*, 271

*Longfellow, Henry W., 5, 48, 97, 213; letter to Clemens cited, 186; letter from Clemens cited, 185-86; "Cadenabbia," 65; *The Masque of Pandora* ..., 106, 107; "The Old Bridge at Florence," 65; *Poems of Places* (ed.), 212; "The Poet and His Songs" (WDH on), 249; "The Rhyme of St. Christopher," 65; entertains WDH or WDHs, 4, 18, 88, 121, 131; on Boyesen's poem, 21; characterized by WDH, 58; at T. G. Appleton's dinner, 88; invited to contribute, 93; response to Whittier birthday dinner and Clemens, 182, 184, 185, 186; attends *A Counterfeit Presentment*, 194; illustrated by W. J.

Linton, 230; on J. T. Fields poem, 233; on Winifred Howells' poem, 268

Longfellow, Henry W., family, 128

Longfellow, William P. P., "The Washington Monument, and Mr. Story's Design" (WDH on), 234-35

Longhi, Pietro, 289

Lord Chamberlain's office, 211

Lotos Club, New York, 269

Louis XV, of France, 197

Lounsbury, Thomas, *286*; Chaucer essay, 286; Shakespeare essay, 286

*Lowell, James R., 5, 138, 248; "Agassiz," 60, 61; "Birthday Verses" (WDH on), 134; introduction to W. B. Rogers article, 82; *North American Review* (ed.), 36; "Ode Read at the Concord Centennial," 93, 97, 98; notice in New York *Tribune*, 101; "Ode Recited at the Harvard Commemoration," 114; "Under the Old Elm," 140; criticizes America, 60, 61; early acceptance of WDH, 83; on WDH and "Private Theatricals," 114; on C. P. Cranch, 115; as Hayes elector, 143; appointments to Spain and England, 149-50, 163, 164, 165, 166, 236; on *The Lady of the Aroostook*, 230, 231-32; invited to contribute, 231

Lutheranism, 108, 256

Lynn, Kenneth S., 15, 41, 302

Macauley, Thomas B., 83

McClannin, R. F., *193*

McKaye, Maria E., 238

McKim, Charles F., *190*, 191, 209

McKim, Mead & Bigelow, 155, 187, 190

Magazin für die Literatur des Auslandes, publishes H. Homberger review of "Private Theatricals," 213

Mahaffy, J. P., *A History of Greek Literature* (reviewed by L. Dyer), 269

Manzoni, Alessandro, *I Promessi Sposi* (*Betrothed*), 70

Marcello, Pietro, *De Vitis principum et gestis Venetorum compendium*, 85, 86

Marie, 89

Marmontel, Jean F., 177

*Mason, Frank, review of *A Counterfeit Presentment*, 177

Massachusetts Historical Society, 222

*Matthews, Brander, 197

Mead, Charles R., 195, 196

*Mead, Edwin D., *59*, 289; *The Philosophy of Carlyle* (WDH on), 288
Mead, Larkin G., Jr., 279
Mead, Mr. and Mrs. Larkin G., Jr., 76
Mead, Larkin G., Sr., 159, 279
Mead, Mary J. N. (Mrs. L. G., Sr.), 93, 98, 136
Mead, Mary N., 98, 209, 233, 282, 283
*Mead, William R., 168, 190, 191, 209, 261; letters from Elinor Howells cited, 191
Medina *Gazette*, 15
Merrill, Mr. and Mrs. Edward W., 191
Meserve, Walter J., 129, 179, 193, 200, 211, 224, 226
Methodism, 69
Middlesex Club, 268
Millerism, 69
Millet, Francis D., 142, *143*
Millet, J. B., *George Fuller* (ed.), 223
Milnes, Richard M., 4, 111, *112*, 229
Mitchell, John G., 132
Mitchell, Mr. and Mrs. John G., 33
Mitchell, Laura P. (Mrs. J. G.), 132, 236
Mitchell, Lilly, 236
*Mitchell, S. Weir, 217
Monteiro, George, 232
Monti, Luigi, *Adventures of an American Consul Abroad* (reviewed by WDH), *279*; Sicilian sketches, 279
Montpensier, Louise d'O., *Mémoires*, *169*
Montreal (ship), 167
Moore, Mr., 299, 300
Moorhead, Rev. Mr., 282, 283
Moravians. See WDH: Religion.
Mordell, Albert, 40
*Morley, John, 224, *225*; "English Men of Letters" (ed.), 242, 245, 262; *Fortnightly Review* (ed.), 225; *Pall Mall Gazette* (ed.), 225; negotiations with Warner, 242, 245
Morris, Marshall, Faulkner & Co., 35
Morris, William, 34, *35*; *Love Is Enough* (reviewed by WDH), 35
Moses, 262
Mott, Frank L., 187
Moulton, Ellen L. C., *53*
Mt. Vernon, Virginia, 253
Mulock, Dinah M., *John Halifax, Gentleman*, *157*
Murray, William H. H., *Music-Hall Sermons* (reviewed by Warner), 10, 11
Museum, Troy, N. Y., 126
Myers, Albert J., *253*
Myers, George, 190, 191

Nation, 19, 25, 98; WDH on its reviews, 5, 12; reviews *A Chance Acquaintance*, 30; publishes James letters, 34; publishes "Forlorn," 37; publishes W. P. Garrison attack, 82; publishes C. F. Adams article, 143-44; notice of B. O. Townsend article, 171; publishes "Concerning Timothy Titcomb," 196; notice of J. B. Harrison article, 205; publishes G. E. Woodberry review of *The Lady of the Aroostook*, 232; publishes W. C. Brownell review of *The Undiscovered Country*, 258-59, 262, 263; publishes W. C. Brownell notice of Aldrich novel, 262, 263
National Academy of Arts and Sciences, 98
National Bank of Illinois, Chicago, 165
National Party, 205
Nautilus Club, 92
New Church school, Waltham, 188
New England Magazine, 59
New England Society, Toronto, 202
Newgate Prison, 85, 86
New Jerusalem Temple, Toronto, 227
Newton Journal, publishes "The Late Horatio S. Noyes," 162
New York *Herald*, 143
New York *Mail*, 296, 297
New York *Post*, 136
New York *Tribune*, 44, 95-96, 136, 217, 268; neglect of *Atlantic*, 100-1; publishes James Paris letters, 106, 107; and Hay, 112, 113, 226; and R. Keeler, 48; and Winifred Howells, 164, 165; and L. Dyer, J. B. Harrison, and *The Undiscovered Country*, 269; publishes WDH's review of *The Prince and the Pauper*, 272
New York *Voice*, 88
Nicholas, St., 116
Nichols, James R., 89, *90*
Nichols, J. R., & Co., 90
*Niles, Thomas, 130
Nobel Prize, 108
"No Name Series," 158
Normal School for Physical Training, Lexington, 288
North American Review, 19, 35, 36, 82, 234, 235; and Perry, 25-26, 27; publishes James review of Gautier book, 26; publishes James review of *Poems* (1873), 39, 40; and Boyesen, 57
*Norton, Charles E., 56, 60, 138, 210, 219, 267; "Florence, and St. Mary of the Flower" (WDH on), 205; *Lowell Let-*

ters, 60, 61; *North American Review* (ed.), 35, 36; "Venice and St. Mark's" (WDH on), 182; at T. G. Appleton's dinner, 88; on Hayes and *Sketch . . . ,* 139, 140; and Lowell's appointment, 163, 164; response to Whittier birthday dinner and Clemens, 182, 184, 185, 186; and Warner, 242, 285, 295, 296; on *The Undiscovered Country*, 258; entertains WDH, 263; interest in Carlyle, 288; and Longhi, 289
Norton, Charles E., family, 26, 27, 40, 42
Norton, Grace, 258
Norton, Susan S. (Mrs. C. E.), 289
Nourse, Miss, 37
Novalis (pseud.). *See* Hardenberg, Friedrich von.
*Noyes, Horatio S., 161, *162*, 207; Boston *Daily News* (ed.), 162

O'Brien, Father, 252
O'Brien, John, *95*
Ohio State Journal, publishes Annie Howells' contributions, 4, 37, 38, 43, 50; publishes item on WDH, 32, 33
*O'Reilly, John B., 124; Boston *Pilot* (ed.), 70
Osgood, Edward L., *291*
Osgood, George L., 134, 138
*Osgood, James R., 60, 75, 103, 104, 138, 172, 179, 299; publishes C. W. Stoddard book, 20, 21; publishes *Poems* (1873), 35; and *North American Review*, 36; and heliotypes, 43; sells *Atlantic*, 47; visits in Hartford, 54, 57; entertains authors, 91, 92, 177; publishes "Choice Autobiographies," 151, 164, 165, 183; contracts with WDH, 152, 273, 274, 275; and *A Counterfeit Presentment*, 175; European trips, 199, 259, 290, 291, 295; terms for W. H. Bishop novel, 223; and piracy, 227; on J. T. Fields poem, 233; and *The Prince and the Pauper*, 271; and H. O. Houghton, 272, 276; publishes R. T. Cooke book, 278; negotiates on *Tuscan Cities*, 280; negotiates on *Mark Twain's Library of Humor*, 280-82. *See also* Osgood, James R., & Co. and Houghton, Osgood & Co.
Osgood, James R., & Co., 167, 243, 251, 252; publishes Warner book, 11; publishes *A Chance Acquaintance*, 13; publishes O. Feuillet and E. E. Hale books, 13; publishes James books, 18, 19; sells *Atlantic* and *Every Saturday*, 39-40, 42; publishes Jewett book, 130; publishes *Out of the Question*, 159; publishes Whittier book, 181; publishes J. B. Harrison book, 205; publishes J. M. Thompson book, 259; publishes *A Fearful Responsibility*, 291; publishes J. E. Cooke novel, 300
Osten-Sacken, Carl R. R. von, 40, *42*
Oxford University, and starving Englishman, 14; and C. Tait, 172; and A. T. Rice, 235; and L. Dyer, 269

Paine, Albert B., *Mark Twain: A Biography*, 282
Paine, J. K., 134, 138
Palfrey, Dr. and Mrs. John G., 18, *19*, 20
Pall Mall Gazette, 225
Papyrus Club, Boston, 252
Paris Exposition (1879), 235
Parker House, 84-85
Parker, Theodore, 285
*Parkman, Francis, 183; "Early Canadian Miracles and Martyrs," 27, 28; "A Great Deed of Arms," 27, 28; *The Old Regime in Canada*, 72, 85; WDH's essay on, 72
Park Theatre, Boston, 243
Parsons, Mr. and Mrs. Theophilus, 20
*Parton, James, "Thomas Jefferson's Last Years," 51
Peabody, Andrew P., 18, *19*, 232, 233
Peirce, Mr., 66, 67
Pendleton, George H., 104, *105*
Pepys, Samuel, 11
Perry, Lilla C. (Mrs. T. S.), 36
*Perry, Thomas S., *North American Review* (ed.), 25-26, 27, 35, 36; review of Georg Brandes book, 78, 79
*Phelps, Elizabeth S., 218; *Friends: A Duet* (WDH on), 290
Phelps, Mrs., 217, 218
Philadelphia *Press*, publishes E. Brainerd review of *Yorick's Love*, 243
Phillips, Laura, 192, 193
*Piatt, John J., *Poems of Two Friends* (with WDH), 138; review of *A Counterfeit Presentment*, 175; visits WDHs, 207
Piatt, Sarah M. B. (Mrs. J. J.), "Folded Hands" (G. H. Warner on), 96
The Pioneer, 102
Poe, Edgar A., 267
Polakoff, K. I., 137

Polaris (ship), 49

Pope, Alexander, L. Stephen book on, 262

*Pope, Charles R., and *Samson,* 62, *63,* 64, 69

Pope's Theatre, St. Louis, 63

Porter, Miss, 286

Porter, Noah, *286*

Premio Real, Count. *See* Lavelle y Romero, José A. de.

Presbyterianism, 69

*Preston, Harriet W., on *A Foregone Conclusion,* 67, 79

Prince, Frederick O., *168*

Procter, Bryan W., J. T. Fields article on, 110, 111

Prospect House, Chesterfield, N. H., 104

Protestant Theological Seminary, Rome, 282

Puritanism. *See* WDH: Religion.

Putnam's Sons, G. P., 34, 229, 242

Quakerism. *See* WDH: Religion.

Quebec *Daily Chronicle,* 201

Quebec *Morning Chronicle,* 201

Quinet, Edgar, 248

Quinn, Arthur H., 126

Rab (WDH's dog), 241

Randolph, Eleanora W. *See* Coolidge, Eleanora W. R. (Mrs. J. R.).

Ratner, Marc L., 256

Raymond, John T. (pseud.). *See* O'Brien, John.

Reade, Charles, 246

Redwood, Abraham, *169*

Redwood Library, 169

*Reed, Samuel R., review of *A Counterfeit Presentment,* 175

*Reid, Whitelaw, 87, 136; letters to and from Hay, 44; review of *The Undiscovered Country,* 269; neglect of the *Atlantic,* 100-1; and James, 107; invitations to and visits by WDH, 196, 213, 269

Republican Party, (and Hayes), 8; (and C. Schurz), 132; (and C. F. Adams), 137; (in 1876), 138, 143; (and A. H. Rice), 168; (and B. H. Bristow), 189; (and E. Hoar), 190; (and B. F. Butler), 209; (and stalwarts), 220, 264; (and J. Sherman), 254; (and Garfield campaign), 267, 268

Rhodes, Mr., on *A Counterfeit Presentment,* 177

Rice, Alexander H., 137

Rice, Allan T., 234, *235*

Richardson, Lyon N., 236

Richardson, Samuel, 160

Riddle, Albert G., *Bart Ridgeley,* 14, 15

Riverside Magazine, 54

Riverside Press, 40, 89, 103, 127, 251; and F. J. Garrison, 67; and Scudder, 87; prints *Sketch of . . . Hayes,* 137; prints *Out of the Question,* 158

Robbins, Samuel D., *228*

Roberts Brothers, 130, 158

Robertson, I. Ross, 264

Robinson, Christopher, family, 100, 101-2, 104, 131

Rochester *Democrat,* reviews *A Chance Acquaintance,* 29

Rochester Knockings, 157

Rogers, William B., "July Reviewed by September," 82

*Rogers, William K., 163, 165, 182; and *Sketch of . . . Hayes,* 135, *136,* 137; visits WDHs, 162; on W. C. Howells' consulship, 170

Roland, Manon-Jeanne P., *Mémoires,* *169-70*

Roman Catholicism. *See* WDH: Religion.

Rosa, 200

Rose-Belford's Canadian Monthly, 201

Rose-Belford Publishing Co., 248, 261, 264

*Rose, George M., 264

Ross, Mr., 111, 112

Rossetti, Dante G., "Hesterna Rosa" (WDH on), 266-67; "How They Met Themselves" (WDH on), 266-67

Rossetti, William M., "The Wives of Poets" (WDH on), 266, 267

Royal Academy, 35

Royal Adelphi Theatre, London, 193

Royal Society of Canada, 208

Rublee, Horace, *145*

Rusk, Ralph L., 52

Russell's Bookstore Group, 10

Russo-Turkish War, 143

Sabellico, Marco A. C., *Rerum Venetarum . . . ,* 85, 86

Salsbury, Edith C., 96

Salvini, Tommaso, 8, 62, *63,* 64, 266

Samson, 61, 64, 69

Sanborn, Franklin B., *Henry D. Thoreau,* 285; review of W. E. Channing book, 36, 37

*Sangster, Margaret, on *A Chance Acquaintance,* 29

Sansovino, Francesco, *Venetia,* 85, 86

Sanudo, Marino, *Diarii*, 86; *La Spedizione di Carlo VIII in Italia*, 85, 86

Saturday Club, 4, 77, 78

Scando-Slavica, 79

Skepticism. *See* WDH: Religion.

Schiller, Johann C. F. von, *Don Carlos*, 226

Schmidt, J. Heinrich, *An Introduction to the Rhythmic and Metric* . . . (reviewed by Boyesen), 212, 213

Schneider, George, 164, *165*

Schurz, Carl, *132*, 150, 168, 241

Scott, Walter, *Ivanhoe*, 244

Scribner, Charles, 282

Scribner's, 98, 282; and James, 6, 39, 41-42; religious reputation, 49, 69, 181; publishes Boyesen stories, 57, 212, 213, 214; and WDH, 80, 81, 103, 104, 106, 107, 121, 122; publishes Harte novel, 106, 107, 118; and Stedman article on Whitman, 250; publishes Higginson review of *The Undiscovered Country*, 260, 265; and *A Modern Instance*, 277, 281, 293; and *Tuscan Cities*, 280; publishes *A Fearful Responsibility*, 282. *See also Century*.

Scribner's Sons, Charles, publishes Boyesen novel, 139; publishes Bryant and S. H. Gay book, 211

*Scudder, Horace E., 54, *87*, 196; "Accidentally Overheard," 219, 220; reviews of Bryant and S. H. Gay book, 211; review of Cable novel, 297; review of C. W. Eliot report, 219, 220; relationship with *Atlantic*, 274-75

*Sedgwick, Arthur G., 153, 195, 196; copyright article, 216; "New York Theatres" (WDH on), 216; political articles, 216; "Presidential Electioneering in the Senate" (WDH on), 216; review of George Eliot novel, 23; "Washington Society," 216

Sedgwick, Theodora, 289

Selby, Charles, *The Marble Heart* (trans.), 192, 193

Sewall, Mr. and Mrs. Francis, 22

Seward, Frederick W., 240, 241

Seyersted, Per E., 62

Shakerism, 100, 101, 103, 120, 133. *See also* WDH: Religion.

Shakespeare, William, 121, 160, 161, 210; *Hamlet*, 196; *Othello*, 260; *Romeo and Juliet*, 125; favored by Winifred Howells, 230; essay by Lounsbury, 286; WDH titles from, 298

Shaler, Nathaniel S., *Autobiography*, 257

Shaler, Mr. and Mrs. Nathaniel S., 257

Shepard, Mr. and Mrs. Augustus D., visit WDHs, 123, 124; entertain WDH or WDHs, 195, 196, 251, 252; entertain John Howells, 206

Shepard, Joanna M. (Mrs. A. D.), 92

Sherman, John, 253, *254*, 264

Simms, William G., 10

Sisyphus, 69

Slayton, Dr., 283

Smith, Charles, 79, 80

Smith, Chloe, 131

Smith, Fanny, 79, 80

Smith, Franklin, "An Hour with Mr. Howells," 214

Smith-Gibson, 6, 54, 62, 64, 67, 69, 75, 76, 84, 85, 91, 94, 95, 109, 110, 112, 124, 137, 141, 162, 183, 185, 186, 200, 224, 237, 239, 248, 250, 255, 256, 262, 266, 268, 271-72, 282, 291

*Smith, Goldwin, 248, 261; *Cowper* (reviewed by WDH), 257, 261-62; "Is Universal Suffrage a Failure?" 234; "Pessimism," 234

Smith, Henry N., 182, 185. *See also* Smith-Gibson.

Smith, Joseph, 288

Smith, Joshua B., *172*

Smith, Roswell, *282*

Smith, Samuel M., *33*, 43; illness, 56, 57; death, 79, 80

*Smith, Susan E. (Mrs. S. M.), 43, 80

*Smith, William H., and A. H. Fréchette, 12, 13, 23; inquiry about Lowell, 143; appointment by Hayes, 183

Smith, William R., 138

Snap (unidentified; reviewed by Warner), 10, 11

"Socialism in Germany and the United States," 224, 225

Society for the Promotion of Home Studies . . . , 285

Solomon, 75

Sons of Temperance, 136

South Mountain, Battle of, 136

Spiritualism. *See* WDH: Religion.

Springfield *Republican*, reviews "Private Theatricals," 117, 118

*Stabler, James P., on *The Lady of the Aroostook*, 221

Standard Oil Co., 154, 271

Standish, Miles, 261

Starke, Aubrey H., 71

*Stedman, Edmund C., 41, 79, 141; "The Carib Sea," 182; "The Creole Lover's Song," 182; "Jamaica," 181, 182; *Li-*

brary of American Literature (ed. with E. Hutchinson), 217; "The Lord's-Day Gale," 48, 49; *Lyrics and Idylls . . .*, 181; *Poems* (1908), 135; *Poems Now First Collected*, 182; *The Poetical Works* (reviewed by WDH), 45; "Provençal Lovers: Aucassin and Nicolette" (WDH on), 181; review of B. Taylor book, 214; "The Rose and the Jasmine," 181, 182; "Sister Beatrice" (WDH on), 135; "The Skull in the Gold Drift," 81; "Walt Whitman," 250; on *A Foregone Conclusion*, 80, 81; on B. Taylor, 213; on WDH's realism, 214; European trip, 228-29

Stedman, Laura, 81, 214, 229, 250

Stedman, Laura (Mrs. E. C.), 286

*Stephen, Leslie, *Alexander Pope* (WDH on), 262; and *Doctor Breen's Practice*, 239

Stewart, George, Quebec *Daily Chronicle* (ed.), 201; *Rose-Belford's Canadian Monthly* (ed.), 201; *Stewart's Literary Quarterly Magazine* (ed.), 201

Stewart's Literary Quarterly Magazine, 201

*Stoddard, Charles W., poem (unidentified; WDH on), 20, 21; *Poems* (1867), 21; *Poems* (1917, ed. Ina Coolbrith), 21; "A Prodigal in Tahiti" (WDH on), 21; *South-Sea Idyls*, 20, 21, (reviewed by WDH) 44; theatrical papers, 20-21

*Stoddard, Richard H., 48, 49, 296-97; "Reminiscences of Bayard Taylor," 215; *Poems* (reviewed by Lathrop), 297

Storer, Marnie, 120, 123, 131

Storer, Robert B., 125, 126

Storer, Mr. and Mrs. Robert B., 121, 251

Storer, Sarah (Mrs. R. B.), 123, 124

Story, Emilyn E. (Mrs. W. W.), 235

*Story, William W., *Conversations in a Studio*, 205; "Do You Remember?" 205; "The Excursion," 204; "In a Studio," 204, 205; Paris Exposition report, 235; "Phidias to Pericles" (WDH on), 107, *108*; poem on G. S. Hillard (unidentified), 234, 235; "The Rabbi's Letter" (unpublished), 204; "Roba di Roma" (WDH on), 204, 234, 235; "A Roman Holiday, Twenty Years Ago," 204, 234, 235

Stowe, Calvin E., 56, 57

Stowe, Harriet B. (Mrs. C. E.), 56, 57, *Uncle Tom's Cabin* (play), 125

Sumner, Charles, *172*

Sun Hotel (or Inn), Bethlehem, Pa., 93

Surtees, Virginia, 267

Swedenborgianism, 23. See also WDH: Religion.

Swedenborgian Society, Waltham, 88

Tait, Crauford, *172*

Tamayo y Baus, Manuel, *Un drama nuevo*, 150, 170, *171*, 210, 211, 242-43. See also WDH, *Yorick's Love* (trans.).

*Tauchnitz, Christian B., publishes *Venetian Life* and *Italian Journeys*, 47, 48; publishes *A Foregone Conclusion* and *The Lady of the Aroostook*, 237

*Taylor, Bayard, 135, 138, 226; letter from Lanier cited, 71; *Don Carlos* (trans.), 226; *Lars* and other poems (WDH on), 46-47, 47-48; *Prince Deukalion* (reviewed by Stedman or Lathrop), 214, 215; Weimar essays, 46, 47; dinner for, 195, 196; illness and death, 213, 214, 215

Taylor, British family, 167

Taylor House, Jersey City, 128

Taylor, Mr., 133

Tennyson, Alfred, 89, 99; *In Memoriam*, 208; *The Princess*, 59

Thackeray, William M., 154, 246

Thaxter, Celia, 47-48

Theatre Royal, Manchester, 96

*Thompson, J. Maurice, "Atalanta" (WDH on), 58; *Songs of Fair Weather* (WDH selects), 259; "A Wild Flower" (unidentified), 58; *Witchery of Archery*, 259; and *A Modern Instance*, 282-83

Thoreau, Henry D., 36, 37, 285

Thurman, Allan G., 189, *190*

Ticknor & Fields, 259

*Ticknor, Benjamin H., 158, *159*

Ticknor, Howard M., 161, 162

Ticknor, William D., 159

Tilden, Samuel J., in 1876 election, *134*, 141, 142; Holmes on, 149, 156; election contest, 189, 190; meets WDH, 196

Timrod, Henry, 10

Tolstoy, Leo N., 8

Toronto *Globe*, 202

Toronto, University of, 261, 262

*Townsend, Belton O., *Plantation Lays . . .* (dedicated to WDH), *84*; "The Political Condition of South Carolina," 84, 171; "The Result in South Carolina," 84; "South Carolina Morals,"

84; "South Carolina Society," 84, 165; advised by WDH, 83-84, 171

Tremont Temple, Boston, 222

Trowbridge, John, *258*

Trübner & Co., 229

Trübner, Nicholaus, *229*

*Turgenev, Ivan, letter to Boyesen cited, 61, 62; *Liza*, 80, 81; *Smoke*, 40, 42; compared with Boyesen, 5, 139; compared with WDH, 8, 67, 213; relation with WDH, 57, 61, 62, 160, 212, 213; on WDH, 78, 79, 241

Turner, Arlin, 298

Turner, Joseph M. W., 197

Twain, Mark (pseud.). *See* Clemens, Samuel L.

Twichell, Joseph H., 56, 57, 75, 76, 249

Twichell, Mr. and Mrs. Joseph H., 76

Union Club, New York, 195

Union League Club, New York, 196

Unitarianism, (and A. P. Peabody), 19; (and *Atlantic*), 69; (and W. L. Gage), 176; (and J. B. Harrison), 205; (and K. Janson), 256; (and T. Parker), 285. *See also* WDH: Religion.

Urbana University, Ohio, 24

Vanderbilt, Kermit E., 264

Van Zandt, Charles C., *168*

Venus de Milo, 30

Vermont Central Railroad, 145

Victoria, of Great Britain, 292-93

Vincent, Mary A. F., 192, *193*

Vinton, Frederick P., *300*

Vorse, 130, 132-33

Wallace, Lew, 58, *59*

Wallack, Lester, and *A Counterfeit Presentment*, 216

Wallack's Theatre, New York, 216

Walthall, Howard P., 102

Walton, Izaak, 110

Ward, Artemus (pseud.). *See* Browne, Charles F.

Ward, Elizabeth S. P. *See* Phelps, Elizabeth S.

Ward, John Q. A., 195, 196

Ward, Samuel, "Nocturne" (WDH on), 64, 65

Waring, George W., Jr., 199, 200, 239

*Warner, Charles D., 5, 59, 72, 86, 153, 157, 183, 187, 244; "The Adirondacks Verified," 175-76; "American Men of Letters" (ed.), 245, 285, 296; *Among the Mummies and the Moslems* (WDH on), 106, 107; "At the Gates of the East," 103, 104; *Backlog Studies* (reviewed by WDH), 10, 11; *Baddeck and That Sort of Thing*, 30, (WDH on), 49, 55, 159; *Being a Boy* (reviewed by WDH), 176; "Equality," 229; "A Fight with a Trout" (WDH on), 175, 176, 187, 188; "From Jaffa to Jerusalem" (WDH on), 116-18; *The Gilded Age* (with Clemens; WDH on), 46, 54; "How I Killed a Bear," 175, 176; *In the Levant* (WDH on), 106, 107, 121, 122, (reviewed by WDH), 144; *In the Wilderness*, 175-76; "Jerusalem" (WDH on), 117, 118; "Lost in the Woods," 175, 176; *My Summer in a Garden*, 176; "Passing the Cataract of the Nile" (WDH on), 96, 97, 98; review of *A Chance Acquaintance*, 30; review of *A Counterfeit Presentment*, 185, 187-88; "Shooting a Loon" (unpublished), 175, 176; *Studies in Irving*, 229; "Washington Irving," 229, 242; *Washington Irving*, 245, 295, 296; visited by WDH or WDHs, 11, 54, 56, 57, 160, 161, 176; advises WDH on fiction, 103-4; on "Private Theatricals," 118, 121, 122; on Lathrop story, 144; miscellaneous visits and dinners, 177, 258, 276, 295; visits WDHs, 268, 285; on *The Lady of the Aroostook*, 218; at Gloucester benefit, 222; interviewed by S. Baxter, 255

Warner, Mr. and Mrs. Charles D., 93, 247

*Warner, George H., *96*, 106, 107

Warner (M. Storer's friend), 120, 131

Warner, Susan (Mrs. C. D.), 56, 117

Warren, Mr., 261, 262

Washburn, Emory, 159-60

Washington, George, 111

Washington, Treaty of (1871), 24, 27

Watkins, Tom, 233

Waud, Alfred R., 181

Webb, Charles H., protest on WDH and Aldrich (unpublished), *44*

Webb, Joseph T., 253, *254*

Webster, Noah, *American Dictionary* . . . , 81

Wecter, Dixon, 256

Welch and Bigelow, 50

Wellesley College, 179, 180, 207

*Wells, David A., "The Creed of Free Trade," *104*; "Our Burden and Our Strength," 104

Wendell, Barrett, *A Literary History of America,* 78
Wesselhoeft, Conrad, *90*
Wesselhoeft, Minnie, *Voreilige Schlüsse* (trans.), 125, 126
Wesselhoeft, Walter, *90,* 296, 302
Westbrook, Raymond (pseud.). *See* Bishop, William H.
Western Associated Press, 143
Western Union, 143
West Jersey Press, publishes Whitman article, 250
Wharton, Francis, *252*
Wharton, Joseph, "National Self-Protection," 104
*Whelpley, A. W., on *A Counterfeit Presentment,* 174-75
Whiskey Ring, 189
White House, Washington, 252, 253-54, 257
White, John W., *An Introduction to the Rhythmic and Metric* . . . (trans.; reviewed by Boyesen), 212, 213
*White, Richard G., "Americanisms" (WDH on), *219*; "Assorted Americanisms," *219*; "British Americanisms," *219*; "Living in London," 218, *219*; "London Streets," 218, 219
Whitman, Walt, "Walt Whitman's Actual American Position," 250; Stedman's essay on, 250; and *Atlantic,* 250
*Whittier, John G., 5, *183*; poem in album (unidentified), 226; *The River Path* (reviewed by WDH), 181; response to Whittier birthday dinner and Clemens, 153, 182, 186; illustrated by W. J. Linton, 230

Wilhelmina, Frederica S., *Mémoires, 169*
Wilkins, Thomas, 217
William, the Conqueror, 89
Williams, Jim (James E.), 270
Williston, Samuel, *145*
Williston Seminary, 145
Winsor, Justin, *203,* 298, 299; *The Memorial History of Boston* (ed.), 222
Woman's Journal, notice of WDH's resignation from *Atlantic,* 54; publishes Higginson article, 292-93
Woodberry, George E., review of *The Lady of the Aroostook,* 232
Woodress, James, 279
*Woolson, Constance F., *Castle Nowhere,* *179*; defense of *Daisy Miller,* 232; on *A Counterfeit Presentment,* 178
Worcester, Joseph E., *Comprehensive* . . . *Dictionary* . . . , 80-81
Worcester (son of Thomas), 77
Worcester, Thomas, 77, 188, 189, 227; *Animals in Heaven* (unidentified), 88
Wordsworth, William, 45
Workingman's Party, 220
World Peace Foundation, 59
Wyman, Morrill, 14, *15,* 31, 32

Yale College (or University), (and D. A. Wells), 104; (and Bishop), 174; (and WDH), 286, 287, 291; (and Aldrich), 291
Young, Mason, 286
Young's Hotel, Boston, 75
Youth's Companion, 268, 291

Zola, Émile, 245

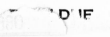